NICKEL CROSS

'Prop' Preller Geldenhuys

Copyright © 2007 by Preller Geldenhuys

The rights of the author of the Work have been asserted by him.
©Copyright in the text rests with the author, Preller Geldenhuys

All rights reserved. No part of this publication may be reproduced, stored, manipulated in any retrieval system, or transmitted in any mechanical, electronic form or by any other means, without the prior written authority of the publishers or the author, nor be otherwise circulated in any form of binding or cover other than that in which it is published and without a similar condition being imposed on the subsequent purchaser.

First published in 2007 by Prop Geldenhuys
Prop@peysoft.co.za

Copyright © Prop Geldenhuys

Design and origination by Prop Geldenhuys
Printed and bound by Lulu.com

ISBN: 978-0-9941309-5-2

Paeroa

2016

To our very Grand children

Courtney Sacha

Brendan Vaughan

Matthew Dylan

Lucy Hope

Mia

And to the memory of

Jake Pey

There is a **right** time for everything

A Time to be born, a Time to die

A Time for War, a Time for Peace

CONTENTS

Introduction	5
Wings	7
Boer War 1899-1902 And World War Ii 1939 - 1945	13
The Rhodesian Connection	20
Wild Blue Yonder	35
The Calm Before The Storm	75
Operations	117
Operation Nickel	146
Business And Pleasure	165
Speed And Courage	205
Strike From Above / Find And Destroy	220
Hurricane	229
Strike 1 - Not-Out	240
Mahogany Bomber / Seek And Strike	249
Nibmar	264
Sabotage – Thornhill	312
Reunions	326
Chimoio	356
Bibliography And War Stories	404

INTRODUCTION

Rhodesian Air Force Operations with Airstrike Log and its companion, *Nickel Cross* was first published in 2007.

These two volumes formed the basis for the author's biography. However, the widespread insterest in only short sections of the 'full story' attracted so much interest that several sections were published to meet demands. Now a lot more wiser and knowledgeable demands that strict editing be applied to sustain the interest – especially the war history aspect.
A lesson in War, and life, results in "to the Victor, the spoils". In other words, the Government in power writes its own so-called 'history'. Where this is lacking, especially in Africa, country name changes occur, followed by the hijacking of City, town and even street names. So, before long, places and names like Rhodesia and even Pretoria will fade into the past (dare I say history?). My own factstory biography covers different aspects the past.
Thebiggest change in this edition is the much larger font used. With own eyesight fading rapidly, the reader deserves to see what one is reading.

OuPey
Paeroa
New Zealand
September 2016

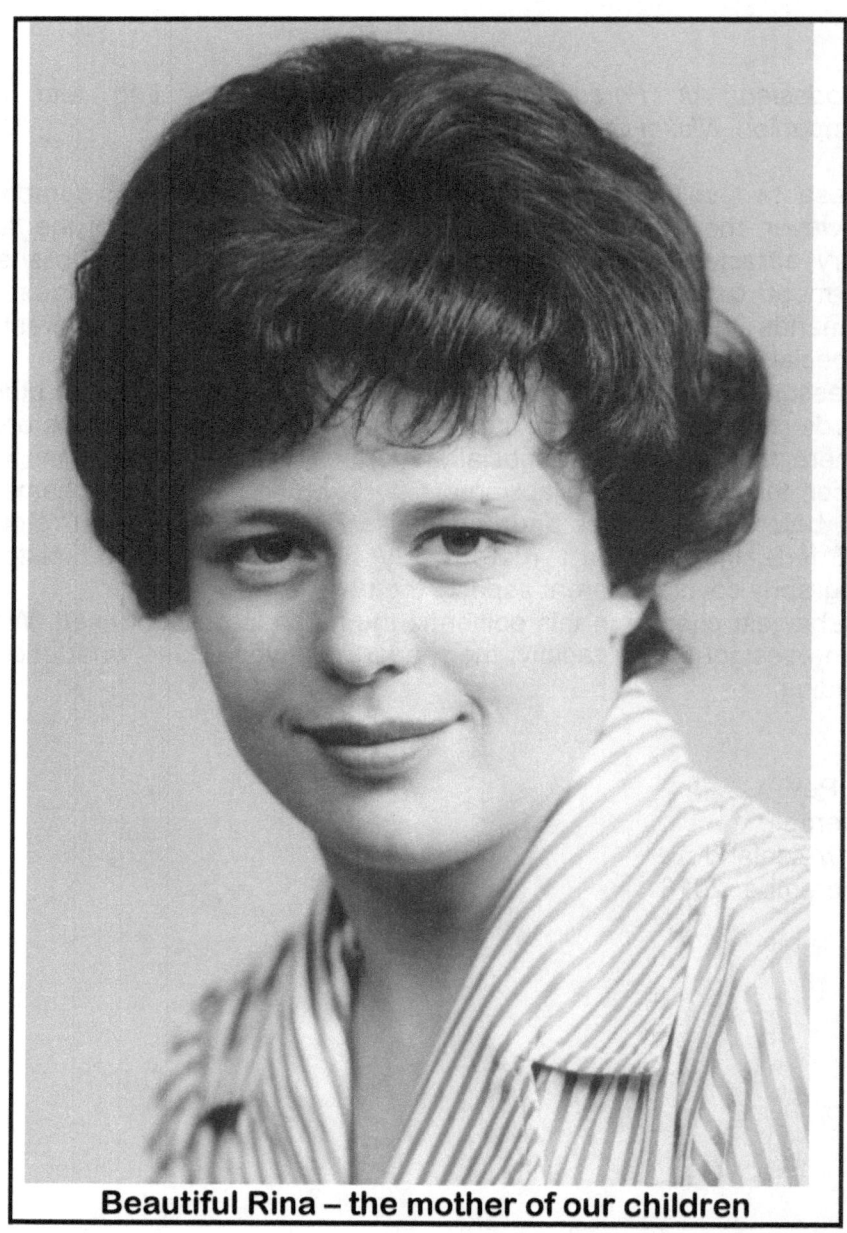
Beautiful Rina – the mother of our children

WINGS

"The Officer Commanding Royal Rhodesian Air Force, Thornhill requests the pleasure of the company of dearest Rina Malan at the Wings Parade of No 16 PTC Officer Cadets to be held at Royal Rhodesian Air Force Thornhill on Saturday, 29th June 1963 at 10h30 to be followed by sherry in the Officers' Mess."
So read the invitation, but unfortunately my future wife was not able to be present. I missed Rina terribly, but was consoled by the fact that I was sharing my very proud moment with the next most loved and respected person in my life - my father.
The moment had finally arrived, after fifteen months of intensive training, to be presented with my Wings - and I understood how proud he must have felt when he was presented with his 'Wings' way back during World War II, on 29th March 1941. That was twenty-two years earlier, at age 25. Here I was, a twenty year old youth, about to embark on a flying career and follow in my father's footsteps.
"Officer Cadet Geldenhuys" bellowed the officer in attendance. Silently, I followed the well-rehearsed drill - attention, shoulder arms, slope arms, quick march - and took the fifty odd steps before coming to a halt in front of the Reviewing Officer, the Chief Justice, Sir John Clayden. I saluted, took a step forward and pushed out my chest whilst the coveted flying badge was clipped onto my left breast. A firm handshake followed then a step backward, another proud salute, smart about turn, and then a quick march back to the squad to take my place as an envied qualified military pilot and commissioned officer in the service of Her Majesty, Queen Elizabeth II.
Nine Officer Cadets of No 16 PTC received their Wings that day, nine of the twelve that had attested into the Royal Rhodesian Air Force on 15th March 1962 to commence flying training. In true, impeccable Air Force tradition, the Wings Parade proceeded like clockwork. We assembled between huge hangars out of sight of all the spectators, invited dignitaries and VIPs. The Parade Adjutant called the three squadrons of airmen, together with the band of the Rhodesian African Rifles (RAR), and lastly the cadets of No 16 Pilot Training Course, to fall in. The march on to the parade ground, or rather hardstanding, in front of the Flying Wing Headquarters, proceeded without a hitch. For the uninitiated, martial music facilitated drill manoeuvres in unison, and this ads splendour to any ceremony. The RAR band played such memorable themes as 'Winged Assegai',

'When the Saints Go Marching In', 'Sweet Banana', 'Those Magnificent Men in their Flying Machines' and 'Auld Lang Syne' at the appropriate time during the ceremony.

Sir John Clayden pinning Wings on Chest

The basic format of the Wings Parade consisted of the March On, the arrival of the Reviewing Officer, General Salute, Inspection followed by the Speech delivered from the dais (all about upholding the high standards and traditions of the RRAF, which were known and acknowledged throughout the world - Sapa). Then followed the Presentation of Wings, announcement and presentation of the Sword of Honour, the privileged March Past in quick and slow time of the newly commissioned officers heralded by a Fly-past. And then the departure of the Reviewing Officer, the honorary March Off of No 16 PTC while being saluted by four Vampire T 11 jets screaming low overhead.

P.M.Geldenhuys   H.C.S.Slatter   W.G.Cronshaw   C.J.T.Dixon   I.J.Bester-Bond   T.McRoberts   B.I.Collocott   A.R.Bruce
P.Molloy   E.R.Wilkinson   Sqdn.Ldr. D.J.Rogers   J.Strachan   K.Welsh

Finally the marching off from the Parade Ground of the three Squadrons followed by the RAR band. So ended the much-envied 'Wings Parade' and the culmination of fifteen months of pilot training and our service as Officer Cadets. We had earned the distinction of wearing the Flying Badge and were commissioned into the Air Force as Acting Pilot Officers. We were no longer dog shit! To record this eventful occasion, immediately after the Parade dismissal, we posed with big smiles for the camera and had our picture taken for posterity.

Pilots WINGS – What it was all about

On Monday morning the Gwelo Times reported: 'Nine cadets of No 16 Pilot Training Course passed out as acting pilot officers at Thornhill RRAF station today when they were presented with their Wings by the Chief Justice, Sir John Clayden. The ceremony was attended by the Chief of Air Staff, Air Vice-Marshal A M Bentley, the Deputy Chief of Air Staff, Air Commodore A O G Wilson and the Minister for Labour and Social Welfare, Mr I F McLean. While the salute was being taken there was a fly-past by Vampires of No 2 squadron. The Chief Justice presented the Sword of Honour to Acting Pilot Officer J F R Strnad. Others passing out were Bruce B J Collocott, C Cronshaw, C Dixon, P M Geldenhuys, T McRoberts, H Slatter and I J Bond. Sir John congratulated them and said he hoped they would uphold the high standards and traditions of the RRAF, which were known and acknowledged throughout the world.'

Chris Dixon had his name misspelled in the papers, but I'm sure that did not detract from the achievement, or the dignity of the "Wings Parade".

FIRST SOLO

It is perhaps also worth mentioning here that going solo for the first time is even better than sex. Having said that I would now like to describe that most terrifying of experiences before going back to the beginning which I should perhaps have done in the first place.

The magic day was Monday, 13th August 1962. The magic aircraft was Percival Provost T Mk 52, No 301. I was still a teenager, wet behind the ears, nineteen years old. My wonderful instructor was Flying Officer (later Group Captain) Peter Petter-Bowyer or P-B, as he was affectionately known.

I had taken off that Monday morning quite unsuspectingly - everything was quite normal, and I had no inkling that I was about to go solo. In fact, I did not have a sortie on the Friday, and so I was not expecting my first solo that day. The pre-solo flight consisted of taxiing, take-off and climb, medium turns, some stalling, spinning and approach and landings. The only strange thing was that we had only been flying for half an hour when Sir P-B instructed me to return to base and announced that I was ready for first solo. Flying Officer Pat Meddows-Taylor, an 'A' Category QFI (Qualified Flying Instructor) gave me my solo check, which consisted of two approaches and landings before he instructed me to 'full stop' - the sortie would last fifteen minutes. I back-tracked and, without switching off, allowed sufficient time for him to tie the red sock to my tail wheel - the symbol to other intrepid flyers that a fly-boy was about to go solo. I hasten to add that the red sock was also a warning to other aviators to give me a wide berth, and for the crash rescue chaps to be on full alert.

Well, the moment had arrived for my youthful ambition to become a reality. I opened the throttle with gusto, felt the kick in the backside and, before one could say "PATCASATNIE" - I was airborne - all by myself without an instructor to hold my hand. To be airborne, all alone for the first time, in a mean machine, with 550 horsepower hurtling you through space at a mean 100 knots, overcoming the force of gravity, feeling free as a bird in the sky, with awesome power at your fingertips, this is a feeling words fail to describe and yet your machine is a deadly one. But now, there I was in the air, all by myself, having done it my way. What do you know? I had gone first solo.

Then the horrifying thought crosses your mind - I got up here all alone, but now I have to get safely back to the ground. An adrenaline rush sobers the mind. Then with 110% concentration, the vital actions come automatically because of the thoroughness of one's instruction. The ground rushes up as one lines up on the runway centreline. Next, the rubber makes contact with the grass. A small hop, skip and jump follows as the Provost settles on the ground. After shutting down in the dispersal area, the ground crew come to meet one with a wheelbarrow?

My first solo had lasted only five minutes, and yet it had taken me twelve hours and ten minutes to prepare for this momentous event - well above average for the course. I will explain later what went through my mind as I flew that wonderful sortie, and also what things I should have done which I didn't.

Going Solo – the early days

The Wild Blue Yonder
The Wild Blue Yonder – Oh, What a wonderful feeling

BOER War 1899-1902 and WORLD WAR II

1939 - 1945

Lizzie Geldenhuys – with Hettie, who died in the Boer War Concentration Camp, Kroonstad, 15-8-1901

LIZZIE GELDENHUYS

My grandmother inspired me to continue the family tradition of documenting our proud heritage. I felt that my father's 'World War II' story, as well as my own involvement in the Rhodesian War, should

be told in a similar vein as that authored by Ou Mam - for the benefit of our grandchildren, and their children.
Her tribute has been published in earlier editions.

JOHANNES ALBERTUS GELDENHUYS

Johannes Albertus Geldenhuys, or Jannie as he was called, was my 'Ou Dad', or grandfather, and was born on 8th July 1877, to Hendrik Jacobus and Elizabeth Schikkerling. He was a direct, eighth generation descendant of Albert Barends Gildenhuisz and Margaretha Hoefnagels. Albert (our "Stamvader" - forefather) arrived at the Cape from Burgsteinfurt, Wesfale, Germany, as a sailor onboard the ship *'Princesse Royale'*. He became a "Vryburger" in September 1661, the year before Cape founder Jan van Riebeeck returned to the Netherlands. He was employed as a farm labourer on various farms, notably with Herman Fer Schekhoven, then Coenelis Claas and then a Jacob Cloete. In 1666 Albert Barends returned to Duitsland and married Margaretha Hoefnagels. He got married, had a son and came back to the Cape in 1672, with his wife and first born, on board the *'Vrye Lieden'*. They had a further seven children, all born in the Cape.

My grandfather, Ou Dad married Ou Mam on 27th June 1899, with the wedding taking place at De Bank, Oupa Preller's farm about three miles from Bothaville. The newlyweds settled initially at Katbos View adjoining De Bank, then later after the Boere oorlog at Rustpan which became well known as the 'familie plaas' - the birthplace of both my father and me. Ou Dad's father, Oupa Geldenhuys' farm, was at Rietgat, approximately twenty-five miles from Bothaville.

Jannie Geldenhuys (sitting) and Abram Preller, Umballa Boer Camp, India 1902

The Anglo-Boer War diaries of Jannie Geldenhuys was published as a separate edition in 2009 while at Durban, South Africa, and subsequently updated with a Lulu.com edition, whilst in New Zealand.

Never-the-less, the photograph ideally sets the scene for the next chapter – World War II but specifically the East African Campaign.

My grandfather Jan, Uncle Henry and my father Preller Geldenhuys - 1940's Army and Air Force service during World War II

LIEUT ABRAM CARL FREDRIC PRELLER GELDENHUYS - SAAF

Dad attested into the South African Air Force at Roberts Heights on 5th May 1940, and served briefly at East London and Bloemfontein before joining pilot training with No 1 Elementary Flying Training School (EFTS) Baragwanath on 9th September 1940.

All Smiles - with First Solo
Going solo – and pranging soon thereafter

Gladiator Prang at Jimma by Ou Dad Geldenhuys

THE RHODESIAN CONNECTION

SAAF INTERLUDE - GREAT NORTH ROAD

World War II ended on the 15th August 1945, on my brother Jan's fifth birthday. Dad last flew with 'A' Flight, No 43 Air School, in Harvard 7342 on 29th August - having logged 1,231 hours and 15 minutes. He completed his tour with 43 Air School on 8th October 1945, having flown 16 types, and was released from the SAAF as Lieutenant on 7th November 1945. Although my ancestors were farmers, and Dad had inherited the "familie plaas Rustpan", he was reluctant to return to farming as a career. He ceded his inheritance to his brother-in-law Steyn Jordaan and persuaded my Mom to head for the Great North Road - or at least to Northern Rhodesia - and give copper mining a go as a trail-busting career.

COPPERBELT - NORTHERN RHODESIA

By the end of the following year, my parents had settled at Luanshya with Dad as a miner with the Roan Antelope Copper Mine. Pioneering prospector William Collier discovered copper deposits in 1902 in what became one of the world's richest copper-producing countries. The Copperbelt mining towns, from north to south, are Bancroft, Chingola, Mufulira, Chambishi, Chibuluma, Kitwe and Luanshya. The Refinery and administrative centre was at Ndola. Dad mined at Roan Antelope (Luanshya) and Nchanga (Chingola). All of the larger towns had flying clubs. But it was not long before he got his bum in the air again, going solo in Piper Cub VP-RBG on my fifth birthday – 20th February 1948. However I had to wait until 15th July for my first air experience. Dad's first passenger was Willem Boshoff, followed by Master Jan and Master Preller Geldenhuys.

At that age, I presume I was privileged to have defied gravity even before starting schooling. What I do recall however, is that the "g" forces terrified me whereas my brother Jan certainly loved it - the sortie lived up to its callsign - not phonetically "Bravo Golf" but "Bak Gat". My brother Jan took to the air like a duck to water.

The following day, my sister Delene, who was then only 3 years old, enjoyed her first air experience (and according to Dad's log books) so much so that she became a regular "hog" - in Air Force jargon, hogging the hours.

Anyway, during the ensuing year, the Geldenhuys children became regular aviators. I enjoyed no fewer than eight sorties and logging up numerous types to my credit, namely Piper Cub, Cruiser, Voyager and a Stinson.

A break of eight years followed, and by 1957 my parents moved to Chingola with Dad now mining at Nchanga Copper Mines Ltd. By July of that year Dad had joined the Chingola Flying Club, and I, the Boy Scouts. It was not long before I again enjoyed flying and logged up another couple of sorties.

Being an intrepid aviator, and a keen Boy Scout I soon set about earning as many Proficiency Badges as I could - and it was not long before I achieved the dubious distinction of being one of the first Copperbelt Scouts to be awarded the Airmanship Badge. Since there were no Air Scouts there at the time, the Badge had to be sent for from Lusaka before the presentation could be made. With my Dad being an active Flying Club member, I had the added advantage of being schooled by my father in the rudiments of Airmanship, and could put into practice the marshalling of the light aircraft operations at the aerodromes. I'm sure Dad was very proud of me for being the first recipient of the Boy Scout's Airmanship award on the Copperbelt.

DAWNIE GELDENHUYS

Dawnie was the first Rhodesian born Geldenhuys. Dawnie, our youngest sister, was born at Luanshya in 1949, and had just grown out of babyhood when my father transferred to Chingola and bought ten acres at Musenga Plots, some ten miles out of town.

One Friday evening, 13th August 1954, a Swahili set fire to our thatched cottage which was occupied at that time only by my elder brother Jan, my sister Delene and six year old Dawnie. Jan and Delene survived the inferno - Dawnie didn't. Jan had woken up to the sound of a gunshot. It was the gun my father had kept next to his bed. The bedroom section curtains had caught alight and the heat had caused the gun to go off. The thatched cottage was filled with smoke and as Jan got down from the top bunk bed, he roused my younger sister Delene from her slumber - no doubt because of the carbon dioxide effect of all the smoke. He searched the bottom bunk bed for my little sister Dawn, but could not find nor see her. He concluded that she had already vacated the bed and was most probably already outside because of the intense heat within the cottage. Jan then dragged Delene out of the raging fire and once outside tried in vain to locate our youngest sister. By this time the thatched roof had collapsed in, and the heat and fire from the thatch so intense that it was impossible to attempt re-entering the burning cottage. In fact, had he done so, he would not have survived the attempt.

My parents were visiting me at that time, having been hospitalised with Malaria. They had gone to catch a movie before Dad went on night shift, while Mom returned to the plot - only to be confronted by the tragic events of that unlucky Friday the 13th.

A Swahili from up North was the prime suspect. The Swahili, who had been recruited as a domestic on one of our frequent fishing trips to the lakes - Tanganyika, Bangwelo and Mrewa - was never brought to justice for his arson. He was thought to have set our caravan and several thatched rondavels alight at weekly or fortnightly intervals. The police would post a guard at the plot, but has soon as the police presence was withdrawn, a further incident would occur. These fires continued for quite a while, and the police was quite useless in taking the culprit into custody, despite all the incriminating evidence.

The loss of Dawnie caused my mother to have several bouts of severe depression - the worst being when she put a revolver under her chin and pulled the trigger - and was fortunately saved by her false teeth. The round deflected off the bottom set, shattered the top plate and exited via the mouth. Apart from having her broken jaw wired up, Mum was indeed lucky to survive the suicide attempt.

I am pleased to record that Mom survived untold "All Things Bright and Beautiful, All Things Great and Small" thereafter, (the tune was Dawn's favourite) - and even outlived my father. Today's date is Friday 13th August 1999 - precisely 45 years ago to the day - that I edited this work. It is perhaps by Divine Intervention, rather than pure coincidence, that I had occasion to witness this tragic event in the Geldenhuys household. Dawnie has been in my thoughts all day. I trust God, in all his wisdom, that the heavenly Angels continue to protect and keep her from all evil, and that God's mercy will continue to shine his light on our offspring in memory of a beautiful lost one. By the time our grandchildren read this, I trust that they would at least live to experience and see out 45 years.

All of the A C F Preller Geldenhuys children had their early schooling on the Copperbelt towns of Luanshya and Chingola. It even included a Convent school, although our schooling was mainly at Government schools.

Jan and I took up boxing and wrestling - but were forced to give it up when we lost our annual subscriptions (We had gone swimming at the local pool, and left the cash in our clothes to be stolen). Jan excelled in wrestling, and was only beaten on points during the Northern Rhodesia Championships. When our renewal subscriptions were stolen, we then took up cycling instead and spent our weekends cycling to nearby rivers and streams to fish. Jan, who was good with his hands, had manufactured professional trailers for our bikes in which to load our tents cooking pots and fishing gear. A favourite fishing spot, within cycling distance, was on the Kafue river that runs from west to east just north of Chingola – on the road to Bancroft. Whilst at Luanshya, our favoured camping site was at Kafulafuta. The junction of the Kafulafuta and Kafue rivers, about 14 miles south-west of Luanshya was also great for hunting, fishing and camping.

Whilst on the Copperbelt, my parents' favourite past-time was to travel to the Great Lakes districts of Northern Rhodesia. These included Lake Tanganyika, Lake Mweru and Lake Bangweulu. To get there, one had to travel through the Belgian Congo, entering at Mokambo, and driving on the right hand side of the road, and exiting at Chembe. The next stop was at Fort Roseberry, the fastest-growing town in the northern province at that time - with its white population of 200 souls. Bangweulu only had a couple of small settlements – at Mwamfuli and Samfya – with dried fish being the main commercial activity. The Lake was generally very shallow, and one could easily kick up mud by the outboard motors of our boats, despite being several miles from the shores. In fact, my father got semi-stuck on one occasion when he dived overboard for a swim. The large Luapula river runs into Lake Mweru, and the area is infested with crocodiles. Tiger fishing was particularly good at Mweru and it was not uncommon for the womenfolk to bottle 600lbs of curried fish during our frequent fishing trips. I recall catches averaged about nineteen fish an hour. The Lake itself is about 80-miles long, but my parents preferred camping along the rivers, about seven miles from the lake inlets. Developments along the northern reaches of the lake were hampered by the lack of decent roads.

To get to Lake Tanganyika from Fort Roseberry, we would travel to Luwingu, Kasama, Abercorn, and then take the treacherous Great Rift Valley road down to the Mpulungu port settlement. Abercorn was the nearest sizeable town to the lake. There is a beautiful waterfall near Luwingu. I remember an occasion when my Dad caught a leguaan by the tail – the reptile is extremely agile and just catching it as it scurried towards the lake was no mean feat. Lake Tanganyika was described in the Horizon as one of the deepest – and most beautiful – lakes in the world. It came thus as no surprise why my Dad had decided to immigrate to the Copperbelt en route to North Africa during World War II.

Jan and I hitchhiked from the Copperbelt to spend time on a farm at Fort Victoria, Southern Rhodesia. It was not long thereafter that my father decided to pack up mining to go farming instead - to Stanmore farm outside Fort Victoria.

SOUTHERN RHODESIA

Once settled as a "plaas japie", I was sent off to boarding school - initially to Guinea Fowl and then to Thornhill High School - both having been Rhodesian Air Training Group (RATG) bases during the war. Dad had passed through the latter during World War II on his way to North Africa. Unfortunately THS had vacated the Air Force base, a term before my arrival, and moved to new premises on the Salisbury road. I thus found myself in a brand new school that had to develop its traditions from scratch.

Thornhill High School, Gwelo – Head boy of Cranwell House

My brother Jan remained on the Copperbelt to finish his Blacksmith/Boiler-maker apprenticeship, in addition to completing a Diesel Mechanic artisan's course. Delene was sent to a farm school at Andrew Louw, Fort Victoria.

My father bought an old Bedford lorry for the household removals from Chingola to Stanmore farm and also to commence farming with. His life savings from mining were used up to buy seed, an old second hand Fordson tractor and basic farming implements. Our first crop of mielies, kaffircorn and castor oil seeds was a disaster. The second crop was not much better.

Farming was not a bed of roses and it was not long before Dad was forced to seek supplementary employment - building the road that leads to Kyle Dam. Not only did he do this with distinction but also received a gratuity for designing an instrument for blasting the approach road to the dam wall site through the granite kopjies which is a natural feature in the Kyle landscape.

Aerial Photo of Thornhill School - Gwelo

Delene meanwhile befriended the Frans and Lettie Malan children at Andrew Louw and then went on to Chaplin School. Hendrik, Philip, Rina and then Frans Malan ended up going to Thornhill High School.
Thornhill High School was good to me giving me a good education - eight subjects at Cambridge University School Certificate / GCE "O" Levels (General Certificate of Education, Ordinary Level). In addition, I was made a Prefect and Head Boy of Cranwell House, the Boys Hostel. I also enjoyed sport - Victor Ludorum at athletics, Captain of the 1st XV-rugby team, played 2nd XI cricket and was a semi-finalist in the Midlands Tennis Championships.
I did not do so well at "A" Level - I bombed out at Subsidiary Level with the excuse of being accepted for flying training in the Air Force.
Meanwhile on the farm, our fortunes declined resulting in my parents settling back in South Africa where my father started selling insurance for Old Mutual in Bothaville. It was not long before he returned to mining at Orkney.

RINA MALAN

I met Susanna Catharina Malan at school. Unbeknown to me at that time, she had already visited my parents on Stanmore with Delene - her shamwari from the Andrew Louw Farm school that they both attended. It is also coincidental that Philip, her twin brother, was my skivvy when he became a boarder at Cranwell hostel, Thornhill High School. Let me add quickly for the record - us "bullies" upstairs took on the "juniors" downstairs in a free-for-all rough and tumble; and they certainly did not come off second best. As a direct result of the beating we received from the skivvies, I developed a healthy respect for my brother-in-law to be.

Rina and I enjoyed many a happy memory at school. Miss Nuttal, in particular, often had us on the carpet for groping and kissing - not to mention all the opportunities in the various Gilbert and Sullivan school Operas - such as Pirates of Penzance, The Mikado and Iolanthe.

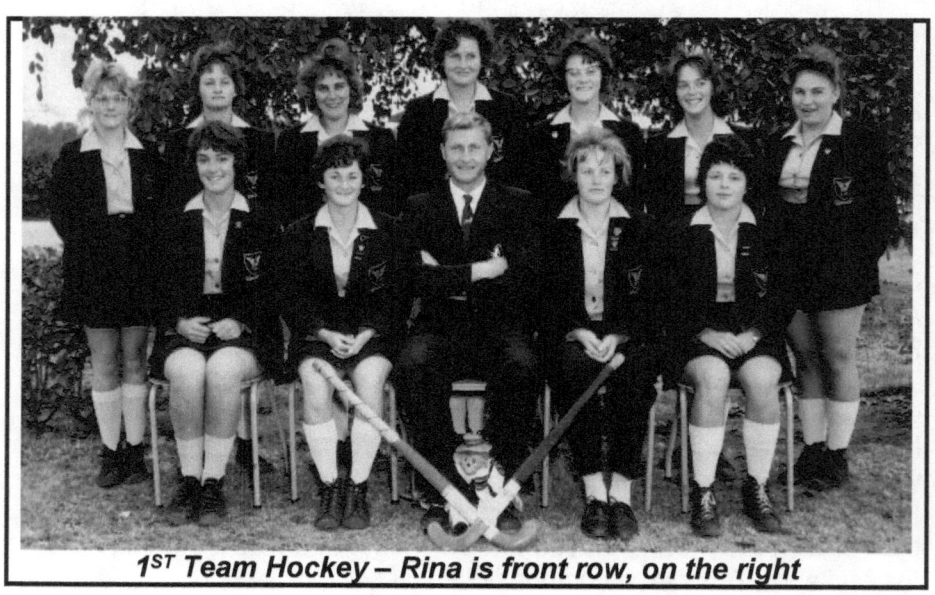

1ST Team Hockey – Rina is front row, on the right

With my parents settled at Orkney, I travelled to school by train from Klerksdorp to Gwelo and return. During a changeover at Bulawayo Station I was accosted, by a "poofta" bum-bandit/poephol pirate, but thanks to my athletic ability I did not become a victim of child abuse. As a result of this unsavoury incident, my generous father gave me a Morris Minor OMB 663 - my first roadworthy car. I had envious wheels to spend some school holidays and all exeat weekends with Rina on their farm.

This brings me to my first meeting with Oom Frans. It was during one of the Schools athletic meetings that Rina introduced me to her parents. The old man took half-a-crown from his pocket and handed me the two-and-six (twenty-five cents) with the words "Vat dit en loop. Ek wil nie snotkoppe hê wat met my dogter lol nie." Like a flustered fool I took his money and made sex my departure - only to be brought back to earth by Rina who convinced me that there was always great humour in the Malan household - no matter what the hardships.

Thornhill High School, Gwelo – Head boy of Cranwell House

During one visit to Kombisa, Rina and I were lying on the bed in the boy's room "resting" after the midday meal. I was becoming annoyed with the twin brother whom I presumed was tugging at my big toe. I retorted angrily "Los ons uit - kan jy nie sien dat ons besig is om te vry nie". Who should stick his head out from the end of the bed but Oom Frans.

During the Nyasaland Emergency the boys from Cranwell were required to "guard" the girls Halton hostel. This was the start of the Federal break-up and "cricket stumps and baseball bats" - a little more about these episodes later on.

The following three photographs are rather interesting – firstly the First, Rugby Team that I captained, and then the Thornhill School Prefects. Of particular interest is my best buddy, Rodney McNeill as we appeared in 1961, and then again 45 years later in 2007.

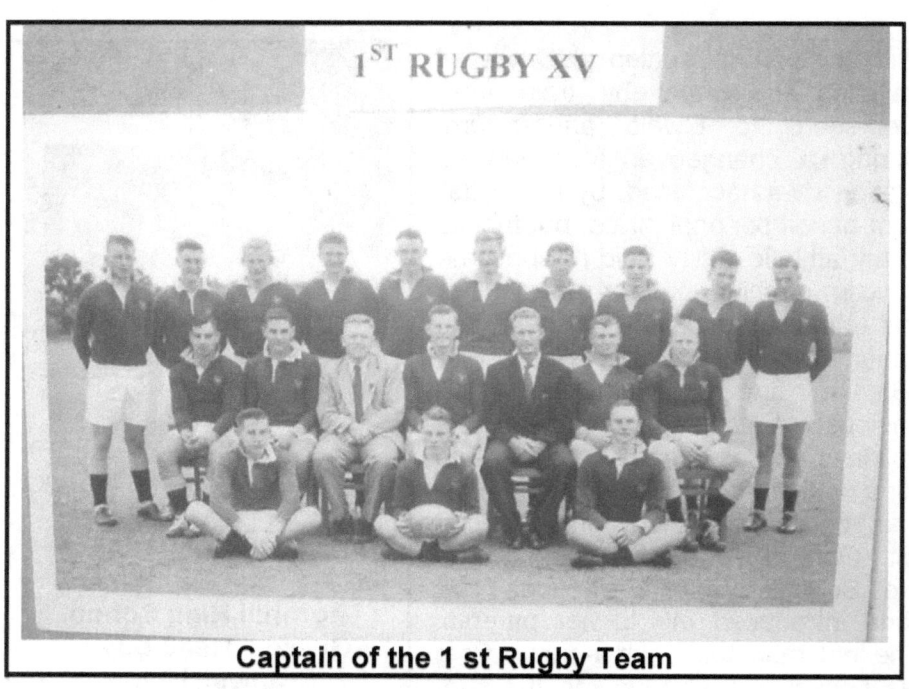

Captain of the 1 st Rugby Team

Louis de Haas, Preller Geldenhuys (Head Boy), Rodney McNeill, Koetie Coetzee and John Perry

Prop Geldenhuys and Rodney McNeill – in 2007

FEDERATION - THE WINDS OF CHANGE

The Central African Federation, the regional political structure, which linked Southern and Northern Rhodesia and Nyasaland had been encouraged and established by the British Conservative Government. It involved five governments - Britain, the Federal Administration, and the three territories - the premise being that in unity there is strength.

Each of the three territories was at a different stage of development when the Federation was formed in 1953. Southern Rhodesia had been self-governing since 1923, Northern Rhodesia (Zambia) was on the way to achieving a similar status, while Nyasaland (Malawi) was still under colonial rule. Southern Rhodesia, because of its more powerful economy and larger white population, tended to dominate the Federation, as did its armed forces. Economically, the Federation proved a tremendous success, and there was great expansion in all fields. The hydro-electric project at Kariba, which my brother Jan and I visited during its construction, was completed. There was vast industrial development, and a fine system of trunk roads, and 'strips', was laid down to link the Federation's main centres.

Yet, despite the many advantages of what was a most complicated structure, the Federation was bitterly opposed by Africans who felt the whole plan had been imposed on them. Black nationalist Joshua Nkomo stood up at a conference in London and stated that he rejected the idea - and yet the British forged ahead with their plans to create the Federation. It was Harold McMillan's era of de-colonisation. Self-determination and Black Nationalism were sweeping down Africa, and the Africans in the Federation wanted their own independence, not junior partnership in a white-dominated country. They wanted Britain to dismantle the Federation and hand over power to the people.

In 1959, African National Congress parties in each of the three territories began a deliberate campaign of rioting and intimidation. In Southern Rhodesia the party was banned and the leaders put behind bars, but the rioting, intimidation, crop-burning, cattle maiming and assaults continued. The British Empire started crumbling whilst I was still at school. Sudan gained its independence in 1956, followed by Ghana in 1957, Nigeria in 1960 and Sierra Leone in 1961. British Somaliland, on the horn of Africa, became independent in 1960 and became part of Somalia.

By the time Tanzania followed in 1961, trouble at home had already started with the Nyasaland Emergency of 1958-59. Thus the opportunity for the Thornhill Cranwell boys to 'guard' the Halton girl's hostel arose. The boarding school boys armed themselves with an array of weapons to defend the defenceless girls. The night patrols certainly provided many an opportunity for the boys to play hanky-panky with their sweethearts - the burglar bars on the windows were no match for the ingenuity of the randy boys - who breached the physical barrier with gay abandon. "It takes a thief to catch a thief".

By the time I joined the Air Force, Uganda had gained their independence in 1962, followed (with all its Mau Mau horror stories) by Kenya, and named after its so called liberator, Jomo Kenyatta - in 1963. Tanzania's independence, in 1963, produced Julius Nyerere, who subsequently proved a thorn in Rhodesia's side for many a year later - always throwing a spanner in the works. The break-up of the Federation of Rhodesia and Nyasaland became very topical. Both Hastings Kamusu Banda and Joshua Nkomo transited Air Force bases - on some occasions whilst I, as the SDO (Station Duty Officer), was required to meet the aircraft and attend to the needs of the aircrews and passengers.

No 4 Squadron's Percival Provosts were always at the forefront of the bush wars in that their primary role was maintaining internal security. Aircraft were deployed for the Nyasaland Emergency and also the Congo border disturbances that followed. January 1964 brought radical changes for the squadron - moving from New Sarum to Thornhill (to swap bases with No 5 Squadrons Canberras) and for the restructuring of flying training.

Harold MacMillan's "Winds of Change" was by now in full swing. Nyasaland's Hastings Banda gained independence for Malawi in 1964 as did Northern Rhodesia's Kenneth Kaunda for Zambia. Gambia followed suit in 1965 - the same year that Ian Douglas Smith defied the British Empire and unilaterally declared independence (UDI) on Armistice Day, 11th November 1965.

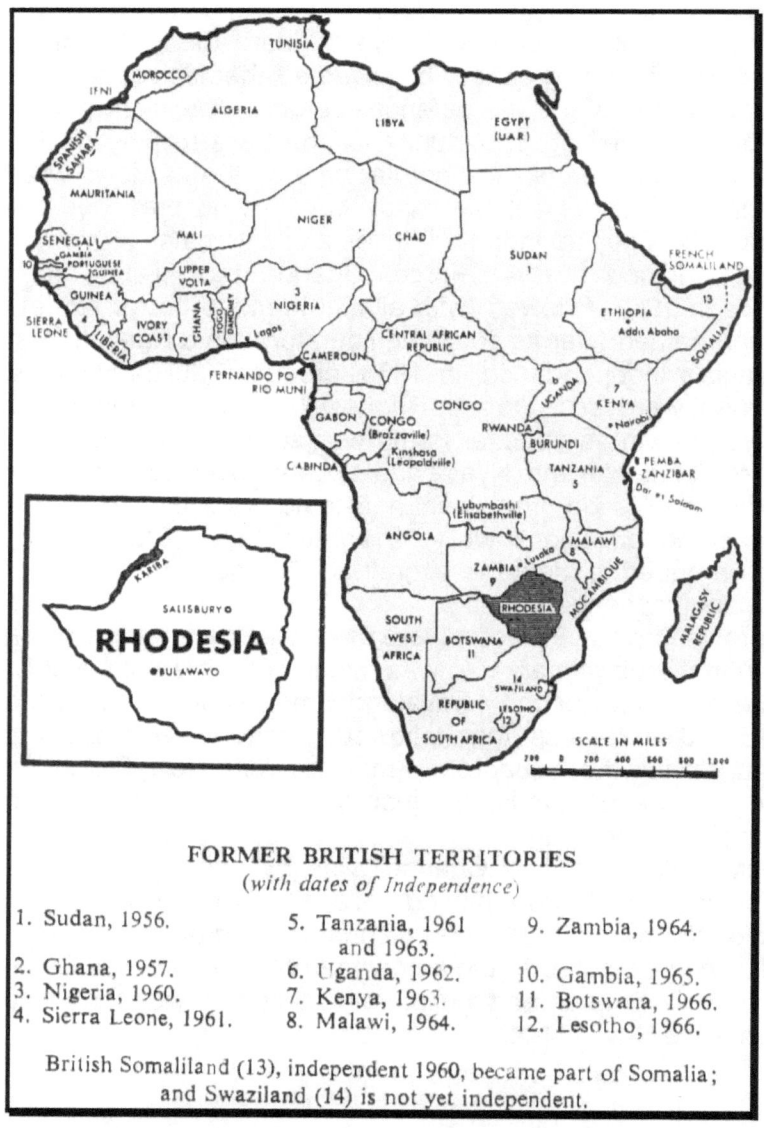

FORMER BRITISH TERRITORIES
(with dates of Independence)

1. Sudan, 1956.
2. Ghana, 1957.
3. Nigeria, 1960.
4. Sierra Leone, 1961.
5. Tanzania, 1961 and 1963.
6. Uganda, 1962.
7. Kenya, 1963.
8. Malawi, 1964.
9. Zambia, 1964.
10. Gambia, 1965.
11. Botswana, 1966.
12. Lesotho, 1966.

British Somaliland (13), independent 1960, became part of Somalia; and Swaziland (14) is not yet independent.

Bechuanaland became Botswana in 1966, and Lesotho gained its independence the same year. Swaziland followed shortly thereafter to establish a Kingdom. By 1975 the Portuguese beat a hasty retreat from their African colonies, leaving Mozambique and Angola in virtual ruins. South West Africa followed and became Namibia - but wait a minute - I seem to have jumped the gun, because much still needs to be told of other 'war stories'.

The mid-1960s were momentous and historical years. It concerned stories of men and nations caught up in the turmoil of war - be they heroes or villains, and sometimes both.

CRICKET STUMPS AND BASEBALL BATS

Nineteen fifty-nine was a memorable year at Thornhill High School. Cranwell Boys' Hostel was given the task of 'protecting' Halton Girls' Hostel and Head Boy Prop Geldenhuys had great pleasure in 'guarding' Rina Malan, especially during the hours of darkness. In effect, it gave the boys licence to roam around the girls' hostel, and indulge in a bit of mischief. We would arm ourselves with an array of weapons, mainly an assortment of sporting bats and cricket stumps, and spend our time dodging the patrolling police car searchlights while we would dream up methods of maintaining body contact with the opposite sex.

Our own arrangement was for Rina to tie a length of wool to her big toe and attach the other end to the burglar bar. I would then come in the middle of the night, scale the wall up to the windowsill, and yank on the length of wool until Rina appeared at the window. Unfortunately though, she had the habit of tossing and turning and would get entangled in the wool thus using up a whole ball, and, much to my disgust, I would have to reel in yards and yards of fleece before she appeared.

A certain Pinky Peters was not as fortunate. His girlfriend was on the first floor and to get to her, he had to scale the toilet drainpipe. This carried on for several nights until one night he was caught red-handed in the girl's ablutions. No schoolboy since has ever been able to emulate his greased lightning slide down the pipe and headlong dash for his own bed at Cranwell, a distance which he covered in Olympic time. He was fortunate not to have been expelled.

The Police - BSAP - meanwhile had successfully completed Operation *Spider* which was a counter-insurgency operation in February 1959 that had rounded up 500 leading nationalists. It was the biggest operation of its kind to date. Joshua Nkomo escaped the net because he was out of the country at that time. This pre-emptive action prevented Nkomo's 'Youth' from causing mayhem 'to create a crisis in Southern Rhodesia' - to coincide with Nkomo's allegations at the United Nations that "Rhodesia was in crisis".

MILITARY FORMATIONS

Under heavy pressure from the nationalists, the British sent a commission to Africa, and the outcome was a suggestion that the Federation should be dismantled. This was not acceptable to the Federal Government. And it became obvious that the Federal Army's structure needed alteration and expansion to cope with the internal political factors.
Until the sixties, Rhodesia had never had a regular white Army. There were four African battalions in the Federation as well as a white territorial force (TF). In an era of black nationalism it was decided to increase force levels by recruiting Europeans into newly-formed all white units: one Infantry battalion, The Rhodesian Light Infantry (RLI); one armoured car squadron; The Selous Scouts; "C" Squadron, Special Air Service (SAS), and the Parachute Training School (PTS) of the Royal Rhodesian Air Force.
On the political front, a new Constitution had been negotiated in 1961 between the Southern Rhodesian and British Governments, which increased the franchise in order to place Africans on the voters' roll - this meant the beginning of the end of the Federation. Harold McMillan's historic winds of change were blowing.
Southern Rhodesia, the wealthiest partner, had strengthened its armed forces, and it was time for me to gaze into the wild blue yonder.

WILD BLUE YONDER

SAAF vs. RRAF

The decision had been taken to pursue a flying career. I applied to both the South African and Rhodesian Air Forces and was duly summoned to present myself at the respective Selection Boards. My father, who was familiar with protocol, accompanied me to SAAF Headquarters in Pretoria. On arrival, and to my utter amazement, the 'Old Man' jumped the queue and was accepted for re-attestation into the force. When my turn came up, I was advised that aircrews needed to do one year's Air Force Gymnasium service starting mid-January and that the next intake selections had already been made. I was advised to return to school and re-apply for the following year's intake. I did not fancy that option.

The Royal Rhodesian Air Force Selection Board followed shortly thereafter, with joining instructions anticipated mid-March. A Rhodesian Herald correspondent headlined his article thus: - "***Africans, 1 Asian seek RRAF jobs***

Salisbury, Friday. – Three Africans and one Asian are among 92 applicants for pilot training with the Royal Rhodesian Air Force. All are from the Federation. Examinations and selection boards will start on January 7.

"An RRAF spokesman said today that there were about 15 vacancies for pilot trainees. "We demand a very high standard and the examination is a rigorous one," the spokesman said. "With 92 applicants we take the cream of the very best."

Applicants were not only assessed on their potential flying ability but also on their general officer qualities, he said.

BASIC FLYING

Successful candidates will undergo a two-year course, which includes four months' initial training. Basic flying training is done on Provost aircraft and jet training on Vampires. Towards the end of their course trainees go to an operational conversion unit where they learn about armaments and battle formations.

Successful candidates will enter the RRAF on March 12.

After borrowing my brother's brand new Saab motor car, I made my way up to New Sarum Air Force Base and met up with Bruce Collocott in the car park. The selection process was really tough, with several batteries of psychometric, aptitude and medical elimination tests. Then the final Selection Board hurdle was surmounted. To my absolute delight I was indeed fortunate to make the grade.

It was now early January 1962 and I had joined my brother for some farming in the Kroonstad area. My father was a miner and staying in flatted houses in Orkney, south west Transvaal. Then during the third week the official offer of employment arrived, to my great relief and joy. The "aircraftman" offer was puzzling, but just the mention of "join the RRAF for flying training has received the recommendation of the Selection Board..." was enough to satisfy me that the opportunity to fulfil my dreams was at least on the horizon. Preparations commenced immediately to report for duty in mid-March.

The letter of offer addressed to me as P.M. Geldenhuys, Esq., 10c Flatted Houses, Kipling Road Orkney, Transvaal, was dated 15 January 1962.

My Dad was most envious. He still had quite a wait for his re-joining instructions for the South African Air Force. However, I would like to think that he was tremendously proud that his son would be following in his foot steps in pursuing a flying career. All those "air experiences" whilst a member of the various Copperbelt Flying Clubs were certainly about to pay dividends.

I did not relish the idea of waiting another year for the much larger SAAF prospect, and jumped at the opportunity of joining the RRAF. It was a wise decision, borne out by the following quotes that I collected many years later.

"The Rhodesian Air Force is rated small, even pocket-sized. But military authorities everywhere count it as one of the most inventive and effective strike forces in the world" - John Lovatt, Contact, 1977.

"Along with the Israelis, Rhodesia had one of the best small air forces in the world. The Israelis, however, get all the latest American equipment whereas the Rhodesians had to make do with ingenuity and sheer guts. Behind the guts was a very high standard of efficiency. A common method of assessing this efficiency is the proportion of men to aircraft. In Rhodesia the figure was about 25:1. The South African figure is about 100:1 and in the USA and UK the rating is between 250 and 400 to one." - Paul L. Moorcraft, Contact, 1981.

"Here is a breed of men the like of which has not been seen for many a long time" - General Sir Walter Walker, former NATO Commander quoted in the London Times, January 1978.

"Professionalism" - General Peter Walls, June 1979, when asked what the greatest strength of the armed forces was.

ORBAT AND HISTORY

The 'Orbat' or Order of Battle of a force refers to the Unit Formations that make up the organisational structures. The Royal Rhodesian Air Force was structured on Royal Air Force lines with its three separate Wings - Flying, Technical and Administrative Wings both on the Stations and at Air Headquarters. The HQ Branches were similarly structured. Both the Air Branch and Flying Wing branch enjoyed seniority over the others. All the 'Units' fell under their respective 'Wing', or 'Branch'. For example, flying units would be named Squadrons, and numbered numerically i.e. No 1 Squadron, followed by No 2, then No 3 and so on and so forth. Each Wing would have several Units, each charged with a specific 'role' or function, plus be suitably equipped to perform its responsibilities.
Command and Control was rigidly enforced, and with set lines of communication - upwards, downwards and sideways. One soon learnt what it meant by "going through the correct channels" in order to convey messages or instructions. Deviation from accepted norms was not tolerated. Traditions were soon established and the tried and tested methods employed by the military stood the test of time. Many a serviceman owes his life skills to the excellent schooling that one gains from any military establishment. The study of Air Force History is an essential aspect of pilot training
Flight Lieutenant Dirk Cloete, MC, AFC, was seconded from the Royal Air Force to the SAAF on 21st July 1921 and appointed Officer Commanding Zwartkop Aerodrome. He was later responsible for the formation of the Rhodesian Air Force in its early stages.
Rhodesia and Nyasaland Airways – RANA – was formed in 1933. Its fleet consisted of de Havilland Fox Moths, Puss Moths and Westland Wessex. In April 1934, the de Havilland Aircraft Company in England floated the de Havilland Aircraft Company (Rhodesia) Ltd. The company became contractor to the Government for the initial training of military pilots.
In 1934 the Rhodesian Government offered the United Kingdom an annual grant of £10,000 for Empire Defence, but the Imperial Government suggested that a more useful purpose would be served by raising and training an air squadron on the lines of the Auxiliary Air Force in Great Britain. The De Havilland Company in Rhodesia was commissioned to undertake the elementary training of pilots, and took on eight volunteers in November 1935 at its Flying School at

Belvedere. The Air Force began with the formation of a Territorial Force Air Unit and the commencement of flying training at Belvedere Airport, Salisbury, in 1935.

In 1936 work started on the first military airfield at Cranborne, and in the same year, provision was made for airmen to join the Permanent Staff Corps of the Southern Rhodesian Defence Force, under the command of Major Dirk Cloete – the Director of Civil Aviation. Major Cloete brought out the first fitters and riggers from England, and six Hawker Hart aircraft from the Royal Air Force (RAF) in 1937. The Unit moved to Cranborne military airfield (also Salisbury) in December 1937. Six Pilots received their Wings in 1938. In September1938, six Audax biplanes added to the unit's strength – and in April 1939, three Gloster Gauntlets were added. Dirk Cloete became the Director of Civil Aviation in South Africa, and was succeeded by Lieutenant Colonel Charles Meredith (later to become Air Vice-Marshal Sir Charles Meredith, KBE, CB, and AFC) in June 1939.

In 1939 the Unit became the Southern Rhodesia Air Force. On August 27, 1939, a few days before the war, this Unit moved to its station in Kenya – the *first* British air unit to cross its borders to take up war duties. Under the command of Flight Lieutenant Maxwell, three Hawker Harts and three Hawker Audaxes flew to Kenya, and all the personnel were soon absorbed into the Royal Air Force, largely manning Nos 44, 237 and 266 "Rhodesia" Squadrons. No 237 Squadron, which later switched to Spitfires, fought its way from Kenya through Somaliland, the Sudan, Eritrea and Libya, into Italy and Southern France. Through North Africa and into Europe its spirit of determination earned for the Squadron a reputation second to none. It remained until the end almost 100 percent Rhodesia.

No 266 Squadron, formed on October 30, 1939, was first equipped with Fairey Battles (the type Ou Dad flew), but by January 1940 was training on Spitfires. Its wartime duties included patrolling, escorting, offensive sweeps along the French and Belgian coasts and the provision of bomber escorts over the Rhine and France. The Squadron was one of the first to be equipped with Typhoons. The squadron took part in the D-Day operations, moved into France, and provided close support for the Army as the advance into Germany proceeded. Throughout the war the aircrew of 266 Squadron were almost exclusively Rhodesian.

The reverse was true with the Rhodesia's bomber squadron – No 44. The country could replace casualties in the fighter squadrons but not, for instance, the 35 men – pilots, navigators, wireless operators and gunners – who failed to return from No 44 Squadron's raid on

Augsburg. After initially flying Hampdens, the squadron was the first to equip with Lancaster's. For the epic raid on Augsburg, to bomb a diesel engine factory that was producing half the requirements for Hitler's submarine fleet, as well as engines for tanks, army transports and warships, six bombers of 44 Squadron and six from 97 Squadron went into special training. The attack was to be from a height of only 50 feet. Of Rhodesia's six bombers, led by Squadron Leader J.D. Nettleton, only one returned. 97 Squadron lost two bombers. But the raid achieved its objective and Nettleton was awarded the Victoria Cross posthumously. A week later 44 Squadron helped sink the German battleship *Tirpitz*. The squadron's last raid was on April 25, 1945. It was the famous raid that devastated Berchtesgaden, Hitler's fortified hideout in the Bavarian mountains.

Air Marshal Sir Charles Meredith, formally of the SAAF, commanded the Royal Rhodesian Air Force during the war.

At home Rhodesians were also making their own valuable contribution. At the outset of the war, the Southern Rhodesia Government proposed the establishment of one training station under the Empire Air Training Scheme. The Imperial Defence Committee suggested that the money be used to set up an air-training unit in Southern Rhodesia. The United Kingdom asked for three – and got them. During the initial stages the RATG (Rhodesian Air Training Group) was formed with training bases at Belvedere, Cranborne and Norton in the Salisbury area, Thornhill and Guinea Fowl in the Gwelo area; and Kumalo, Heany and Llewellin in the Bulawayo area. It owed its existence to the events leading up to the war, when the Rhodesian Parliament voted a sum of money to be used to help in the defence of the British Empire. In the later stages of the war the RATG had no less than 11 stations, training thousands of fighter and bomber pilots, navigators and air gunners for the RAF. The training schools continued after the war, the numbers gradually decreasing until the last shut down in March 1954.

On 28th November 1947, Colonel S Garlake, Acting Secretary, Department of Defence and Air, gazetted Government Notice 945 that reformed the Southern Rhodesia Air Force on a permanent basis, - largely as a communications unit. Its main purpose was to provide transport for Government officials between various centres. Slowly, more aircraft were added. The South African Government in 1948 donated a Douglas Dakota DC3. By June 1949, two North American Harvard Mk II A ex RATG were acquired, followed by another six Harvards for OCUs and a further 12 Harvards from the SAAF for

Advanced Flying School pilot training. The scope of the communications unit gradually increased until in July 1949, flying training of territorial volunteers started. Other less publicised additions were an Avro Anson Mk 9 and two Austers - marks J/1 and J/5.

No 1 Southern Rhodesia Auxiliary Air Force Squadron was formed and manned by ex-combat pilots living in Salisbury, who volunteered to carry out squadron training in the early mornings, evenings and at weekends. The deterioration of the international situation over Korea in 1950 led to the need for accelerated training and the Short Service Unit came into being to give pilots a concentrated two years of full-time training.

Supermarine Spitfires Mk 22s were acquired in 1951. The Spitfires added a significant boost to the fledgling Air Force and became perhaps one of the few classical types an air power could possess. Its association with the Battle of Britain during World War II made it one of the most sought after types by pilots the world over. The Spitfires augmented the Tiger Moths and Harvards used until then. The Air Force personnel wore khaki uniforms and used Army ranks.

Then in December 1953 the Air Force acquired its first "strike" jet aircraft with the arrival of four de Havilland Vampires Mark FB 9 aircraft. This Fighter-Bomber was a single seat jet but its greatest drawback was the absence of an ejector seat for the pilot. In the event of an emergency, the pilot needed to have sufficient flying control to trim the aircraft nose-down, blow the canopy, roll the aircraft inverted, loosen his seat straps, fall clear of the aircraft, and then deploy his parachute. These first four Vampires were allocated for Operational Conversion Unit (OCU) training.

In the same month, two Hunting Percival Pembroke's were added to the Transport Flight. Then No 4 Squadron was equipped with 12 Hunting Percival Provost aircraft, Mark 52. The T Mk 52 was the armed version. An additional four T1, or "cleaner" trainer aircraft for No 4 Squadron followed on the heels of the T Mk 52 aircraft. No 3 Squadron was also boosted with the acquisition of six plus one (7) Douglas C-47B Mk 4 Dakota aircraft. The DC-3, or Dak, as it was also popularly known by, completed a rather impressive re-equipment programme during December 1953.

Then in April 1954, thirty-two Vampires were acquired. The first batch of 12+4 de Havilland Vampire FB 9s went to No 1 Squadron and then 16 two-seater Vampire T 11s went to No 2 Squadron. The trainer version, T 11, was fitted with ejection seats - much to the relief of pilots. However, apart from the nose hatch and engine cowlings, the Vampire fuselage was predominantly constructed with balsa and other suitable wood - hence very little was left of the cockpit area whenever a Vampire "fell to the ground".

With the creation of the Federation of Rhodesia and Nyasaland, in October 1954, the Queen gave permission for the Royal prefix to be added to the title; and the Force adopted Royal Air Force style uniforms and ranks; and adopted the title "Royal Rhodesian Air Force". In April 1956 Thornhill Airfield was reopened, and reconstruction of the runway and installation of the latest Radar equipment began. Interestingly, Operation *Show Plane* entailed wheeling a Provost from Thornhill into town, to display the aircraft at the Gwelo Show, in August 1957.

Above: A formation of Percival Provosts of the Royal Rhodesian Air Force

A formation of Provosts in 1960 – as seen from Thornhill High School

A five year break followed before the next major acquisition - 15 English Electric Canberra B2 light Bombers, from Britain, for Nos 5 and 6 Squadrons, in 1959. That same year, No 3 Squadron's transport capability was significantly enhanced with the addition of a Canadair C-4 aircraft. These two types of potent aircraft added such a massive deterrent aspect to the Royal Rhodesian Air Force that its influence had a profound affect on the emergent Black states throughout Africa.

By this time I was a sixteen-year-old schoolboy at Thornhill, and I often marvelled at all the jet activity at the base from which the school owed its origins. Even to this day, I still cherish a Rhodesian Herald newspaper clipping that heralded the event of the Canberras arrival. I was convinced the "Wild Blue Yonder" was the life for me – and made it a life goal to one day fly one of those magnificent flying machines. This was a dream that I achieved.

Five French Aerospatiale Alouette III helicopters for No 7 Squadron followed in 1962. The next year No 1 Squadron was re-equipped with 12 Hawker Siddeley Hunter FGA 9 aircraft - but wait awhile - by this time I had joined this elite band of airman and I can now continue with my tale of personal experience of the history of the Royal Rhodesian Air Force - during its heyday in Federal times.

In 1962, the RRAF manned two bases – New Sarum in Salisbury and Thornhill at Gwelo. The Air Headquarters were at Dolphin House, commanded by the Chief of Air Staff, Air Vice-Marshal Bentley. The Squadrons at that time were:-

Thornhill –
    No 1 Sqn – equipped with Vampire FB 9s – the fighter squadron
    No 2 Sqn – equipped with Vampire T 11s and Provost T Mk 1 – the training squadron
    No 6 Sqn – equipped with Canberra T 4 and B 2s – the strategic Bombers

New Sarum –
    No 3 Sqn – equipped with DC 3 Dakota's and a Canadair – transport
    No 4 Sqn – equipped with Provost T Mk 52s – the Internal Security squadron
    No 5 Sqn – equipped with Canberra B 2s – light bombers and Photo Reconnaissance

The Role of the RRAF, simply put, was mainly threefold:- (1) Defence and Security of Rhodesian air space (2) Support of the ground forces and (3) To assist the civil power in the maintenance of law and order.

Command and control was exercised through a three-pronged organisational structure, from Air Headquarters down to Air Force Station formation levels – namely:-

Air Staff – Air operations – the steely blue-eyed boys
Technical Staff – aircraft maintenance and serviceability
Administration and Organisation – all support service functions

I was just itching – and raring to give it a go.

ATTESTATION

The educational qualifications required by the Selection Board were a minimum of five 'O' Level passes and these must include English, Mathematics and Physics. But the Selection Board seeks much more than mere paper achievements. The future pilot, who will automatically be an officer, has to possess other personal qualities and abilities as well. In the case of No 16 PTC, the Board only selected 12 pilot trainees out of 200 applicants and 92 Selection Board candidates. Aptitude tests, academic tests, psychological tests and a thorough medical examination are all part of the intense scrutiny of each aspirant. Motivation is studied carefully - the desire to follow Dad's footsteps in a pilot's career was to my advantage.

It can be said that the Air Force Selection Board's system is proven - it may very occasionally select a borderline case and invariably that chap will remain borderline throughout the rigorous pilot training course. My joining instructions that followed my letter of offer read as follows:-

R.R.A.F. Joining Instructions: "Reference is made to your letter of acceptance and this Headquarters' letter concerning your successful application for Flying Training in the Royal Rhodesian Air Force, you are requested to report to the Guard Room, R.R.A.F. New Sarum, by 1900 hours on Wednesday 14th March, 1962. You are advised to bring with you civilian clothing including a lounge suit, and whatever sporting equipment you wish.

"Please inform this Headquarters as to your mode of travel, place and time of arrival in Salisbury, so that transport and accommodation arrangements may be made if necessary.

"Your attention is drawn to the fact that previously you were advised to report on 12th March, 1962. Please note the correct time and place.

"The letter was once again signed by Flight Lieutenant van Ryneveld, for Air Vice-Marshal, Chief of Air Staff, Royal Rhodesian Air Force."

My first priority was to get a decent suit. Up until now I had been used to my school blazer. My Mom took me along to those cheap Indian shops in Pretoria's Church Street, and I was able to select two suits - for the price of one. My sporting equipment consisted of tennis and rugby kit. Interestingly, my rugby jersey looked like the Western Province blue and white striped jersey and the stir it caused may well have influenced the Air Force selectors in deciding on their team selections. However, let me hasten to add I did play 1st Team at school, and also captained the side. Any way, I reported to New Sarum at the appointed time, booked into the Officers' Mess and joined the rest of guys who would become branded as No 16 Pilot Training Course.

No 16 PTC

The fortunate twelve guys that comprised No 16 PTC - Pilot Training Course were:-

Ian Bester-Bond	- a natural sportsman and very talented rugby player
Al Bruce	- a real nice guy, who later went commercial flying
Bruce Collocott	- the 'old man' of the course. A true lover of music
Graham Cronshaw	- the youngest, but fond of name dropping
Harry de Kock	- a pipe smoker, straight from Jameson School
Chris Dixon	- jovial, called Noxid - name spelt backwards
Andre du Toit	- a strange sort of guy
Prop Geldenhuys	- 'prop'Preller - yours truly
Roy Hopkins	- a re-mustered Tech, never say die type
Trevor McRoberts	- a real 'pom'
Hugh Slatter	- university graduate, and born leader
John Stracken	- also graduate, changed his name to Strnad (due to abused childhood).

Nº 16 PUPIL PILOT COURSE

H.C.G. de Kock B.I.Collocott A.R.Bruce A.P. du Toit R.D.Hopkins C.J.T.Dixon
W.G.Cronshaw I.J.Bester – Bond J.F.R.Strnad P.M.Geldenhuys H.C.S.Slatter T. Mc Roberts

16 PTC – BFS (Basic Flying School)

GTS - ITS

Our feet only touched the ground momentarily when we landed by Dakota at Thornhill - to be met by the No 2 Ground Training School drill instructor, Paddy Malloy. After a brief welcome by OC Ground Training School we were ordered to fall-in, with kit bags slung over our shoulders and at double quick time marched / ran down to our billet. This consisted of a corrugated iron barrack that we would call home for the next four and a half months.

Most of No 16 PTC "thought that they were fit?" But, we were all very wrong regarding our physical fitness for pilot training. All movement during our Initial Training School (ITS) was at low flying pace. Our day started at dawn, reveille at 05h00, billet inspection at 05h30 then at least 1½ to 2 hours square bashing on the parade ground. Lo and behold the cadet who would dress up with his jersey underneath his shirt for the early morning basic drill sessions - for eagle eyed Paddy Malloy would drill the squad until the sweat showed on everybody's back. When a jersey was worn to fend off the early morning cold, it would take that much longer for the 'saturated' hidden garment to allow sweat to appear through the shirt.

A quick cold shower or swim, summer or winter didn't matter, no matter how freezing it was outside, followed the basic drill sessions. Then a hurried breakfast, also at double quick time, before being marched to Ground School - for lectures from 07h30 to 13h00. The subjects were fairly high powered - maths, physics, aerodynamics, navigation, airmanship, service writing, roles and history of the Air Force, Air Force Law, general duties studies, current affairs, etiquette etc. I seem to recall something like 16-18 subjects, with weekly and monthly progress tests cum examinations, in order to advance to progressively difficult phases.

Physical fitness played a major part of ITS - with another drill session after lunch, gymnasium work-outs and participation in all sports. Late afternoons would be devoted to route marches and or cross-country running.

UMGULUGULU

Shortly after attestation, 16 PTC were challenged to better 14 and 15 PTCs graffiti on Umgulugulu. We had no clue what it entailed - or where Umgulugulu was. It was all part of the Air Force method of officer character building and designed to test initiative.

UMGULUGULU
Yours truly is on the extreme right. L to R are Hugh Slatter, Hoppie Hopkins, Harwood de Kock, Graham Cronshaw, Andre du Toit, Trevor McRoberts, Ian Bond (sitting), Al Bruce, Chris Dixon and Prop Geldenhuys. Bruce Collocott took photo.

Umgulugulu is in fact a mammoth granite kopje in the jet general flying area, situated in a triangle roughly between Selukwe, Mashaba and Shabani. This pilot training tradition was first introduced by 14 PTC whose rather feeble effort does not warrant special mention, except perhaps for the fact they were the pathfinders, and albeit that they used paint brushes. 15 PTC did not fare all that better, but their course number was painted nearer the summit, with paint rollers. Our challenge was "do better" - but we had no idea of what size to expect, what quantities of paint were needed or where we would have to paint our course number. One bright idea adopted early on was the use of brooms, or was it perhaps laziness? I think not.
Undaunted, we set off early one Sunday morning - having done all our 'shopping' on the Saturday. Although one could see the massive kopje from miles around, it was another thing just getting to it - one had to

travel through a densely populated TTL with all its kraals and winding pathways. But by mid-morning we arrived at the base of the kopje - which by now turned out to be a 'mountain'.

Our course number 16 painted on the top of Umgulugulu Mountain. Note "Bogom", and names to extreme right of the photo

Defying gravity on Umgulugulu

It was indeed ginormous - we lugged up the paint and climbed to the trig beacon encased in a concrete plinth. We then painted the outline of our figure "16" and took turns using brooms to fill in. The left over paint was used to autograph our masterpiece, we had a ball on top - and returned at sunset. During the next week, we were commended for our efforts when several jet pilots reported that our "16" was clearly visible from 20,000 feet Above Ground Level.

Our record did not remain for long. When our turn came to pass on the tradition to our junior course, they had an easier number seventeen to paint on top of Umgulugulu. Theirs was basically two long lines with a short crosspiece to form the number "17". The "18" that followed "17" was even less impressive than our own "16". By the time it got to No '21' Course in 1967, their number was measured to be 120 yards across and 100 yards high. As this exercise had now reached ridiculous proportions, both in magnitude and expense No 22 Course were allowed to make their number smaller.

OUR SIGNATURE TUNE - 12 DAYS TO CHRISTMAS

At our initiation, a tradition with the entire 'junior' pilot training courses; we were required to entertain the Officers' Mess members to a Course Concert. One was ridiculed for deviation from originality - and for your efforts would be rewarded with all forms of UFOs - ranging from verbal abuse to rotten tomatoes. As it was, during the whole period of our ITS we were required at dinner in the evenings to wear flowers stuck in a 'lug' ear hole - and woe betide if you presented yourself improperly dressed.

At our traditional Course Concert, because we were twelve cadets, we chose the 12 Days to Christmas as our signature tune.

It was sung something like this: -

> "On the First day of Christmas my true love said to me,
> Nine knackers knocking
> Eight vicars wanking
> Six lesbians leaping
> Five Choir Boys
> Four dirty whores
> Three shit house doors
> Two pairs of drawers
> And a French letter on a fir tree."

I was saved from a bolt of lightning - I was No 5 - but I also incurred the audience's wrath for lack of originality. However, I was fortunately consoled by Flight Lieutenant Basil Ledderboer who was a legend in his own lifetime. Basil was well known for his "Titch titch - Darkest Africa." accompanied by the right hand raised, forefinger and pinkie extended four inches apart and with thumb holding the other two fingers closed. It was a cardinal sin to use un-gentlemanly language, especially in the presence of ladies. To earn his thumbs up, and especially "Darkest Africa", meant that our 12 days to Christmas was Aye Okay.

I often wondered whether the Rhodesian African Rifles catchy tune "Sweet Banana" and the all white Rhodesian Light Infantry's "When the Saints Go Marching in" and even our junior course's "Raindrops keep falling on my head" popularised the hit songs of the day. "Those Magnificent Men in their Flying Machines" was popular at Wing Parades and the Air Force's signature tune was in fact "Winged Assagais". Isn't it strange how nostalgia sets in whenever one happens to hear a song of beauty from days gone by. The national anthem "Ode to Joy" lingers to this day.

MISTER VICE - A BOOB

As a Cadet, one was schooled in Air Force etiquette and it was expected from the Officer corp to foster the fine traditions of the force. It was expected of one to frequent the Grog Spot on Friday evenings, for example - other traditions included behaving like an officer and gentleman at all times - and this included ones behaviour at Dining In/Out Nights.

The purpose of Dining In new officer arrivals or Dining Out retirements or officers posted away from base was one of those affairs that demanded behaviour above reproach. In fact, misbehaviour was unforgivably scorned and could indeed blotch a career officer's whole career. So strict were behaviour norms that one could just not afford to blotch up. The PMC - President of the Mess Committee - was accorded the most senior status, even above the Commander of the Air Force or President of the Country for that matter irrespective of the PMC's rank. On the other end of the scale, Mr Vice was considered the most junior, but not every officer in the Force gets the opportunity of experiencing this dubious honour. However, yours truly can count himself unfortunate enough to be counted among the cast of thousands.

It was customary, after the meal, which would last several hours, and before the commencement of the speeches with cigars and liqueurs, that a toast to the Sovereign was proposed. The norm would be - the PMC rises, calls for quiet and announces "Mr Vice". Mr. Vice stands up, raises his glass of port and says "Gentlemen," and waits for

49

everyone else to rise, with glasses charged, before proposing the royal toast "The Queen". Everybody then repeats "The Queen", and all fall down - I mean sit down.

Well, my moment of glory had arrived. The PMC stood up and gave me my cue, "Mister Vice". I duly stood up, raised my glass and toasted " Gentlemen, the Queen" - took a gulp and sat down even before all the other diners could stand. What an insult for not pausing between "Gentlemen" and "The Queen" - and duly earned the icy steely eyed stares for my unforgivable boob.

To add insult to injury, at the conclusion of the Dinning In/Out - once the PMC leaves the dinning room, Mister Vice takes the PMC's place at the head of the table to keep an "eye" on all the silver cutlery and trophies until the last chattering hanger-on departs. This I did, until the last person left - but failed to ensure the safe storage of all the silverware - another boob.

It is appropriate at this stage to recall the "Affluence of Incohol" which should only be digested once truly blotted, after the one too many. Please read carefully less you miss the moral of the story.

AFFLUENCE OF INCOHOL

The influence of alcohol makes nonsense of the traditional Friday night "Grog Spot" drinking sessions. During pilot training I found the poem witty but one needs to be not quite sober to appreciate the humour. It goes like this: -

I had eighteen bottles of whiskey in my house and I was told by my wife to empty the contents of each and every bottle down the sink, or else...

I said I would and proceeded with the unpleasant task.

I withdrew the cork from the first bottle and poured the contents down the sink with the exception of one glass, which I drank. I extracted the cork from the second bottle and did likewise with it, which I drank. I then withdrew the cork from the third bottle, poured the whiskey down the sink, which I drank. I pulled the cork from the fourth bottle down the sink and poured the bottle down the glass, which I drank. I pulled the sink out of the next glass and poured the cork down the bottle. I pulled the bottle from the cork of the next and drank the sink out of it and threw the next down the glass. Then I corked the sink with the glass and drank the pourer.

When I had everything emptied I steadied the house with one hand, counted the glasses, corks, sinks and bottles with the other which were

29, and as the house came by for the third time I counted them again, and finally had all the houses in one bottle, which I drank.
I am not so under the affluence of incohol as some theeple pink I am. I am not half so thunk as you drink. I fool so feelish that I don't know who am me, and the drunker I stand the longer I get. Oh. me . . . . ..

SURVIVAL EXERCISE - BINGA/KARIBA - 1962

Aircrew survival was a vital part of Air Force pilot training. Numerous exercises were carried out in and around Thornhill base, Selukwe foothills, Gwenora dam, rifle ranges and even as far afield as Lake Kariba. One of the first escape and evasion exercises took place between the Gwelo Rifle Range (behind the Gwelo Kopje), and Gwenora Dam. Flight Lieutenant Archie Conlin was our ITS Course Officer. Archie was a 'pom', ex- Royal Air Force navigator, who used to fly with Flight Lieutenant Ossie Penton on Canberras, but met with an unfortunate motor accident. He was unable to return to flying duties and was posted to No 2 Ground Training School as a Navigation Instructor.
The Cadets were split into two groups. One group was tasked to "secure" the DS – Directing Staff base camp, and were sent on foray patrols to search for the second group – whose mission was to move through "enemy" lines, to so-called 'safe havens'. I was in the latter group with Roy Hopkins, Andre du Toit, Trevor McRoberts and a couple of others. We managed to successfully evade the 'hunters' and breached their base camp defences. While Roy had a ding-dong battle with defender Ian Bond, firing blanks from our 303 rifles, our group managed to 'capture' Archie Conlin and forced marched him to our camp some miles away. When our Course Commander tried to resist apprehension and made a heroic bid to escape from our clutches, we tied up his hands with his boot laces. En route through the bush, Archie somehow lost his footwear. By the time we got near our camp, his socks were covered in grass seeds, and his feet looked even worse for wear. Meanwhile, one member from our group managed to commandeer an Air Force troop carrier that had negligently been left with the keys in the ignition.
We bundled our sporty Course Commander in the back of the vehicle, still with his hands tied behind his back, and raced off to the Guardroom at Thornhill. The Provost military police were initially very sceptical taking a Commissioned Officer into custody. He was admitted only when Archie Conlin confirmed that the Cadets were

being exercised in Escape and Evasion ground training exercises that the Military Police placed our Course Commander in the cells. To our horror, we noticed that our Officer's hands had turned 'pot-blue' during his ordeal, and we were convinced that we would end up in hot water for displaying initiative, albeit bending the rules of the escape and evasion exercise. We were much relieved to be assessed A-okay, and not a word was said for all the mistreatment that we had subjected our Instructor to. But, we were not out of the woods, because one of our course guys had 'lost' his service rifle. The next day we were ordered to go and find the missing weapon – and not to return unless found. However all is well that ends well – after forming a long line abreast, we backtracked our routes through the bush and managed to find the missing rifle. Our next bush exercise was a 'survival' exercise in the Zambezi Valley. This was a totally different kettle of fish.

Most pilot trainees viewed the Chete Gorge survival exercises with some trepidation. The Course flew to Binga by Dakota. We were met by the local District Commissioner and travelled by his motor launch, the Sir Patrick Fletcher, to Chete Gorge from where we had to bundu-bash our way back inland to Binga. No 16 PTC - 12 Pilot trainees were split into three groups of four. As is common in the Valley, we followed numerous game trails but would still come to a standstill because of the dense wag-'n -bietjie thorn bush, which grew abundantly in the Zambezi Valley. It was tough going - some 25 miles to do in 12 hours foot slogging. We could hear rhino and elephant crashing through the bush, often only metres away, which only spurred us on.

Some four miles short of our target we noticed a red Very flare illuminating the night sky - it was "Bundu Harry" Harwood de Kock wanting to find out how these emergency flare things worked. Flurries of vehicle were very soon upon us and with our somewhat anxious BFS Course Commander Eddy Wilkinson wanting to know why the distress signals? Red faced Harry was not popular. Our team on the other hand was only too relieved to bum a ride for the last couple of miles back to Binga.

RHINO ENCOUNTER

The following day we travelled by District Commissioner's truck to the base of the Zambezi Escarpment to visit a Batonka tribe (a strange primitive people who cake their naked females with red mudpacks to make them less attractive). We were then required to climb the escarpment and trek 12 miles on foot to Manzituba vlei, famous for its white rhinos.

Each 'survivor' had to carry their own night stop equipment and there was no way yours truly was going to lug bed roll etc for 24 miles - so I decided I would survive the exercise with my flying suit and vellies [veldskoene]. The hike to Manzituba was uneventful and we saw a fair amount of 'wild' animals at close range.

"On top of the World"
Top to Bottom – Prop, Chris, Roy, Trev, Bruce, John, Ian, Hugh, Harry, Graham and Al

That night, whilst trying to get some kip, with five log fires burning around the camp site, I had my head pointed to one of the fires and my feet facing another. It was difficult to get some sleep - my head and feet were okay but my torso was freezing. Anyway, a disturbance nearby attracted a few curious cadets who in turn were assured by our game-ranger that it was only a curious rhino, attracted by the campfires, who would not venture near the burning fires. I for one took his advice and tried to get some more sleep.

Shortly thereafter I was rudely awakened from a deep sleep by a commotion that sounded like a thundering rainstorm -- the curious rhino had decided to charge through the camp. No sooner had I stood up than I had this burning sensation on my feet. With every step I took the molten crepe soles of my vellies was collecting more and more sand. I soon realised the twinkle toeing around the campfire would not survive a rhino charge and then headed for the nearest cover - burning feet and all.

I took refuge behind another guy only to discover that there were about four others ahead of me in the queue - all line astern with the front guy trying to grovel behind a tiny bush only about half a metre high. The so-called protection was not a match for a raging rhino in headlong flight.

Colleague Hugh Slatter tells another rather interesting tale - he was rushing to take cover behind a tree when he passed our Course Commander Eddy Wilkinson who was still asleep in his fartsack. He paused for a moment to warn Eddy Wilkinson to take cover but thought it best to save his own bacon first. The story is told that Eddy Wilkinson in fact was even quicker to hide behind an adjacent tree despite Hugh Slatter legging at high speed. Eddy Wilkinson had hung up his under rods to air the night before on a branch of the tree that he had taken cover.

I'm not so sure - I think it was after the rhino charge. In any event, the Boss's movement was greased lightning if ever that were so. Our trek the next day was uneventful albeit that my vellies, with no soles left, had seen better days. Back at Binga the hot spring was magic to our tired bods.

BRAVE, BRIGHT OR SENSELESS?
At the hot spring, not to be outdone, 'Bundu' Harry had to prove that only the thick-skinned could walk barefoot all the way from the pool to the eye of the hot spring. Each chap would `claim' that he had broken the previous record - then along would come old Harry, grit his teeth and with a smile go that extra distance until he walked the whole way.

Binga and Manzituba Survival Exercise – 1962
L to R: Chris, Andre, Al, Bruce, Harry, Trevor, Hoppie, John, Ian, Hugh and Game Guide. **Kneeling:** Prop, Paddy Malloy, Ranger, Eddy Wilkinson, Ken Welsh, and Graham

Our last night, as normal, ended with a humdinger booze-up. Al Bruce had timely made a super bed under the African stars - so that he would not have to find a sleeping place late at night. It just so happened that my possie was not far off. Anyway, after our fair share of chibulies and campfire singing into the wee hours, we both hit the sack. During the night I understood why Al had taken a beer bottle to bed -- whenever the call of nature came, Al would empty his bladder into the bottle, reach out arms length and deposit the contents until the next time. This obviously carried on several times during the night. However when Al woke up the next morning, who was in his bed? It was the remainder of 16 PTC while Al found himself lying amongst all his beer bottle/bladder deposits.

Brave, bright or senseless? That is for the reader to decide. After my twinkle toe episode, I'm not too sure.

Our jungle survival, and escape and evasion training came to an end. We boarded the Dakota sent to Binga to do the uplift - and returned to the bump and grind of schoolroom stuff at Thornhill. Physical fitness was an essential aspect of our initial training phase. As Cadets we were challenged to participate in all sports, as well as being subjected to one bush exercise after another. The following couple of pictures gives an idea of what we were expected to do.

Loading the truck; Baked beans and Bully Beef; and Fartsack relaxation (bowel exercises)

Kaalgat – "Geronimo"

The author and Bill Jelley – taken from the Team Photo above

Our Initial Training School phase came to an end on 20th July, but not before the exciting issue of all our flying kit.

Being kitted out with ones own personal flying helmet (bone dome), boots, flying overalls and kid leather flying gloves. Individual lockers were allocated in the Safety Equipment section - as were parachutes that required frequent checking and servicing. It was Friday, and we were instructed to report to No 2 Squadron on the Monday morning for a mass brief to commence our Basic Flying phase on the Hunting Percival Provost aircraft.

BASIC FLYING SCHOOL

No 16 PTC was posted to No 2 Squadron commanded by Squadron Leader Bob Woodward, on 23rd July 1962. The squadron was equipped with Provost T Mk 1, side-by-side seating, powered by a nine cylinder radial Leonides engine, 550 shaft horsepower, with a three-bladed variable pitch propeller. Basic Flying School got off the ground to a flying start, on that very same day. My allocated instructor Flying Officer Petter-Bowyer (Flg Off P-B), showed me the pre-flight checks and logged "Ex 4 – DCO" (Exercise 4 was Effects of Controls and Elementary Handling – duty carried out) after our landing 45 minutes later. The air experience sorties on 11th May with Flying Officer Pat Niemand, and again on June 29th with Flying Officer Pat Meddows-Taylor was no doubt to whet our appetites and also to re-motivate lagging spirits for the potential drop-outs. The first two flying experiences were basically as a passenger in awe. The latter was 'extractum digit' or pull finger out – because this was now real flying – and a taste of what our whole future depended on.

On the sports field, the pilot trainees were also expected to perform. Three Cadets from No 16 P.T.C. made the grade. Rob Tasker, Randy Du Rand, Varky Varkevisser, Bill Jelley, Eddy Wilkinson, Rich Brand and Tol Janeke would all play a significant role in my career as an aspiring pilot in the Air Force.

The following picture, taken from the Team Photograph, shows me with Bill Jelley. I was nineteen years old, and Bill my senior aged twenty-seven. At this time, Grahame Jelley was a three-year old baby. Grahame is mentioned because many years later he became my son-in-law! Looking at this 1962 rugby club photograph, who would have guessed correctly that Bill and I would one day become related?

The 13th August arrived and after a rather short sortie of 30 minutes my instructor Flying Officer P-B taxied back to the hardstanding and handed me over to Flying Officer Pat Meddows-Taylor for my solo check. Another 15 minutes later, my moment of eternal glory arrived.

Would you believe this glorious moment only lasted a mere five minutes. But wow - what a wonderful feeling it was to experience, and savour the achievement of going "First Solo". I am sure Ou Dad Preller was the only one in the world who could relate to that moment. I bet, he must have been very proud.

Basic Flying School instruction consisted of Taxiing, Straight and Level, Climbing, Descending, Stalling, Spinning, Take-off and Climb, Approach and Landing, Advanced Turning, Low Flying, Aerobatics, Instrument and Night Flying, Pilot Navigation and Formation Flying. I passed my progress check on 11th September and went on to scrape through my Instrument Rating test on 17th October. In the intervening period I was somewhat fortunate to experience the real thing when P-B, my instructor, took me along on my first taste of Internal Security work - we logged a 15-minute non training police recce sortie. There was also a lengthy 1½ hour, the longest to date, search and rescue sortie, of which 35 minutes was logged as non training. I wasn't complaining.

Three sorties warrant special mention. The first was one of those days when nothing went right. I guess I was not very receptive, for somehow the sortie was curtailed and as soon as we had taxied onto the hardstanding, Boss P-B instructed me to make sex my departure. I responded politely that I would wait the two minutes it took to run down the engine. As I climbed out of the cockpit, my parachute deployed. There I was, with miles of streaming silk fluttering in the breeze and me trying to look dignified in my rather ridiculous appearance. I must hasten to add that although I had had a bad day, it was not quite as bad as some of the other unfortunate cadets. They would be seen running in front of their instructors, having been dropped off at the end of the runway, and told to run all the way back to the squadron, lugging their parachutes over their shoulders.

The second sortie made the history books. Boss P-B was instructing me in short take-off techniques. We climbed steeply to about 300 feet, when he suddenly cut the engine, catching me completely unawares, and said we would 'force land' back on the runway. Well, things started happening very rapidly, as mother earth came up to meet us. As we hit the ground, the engine roared to life and we found ourselves airborne again. My port wing, the wing on my side, was looking somewhat sad, angled downwards at a very peculiar angle. An escort aircraft was scrambled to conduct an aerial inspection. This was the first time I had seen another aircraft in close formation, occupying our flying air space. If I thought that was frightening, then more was to follow.

The report sounded something like this "The dihedral on your starboard wing is greater than the port side. Tail wheel has been pushed into the fuselage. Starboard undercarriage is bent inwards and may collapse on landing.

BASIC FLYING SCHOOL: Graham Cronshaw, Prop Geldenhuys, Flying Instructor Peter Petter-Bowyer, and Chris Dixon

Stalling characteristics is unknown - suggest you try and burn off as much fuel as possible, carry out a slow speed handling check and decide whether a wheeler landing should be attempted." And I thought the wing on my side looked badly. The chase aircraft remained with us during the climb to a safe altitude; the slow speed handling and stall check and then followed us for the approach and landing. The circuit was cleared and all the fire engines on the base took up strategic positions on all the runways. Boss P-B skilfully selected one of the cross-wind grass runways (because of the bent starboard undercarriage), came in shallow with a lot of power and half-flap selected - and carried out a perfect "greaser" of a roller landing. He used a lot of power to keep the tail up, and with gentle brake application, was able to lower the tail gently onto the runway - without the oleos collapsing. The landing was like a cat p---sing on velvet. A Hobart tractor was dispatched to tow the aircraft back to the squadron.

No sooner had we landed, than P-B said he considered ordering me to bale out before attempting to land the crippled Provost. I was relieved he didn't - I think it would have taken ten strong men to throw me out of the aircraft. I must admit I felt a lot safer with my instructor beside me, than to take my chances parachuting to the ground. The technical investigation found that the instructors ASI - Air Speed Indicator - was over-reading by five knots. Parallax error with the port Air Speed Indicator was such that the discrepancy was difficult to detect. This incident became famous for the first "Stuka" (well-known Junker 87 German high-dive bomber during World War II) aircraft on No 4 Squadron. The experience was to stand me in good stead, when I was faced with a forced landing many years later.

During early November 1962, I had a change of Provost flying instructor, from Boss Peter Petter-Bowyer to Flying Officer Wally Galloway. He instructed me in night flying and I then went night-solo on 8th November. Squadron Leader Bob Woodward gave me a Provost progress check on 21st November

The next noteworthy sortie concerned our final cross-country exercise. Because of our somewhat large course, there was not sufficient Provost aircraft for all of 16 PTC to fly this particular exercise. I was only too happy to forfeit my sortie - and in return, was rewarded with two sorties in a Vampire jet aircraft. I believe I was the envy of all my fellow colleagues. AFS was just round the corner, so to speak, and I would benefit most by experiencing what lay ahead.

HEY KROKODIL - DECEMBER 1962

Our trip to Livingstone was eventful. I was the lucky guy to fly with Boss Woodward in the Vampire. At our first turning point I blacked out completely - the 'g' - gravity forces were not only much higher than in the Provost, they were also more sustained. I wondered whether the Boss was unimpressed with me slumped in a heap at the bottom of the cockpit, or whether he intentionally sustained the high-g turn to make a point. The obvious highlight for me was to get my hands on a jet aircraft well before any of my fellow course mates. Our jet-trip lasted one hour, whereas the Provosts took nearly three times as long.

We arrived on the morning of December 1st, to a very enjoyable jolly that lay ahead - combining business with pleasure - sporting events and the odd mischievous incident. In the afternoon we played hockey against the local sports club. Despite our pre-match practice held prior to our final cross-country flying exercise, we were no match for the locals and had to contend with a resounding beating. A soccer match also followed as had been arranged. 16 PTC was determined to avenge their hockey match defeat and played like demons. Defeating a Livingstone Invitation sports club team 6 to 2 justly rewarded us - but not without casualty, with yours truly being one of the unfortunate victims.

I was playing right wing. Having received a pass on the half way line, I raced towards the opponent's goal and in the process managed to beat off most of the defenders. With us already leading the score, the opposition had perhaps resigned them to a defeat by the very fit Officer Cadets. Anyway, a good opportunity presented itself and I had no option but to shoot at goal. My mighty kick connected - not with the ball but against a big grop's size ten boot. His boot studs sunk into my right shin about four inches above the ankle. A stud penetrated the shin and caused an indentation, which could accommodate my small finger. Suffice it to say that I carry the scar to this day and will no doubt take it to my grave.

The rest of the afternoon was spent with a leisure trip to Victoria Falls followed by much jollification - and ultimately the untimely demise of poor old Krokodil. It was thus with some trepidation that we attended the reception that evening, held in our honour. All the local dignitaries headed by the Mayor were in attendance. At the dinner-dance, females were in short supply with the result that most of the chaps spent their time talking to bottoms - beer glass bottoms.

As can be visualised, after a few too many Chibulies, the bunch of frustrated airmen were ready to take on anything. It so happened that just outside the Livingstone Hotel a crocodile pen contained a medium sized crocodile specimen content to while the time away in what appeared to be a constant drunken stupor. Needless to say, the local pet was always on the receiving end with boisterous abuse hurled with gay abandon.

Little did we realise that the event that was about to unfold would make such an impression on those that witnessed "Hey Krokodil.". As was the custom during our visit to Livingstone, the poor specimen always happened to be on the receiving end of our constant assault. Various ingenious methods were used to stir the poor old croc from its lethargic existence - from the non-violent "Hey Krokodil" verbal abuse to some fairly king sized bricks hurled with brute force. The croc invariably just ignored the commotion. However, the poor old croc was not immune to the size of the rocks needed to solicit a response or movement. For the most part of that night, sounds of "Hey Krokodil" could be heard - accompanied with shrieks of laughter or encouragement every time the crocodile as much as batted an eyelid.

"Hey Krokodil" became a battle cry for No 16 PTC for some considerable time and was well used with enthusiasm to describe various moods or reactions. However, I need to add that an article appeared in the local press - a day or two after our departure - announcing that the unfortunate reptile was no more; the poor creature having been killed by unscrupulous hooligans who will remain nameless. We beat a hasty retreat back to Thornhill - my jet trip taking a mere fifty minutes.

We were fortunate to escape the wrath of the SPCA.

My FHT – final handling test – was flown with the 'A' Flight Commander, Flight Lieutenant Mark Smithdorff on 18th December. Our Basic Flying School ended the next day, on 19th December 1962, having taken 103 hours 45 minutes flying time, and five months since 23rd July. I was assessed as an Average BFS Student, but my instrument flying was below par. No 16 PTC was then granted a spot of Christmas leave.

ADVANCED FLYING SCHOOL

Our Advanced Flying School commenced in the 1963 New Year. I was allocated Flying Officer Rob Tasker who took me up for my first formal Vampire sortie on 21st January. Flying Officer Keith Corrans gave me my solo check, which was duly flown in Vampire No 400 on 13th February – one week before my 20th birthday. I can thus claim having gone solo in a jet aircraft whilst still in my teens.

Going Solo in a jet warrants special mention. Unlike Basic Flying School which only lasted the five minutes it took to take-off and land, the Vampire Solo was a respectable 20 minutes - just under half of the solo check which took 50 minutes. A 'dummy' is strapped into the instructors' ejector seat, to secure all the harnesses and leg-restraining straps. (These were straps attached to the cockpit floor, then passed through buckles that the pilot wears above his calves, and draws the pilots legs up against his seat - thereby protecting his legs as the ejection seat is launched out of the confined cockpit). As is normal, all other flyers keep a healthy distance away from the about to be soloist. What a thrill as the pupil pilot opens the throttle, releases the brakes and starts accelerating down the runway? The nose is lifted gently off the ground and the jet propels the intrepid airman into the wild blue yonder.

Speed increases rapidly and the pilot needs to keep his wits about him to turn on the cockpit pressurisation, raise the undercarriage and the flaps in quick succession. Before you know it, one is already 'miles' off the ground, climbing at an astonishing four thousand feet a minute. After a couple of steep turns at medium level, the circuit is joined by calling 'initial' which is some six nautical miles short of the runway - the Air Traffic Controller knows that within minutes the solo pilot will be 'driving his flying machine into the ground'. Flying at five miles a minute (250 knots), the pilot "breaks" onto downwind - steep turn port, throttle back, airbrakes out, maintain level flight as the speed reduces to 175 knots, roll out onto downwind and lower the undercarriage. I still remember the pilots' checks well - after 37 years. Airbrakes in, U/C down, engine settings, fuel, flap, harness tight, brake on then off. By this time it is already necessary to turn and call 'finals' to the Controller, check three greens (wheels down and locked), apply full-flap, for the approach and landing. Line up, flare-out and land at 105 knots. Then throttle back, airbrakes out, and brake gently to slow down the six tonnes of jet propelled magnificent flying machine. What do you know - I've gone solo in a Vampire. Although more enjoyable than the first time round - it certainly was the next best thing to sex.

Squadron Commander Mick McLaren had taken over the Squadron from Bob Woodward, and Wing Commander Charlie Paxton was OC Flying Wing.

The flying was quite different. With jets the pilot needs to constantly wear oxygen masks - and lo and behold the pilot who forgets to lower his undercarriage for landing. AFS consisted of some 18 flying exercises, ranging from ground handling to formation flying. Exercise No 11, which was "Effects of Altitude and Compressibility" was exhilarating - at high altitude the aircraft wallows like a duck in the rarefied air. The high-speed runs would be flown to the aircraft's limits. This entailed going into a steep dive, full power, watch the Mach meter inching up to .84 of the speed of sound, the aircraft starts porpoising, then recovering before control is lost. At compressibility, the Vampire hits a "brick wall" as the shock wave moves forward and backwards along the airfoil shape of the wings, which thus causes the porpoising-flying characteristic.

Vampire T11 – First Solo on type – 13 February 1963

Spinning is something else. Only four turns were allowed, because the Vampire tended to tighten its rate of rotation in its nose dive fall earthwards. Pilots make sure they have well rehearsed ejection drills, which they would need to take if recovery from the spin is not effected whilst descending through ten thousand feet above ground. The aircraft's maximum speed is 520 miles per hour at 30,000 feet (and its maximum altitude 38,000 feet). Its normal operating height in Rhodesia is between 15,000 and 22,000 feet.

Although Rob Tasker was my primary AFS instructor, I also flew with Flight Lieutenants Mark Smithdorff and Eddy Wilkinson, Flying Officer Roy Morris and Pilot Officer Brian Strickland. Squadron Leader Mick McLaren gave me his Squadron Commander's check on 9th May and 12th June 1963. I flew my FHT - final handling check with Wing Commander Dad Cunnison on 26th June 1963.

Aerobatics is a real joy in the Vampire. The Goblin jet engine pushes out over 3,000 pounds of thrust and moves the six tonnes of aluminium and wood through the air like a toy. The Vampire is comparatively easier to fly than the piston engined Provost. It can do a near perfect "loop", whereas in a Provost the loop is more egg shaped. Rolling the aircraft is also a lot easier.

Cross-country flying was very interesting as well. This ranged from high-level, low-level, medium-level and night flying. Places overflown included Gutu, Shabani, Rutenga, Antelope Mine, Sabi/Lundi Junction,

West Nicholson, Bulawayo, Binga, Kariba, Sinoia, Salisbury, Bindura, Rusapi, Bangara Falls, Filabusi, Fort Rixon, Fort Victoria, - and of course Umgulugulu - to admire our grand No 16 painted on the granite mountain. We also flew to Feira, Lusaka and Livingstone on our high level sorties. One certainly got around as a pilot - and all in double quick time.

"Thumbs Up" for solo on Vampire T11

It may interest the reader to compare formation flying in jet aircraft as opposed to piston aircraft. In the Vampire it was more difficult because of inertia - when you throttle back, the aircraft just keeps on going. Unlike the Provost with its huge propeller - which acts like a massive fan or airbrake. The Provost slows down immediately upon throttling back, and is thus easier to hold ones position in formation flying. Greater, and more accurate anticipation was needed on jets, for acceleration and deceleration. It is likened to a big oil tanker at sea that requires several nautical miles to slow down and stop. By the same token, a lot of power, or thrust is needed for the tanker to change its velocity. So it was with jets compared to piston engined aircraft. Size also had a big influence - say Vampire versus Canberra.

With John Strnad at Livingstone in June 1963

I had flown 117½ hours in the Vampire T 11 on AFS - plus the BFS Provost total of 103 hours gave me a grand total of just over 221 flying hour's experience. It may be of interest that I was to become Roy Morris's 'B' Flight Commander many years later on No 1 Squadron - flying Hawker Hunter aircraft.

The most significant event of June 1963 was the Award of Wings and our Passing-Out Parade as Commissioned Officers in the service of Her Majesty Queen Elizabeth of Britain.

This grand occasion occurred three days after my memorable sortie in Vampire T 11 408. With all the examinations and flight tests behind us, we only had a couple of days to rehearse for a moment of glory. But true to Air Force tradition, timings for the completion of No 16 Pilot Training Course went like clockwork - one could literally set ones watch to impeccable Air Force timing.

No 16 P.T.C. WINGS PARADE

Our Wings Parade for the coveted Flying Badge was already mentioned at Chapter 1. Suffice it to add that all the Officer Cadets had their proud parents and girlfriends in attendance. The visitors were given VIP treatment and took up their seats positioned either side of the Reviewing Officer's dias. The Parade, Presentation of Wings and

Flypast by a formation of four Vampires (by our instructors) went off without a hitch.

L to R: Group Captain Jock Barber (Station Commander), Squadron Leader Eddy Wilkinson, Air Vice-Marshal AVM Bentley, Sir John Clayden, Officer Cadets Prop Geldenhuys, John Strnad, Chris Dixon and Hugh Slatter

The Wings Parade is the highlight in every pilot's career. The Air Force pulled out all the stops to imprint in the memories of the aspiring aviators an event that would last them the length of their days. This fine tradition has continued over the years - and ones own wings parade makes it that more special when compared to any other. I pay tribute to everybody who played their particular role - such as all the airmen and officers parading in squadrons, the grounds-men who erect grandstands and prepare the park-like surroundings, to the caterers and barmen for the food and drinks. And the military bands providing martial music during the parade as well as playing during the Sherry Party and at the Ball itself. Then there is the entire organisation to attend to all the dignitaries and invited guests. Last but not least are the aircraft flypasts. Close relatives are able to witness the aircraft in action on which their loved ones had qualified during their pilot training.

Inspection, and Presentation of Wings, by Sir John Clayden

The heady Officers' Commissioning Parchment reads as follows: -

By His Excellency, The Honourable Sir Humphrey Vicary Gibbs, Knight Commander of the Most Distinguished Order of Saint Michael and Saint George, Officer of the Most Excellent Order of the British Empire, Acting Governor-General and Commander-in-Chief in and over the Federation of Rhodesia and Nyasaland
To   Preller Matt Geldenhuys
Greetings.
Know you that by these Presents I, Humphrey Vicary Gibbs, acting in the name of and on behalf of Her Majesty the Queen, reposing especial Trust and Confidence in your Loyalty, Courage and Good Conduct, do , by these Presents, constitute and appoint you to be an Officer in the Air Force of the Defence Forces of the Federation of Rhodesia and Nyasaland from the 29 th day of June 1963. You are therefore carefully and diligently to discharge your Duty as such in the Rank of Acting Pilot Officer, or in such higher Rank as I, or my Minister of Defence, may from time to time hereafter be pleased to promote or to appoint you, of which a notification will be made in the Federal Gazette, and you are at all times to exercise and well Discipline in Arms both the inferior Officers and the Men serving under you and to use your best endeavours to keep them in good Order and Discipline. And I do hereby command them to obey you as their Superior Officer,

and you to observe and follow such Orders and Directions as from time to time you shall receive from me or any Superior Officer in accordance with the provisions of the Defence Act, 1955, and the Regulations and Rules made there under and any further Acts, Regulations, and Rules as may be framed for the Regulation and Discipline of the said Forces.
    Given at Salisbury this 18 day of October 1963
    By Command of His Excellency the Acting Governor - General-in-Council
Minister of Defence

Really heady stuff, isn't it? The awesome responsibility did not sink in for some time - we were really only interested in flying aeroplanes. However, as time progressed we learnt that our whole grounding had been to turn schoolboys into Officers and Gentlemen.
SHERRY PARTY

The Air Force certainly knew how to plan and organise functions. The Sherry Party followed immediately after the Wings Parade, and was held at the Officer's Mess where a large marquee had been erected. Tables and chairs had been laid out, both in the marquee and the tented area alongside. Tables had spanking white table-clothes and were adorned with flowers, sherry glasses, Mess silverware and with several bars just about everywhere. One did not need to stand queues in order to be served drinks. Whiskey and all forms of hardtack for the old timers were readily available - including much champagne for the recently commissioned officers and their guests.

WINGS AWARD

Champagne flowed freely as the recently qualified pilots sported their Wings, and their Pilot Officer's badges of rank. The white flashes from the No 1 tunics and the white band around the caps had by now been unceremoniously removed. The ex-student pilots introduced their next-of-kin to the aircrews who had taught them to fly aeroplanes. After a couple of rounds of drinks, the guests departed for some shut-eye for the Ball that was to follow.

The ex-cadets were expected to complete the final touches to the Mess for the Wings Ball. Air Force aircraft had flown to the Coast to uplift Cape wines, to Mozambique for shellfish, cashew nuts, and other delicacies to test the taste buds. I think even caviar was available. Unfortunately, Rina could not make it - so I was without a partner. I did however spend a most memorable evening with my parents. Mum and Dad had come up from Pretoria and retired rather early.

The newly commissioned pilots were given a short absence for leave before joining the various squadrons that they had been posted to.

No 16 P.T.C. WINGS PRESENTATION 29TH JUNE 1963

P.M.Geldenhuys H.C.S.Slatter W.G.Cronshaw C.J.T.Dixon I.J.Bester-Bond T.McRoberts B.I.Collocott A.R.Bruce
P.Molloy E.R.Wilkinson Sqdn.Ldr D.J.Rogers J.Strachan K.Welsh

I was posted to New Sarum to join No 4 Squadron - but was granted leave to spend some time with my parents - who were off to Hot Springs before returning to Pretoria.

And so, on the Sunday, I packed my kitbags, vacated my comfortable single quarter and signed out of the Officers' Mess. I loaded my car and set off for Hot Springs to join my folks for a spot of camping at the mineral spring. It was there that I noticed my father getting out of breath with minimal effort. I was to learn years later that the ailment was a narrowing of the arteries - most probably from smoking - that eventually led to his death.

After the short spell with my parents, I set course for 'Bamba Zonke' to join Squadron Leader Oswald D Penton's No 4 Squadron, to fly Provost aircraft once again. My posting would last to September 1967 - and 1550 flying hours later (having joined No 4 Squadron with just over 220 flying hours).

OPERATION MAYIBUYE – MAY-JULY 1963

Operation (Africa) *Mayibuye* (operation for its return to the masses) was formulated by the South African Communist's Central Committee and the Umkhonto we Sizwe (MK) High Command in May 1963. It was a plan to overthrow white-ruled South Africa.

Details of the operation were revealed when the Rhodesians arrested eight Ethiopian-trained MK cadres that were in transit to South Africa. It transpired that the head of MK, Stalinist Joe Slovo, had secretly recruited terrorists for training in Algeria, Egypt, Ethiopia and Tanganyika (Tanzania). A few were dispatched to the Peking (Beijing) Military Academy. The operational plan involved the manufacture or procurement in South Africa of grenades, anti-personnel mines and various other explosives. Proposed targets were detailed on a series of 106 maps and included police stations, pylons, power stations, houses of black policemen, railway installations and so on.

The details emerged during the police raid on Lilliesleaf Farm, Rivonia in July 1963. Ten ANC/SACP leaders were arrested, and charged with conspiracy to overthrow the South African Government by violent means, and brought to court what became known as the Rivonia Trials. Nelson Mandela, Walter Sisulu and eight others were convicted and sentenced to life imprisonment. Co-conspirators Oliver Tambo, Joe Slovo, Joe Modise, and Ronnie Kasrils fled the country to Dar-es-Salaam.

The significance of Operation *Mayibuye* in this biography is three-fold, namely: -

≡ The Rhodesians arrested the eight Ethiopian-trained cadres in transit to South Africa. This resulted in the raid and Rivonia Trials. Four years later, Umkhonto we Sizwe (spear of the nation) terrorists would clash with Rhodesian Security Forces during Operation *Nickel* in the Wankie area.

≡ I recall my late father blowing his gasket. He had fought in Ethiopia during World War II to keep Emperor Haile Selassie in power. He was mad as a snake that Ethiopia was now training terrorists for armed insurrection against the hand that fed them with South African blood and tears.

≡ This operation received only a very brief mention in my "Rhodesian Air Force Operations" book, but because of the Rivonia Trial significance warranted further elaboration which will soon become apparent. I had just qualified as a fully-fledged pilot in the Royal Rhodesian Air Force – and would be destined to confront the terrorist invasion during Operation *Nickel* and many other counter-insurgency operations that lay ahead during my flying career.

THE CALM BEFORE THE STORM

No 4 SQUADRON / OPERATIONAL CONVERSION UNIT

I was posted to No 4 (Provost) Squadron for my OCU and duly reported for duty mid-July 1963. The Squadron was based at New Sarum, Salisbury and commanded by Squadron Leader Ossie Penton. No mention of the Rhodesian Air Force will ever be complete without mention being made of the "pint-sized General". Boss OD or "Ossie" whom everybody knew him by, was one of those people that made a lasting impression on everyone with whom he came into contact with. He fitted the apt description of "Dynamite comes in small packages." It was an exciting change for me to be based at 'Bamba Zonke' instead of dreary Gwelo. One of my earliest recollections had world-renowned repercussions.

I was possibly the first person in the Officers' Mess to hear that American President John F Kennedy had been assassinated in Dallas, Texas. A couple of Officers were sitting around the Bar, and quite a few were playing billiards in the Snooker Room. I was the only one watching television at the time. When the news flashed across the screen, I couldn't believe my ears. The consequences were just too ghastly to contemplate – America was in the middle of its Cold War with Russia, Kennedy had issued an ultimatum to Cuba to dismantle their Missile Sites, and the Space Race was going ahead at full steam. I rushed into the Snooker Room to spread the news and soon the small TV room couldn't contain the crowds that came streaming in. There was much speculation as to 'Who-done-it' – and the likelihood that World War I I would erupt. Within a matter of days, Lee Harvey Oswald was arrested and taken into custody as the most likely suspect. Americans were devastated by the death of this very popular leader. However, before Lee Harvey Oswald could appear in court, Jack Ruby gunned him down. The Warren Commission was convened to investigate the circumstances surrounding the assassinations, and their findings resulted in many claims and counter-claims that ranged for a good forty years later.

I learnt many years later about "flash-bulb memory" – events in a person's lifetime that would remain with them till their dying day. The Kennedy assassination was one of those in my case. And so it was also with the many highlights during my career in the Air Force – events that impacted on my life, and which I trust I will be able to relay in this biography. For example, 24th September 1976 and March 1993 are two other "flash-bulb memory" events that I will cover shortly. For now, however, permit me to return to my good old Provost days.

I had not flown the Provost since Basic Flying School, and I needed a quick re-familiarisation on type. And so my BFS instructor, Flying Officer Peter Petter-Bowyer once again instructed me, on 15th July. My conversion required familiarisation with general handling, low flying, formation, night flying, and the dreaded instrument flying. Squadron Leader Ozzie Penton carried out his Squadron Commander's check on me on 23rd July - that is, within a week of my joining the Squadron. Squadron Leader Oswald Dennis Penton had vast flying experience – having soloed in the year that I was born, and flew Hurricanes and Spitfires during World War II – serving in North Africa, Italy and the Mediterranean.

I had flown with Flying Officer Ian Harvey five days earlier, on the 17th, Pilot Officer Mike Hill on the 23rd, Flying Officer Gerry Craxford and Pilot Officer Bruce Smith on the 25th, and Pilot Officer Alec Roughead on 31st July 1963. Gerry Craxford was tasked to get me 'Instrument Rated', which he duly did on the 7th August. Mike Hill and Alec Roughead were both to die in aircraft accidents. Ian Harvey was destined to become the Air Vice-Marshal of the Air Force of Zimbabwe in the 1990s (some years after our fellow No 16 Course member Hugh Slatter had become Second in Command, and following his scandalous sabotage torture and deportation).

On 26th July, P-B checked me out on formation flying - with six, yes, no fewer than six Provosts in the same airspace. Up until this time the largest formations were only four aircraft. That was the difference between pupil pilot training and an operational Squadron. In addition, a new type of formation, known as Battle Formation, was also taught. This is where large formations are able to provide cross-cover for one another, and at the same time allow maximum manoeuvrability during turns.

During August 1963 I flew with Flight Lieutenants Randy du Rand and Ted Brent on OCU air-to-air quarter attacks. The Provost was fitted with a fixed gunsight and this meant that the pilot needed to compute the range, line and deflection during aerial combat - very much like the pilots did in the earlier air warfare days. In other words, the 'aircraft' is aimed ahead of the target, allowing the correct 'aim-off', angle, distance ahead, above or below depending on whether the target is climbing or diving. All these calculations had to be done in a fraction of a second if there was to be any success. All these sorties were cine-filmed, then viewed and assessed on the ground to determine whether any 'kills' were scored in the aerial combat exercises.

September 1963 was an interesting month. I flew as safety pilot to Boss Ozzie and then the next day with Pilot Officer Henry Elliot, who instructed me on instrument flying. It may be of interest that I flew a second sortie with Henry on quarter attacks on 14th October. Fourteen months later he died in an aircraft accident. Henry Elliot was one of our "Senior Course" members who had always treated me like an officer and a gentleman. Shortly after my second sortie with Henry, he was posted to No 2 Squadron in Gwelo. On the day he died he had complained of an upset stomach, but nevertheless took off on a night cross-country sortie to Bulawayo. On his return, near Moffat airfield, the Vampire FB 9 aircraft disappeared off the Thornhill Radar screen. It appeared he had lost consciousness and ploughed straight into the ground. My pilot's logbook records the event on 20th December 1964.

I also flew with P-B on a non-OCU "Army radio air test" mission. These sorties were important because they sorted out ground to air radio communications, which proved to be essential in all the COIN - Counter Insurgency operations that occurred in the Rhodesian Bush War.

However, what made September so special was the Kutanga Range air weapons camp, where for the first time live ammunition was fired from aircraft. This was the real thing. It was the reason why the government was spending thousands of pounds on our training - so as to be able to use aircraft as weapon platforms - as well as for the development of air power. We arrived at Kutanga for our weapons detachment, from the 9th to 24th September 1963. The Range Warden was Warrant Officer Nobby Clarke, ably assisted by "Kutanga" Mac John McKenzie. And what characters they were too.

My Pilot Attack Instructors (PAI) were Flight Lieutenants Randy du Rand and Ted Brent. On my first 100x·303 air to ground dual instruction sortie with Ted we scored 37%, The second, with Randy, we scored slightly better with 40%. My third sortie, solo that is, also on the 9th, I scored 56%. The next day I flew five sorties, all solo, scoring 50%, then a disastrous 16%, recovered with a respectable 57%, and then deteriorated for the last two with 44 and 31% respectively. But scores aside, it certainly was great firing a total of

800 x ·303 rounds live ammunition on air to ground targets - albeit only square cardboard targets. The smell of cordite in the cockpit was something else. It was also great fun going out to the targets with Mac's ground parties to patch all the bullet holes with brown sticky paper.

Then followed rocket firing. These were four-inch diameter rocket tubes with 60lb concrete heads. A total of four were carried, two on each wing. The average academic sortie took half an hour to fire all four rockets, but only seconds to watch their trajectory as the rockets white cordite trail streaked towards the target. Ted was a mean rocketier - scoring an average 10·5 yards. My sortie with Randy was nearly double at 20.5 yards, whereas my solos produced 18.25, 17.3, 18, 22.5, 30·5 and 22.5 yards respectively.

Then from 16th September we commenced our high-dive and low-level bombing - dropping 8 x 12lb bombs (4 x HD and 4 x LL). My high-dive bombing wasn't great, about 17.46 yard average, with best three consecutive sorties scoring 14.25 yards. Low Level was much better, the scores being 7.75 and 5.5 yards respectively. My best high dive was a mean 8.25 yard average for four bombs, and my best was eight consecutive low level bombing was a very good 4.25 yard average. A total of 48 bombs were dropped.

On 23rd September I was exposed to tear-smoke dropping - flying six sorties for the day. It took only twenty minutes to drop eight canisters. The weapons detachment was concluded with a FAC - Forward Air Control where the pilot is committed to firing 100 rounds ball ammunition and two 60lb rockets on first-run attacks.

Kutanga Range detachments were something to be really appreciated. They warrant elaboration later on. The month ended flying a cross-country with Squadron Leader Ossie Penton, to Wedza, Inyangani, Vumba and return to Salisbury.

Part of October was used to wrap up my formal Operational Conversion Unit to be certified as a Provost pilot in Internal Security Duties - qualifying on 17th October 1963. I had, up until now, flown in Provosts numbers 300, 301,302, 303, 304, 305, 306, 308, 309, 310, 311, 312 and 313. These aircraft numbers are recorded in case one day I should come across a museum piece Provost, and would be able to confirm whether I had flown that particular aircraft. In any event, I was now ready to join No 4 Squadron as a fully-fledged Squadron "jock".

No 4 SQUADRON JOCK

Having qualified, as a fully-fledged IS - Internal Security Pilot on Provost aircraft, I was now set to play my part in this exciting period of Rhodesian history. Flying duties became more challenging and meaningful. The pilots of No 14 and 15 PTC, as well as the more senior squadron jockeys also accepted me.

Echelon starboard pansy formation, turning starboard. Note: Chase aircraft, with the photographer, has also captured excellent cloud in the background

During early November a very extensive flying exercise was carried out. I teamed up with Bruce McKerron, and early Monday morning on the 11th we took off from New Sarum for a low-level battle formation and reconnaissance sortie, landing three hours later at Thornhill for lunch and re-fuel. In the afternoon, we flew another battle formation sortie, returning to Thornhill for a night-stop (jolly). On the Tuesday I teamed up with P-B (Petter-Bowyer) and we logged seven hours for the day - carrying out reconnaissance to the west of Gwelo and south of Bulawayo. After another Thornhill night-stop, I again teamed up with Bruce McKerron for a recce extending south-east of Fort Victoria, landing back at New Sarum base. The three-day exercise had traversed the whole of the country, and took a total of 16 flying hours. A memorable exercise included bombing No 1 Squadron with "bog rolls". But the week was not over yet.

On Thursday I flew an instrument flying sortie with Alec Roughead as my safety pilot, and then a sortie of night circuits and landings. Then on Friday, I was one of six Provost pilots that got airborne to practice pansy formation in preparation for Federal Prime Minister Sir Roy Welensky's farewell. Fortunately, the easier position of echelon starboard was given to the less experienced squadron jocks like yours truly.

Sir Roy Welensky's farewell flypast was flown on Monday 18th November 1963. It was a proud moment for me to participate on this major air effort by the Air Force. No 4 Squadron fielded seven Provosts, and we preceded the slightly faster Dakotas of No 3 Squadron. Alouette Helicopters from No 7 Squadron led the Flypast over the Salisbury Showgrounds, with the lead chopper dangling the national flag on a massive ball-weight fluttering below its belly. The faster Vampires and Canberras followed the Dakotas. With the national anthem in full swing, and as the salute was taken on the parade ground, the whole Air Force flew over with immaculate timing. It was this awesome display of air power that brings lumps to the throat of airmen. Meanwhile, in the cockpits (mine in particular), there was much "kicking and gouging, thrashing of throttles and sweat pouring from brows" to maintain ones position in a rather crowded sky.

Flypast of six Provosts – our relocation from New Sarum to Thornhill

Sir Roy was born in Salisbury in 1907. He left school at the age of fourteen (he was the thirteenth child) to become a storekeeper. At age seventeen he joined the Railways as a fireman, and in 1926 became the Heavyweight Boxing champion of the Rhodesias - a title he held for two years. In 1928 he got married and moved to Wankie.

Then in 1933 he moved to Broken Hill and became the chairman of the Railway Workers Union and in 1938 he was elected to the Northern Rhodesia Legislative Council. He was knighted in 1953, and became Prime Minister of the Federation from 1956 to 1963.

But the new week was not over yet. Bruce McKerron and I continued with our tour of Rhodesia - flying 7½ hours on a recce south-east of Salisbury, landing at Thornhill to refuel, then west of Bulawayo (and refuelling there), and back to New Sarum via Thornhill. Towards the end of the month, I covered Salisbury north with P-B, landing at Mount Hampden. Then in early December, P-B and I recced the Eastern Districts - which also included formation take-off and formation landings. Getting to know the country so well would stand me in good stead, because African Nationalism was starting to get out of hand. Also, during the early part of the month, I flew my only sortie with Tony Gassner - a member of 14 PTC.

Towards the latter part of December I flew with the three senior course pilots who subsequently lost their lives in flying accidents. The first to die a mere six months hence was Bruce McKerron, then Mike Hill and followed by Alec Roughead. Bruce had been posted to No 2 Squadron in the New Year and was killed in a Vampire. Mike Hill died in an Alouette crash and Alec would die in a Canberra. But I still need to tell the story of Alec and his booby traps with cordite in "squash balls".

The Federation of Rhodesia and Nyasaland lasted for ten years from 7th November 1953 till 31st December 1963.

And so 1963 drew to a close. With the postings announced in early December, the New Year was to bring about many changes. No 4 Squadron lost Boss Ozzie Penton, with Ted Brent standing in as acting Squadron Commander, pending John Mussell taking over. (Author's note: Rob Thurman published *"Half a Century in Uniform"* – the Life Story of Group Captain O D Penton AFC OLM Rhodesian Air Force Volunteer Reserve (Ret'd), with my copy being printed in April 2000. This unique story has added value to my prized possessions). No 4 Squadron would also swap bases with No 5 Canberra Squadron, and No 6 Squadron would be disbanded as a result of the Federal break-up. There was a need to rationalise the Air Force within Southern Rhodesia's limited resources to sustain a "pocket air capability". Swapping bases meant us 4 Squadron blokes would leave Bamba Zonke Salisbury for "Lay-by with Lights" Gwelo.

Although we didn't fancy leaving the Big City, the pending change to a new environment presented challenging opportunities. In any event, it would suit pilot training better, as well as make the 'main manna' IS Squadron more centrally situated - to react more speedily to all four corners of the country.

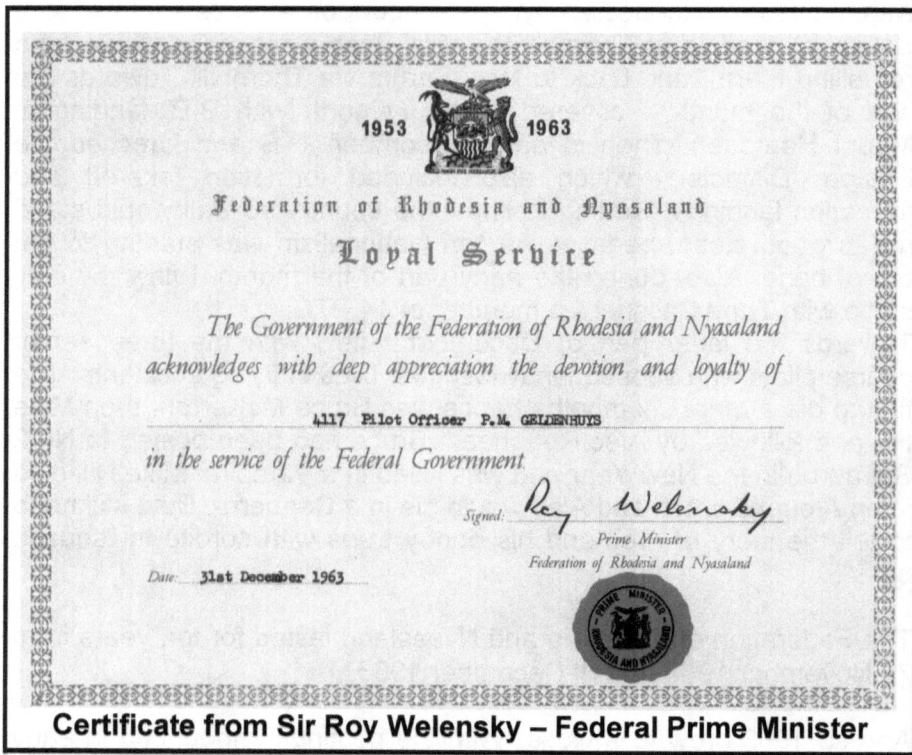

Certificate from Sir Roy Welensky – Federal Prime Minister

On 14th January 1964, I was one of the six aircraft positioning at Thornhill to set up our new home. But not after a duly impressive "Flypast" at our new base, which lasted over 20 minutes formation flying and then "breaking" to attack No 1 Squadron crew-rooms with some more bog rolls. Air Traffic Control kindly gave us free rein with regard to the base beat-ups. But Thornhill was a shambles - I mean taking over No 5 Squadron buildings. The bomber squadron was only scheduled to depart two days later - and they took all their furniture, including telephones. Alas, the swap-over had not been co-ordinated too well. We were given a week off to bring our cars, as well as Squadron equipment and furniture down.

> # CERTIFICATE OF AUTHENTICITY
>
> This is to Certify that this Copy
>
> of
>
> # Half a Century in Uniform
>
> The Story of
>
> ### Group Captain O.D. Penton
> AFC, OLM
>
> Rhodesian Air Force Volunteer Reserve (Retd.)
>
> has been specially printed for
>
> Prop. (Propeller) Geldenhuys
>
> Signed
>
> O.D. Penton
>
> Copy No 19   05 April 2000
>
> **The personalised copy of Ozzie Penton's book**

The new No 4 Squadron was now tasked to take on the additional role of handling basic flying training (hence the move to Thornhill) and flying began on 21st January with 12 pilots, 15 ground crew and 13 Provost aircraft. I myself got airborne that day on a general, low flying sortie. Two days later I flew up to New Sarum for a night stop with squadron Qualified Flying Instructor Flight Lieutenant Meddows-Taylor to attend to unfinished business. By the end of the month I had also flown with our senior course colleagues Pilot Officers Dave "Spas" Currie and Dave Hume. The sortie with Spas was to Shangani (of Alan Wilson last stand fame), Lupani - in the middle of nowhere, Gokwe and return to base.

February 1964 was reasonably quiet, except for a 3½-hour recce in north-west Rhodesia with Brownjob Lieutenant Garnett and followed by a similar sortie with fellow course member Pilot Officer Hugh Slatter, who had joined the squadron for QFI conversion to train BFS students. March followed a similar pattern, but this time I flew Junior Technician Mazaris on a low-level recce in south-east Rhodesia. Aircraftsman Pete Badenhorst was also frightened "passing-windless" on a tail chase sortie. A couple of simulated air-strike sorties were also carried out but the quiet before the storm was not to last long.

During early April, preparations were made for a major "Forcex" - Air Force exercise, to demonstrate the effectiveness of air power to Government officials (Sir Humphrey Gibbs et al). The 'Tactical and Air Weapons Demonstration' was scheduled for the weekend of the 11th and 12th. Five days earlier, I was tasked to carry out the timing runs - to ensure that the Provost demo would slot in with the other force aircraft. On the 8th, I flew two sorties, with the second sortie entailing the air-to-ground firing of 200 rounds of ·303 i.e. 100 rounds from each Browning front gun. Up until this time, the most I had fired was 2 x 50 = 100 rounds. This was just a practice for the big event. The following day, another practice sortie was flown to fine-tune the preparations for the big day.

The Governor-General Sir Humphrey Gibbs, accompanied by the Minister of Internal Affairs, Jack Howman and the Director of the Central Intelligence Organisation (CIO), Ken Flower, flew down to Thornhill on the Saturday to view the static display. The Minister of Defence, Winston Field had cancelled his attendance at the last minute. The following day, the dignitaries were flown to Kutanga (it transpired that the Prime Minister was about to dismiss Field). Then on Sunday 12th April 1964, the grand finale unfolded spectacularly for all the assembled guests. Although I say with all modesty, gunnery seemed to be my speciality, I was duly loaded up with 400 rounds of ammunition to attack the 'huts' which range wardens Nobby Clarke and John "Mac" McKenzie had constructed at the Kutanga Bombing Range east of Que Que. With both guns blazing away, I was duly able to record DCO - duty carried out, on the Air Weapons demonstration.

As a matter of historical interest, Monday the 13th was the last day in office for Winston Field. This day marked the fall of Field and the advent of Ian Douglas Smith

The other highlights of the month were a practice diversion sortie to Bulawayo with RAF qualified pilot Acting Flight Lieutenant Phil Pile (of Hawk aircraft sabotage fame). I think this was the only time that I actually flew with Phil, or knew of him flying for that matter. I suspect there was a problem, but being a very able and capable airman, he was destined for various staff appointments. The other highlight was being tasked to uplift our Officer Commanding Flying Wing, Wing Commander Sandy Mutch, from Bumi Hills opposite Kariba. I suspect the WingCo was involved with operational planning. Then on the last day of April, I was the poor sucker ending up as number nine in a squadron formation flying exercise. The whiplash as number nine in echelon formation is something to experience. In a gooseneck or arrowhead formation one flies arse end Charlie in line astern position.

OPERATIONS COONDOG & HEDGEHOG

Border reconnaissance sorties were still in their infancy. At the end of April, I had flown a lengthy night cross-county sortie with Pilot Officer Hugh Slatter to Umtali and the return to Gwelo via Fort Victoria. The next day, 1st May, SAC Rich Bean was my passenger cum observer on a Bumi Hills "Operation *Coondog*" mission - associated with the business that Wing Commander Mutch had arranged some nine days earlier. Why Coondog, I don't recall? I doubt very much that any racial connotations were intended - but in retrospect, "hound-dog" may have been a better choice of codename.

On the Monday morning, 1st May, I got off to an early start and departed Thornhill for Salisbury to uplift Army Captain Hugh Rowley for Operation *Hedgehog*. The airtask detailed a reconnaissance of the north-east Portuguese border. I still remember that the Avgas fumes in the cockpit proved a problem for the Army Captain. Every time I banked the aircraft, poor old Hugh was apt to spread second-hand carrots all over the instrument panel. He was okay flying straight and level - but at some stage one needs to turn around - lest one runs out of fuel. Also, a recce, of necessity, entails orbiting ground troops or banking the aircraft to get a better view of the ground. I did my best to turn the aircraft with minimum aileron, applying a boot full of rudder, and yawing the aircraft around turns. Flying cross controls at low level is not such a good manoeuvre - but it was a better option than having to contend with all the "honk" floating my way. After a trying 2¼-hour torture for the poor Brownjob, we called it a day.

After a comfortable night-stop, I was airborne on Airtask 062, but this time with Lieutenant Brian Robinson. As the future SAS - Special Air

Service squadron commander, Brian took to the air like a duck to water. In other words, he was as happy as a pig in manure. Our mission was a three hour thirty-five minute recce in the Kariba area. After landing back at New Sarum, Ian Harvey joined me on the flight back to Gwelo. Then on 13th May, I was off again on a recce of the Gokwe area with Army Captain Ellis. I don't recall much of this sortie, but I do recall the one the next day. My logbook records a 'quickie' exercise to Trickling Waters. Trickling Waters was the name of the farm on which my future father-in-law farmed. Unbeknown to the Boss, this invariably entailed stupid low-level beat-ups - fowls not laying eggs, farm labourers scared out of their wits, and yours truly nearly ending up in a box. As it was, I was nearing the dangerous 500-hour stage that my good father had wisely warned me against.

Anyway, I suspect that my behaviour back at the Squadron may have given my high spirits away as I found myself flying with the Boss, Squadron Leader John Mussell. On a dusk navex (navigational exercise), to Enkeldoorn, Kutanga Range for a 1 x 25lb bomb first run attack, then on to Umvuma and a night landing back at base. This was the first time the Boss had flown with me since taking over from Ozzie Penton.

Army FAC – (Forward Air Control) Course flying involved the Army ground callsign would giving a target grid reference point and direction of attack. The IS pilot would then proceed to an IP - or Initial Point, calculate a pull-up point and then advise the army unit of estimated time on target - or TOT for short. The pilot then flies at very low level to his pup (pull-up point) in order to maximise surprise, climbs at full power to 1000 feet above ground level, and then relies on the army unit to direct him onto the enemy target position. The purpose of the FAC Course for the Brownjobs was to give them air experience as to how quickly things happen in the air. There is no time for mucking about. The Brownjob needs to have his finger out i.e. extractum digit. My second sortie with Geoff was a recce in the low-flying area where we simulated several FAC attacks in order to give them pointers in selecting appropriate landmarks. For example, the Brownjob may select a "big tree", or a "line of trees". From the pilot's viewpoint, the Army guy then realises that his "big tree, or line" disappears into insignificance, because he then sees thousands of big trees, or his line of trees is in fact a whole plantation. Anyway, it was these types of Army Co-operation exercises that enhanced appreciation of each other's limitations in close air support operations.

The next day I concluded my involvement with Operation Hedgehog.
It was a long, hectic day, with an early start for Bulawayo. I landed at Kumalo to uplift Major Johnson for a recce in the Kariba area, landing Wankie to refuel. We returned to Bulawayo at night, and then I continued on to Thornhill. I need to add that I, as with all pilots, always enjoyed the free nite-flying supper perk. It consisted of two fried eggs, bacon, two pork sausages and buttered bread - a meal I still enjoy to this day.

No 4 Squadron, by the way, was affiliated to Umtali. No 104 Volunteer Reserve Squadron was based there, and the VR would go out of their way to make life comfortable for the Bluejobs. The Queen's Birthday celebrations were coming up and No 4 Squadron would spend an enjoyable three-day jolly there. A practice Air Display was carried out on 5th and 9th June, and then early morning on the 11th the Squadron positioned New Sarum. Hugh Slatter then joined me for the Umtali Flypast. We flew to Umtali and landed at Grand Reef. We got airborne in the afternoon as the standby aircraft for the Air Display over the town. After landing, we were treated like royalty, and enjoyed Portuguese fair before bedding down for the night. The next morning I was required to take Flight Lieutenant Petter-Bowyer to Salisbury, where we stayed overnight. Early on the 12th, we returned to Grand Reef to effect the necessary repairs to one of the unserviceable Provost aircraft. Then later on in the afternoon, we returned to Thornhill, routing via New Sarum.

A FAC simulated strikes (two hours sortie duration - which was in fact quite lengthy) was carried out for the benefit of our southern neighbours. Rhodesian inter-service was good, thanks to Nos 4 and 7 Squadrons' close army co-operation. The South African pilots could only benefit from our experience, as inter-service jealousy was still rife down south. In retrospect, the South Africans were in fact shrewd to observe and "use" the Rhodesian pawns in preparation for their own "swart gevaar".

The other albeit tragic highlight was the fatal air accident on 22nd June 1964 in which Flying Officer Bruce McKerron was killed. I was needed to take my old flying instructor P-B to Salisbury for the Board of Inquiry that was convened to investigate the circumstances surrounding the crash. It may be recalled that I had last flown with him on 17th December, and in the month following my Operational Conversion Unit, had in fact traversed most of the country with him. As was customary, the entire flying wing pilots would adjourn to the pub and get plastered for the day. Anyway, the show must go on and the next day I departed for our twice-annual weapons camp to Kutanga Range.

KUTANGA DETACHMENTS

My third camp to Kutanga Bombing Range lasted from 23rd to 30th June 1964. The first camp was during our earlier Operational Conversion Unit shortly after "Wings". I was then still wet behind the ears and overawed at discharging lethal air weapons. As JPs, we junior pilots were largely left observing how things were done. This was collecting all the dollies from Que Que for the numerous bashes held, apart from doing dog's body work. Orgies were perhaps a more accurate description of normal antics. I remember some of the rather strange happenings well. A troop carrier would be dispatched to round up the gorgeous gals who would then be lined up, and paraded for the sex-starved bunch of airmen. A Squadron Commander, who will remain nameless, would then choose the pick of the bunch, and quietly disappear for the night. Then there was the one-eyed beauty, - who would extract her glass eye and leave it staring at all and sundry, or purposely drop it into some unsuspecting airman's drink.

The Bossman would appear hours later, neatly attired, hairstyle unruffled, partake of a courtesy drink at the pub, and then blow the whistle for the troop carrier to take all the lovelies back to town. Bruce Smith, our senior course Maths Instructor, would on occasion become so inebriated that the ground crew would tie him to one of the marquee tent poles - to prevent him from falling over. Bruce would go into fits of giggles, invariably when any dolly wandered close enough to his

Bruce Smith

groping limbs. Bruce was also an ace guinea fowl slayer. Our hunts along the range firebreaks would result in flying dismounts from the still moving vehicle, kicking one poor bird to death, wringing the head clean off another, and swatting a third with his free hand - all in one simultaneous movement. Henry Elliot was another mean Guinea fowl slayer. But enough said.

I need to digress for a moment. I've already mentioned Alec Roughead and his cordite pranks - bless his soul. Alec had an incurable habit of collecting all the cordite from expended rockets. He would throw chunks of cordite explosive into braai fires; blow bully beef tins sky high, and make all sorts of bombs and booby traps. A favourite pastime was stuffing cordite into a squash ball and then inserting the filament of a broken light bulb into the squash ball containing the cordite. Alec would then choose a victim, sneak into the unsuspecting sucker's single quarter and cleverly place his 'bomb' in the light socket. Now our quarters had two ceiling lights and the light switches were positioned back to back, near the entrance doors. Before long, yours truly became a target of Alec's pranks. A typical incident - or rather series of incidences would unfold thus: I would return late at night (after a night out, or just watching TV at the Mess), unsuspectingly switch on my billet light in pitch darkness, and be momentarily 'blinded' by the flash and explosion as the cordite would ignite when the electric current was switched on. This invariably left a big, black circle around the light fitting. Shrieks of laughter from Alec's room left no doubt who had succeeded in claiming another victim.

In my case, that was not the end. Very shortly after having fallen victim, Alec fooled me by placing a second 'light special' in my remaining ceiling light. Believing to be inspector Clousseau, I would suspiciously not switch my already blown-up light on, but reached round the corner in the darkness to put the 'other' light on - only to once again fall victim to Alec's antics. Well, enough was enough, except that the phantom bomber was not of like mind. The following night, having watched a good detective movie on TV, I tried to outwit the Smart Alec. I claim to have approached my single quarter cautiously — once bitten twice shy. I wasn't going to take a chance and blow up my already blackened ceiling so opted to fumble in the darkness for my bedside light. I took the extra precaution of sticking my finger into the lampshade and felt, what I thought to be, the 'normal small light' as found in the bedside lights. Guess what happened? As I pressed the button to switch on my bedside light, I nearly blew my hand off. Alec had succeeded in fooling Inspector Clousseau a third time. I can only say again; Alec, Bless your Soul.

I flew Peter Hosking on a three-hour recce of the Mfungabusi Plateau. I then returned to the Range with P-B on the 29th to complete my high dive and low-level sorties - dropping all told 48 x 20lb smoke bombs. My gunnery scoring was improving all the time, with a high of 89 % and an overall average of 66.2 %, High dive average of 22.1 yards and a low-level bombing average of 8.2 yards. During July, I flew our Station Commander Group Captain Doug Whyte to the Range and return. As a JP, I was a trifle nervous with flying such a senior Air Force officer. It is natural to be on ones best behaviour, and for it to be seen that the Force was fully justified for entrusting even junior, fairly inexperienced pilots with expensive machines plus the lives of its senior officers. The thought comes to mind that in the event of an accident, a lot of career minded blokes will jockey for promotion opportunities. Not so much my lowly vacancy - but certainly down to Squadron Leader level. A Wing Commander would be promoted to Group Captain; Squadron Leader to Wing Commander, Flight Commander to Squadron Leader and then a Flight Lieutenant would fill the command vacancy. There was no merit in my committing 'hara-kiri', although I guess there were some feeble minded aircrew around that would have cherished the thought. In any event, my mission was carried out successfully, albeit my landings at Kutanga and back at Thornhill were not of the greatest with the Group Captain aboard. I might add that Groupie Whyte was a terrific Station Commander, who new the names of all the service wives in Married Quarters, and more often than not, most of their offspring as well.

In August, I had a particularly interesting sortie. I again flew to Kutanga to uplift Range Warden Warrant Officer Nobby Clarke for a recce of Zimbabwe Ruins and Lake Kyle. We landed in order for Nobby to survey a lake campsite which the Air Force Welfare organisation intended developing. Nobby was a master at scrounging the necessary material and resources to construct comfortable rest shacks. Once he had seen his fill, I then returned him to Que Que and proceeded home to Gwelo. The Campsite was to become one of the most sought after week-end retreats for Air Force personnel.

About mid-month I was again selected to fly Group Captain Doug Whyte. This time he needed to attend a military conference in Bulawayo. Another strange mission during the month was to carry out a 'bread' drop to Gokwe and then continued on to Bumi Hills. A couple of days later I was tasked to the diagonally opposite side of the country - to Chimanimani and Chipinga. The trips were flown with Army Captain Geoff Atkinson, which included landings on the Chipinga airfield. I trust Brendan Jelly will one day realise that his Oudad actually visited his town of birth some 35 years before he was born. In fact, the airfield is within a stones throw from the mansion that his father has developed. At the turn of the century, Grandpa Bill

Jelley also flew his aircraft in to Chipinga airfield, to visit the younger Jelley's.

Another illustrative perk of being a bush pilot is the opportunity of visiting all corners of the country with regularity. The No 4 Squadron pilots certainly managed to get around - and got to know the country fairly well.

Before Renene chastises me, let me return to the matter at hand. It certainly wasn't all play. On that 23rd June, I actually flew a mammoth eight gunnery sorties, firing 7 x 100 rounds ball ammunition, with the ninth sortie being cancelled. After such a hectic day, one would flop into bed. My range detachment was interrupted to uplift Army RAR Captain Peter

In September, FRA (first run attacks) were carried out at the Range - gunnery as well as bombing. Then in November I improved my high dive average marginally to 21.3 yards - my best was a mere 7.6 yards average but a disastrous thirty-five yarder spoilt it.

Bombed up and ready to go

It is opportune to jump the gun and record latter detachments at this juncture. Our next camp was from the 18th to 25th January 1965, then the 2nd to 6th August, followed by the 20th to 26th January 1966. I managed to improve my gunnery scores to 93 % academic and 79 % FRA. My best high dive was 13.3 yards with low level hovering around 7.6 yards. These achievements earned me a "Master" category in both gunnery and low-level bombing, and an "A" category in High Dive. I was giving my ace Pilot Attack Instructor Varky Varkevisser a run for his money, and in all modesty admit that I treasure the low-level Bombing Trophy that I presume is still displayed nowadays in No 4 Squadron crew-room.

At Kutanga – Bombed up with 8 x 20lb Smoke Bombs

AN ILL WIND BLOWS

On 10th July, Bruce Smith and I carried out a reconnaissance sortie in the south-east of the country - to show the flag and publicise 'air power'.

On 1st September 1964, I was tasked to uplift Major General 'Jock' Anderson from Boli to Salisbury. He had conferred with Nkomo regarding nationalist feelings. I suspect that the poor General had fallen from favour with the Rhodesian Government; otherwise they wouldn't have subjected him to the discomforts of a Provost. I obviously needed to take a spare parachute and Bonedome for him to wear for his one hour forty flight to New Sarum. Boli was a dusty airstrip in the middle of nowhere in the south-east Lowveld. I sensed that the bonedome was a couple of sizes too small, and the poor fellow was sweating profusely in the cockpit. I offered him the opportunity of taking over control (at a safe altitude I might add), but he politely declined. He was not very talkative on the rather long journey to Salisbury, but did thank me on landing for having saved him a somewhat long road journey. As the GOC - General Officer Commanding the Rhodesian Army, he was the most senior militiaman I had the privilege to fly with. Major General Jock Anderson, incidentally, was a founder member of the Operations Co-ordinating Committee. The Air Representative was Air Vice-Marshal Bentley, later replaced by Air-Vice-Marshal Harold Hawkins.

National Servicemen were being called up left, right and centre. I am sure Philip Malan, my future wife's twin brother, will not quickly forget 14th September 1964. He was passing through Gwelo on his motorcycle en route for Army call-up, when he met with an unfortunate accident at the first roundabout. He was quickly patched up at the Station Sick Quarters and discharged. I managed to wangle a general, low flying sortie in Provost 302 for him. After kitting him out with the necessary flying gear, we took to the wild blue yonder. He certainly appeared to enjoy the treetop hopping, but did not take a liking to the aerobatics. I could see he was trying to remain conscious during the high 'g' manoeuvres, but when the smell of Avgas entered the cockpit, I had a problem once again of scraping the second hand carrots off the instrument panel. Airsickness effects are at their worst after the event, because of the resultant migraine headaches, which sets in whenever a stomach is emptied. Despite my being kind to my brother-in-law by curtailing the sortie to a mere thirty-five minutes, Phil has been getting me back ever since.

On a more serious note, let the record show that Phil Malan, like Rina's younger brother Frans Malan, played their fair share during the bush war. Some of his episodes included no fewer than four 10th Battalion, Rhodesia Regiment call-ups, for Zambezi Valley border control operations. To name but a few would not do justice to the role played by the Territorial Force. One needs to know Phil, to appreciate his good humour and downplay his own personal contribution to the Rhodesian war effort. He recalls a stint at Photo Corner in Kariba when on his instructions he ordered his men to drop their kit but hang onto their rifles whilst on boat patrol duty. Although he literately landed in deep water, his main concern was the safety and wellbeing of his colleagues. On another occasion, whilst eyeballing the enemy with powerful binoculars across the Kariba dam wall, his mate quite seriously suggested "Why don't we just go over and blow up the Zambian side of the dam wall? That will really bugger up the Zambians, while we will be okay Jack."

On yet another occasion, while doing a 36-day stint in the Zambezi Valley (believed sometime during November 1974), it rained continuously for the entire six weeks. They were wet through and through, and amazingly, not one of them caught flu or got sick. The patrols had to fight their way through the thick Valley Jesse-bush and often made up lost ground by following game trails. However, these game trail excursions also had their unique hazards – like elephants – which were in fact more feared in the bush than stumbling on infiltrating terrorists. On more than one occasion the patrol walked slap-bang into the backside of a grazing elephant.

However, before I jump the gun too far ahead, I will return later to other Phil Malan escapades in the Zambezi Valley – such as Mukumbura "By The Sea", drinking water contaminated with elephant urine, and following tracks for no less than 35 kilometres.

ARMY SHAMVA OPERATION 16 - 20 SEPTEMBER 1964

Two days after that eventful sortie with sporting Phil Malan, I set off for a five day Army detachment in the Salisbury area of Shamva. I routed via Salisbury to drop off Flying Officer Spaz Currie. Then followed an armed reconnaissance sortie in the Shamva area that also involved the BSAP Air Wing, the sortie lasting two hours twenty-five minutes. That night, the kind hospitality of the Army field Mess was enjoyed. They certainly knew how to live in the bush with very little mod cons. The troopies did not quite enjoy the same standard of living; they had to make do as best they could with what they could carry on their person. My logbook entry records "destroying enemy" for 17th September, but I suspect these were simulated Forward Air Control ground attacks, to exercise Army units in this form of Internal Security operational tactics. On the next day I flew two sorties totalling just over three hours, which involved the police Air Wing in FAC simulated strikes. I presume radio problems were experienced, because my task the next day entailed uplifting radio mechanic Flying Officer Sandy Steele. The night of the 19th was spent at Salisbury, kipping at New Sarum Single Officers' Quarters. The Army exercise ended with my return to Gwelo on the 20th, this time having Flying Officer Bruce Smith as my co-pilot for the New Sarum to Thornhill leg.

On 22nd September I flew a British soldier, Lieutenant Smart, from the Scottish Guards Regiment on a flag waving "show attractions" in Rhodesia sortie. I can't recall whether this was an English 'spy', or whether the intention was to 'poach' or attract foreign soldiers to join the Rhodesian security forces. I do in fact remember an 'import' Air Lieutenant John Smart, who was subsequently killed on active

service in the Ruya Game Reserve, with Sergeant Kevin Tinker Smithdorff, in an Alouette helicopter on 21st February 1973.
The month ended with a 100 x ·303 front gun and 2 x 25lb bombing dusk strike. October got off to a flying start with a variety of sorties with Wally Galloway, Bruce Smith, Hugh Slatter, Barry Matthews and Aircraftman Johnson. A couple of days before Operation *Phoenix*, I again flew Group Captain Doug Whyte to Kutanga Bombing Range, and return. The Thornhill Station Commander was starting to make a habit of using me as his air-taxi driver. On 15th October, Acting Pilot Officer Barry Matthews flew with me to the Bulawayo area to carry out a reconnaissance of all the surrounding kraal locations.

OPERATION PHOENIX - 1964

I had hardly finished my Operational Conversion Unit (OCU) training on No 4 Squadron, RRAF, when I was whisked away to Bulawayo. Barry Matthews and I, accompanied by Wing Commander Mutch, flying two Provost aircraft, were to base up with 1 Brigade, Brady Barracks, Bulawayo. Brady Barracks was an ex-RATG World War II aerodrome that had been turned into a grand prix-racing track, with car tyres down the centre line. The purpose of our deployment was to fly over all the chiefs' and headmen's kraals in Matabeleland while the 'Indaba' took place in Salisbury.
On 16th October 1964 I flew Provost 312, with Barry, to Kumalo. Later the same day, we flew the ten minute return trip to Woodvale to refuel (Woodvale was the Bulawayo International Airport). The next morning I got off to an early solo start for the lengthy 3hour 40minute Matabeleland North reconnaissance route. On landing back at Kumalo, I uplifted Corporal Mick Fulton to help with refuelling at Woodvale. On the 18th I flew the northern circuit with one of the No 101 (Bulawayo) Volunteer Squadron crew, Pilot Officer Eddie Hobbs. The 18th was a mammoth morning 4hour 25minute sortie with Barry, to Bubi, Nkai and Lupani, followed by three-hour trip to Bulalima Mangwe in the afternoon - not bad for nearly seven and half-hours flying for the day. This pattern of flying would repeat itself until the end of the month. As the days progressed, the flying became more interesting. I also flew with VR Flying Officer Ruby. We landed at Tjolotjo, Nkai and Lupani. I met BSAP Air Wing pilot Peter Scales and enjoyed a seven-hour sortie in his Cessna, VP-YTV. I was destined to meet up with him again during Operation *Nickel*. Before

my flying bores the reader, let me detail the reasons for Operation *Phoenix*.

The 'indaba' - a meeting - was held to gauge African opinion: the indaba consisted of consulting six hundred and twenty-two African chiefs and headmen. Since Smith was very wary of intimidation amongst the blacks, the Army/Air Force were mobilised and deployed to the six hundred and twenty-two locations, while all the chiefs and headmen in the country were summoned to state their opinions.

The Army chaps were deployed with white bed sheets, which were placed on the ground in a square panel. As soon as the 'Blues' spotted the square panel, signifying all was well, we would continue on to the next kraal, and so on and so forth. If all were not well, the panel would be folded into a triangle and the Blues would then radio base and advise them accordingly. However, cognisance was not taken of natural local limitations like goats, which caused the odd false alarm after chomping up half the panel sheet.

The public generously donated newspapers, Daily Mirrors, Readers' Digests, Personality, and various men only magazines. We would then take bundles with us and try to bomb the troopies with them. I had some narrow escapes for, after scoring a couple of direct hits, I would carry out a victory roll, only to be confronted with magazines floating all over the cockpit after having turned inverted. One would then spend the rest of the time flying the next leg while picking up paper from among the rudder pedals, long range fuel tanks, and every nook and cranny in the cockpit.

Often, when no response was forthcoming from the ground troops - especially after a three to four hour sortie - I would carry out a low level beat up, and I was indeed very lucky to have survived the umpteenth blue gum tree, power line, telephone wires, and even stampeding cattle.

Blue jobs were fortunate to return every evening to the comfort of a barrack block bed, whereas the Browns in the field would have to rough it out in the open. The Brigadier, VR Squadron Commander, and even the Mayor often invited us out to dinner. Officer Commanding No 101 (Bulawayo) Squadron was Squadron Leader Ted Strever. He invited us quite a few times to his home for dinner (Ted Strever died at Haenertsburg in 1996). Most of these dinner parties were semi-formal, and we expected to be on our best behaviour. However, I suspect our hosts were sometimes embarrassed by the Bluejob behaviour. On one such occasion, Wing Commander Mutch fell foul of his host when he (1) recounted an earlier experience of making love to a girl while her parents were out, and (2) because he insisted on popping his hostess's cigarette butts into a spittoon.

In the latter, hardly had the dignitary's wife finished smoking her cigarette, that Wing Commander Mutch would insist on ejecting the stompie from the cigarette holder (he was apparently fascinated by the holder's mechanism). And he appeared not to realise that the lady was becoming increasingly annoyed at having her cigarettes prematurely extinguished.

In the former incident, he recounted the story of making love on the carpet in front of the lounge fireplace, when the girl's parents returned unexpectedly early. Having hastily dressed, they took their seats and, when the mother brought in the tea, he duly jumped up to take the tray. In doing so, the French letter slipped down his trouser leg and landed on the floor at his feet. Quick as a flash he put his foot over it, and then refused to budge from the spot. There he was, pivoting around on one foot trying to serve the tea. When he finally finished he could hardly walk back to his seat and thus expose the incriminating evidence. Instead, he had to perch on the very edge of his seat with his legs stretched out in front of him wide apart. He spent a very uncomfortable evening in this peculiar position until the parents finally went to bed and he could recover the telltale French letter. Needless to say, he never returned to explain his extraordinary behaviour of that evening.

From a flying point of view, I had the opportunity of gaining valuable experience, making and maintaining regular army contact, and learning to fly up to eight hours a day (take off early in the morning, land, refuel, lunch, and off again, returning at dusk). Wing Commander Sandy Mutch joined me for quite a few sorties. When I first came in to land on our first trip, there was some fool standing on the runway threshold, obviously curious at our antics. I'm surprised that he did not hear Mutch's screaming and shouting from the air while I did several low approaches trying to force him to move off. However, that was not to be, and I accordingly landed deep to avoid hitting the obstruction, much to Mutch's relief, but it did nothing for my anxiety as I tried desperately not to overrun the short runway and land up on the Bulawayo / Gwelo road with burst main wheels.

The Wing Commander flew with me on no less than seven sorties - logging over 21 flying hours within six days. That would have been a lot for OCFW. Also, bearing in mind my two sorties with the Station Commander, I had in this month alone flown with the top Thornhill Brass. I logged a phenomenal 79·55 hours for the month

Operation *Phoenix* ended on 30th October 1964. The end result of Operation *Phoenix* was that the battle was won but the war was lost - a sorry tale that repeated itself with the demise of Rhodesia. Let it be known and appreciated that the Rhodesians never lost militarily in battle - it was international politics that lost the war. The Chiefs and headmen supported Ian Smith / Alec Douglas-Home's call for independence, but by then Britain had a new Prime Minister, Harold Wilson, and his Labour Party refused to accept the meeting with the chiefs as a valid indication of black opinion.

Britain was not going to grant independence until majority rule was guaranteed - and that meant African majority rule - NIBMAR - No Independence Before Majority African Rule. Ian Douglas Smith, the first Rhodesian-born Prime Minister, had no option but to unilaterally declare Independence, despite eleventh hour flying visits from fatso Arthur Bottomley.

OPERATION SLIPSHOD

During October, Squadron Leader Ken (KAS) Edwards took over command of the Squadron from John Mussell. I had last flown with my ex-Boss way back on 19th May.

November got off to the normal humdrum squadron flying - aircraft air tests, low flying exercises, formation flying, bombing sorties at Kutanga Range and instrument flying in preparation for my rating test. I flew with Mike Hill, Derek Nightingale and my last sortie with Henry Elliot. Surprisingly, Flight Lieutenant Dave Thorne tested my instrument flying and rated me a lofty 'Green Card'.

Operation *Slipshod* was from Kutanga, on 14th November 1964. I positioned at the Range with Corporal Fulton for a night stop. The next day I was given two air tasks, to carry out reconnaissance sorties to the south of Gwelo in conjunction with the Army School of Infantry. On landing back at Kutanga, I again uplifted Corporal Mick Fulton for Thornhill. Towards the end of the month, I flew safety pilot for the Boss, Squadron Leader KAS Edwards. Now he was a good boss, perhaps even better than Boss Ozzie Penton. On the 28th of the month I flew and dropped off Flight Lieutenant Erasmus at Kyle Dam.

Two instrument flying sorties were flown with Boss KAS Edwards, one of which was a night QGH/GCA, during December. A QGH is where the pilot transmits to the Air Traffic Controller, requesting a ground controlled 'let-down'. The Controller had a dial that shows him the aircraft's bearing relative to the airfield and then directs the pilot to fly over the radio beacon. Once overhead, the pilot is 'ground controlled', and flies a descending tear drop pattern, then turns inbound, continues his descent to a break-off altitude, - and if all things work out, the pilot is then ideally positioned to carry out a direct approach and landing on the runway. A GCA - or Ground Controlled Approach is where the pilot flies totally under radar surveillance and the GCA Controller 'talks the pilot down to touch-down' on the runway.

Two other notable sorties during the month were a formation drill sortie with fellow No 16 PTC Course member Pilot Officer Graham Cronshaw, and the second was with Flight Lieutenant Varky Varkevisser - on a re-familiarisation on type sortie. I think Varky had been posted to the Provost squadron from Canberras. Varky would have a profound affect on my career as well as development of flying skills.

Then on 10th December 1964 I had two interesting sorties, dropping supplies to Army callsigns, and the second was an hour's search for escaped convicts. I can't remember whether we actually located the convicts, but would think the Army was assisting the police to track the escapees - hence the supply drop to the ground forces, and followed by the air search to slow down those on the run.

My last sortie for the year was flown with Hugh Slatter on Friday the 17th. I had been granted a month's leave and left Gwelo the next day for a visit to my folks in Pretoria, routing via Fort Victoria where Rina was working for the Cold Storage Commission abattoir.

On the Monday night, 20th December 1964, Henry Elliot had gone and got himself killed in a Vampire FB 9 aircraft accident near Moffat aerodrome, whilst on his way back from a night flying sortie to Bulawayo. I'm sure I covered the details earlier.

I was a pallbearer at his impressive military funeral. Even now, many years later, the playing of the "Last Post" by bugle has a special significance for me.

January 1965 started off with our normal Kutanga Range Detachment, from 18th to 25th January. My academic days were over and I went straight into 'categorisation' sorties with FRAs - first run attacks. I expended 700 x ·303 rounds air to ground front gun, and 31 x 20lb high dive and low-level bombing attacks. My scores kept on improving, as recorded earlier under the Kutanga side heading. The beauty of these latter air power strikes was that they were flown mostly solo. My only 'dual' sortie for the entire month was with Mike Reynolds.

On 2nd February I flew to Kutanga again for 4 x 20lb fragmentation bomb trials. A further four fragmentation trials were carried out on the 9th, with me flying armourer Corporal Steve Stead to the Range for arming the lethal bombs. This goes to show how far sighted the airmen were in our own research and development plans. Up until now, we were using a British 'steel coil spring' bomb that on detonation, fragmented into thousands of lethal steel slivers, blown in all directions. The powers to be at the Glass Palace (Air Headquarters) had foreseen the necessity for the force to become self sufficient in the design, manufacture and supply of air weaponry. As mentioned previously, Wing Commander Sandy Mutch played a major role. Bear in mind that UDI was declared 11 November, and the arms embargo that followed.

It is perhaps pertinent to mention that these trial bombs, designated the Mk 1, were designed to detonate just above the ground. The fuse had a reversible diaphragm, to which was attached the firing pin that would strike a percussion cap. The diaphragm would reverse due to the air pressure build up as the bomb neared the ground, thus initiating the firing mechanism. A metal cap protected the diaphragm with vanes that would spin or screw itself off once an arming wire, fixed to the bomb rack, extracted when the pilot pressed the release button. Whilst refinements were carried out, a malfunction would many years later cause the loss of a Canberra, together with the instant death of the crew (one of my 1974 students, in fact).

Steve Stead's path was destined to cross mine several times in the future, including being blown up in a fragmentation tank bomb – "frantan" for short (a form of napalm bomb) which destroyed my Provost aircraft. Wait, Prop - I seem to be jumping the gun again, figuratively.

On 1st March 1965 Flight Lieutenant Varky Varkevisser instructed me on my PAI - Pilot Attack Instructors Course.

PILOT ATTACK INSTRUCTOR - PAI

A sense of great satisfaction and achievement was to qualify as a PAI in the Air Force - as a DF/GA/IS Pilot Attack Instructor. There were one or two hiccups - flying with a broken wrist, and/or reconsidering my future as a rugby player. The PAI course commenced on 1st March 1965, and I qualified on 31st May. During the three months, several events happened, which I wish to mention as they unfold.

The first two weeks was devoted to flying Battle Formation, with my 'students', for practice purposes, being Varky himself, Barry Matthews, Hugh Slatter, Aircraftsman Dave "Unc" for Uncle Stone and Butch Graydon. Squadron Leader KAS Edwards gave me a PAI Course test flight on the 10th (the day before, I flew safety pilot for Bruce Collocott).

On the 14th, my training was interrupted for a day to participate in a Police Reserve Air Wing operation held at Kutanga Range. I flew one sortie with Corporal McKenzie - of John Mac Kutanga fame - and another sortie with Police Air Wing pilot King. By a strange twist of fate, John McKenzie and his good lady June invited Rina and I to Swaziland 34 years later - 13th November 1999, to a UDI function with my PAI Instructor Varky and his good lady Amy

On the 15th I flew as a number three in a formation "tail chase". This was a tricky exercise of follow my leader. The leader performs various aerobatics manoeuvres, while the other aircraft follow in the leader's wake. During looping manoeuvres, there is much concertina ring as the tail catches up when the leader climbs vertically, but then the leader accelerates away as he goes over the top of the loop. As the number three, the pilot anticipates the flying characteristics by power application and flying skill to minimise distance variation, including cutting the corners or flying a wider circle. However, every time one flies through the slipstream of the lead aircraft, the flight effect is to throw one off-course. Most pilots enjoyed tail chases because it tended to hone one's flying skill. However, tragic consequences were about to unfold.

OPERATION BROKEN ARROW 18-24TH MARCH 1965

Then on 18th March 1965, I was dispatched to Tjolotjo on Operation *Broken Arrow*, where Mike Reynolds and Barry Matthews had deployed in support of Army and Police forces. But I need to tell a tale where I took a chance in order to avoid facing embarrassment for a lack of professionalism. It was near lunchtime when I was tasked to be on standby for take-off at short notice. I had hurriedly filed my flight plan, dashed off to the Mess for a bite to eat, and then rushed back to the squadron crew room for a cup of coffee, when the call came to scramble. I duly headed in the general direction when I discovered that I had left my route map behind - in the squadron crew room. No ways was I going back for it, but then I was also taking a great risk of getting lost because I did not have a map with me.

Tjolotjo lies in the middle of Nyamandlovu north of Bulawayo, in the middle; I mean middle of nowhere. I was fortunate to draw on my previous experience of the countryside to feel my way to this 'dot' in Africa. Someone up there was looking after me and I managed to arrive safely at my destination. Barry kindly lent me a spare map for my return journey - which I might add took five minutes longer flying back to Thornhill, than the trip to Tjolotjo without a map.

On the 23rd and 24th, I flew in a formation of three, then four Provosts. On landing, we received the tragic news that Pilot Officer Barry Matthews and Chief Technician Sandy Trenoweth had been killed. A Dakota had arrived to take the Board of Inquiry down to Tjolotjo, and at the same time uplift me, as I was charged with returning Mike Reynolds's Provost to Thornhill. On landing there, I saw at first hand the wreckage, which had claimed the lives of the two people I knew very well. Mike had been "grounded" for leading the tail chase at the conclusion of Operation *Broken Arrow*. They were doing a barrel roll when Barry caught up with, and hit Mike's slipstream, going over the top of the loop cum roll. The effect was a 'flick' in the opposite direction of the roll. Instead of just recovering from this unusual attitude, it appears that Barry had mistakenly elected to 'follow his leader'. He soon found himself at the point of no return - heading at high speed towards the ground. There was then nothing he could do - he was heading for a crash. When the Provost hit the ground, the bakelight seat pans (that house the parachute, and to which the harness is attached) fractured,

R.R.A.F. THORNHILL — RUGBY TOUR — 1965

(Standing): J. Pinner, P. Geldenhuys, D. Smith, P. van Zyl, N. Walsh, B. Wheaton, I. Bate, S. Kesby.
(Sitting): R. Stewart, C. Tubbs (Club Captain), D. Deysel (Vice-captain), K. Edwards (Manager), G. Wright (Captain), C. Whi
R. Graydon, S. Maitland, M. McLean, P. Juncks, W. du Plessis, J. McKenzie, G. Butters, D. Strydom.

causing the harness to slide up as the crew bodies were thrown forward in the absence of the now ineffectual harness. In Sandy's case, the back of his neck struck the gunsight with such force that it dislodged it completely from its mounting. By this time the harness buckle continued its upward travel as the momentum of the forward moving bodies continued - completely shearing the faces off their victims. It was a gruesome sight - but which hardened pilots came to accept that when an aircraft bites back, it does so with a vengeance. Anyway, let's get back to things more pleasant, like my PAI Course.

The actual course was not too tough. I believe my weapons results secured my selection for the course. But I also needed to earn my selection by acquiring the appropriate flying skill and abilities necessary to teach other pilots how to handle an aircraft as a marksman would a handgun

Varky and Bruce Smith instructed us in the techniques of Ranging and Tracking, as well as Level and High Quarter attacks - during the next three weeks in April 1965. But an incident mid-April nearly put paid to my career as a Pilot Attack Instructor - a Scaiphoid fracture. I fancied myself as a prospective rugby star, but in reality was just happy enough to be selected for the Air Force Touring Rugby Team - to South Africa.

Having captained the Thornhill High School First XV, I continued playing club rugby in the Air Force. We even played in the Midlands Provincial League and were fortunate to travel 'first class' by way of Air Force Canadair C4 aircraft between match fixtures. Anyway, I was selected for the Thornhill (Air Force Base, that is), to play rugby in Natal. This meant an interruption in my PAI Course - which I didn't mind at that time. John Pinner, the Air Force Accounts Officer, used his station wagon for the necessary road transport. As the official team 'Imprest holder' to settle all the accounts it suited me just fine to bum a ride with him. John McKenzie and I sat in the back. Our first night-stop was at the Ranch Motel, between Pietersburg and Potgietersrus, then on to the best fish and chips lunch at Marble Hall, next night-stop Andrews Motel at Volksrust, arriving at the Butterworth Hotel in Durban as our base. We played rugby against Port Shepstone Sports Club, and then proceeded to Margate where we played the South Coast teams. On our way back we played rugby against the Durban Country Club team as well as against Glenwood Old Boys. Varky and I played centres, Randy du Rand 8th man, and Mac McKenzie in the scrum.

A couple of amusing episodes occurred on this tour, which would be amiss if I didn't mention them. A trip to a brothel type night-club called Upstairs and Downstairs in the Point Road of Durban resulted in a couple of highlights. Dux Deysel parted with his hard earned cash (by a shrewd pick-pocket, thus preventing him catching Aids from some well endowed hostesses), frisking the ladies, drunken brawls, a couple of well intentioned 'officers and gentlemen' needing baling out of jail, and the team coach being highly upset that his team were expending their energies between their legs and not saving it for the rugby field, to name but a few. At Margate's Kings hotel, a drunken guest disappeared down the lift shaft. Fortunately, he did not have far to fall – he had hurried over to the lift in hot pursuit of a lady friend who had already departed in the lift for a higher floor. He duly wrenched the lift door open, took a step into space, and promptly fell down the hole because the lift had departed moments before. A bunch of helpful guys assisted in extricating the poor fellow from the lift pit.

In my case, I sustained an injury to my left wrist in the match against Old Boys (the only opponents I recall that we lost against). I had it bandaged but it was only on my return to base that x-rays revealed a fracture of the Scaiphoid - those small bones between the arm and wrist. The plaster cast set the wrist in a near right angle - so much so that the awkward angle made flying from the instructors' side extremely difficult. In those days, before UDI, the Provost Leonides engine was still started by firing a cartridge. The starter mechanism consisted of lever between the two seats, at cockpit floor level, which required to be lifted to fire the cartridge. At the end of the starter lever was a button to prime the combustion chambers with fuel to facilitate engine ignition. When flying the Provost from the pilots (or students seat in the case of dual instruction), the left hand operated the canopy, throttle and pitch levers. However, when flying from the right hand instructor's seat, the left hand had to be used for aircraft starting as well as flap and engine air intake operations.

Anyway, the nature of my rugby injury was of such a magnitude that my continuance on the PAI Course was in jeopardy. And so, after much debate, it was decided to put me to the test and I was accordingly drilled by Varky Varkevisser on my quarter attack sortie flown on 24th April 1965, from the gruelling right hand seat, I might add. Three days later I was cleared to fly. My next eight sorties were conditional with my having to fly with another instructor, or pupil, on board. The exercises included air-to-air quarter attack manoeuvres, night flying to Bulawayo with landings, and air-to-ground gunnery firing 4 x 100 x ·303 front gun. Phew, what a relief. I scraped through this trial period by the skin of my teeth.

On 29th April I flew with Spaz Currie in a Vampire 60 x 20mm cannon sortie. That same day I was entrusted with carrying out a solo air test, after a propeller change, all by myself. Not only was it necessary to study air-to-air tactics as well as air-to-ground attack, but there were a host of other subjects that a PAI needed to master. My own particular speciality was "fixed gun sighting" and I became somewhat expert in the three techniques - lengths ahead, fly through method and the aim-off required for quarter attacks. Gyro gun-sighting made air-to-air a lot easier for jet pilots, but once the rudiments of fixed gun sighting was grasped, a lot of things just fell into place.

Whilst I also enjoyed flying battle formations and bombing, with its whole range of loads and variable methods and also rocketing, fixed gun always gave me the greatest pleasure. I soon learnt that all those schoolboy comics about "Dogfight Dixon" were a load of hogwash. I also learnt a lot from OuDad, and his operational wisdom from the North Africa campaigns. Presumably, Sailor Malan, the World War II fighter ace, was a distant relative of the Malans that I married into. His rules of air combat warrant repeating, since even the Korean War and the subsequent American air combat jet jocks as late as 1987 made reference to Sailor Malan's SOPs.

These Standard Operating Procedures or Rules were: -
1. Height gives you the initiative.
2. Always turn and face the attack.
3. Wait until you see the whites of the eyes. Fire short bursts of one to two seconds, and only when your sights are definitely 'on'.
4. Whilst shooting, think of nothing else. Brace the whole of the body, have both hands on the stick, concentrate on your ring sight.
5. Always keep a sharp lookout. "Keep your finger out".
6. Make your decisions promptly. It is better to act quickly even though your tactics are not of the best.
7. Never fly straight and level for more than thirty seconds in the combat area.
8. When diving to attack, always leave a proportion of your formation above to act as top guard.
9. Initiative, aggression, air discipline, and teamwork are words that <u>mean</u> something in air fighting.
10. Go in quickly - Punch hard - Get out.

I promoted height or speed - especially in jet aircraft where speed could easily be converted to height during air-to-air manoeuvres. For air-to-ground gunnery attacks, I was apt to give only several short bursts, only when my pipper was on target. Target fixation was a very real problem - and I have no doubt that several casualties during the war were due to ground attack pilots flying straight into the ground.

No disrespect is intended for lady readers, but 'keep your finger out' meant that no distractions, albeit sexual, was tolerable. Air Force jargon of "extractum digit" basically said get a move on.

Much fun was had "mixing it" with our SAAF colleagues - with our Vampire and Hunter aerial combats against their Sabre and Mirage intercepts. I hope to recount experiences and lessons learnt.

I would also commend the reader to refer to my first printed and bound story on Geldenhuys Genealogy, dated Christmas 1999, with specific reference regarding the fighter ace exploits of 'Chris' Johannes Le Roux and Adolf Malan.

Anyway, getting back to 29th April. I also flew two FAC attack sorties with Army Captain Peter Burford and Lieutenant Meyer. I think they were not too impressed flying with a pilot who had his left hand all encased in plaster of Paris. The day ended with a total of five sorties - ·303 gunnery, a Vampire 20mm cannon firing sortie, prop change air test and two Army Forward Air Controllers familiarisation sorties. The cherry on the top was the interception and slaying of seven terrorists in the 'Battle of Sinoia ', or the first day of the so-called liberation Chimurenga Day, which will be covered later on.

The month ended with a further two sorties flown on Army FAC attacks - the second sortie being with Corporal Danny Strydom. These sorties were fairly lengthy, averaging an hour and three-quarters. My Scaiphoid fracture seemed to be standing up to the pressure.

On 1st May 1965 I and all our No 16 PTC Course members were promoted to Flying Officers - equivalent to full Lieutenant army rank - plus the welcomed salary increment that came with this advancement. But there was no let-up on our PAI Course, and Flight Lieutenant Varky began instructing me on the first of eleven bombing sorties. Co-instruction sorties were carried out with Bruce Smith, Hugh Slatter, and Derrick Nightingale. We were using a combination of 20 and 25 pound bombs, on High Dive and Low Level bombing. The bombing phase was completed with a practical instructional test with the Boss, Squadron Leader KAS Edwards on the 17th. In the intervening period a variety of other sorties were also flown, such as instrument flying safety pilot for my AFS instructor Flight Lieutenant Rob Tasker, battle formation, low flying, and night flying controlled radar letdowns (Conrad) at Thornhill and Bulawayo. Then from 18th to 20th May, we completed the Tear Smoke phase - pin point and screen-lay - over nine sorties and dropping a total of 107 tear smoke canisters. Then on 21st May the Squadron Commander tested me on 100 x ·303 front gun.

Squadron Leader KAS Edwards awarded me my PAI category on 31st May 1965, and I was duly appointed as a Pilot Attack Instructor pilot in Day Fighter / Ground Attack, despite qualifying with a plaster cast still around my left wrist.

COMMISSIONER'S TROPHY

I was selected to crew up with my PAI instructor Flight Lieutenant Varky Varkevisser to compete against the top Police Reserve Air Wing pilots for the Police Commissioners Trophy. All aircraft and crews assembled at Gatooma airfield for the four-day exercises that started on 8th June. My counterpart, Nobby Nightingale, was crewed with the second Provost.

We flew on average just over two sorties per day. Competitions included navigational cross-countries, search and rescue, reconnaissance, message bag dropping, field exercises, forced landings, ribbon/tape cutting, spot landings and scrambling. In addition, there was also a night escape and evasion exercise. All of the individual exercises had their highlights - some of which were truly hilarious - perhaps not so much for the unfortunate victims. PRAW pilot Bill Springer, from Chipinga, literally carried out a real forced landing when he was scrambled at short notice - and got airborne before he realised that he had insufficient fuel for the task at hand - and ended up in a mealie field. There is no first prize for guessing who was awarded the "wooden spoon" at the awards ceremony. (Bill Springer was killed in an air accident on 19th July 1969).

Varky Varkevisser

Varky and I had practised our teamwork immediately prior to our deployment to Gatooma. It needs to be remembered that I still had my left wrist in plaster as a result of the rugby Scaiphoid fracture. The handicap restricted the full use of pilot's tools - his hands. My pilots' logbook shows that we had got our timed landing down to an accuracy of a mere two seconds. We knew that our technique would take some beating - I would lift the flaps moments before the required time, while Varky expertly maintained the controlled crash cum arrival cum contact with the runway. Our message dropping was also perfected - no doubt expected with both him and I being PAIs as well as having been categorised "Master" low-level bombing pilots.

Our spot landing competition result warrants mentioning. The landing spot was a whitewashed cross on the runway. Just short of the cross was a suspended tape strung some ten feet or three metres high, attached to a pole on both ends and held up by two somewhat very brave souls. This obstacle was designed to make the spot landing that much more difficult - for those pilots who were apt to 'drag' their aircraft on a very shallow glide path and 'chop' their engines to control their resultant crash to mother earth. Some pilots opted for hairy side slipping approaches, with a steep approach angle. In our event, things did not quite work out as planned. But the result was outstanding. We crossed the threshold fast and low. On approaching the obstacle, I dropped the flaps to fully down, with the additional lift being just sufficient to clear the tape. We both simultaneously realised that we would overshoot the mark if drastic action were not immediately taken. True to 'Sailor' Malan's rule number six, I raised our flap while Varky cut the engine and stuffed the nose down (please note - a trim change takes place with flap selection - lifting flaps requires easing the stick back, and vice-versa).

Our combined action was the exact opposite. Needless to say, we duly "arrived" nearest the spot, albeit in a very ungainly fashion, and much to the astonishment of all the onlookers.

NOTICE. Police Reserve Air Wing. Commissioner's Trophy, 1965.

ie results of the Commissioner's Trophy, 1965, are notified for general information:—
1. F/Lt. Varkevisser, R.R.A.F., and F/O Geldenhuys, R.R.A.F.
2. No. 1424OC, P/R/Pilot Brittlebank, and No. 14559Z, P/R/Observer Barnett.

For our efforts, Varky and I were awarded the Commissioner's Trophy - to much shouting of 'fouls and boos', or utter surprise that a plastered pilot could be in the top awards. Several PRAW pilots felt they were done in by the professionals, or had no hope in hell of competing against those 'air force types'. I wasn't complaining. The miniature trophy enjoys pride of place amongst my displays to this day. This was not something one can buy, or get by mere participation - it was earned, and was a just reward for professional teamwork.

The very next day, June 12th, I flew with our squadron commander, Squadron Leader KAS Edwards to Umtali our affiliated town for the Queen's Birthday flypast. After the flypast, we landed at Perrem airstrip in the town and attended the mayoral functions. The Volunteer Reserve members entertained us to a peri-peri chicken lunch across the border in Mozambique, after which the formation of Provost aircraft flew back to Gwelo.

14th June 1965 was also a noteworthy day in that at long last my plaster cast came off. I had flown nearly 64 hours with the cast on, which had threatened my career as a PAI student. But I had managed to fly Army Forward Air Control sorties, had been permitted the opportunity to compete for the Commissioner's Trophy, and also to participate in the Queen's Birthday formation flypast.

Later in the month I flew Lieutenant Ian Pullar, plus two other officers, on Army FAC familiarisation sorties. The army co-operation included FAC simulated strikes to allow the Brownjobs to practise their newly acquired COIN operational skills

On 29th June, whilst flying with Varky on a night cum instrument flying sortie which included radar controlled ground approaches, we experienced a minor emergency with generator failure. We curtailed our sortie in order to land before we lost our electrics. The next day I flew a short air test to check on engine performance.

EXERCISE PANTHER: 24-26 JULY 1965

July started off with a recce in the Kariba area with Brownjob Captain Morris. This was followed by two weeks of range work at Kutanga and included one sortie of 4 x 20lb high dive-bombing with my PAI instructor Varky Varkevisser. In the third week, I flew Senior Technician Gibson on a lengthy four-hour sortie on a low level squadron exercise with message drop to Chiredzi in the Lowveld.

Having traversed Rhodesia, the time arrived for Exercise Panther.

Early on Saturday morning the 24th, I positioned at Salisbury to uplift Volunteer Reservist Flying Officer Derrick Purnell for Mount Darwin, followed by an afternoon recce after lunch, and then a patrol in the Spill area the following day. Derrick was my observer during the whole exercise. Later on the 25th we returned to New Sarum, followed by a recce exercise in the Truss area before landing back at Mount Darwin for our second bush night-stop.

The article in the Rhodesian Herald was headlined thus "'Exercise *Panther*' full scale operation for Reserves', and I quote: - "A Royal Rhodesian Air Force two-day exercise this weekend -'Exercise Panther' - will be the first full-scale operation for the force's Volunteer Reserve since reorganisation after the break-up of Federation, an RRAF spokesman said yesterday. About 200 VRs and some Territorial Forces in planes and self-contained road convoys will deploy to six advance and three main air bases throughout the country early tomorrow morning. Their task will be to occupy these fields, establish and man communication equipment, distribute fuel and generally make the bases operational.

About 150 Air Force regulars will also take part, and members of RRAF Command, headed by the Chief of Air Staff, Air Vice-Marshal H Hawkins, will fly to the various bases on inspection. Hawker Hunter and Canberra jets, Provosts, Dakota transports and helicopters will take part in the exercise. The advance airfields to be used are part of a net of airfields owned by individuals, the Department of Civil Aviation and private companies in Rhodesia which can be used by the military if the need arises, the spokesman said.

The VRs, many of them Second World War veterans, "are held in the highest regard by the air force regulars," the spokesman said.

"They are citizens twice over. They hold full-time jobs and on weekends serve the air force with no pay. They perform an invaluable service."

"Exercise Panther" is "designed to try out and prove all elements of the Volunteer Reserve in the various duties with which it has been individually charged," the spokesman said. The exercise will form part of the initial training for some of the VRs and as a refresher course for others. In the past minor exercises have been held for specific units, but this exercise combines all the forces of the RRAF VRs and elements of the regulars, the spokesman said.

Representatives of the Press, radio and television will accompany officers in a Dakota."

Late Sunday, I flew Derrick Purnell from Mount Darwin back to Salisbury. I night-stopped at New Sarum and returned to Gwelo on the 26th. What was left of July was taken up with preparations for our next Kutanga Range Detachment that entailed ten days of fairly extensive flying. And the opportunities to put into practice my recently acquired PAI skills.

PAI INSTRUCTION

My first formal "students" were Flying Officers Hugh Slatter and Harold Griffiths on High Dive Bombing, on the 2nd August 1965 - on my father's 49th birthday. As I write this, my father was younger than I am now - nearly 59. The next day I instructed Flight Lieutenant Rob Tasker on high dive and low level bombing. It will be recalled that Rob taught me to fly Vampires - and it felt good to demonstrate my weapons skill to my former instructor. I also had the opportunity to instruct Flight Lieutenant Pat Meddows-Taylor on bombing and frantan. The frantan always impressed one, because when the 'fragmentation' tank burst on impact, it spewed diesel fuel all over the target area and burnt everything the gel made contact with. However, Acting Pilot Officer Chris Weinmann would be my first full time OCU Student, but, as would occur time after time, the students would have to contend with the frequent interruptions in their training schedules as dictated by Force needs.

The current Kutanga Detachment ended on the 10th August. I had flown no less than thirty-one sorties all told - and then only in the space of ten days. That same day, at Thornhill, I took Corporal Tom Crawford up in Provost No 308 for an air test post Minor scheduled aircraft service. This particular Provost was destined to tax my flying skills as well as serve me well in various operations and exercises in the future.

The next four days was practising formation flying, with a Flypast Rehearsal logged on the 13th. I flew Derrick 'Nobby' Nightingale up to Salisbury for timing runs over the Show Grounds. Then on the following day, the 14th, the Squadron made its contribution with the real McCoy, with the Salisbury Show Flypast taking 2½ hours, which included take-off and landing at Thornhill.

Then on the 18th August I flew my first OCU instructional sortie with Acting Pilot Officer Chris Weinmann. A repeat formation instructional sortie was also flown with Chris the next day as well - logging three hours for the two days. The 20th was quite hectic in that I flew

Graham Cronshaw to Kutanga Range, followed by OCU formation, then back to Kutanga to uplift Graham for Thornhill. Chris's OCU was then interrupted because we then had to prepare for another detachment for Internal Security Operations in the Karoi area.

Exercise Longdrag was destined to make a lasting impression on me. It is always easy, in retrospect, to realise the wisdom and foresight of the powers that were.

EXERCISE LONGDRAG. 23rd AUGUST - 1st SEPTEMBER 1965

On 23rd August I flew to Karoi with Chris Weinmann in Provost 308, on an Army exercise. The next day we carried out a local reconnaissance mission. On the 25th, we flew a lengthy three-hour sortie of the Kariba area, but concentrated our reconnaissance along the Sanyati Gorge and Umniati River that runs into the Lake. Our first sortie of the 26th is recorded as the "Battle of the Angwa River". It is rather ironical that I would, a couple of years hence, actually fire live weapons in a Vampire airstrike during Operation *Cauldron* (in 1968, with Bill Jelley). Then later that day, I carried out an "umpire flight" to evaluate troop deployments by Army Major Conn. The next three day's flying missions were rather uneventful - Chris and I flew another reconnaissance sortie to the Kariba area, followed a day later by a recce along the Kariba power line. This sortie was 3½ hours duration, with a detour to Anker plaas, where Hansie and Gerta Bezuidenhout farmed tobacco. I was engaged to Rina, and could not resist 'beating-up' my future sister- and brother-in-law. Then on the 29th, we carried out a recce of the Tengwe River area, where the fledgling town was still in its infancy. Once again, a surprise visit to Anker was carried out.

Then the most eventful flight of Exercise *Longdrag* occurred. I was tasked to fly Major Conn down the Umniati River to Lake Kariba. We duly took off in Provost 308 and set course for the gorge. No sooner had we got airborne than one of the nine cylinder heads of the Leonides engine 'blew its top', spewing engine oil all over the windscreen. The good news was that it was one of the 'top' cylinders, and not a bottom one. The bad news was that the oil spattered windscreen obscured forward vision, there was insufficient power available for prolonged level flight, but worst of all having to contend with a panic stricken Army Major on my hands. Had one of the bottom cylinders failed, all the engine oil would have drained in a matter of seconds, seized the engine, and resulting in the Provost dropping out the sky like a ton of bricks. It was just as well that we had the engine partial failure shortly after take-off. Had it occurred down in the Umniati Gorge we would have been in a much more serious predicament. We would then have gone down in the bush somewhere.

Well, there I was, with a panic stricken Brownjob, who took some quieting down. I kept him busy with tightening his parachute straps, going over the bale-out procedure, and generally trying to keep him out of my face. But, fortunately, within ten minutes we were able to carry out a partial engine failure forced landing back on Karoi airstrip. The oil-splattered windscreen was a bit of a problem, and the landing was probably not one of my best. We were just thankful being on terra firma, without bending the aircraft further. Although I can't confirm those final minutes, it would not surprise me if the Major were preparing himself for the last rights.

Anyway, the show must go on. The Major and I boarded another Provost and we were able to log a 'duty carried out' reconnaissance sortie of two hours ten minutes down the Umniati River to Kariba Dam. Major Conn was rather subdued albeit somewhat fidgety while flying low level down the steep-sided gorge. Our technicians back at Karoi had meanwhile wasted no time in relaying their requirements to Thornhill.

Operation Longdrag - With Chris Weinmann And Bill Buckle

Upon landing, I joined the ground crews to dismantle the Leonides engine. A replacement arrived during the night, together with the necessary tripods, additional engine experts and specialised tools to effect a complete engine change in the field. All credit goes to our magnificent men in doing the engine change in record time. That is, one day, including the ground runs. And so, early on 1st September, Varky Varkevisser and I carried out a thirty-minute engine change airtest, and declared Provost 308 fully serviceable. Chris Weinmann had meanwhile packed our bags and helped the ground crews strike camp. After a good pre-flight check, Chris flew the one hour thirty minutes sortie with me from Karoi to Thornhill.

After a short break of six days, I resumed normal squadron flying duties. On 9th September, Chris again flew with me on a rather interesting mission. We loaded a Provost up with 200 rounds of 303 and four fragmentation bombs, for a "Rhodesian Chiefs Weapons Demonstration". This was a 'win the hearts and minds' exercise to get the chiefs on sides. They had been assembled at Kutanga Range where John McKenzie had laid on special arrangements designed to impress them. I might also add that when 'frag' bombs explode they certainly go off with a bang, plus plenty of black smoke and make a complete mess of all the old motorcars that John used as targets. It was a wise move by the Government to lay on these sorts of exercises in order to impress upon the future rulers of the country the value of air power. It also needs to be realised that Ian Smith's UDI was a mere six weeks away.

Provost Aircraft, Minus Its Leonides Nine-Cylinder Engine

Another view – side on. Look at all those 'connections'

October 1965 was a hectic OCU instruction month. I was able to resume my main pupil's (Chris Weinmann) OCU course, but also instructed various other pilots in attack techniques. These included Acting Pilot Officer John Bennie on instrument flying and Ranging, Acting Pilot Officer Bill Buckle on gun sight, Ranging, ¼ attacks and Range work; Acting Pilot Officer Blake Few on general; and Pilot Officer Mark McLean on Tear smoke. The OCU Kutanga Detachment lasted five days from 26th to 30th October 1965 - that is, mainly weapons delivery for Chris Weinmann. We ended the detachment with a 4 Squadron Flypast over Thornhill, followed by one of those famous 'breaks' that Varky had devised. We would fly echelon starboard at three thousand feet, each aircraft then half-rolls, pulls out of the dive at a thousand feet on the downwind leg, and glides around finals for a roller-landing.

The 1st November 1965 was a career highlight for me. Squadron Leader KAS Edwards saw fit to appoint me "Deputy Flight Commander". This was a similar command appointment that my father enjoyed way back in 1943 when he was appointed Battle Flight commander of No 45 Air School in Oudtshoorn - in the year when I was born.

OPERATIONS

ISOPS

Internal Security Operations, or ISOPS, were dictated by the civilian authorities, the BSAP (British South African Police), who were charged with intelligence gathering through their SB (Special Branch) and INTAF (Internal Affairs). The primary role of the Air Force is the security of its air space, and in this theatre of war Rhodesia was never seriously challenged, for they enjoyed total supremacy of the air. However, it was in its secondary role of 'to assist the civil power in the maintenance of internal security' that the Air Force contributed its fair share in all ISOPS.

Whereas the Rhodesian Army and Air Force had learned from their overseas experiences, the Police, who had never been out of the country, didn't have this fund of experience to draw upon. They refused to accept the lessons learned in Malaya, and furthermore they were not attuned to trying new methods. In addition, the country's top level Security Council supported the view that the Police knew best. INTAF on the other hand were a law unto themselves.

In 1963, I had completed my OCU on Provost T Mk 52 aircraft of No 4 Squadron, and was a fully-fledged IS pilot. However, many of the earlier joint operations involving the Air Force, Army and Police soon proved that ISOPS were outmoded. And the need arose to evolve COIN OPS (Counter Insurgency Operations) to fight the terrorist menace - with the Air Force and Army playing just as important a role as the Police.

COIN OPS

Counter Insurgency lessons learnt in Malaya, and applied in the Portuguese Provinces, were introduced into Rhodesia - like the PV (Protected Village) concept where the vulnerable, unarmed local population were moved and resettled into fenced and guarded villages in order to deprive the enemy of its target and means of support, while providing better community facilities and a more sophisticated infrastructure. Much resistance was encountered from the civil authorities; and the Army and Air Force commanders often found it necessary to force their proposals through.

While I was at Mtoko, I was party to the CV concept (Consolidated Villages) which was a compromised PV - without the strict security fencing and designated plots allocation, as was the case with PVs. Furthermore, a closer co-operation between the various Security Forces evolved, and a more harmonious relationship developed between them. Up until then, each military unit had jealously guarded its own integrity with no give or take, often resulting in abortive operations with a consequent excessive wastage of valuable manpower, materials and scanty resources which Rhodesia could ill afford. In retrospect, I admit that I had my fair share of disagreements with various Army and Police commanders, and personal dislike of individuals clouded my better judgement which was sorely needed to promote the war effort.

COIN OP techniques were perfected in Rhodesia, often to South Africa's benefit, since innovative methods were presented with ideal testing conditions. Understanding basic guerrilla strategy was crucial to the development of counter-insurgency tactics. In guerrilla warfare the insurgent selects the tactic of seeming to come from the east and attacking from the west; avoid the solid, attack the hollow; attack, withdraw; deliver a lightning blow, seek a lightning decision. When terrorists engage a stronger enemy, they withdraw when he advances; harass him when he stops; strike him when he is weary; pursue him when he withdraws. In guerrilla strategy the enemy's rear, flanks, and other vulnerable spots are his vital points, and there he must be harassed, attacked, dispersed, exhausted, and annihilated. The tactic most commonly employed was referred to as "shoot and scoot" – and was employed by both sides – I might add.

COIN OP developments included leap frogging trackers; ground coverage; frozen areas; pseudo operations; fire forces; establishment of FAFs (Forward Air Fields); FASOCs (Forward Air Support Operational Centres); TAC HQs (Tactical Air Headquarters); JOCs (Joint Operation Centres); Search and Rescue Techniques; Cordon Sanitaire; Psychological Operations specifically to win over the hearts and minds of the local populace; HALO (High Altitude, Low Opening) path finding freefalling; propaganda campaigns and paratroops; PVs/CVs (Protected and Consolidated Villages); Vertical Deployments and many others, too numerous to mention. Each aspect warrants its own chapter, but let it not be forgotten that invariably the Air Force had a hand in it as well - in some cases more so than the other military/civil branches.

OPERATION REPTILE – 1966

Pseudo-terrorist groups were first formed in 1966. Prior to Federal break-up days, in the early 1960s, Rhodesian-born hunter and ecologist, Allan Savory, ultimately to become a controversial figure in Rhodesian politics, tried unsuccessfully to convince the military to develop their expertise in tracking. He foresaw the value of a tracker-combat team, a pseudo gang consisting of both soldiers and Special Branch. His endeavours failed because many of the African Special Branch members said that if they wanted to become soldiers, they would have joined the Rhodesian African Rifles. Most of the Special Branch whites held a similar viewpoint and this resulted in the Special Air Service going it alone.

The School of Infantry established its Tracking Wing at Kariba, and employed Air Force Flying Officer Basil Moss, during Operation *Reptile*, to develop exercises at operating pseudo gangs. The value of good trackers came to the fore during Operations *Nickel* (1967) and Cauldron (1968). Skills were honed and as more and more "turned" terrorists, or guerrillas, grew in number, the pseudo operator concept was resurrected and several years later, from these groups, evolved the Selous Scouts.

CONVENTIONAL OPERATIONS

Classical War, Limited War or Conventional operations - call it what you will - never really developed in the Rhodesia/Zimbabwe situation. Although as airmen we were trained to regard our primary role as the security of airspace in the defence of the country, in conventional war methods the principles of war are the same: they apply equally in ISOPS and COIN OPS situations.

The Principles of War - (SMOCEFSCCA) - Surprise, Mobility, Organisation, Co-operation, Equipment, Flexibility, Security and Intelligence, Co-ordination and Administration.

Air power is an integral, albeit modern, part of conventional operations. It is likened to the use of artillery for ground forces. A warring nation can apply guerrilla warfare or coin-ops without air power, but not so in the case of classical warfare. Although air power centres on the defence and protection of air space, air power entails several specialities. These include air-to-air aerial combat as in 'day fighter/ground attack', night interdiction, strategic and tactical bombing, aerial resupply, photo-reconnaissance, vertical support operations, para-trooping and a host of other ground support functions. Air power can also be applied independently of the other arms of military forces, but its most efficient application lies in co-ordinated inter-action with the other military arms. A pilot trained in conventional operations can easily adapt to coin-ops, but not so easily in a vice-versa situation. The Royal Rhodesian Air Force pilot is schooled in all facets of air power, and as such, is rated exceptionally highly by the other world air forces.

OPERATION BREAMPOOL: 1 to 2 NOVEMBER 1965

Operation *Breampool* was an Army affair at Chirundu. I took off early from Thornhill on the 1st, dropping Chris Weinmann off at New Sarum. I proceeded solo to Kariba for fuel and then flew the short hop down the Zambezi River, from the Dam wall to Chirundu for a night-stop at the Army camp. Five missions were flown the next day. The first was with Brownjob Captain McConnell for a reconnaissance along the road from Chirundu to Makuti and return. We flew to, and landed at Kariba.

Late that afternoon, I returned to Thornhill for a couple of days R&R - Rest and Recuperation. Just as well. The Army were familiarising themselves with the harsh Zambezi Valley conditions, reassuring the local Sugar Cane growers, and for me it was a fortuitous pre-UDI introduction to the Kariba and the Army's No 2 Independent Company headquarters on Kariba Heights. A couple of Instrument sorties followed before I was whisked away to Kariba for the start of Operation *Wizard* and the historical UDI - Unilateral Declaration of Independence, when Ian Smith defied the World.

UDI - 11th NOVEMBER 1965 - OPERATION WIZARD

I was deployed to Kariba the day before UDI. The Provost aircraft was armed with 1300 rounds of .303. While the army units were preparing their defences, Peter Piggot invited me to help check out runway security and surrounds. We boarded his Alouette helicopter number 501 for a fifteen minute "chasing game" ride. It was the finest and most enjoyable chopper ride I have ever had - he would run the nose wheel along the runway centre line and only lift off at the last moment to avoid colliding with the obstructing LRs. At the end of the runway he pulled the chopper into a steep stall turn, and I found myself floating on the cockpit ceiling because I had not bothered to fasten my seat belt - he was damn lucky I did not grab the collective in my scramble to get hold of the seat belt (I was sitting next to him to observe the flight instruments and flying technique).

At the other end of the runway, where the dry Nyanyana riverbed runs at right angles towards the lake (this also happens to be the natural elephant trail to the water's edge), Peter Piggot promptly proceeded to tantalise a particularly mean-looking jumbo. While lowering his nose wheel on to the elephant's head with the rotor blades only inches from the steep sides of the riverbank, Peter was trying to agitate and annoy the elephant - a task in which he succeeded. As the elephant raised its trunk in an attempt to grab the undercarriage and throw the chopper to the ground, Peter would lift off at the last possible moment, much to the annoyance of the elephant. I can't remember what I was most afraid of - either being trampled to death by an angry elephant, or striking the rotor blades against the riverbank and dying in an aircraft accident.

But that was not the last of the jumbo story. No 2 Independent Company, a Territorial Army Unit based in Kariba, were supplying us with our daily rations. On one particular day, the ration delivery drivers advised us that a jumbo was adjacent to the airfield, on the Kariba-Makuti road. Polly Postance, Monty Maughan and I decided to investigate. We set off through the mopani scrub in the Zambezi Valley and soon came across a very old, wrinkled elephant ambling along the tar road towards the Nyanyana River. We approached the old jumbo to within about thirty yards and because of its apparent disinterest in our antics we then started hurling abuse, sticks and rocks at it. Then all of a sudden it charged us and off we ran, I through the thick jesse and Polly and Monty back towards Kariba along the road. We caught our breath about two hundred metres further on, regrouped, and decided that the elephant had only charged us to frighten us off, which he certainly had succeeded in doing.

As we strolled back to camp thanking our lucky stars that we had survived, navigator Polly Postance suggested we go back to the elephant. Monty had had enough and returned to the airfield. I didn't want to be chicken and elected to go with Polly. By now the old jumbo had left the road and drifted off into the bush towards the lake. It was not long before we accidentally stumbled upon him as he was perfectly camouflaged by the surrounding foliage. He was having a meal of branches, leaves and all, from the mopani trees. Once again Polly taunted the elephant, and before long we were again subjected to an elephant charge. This time I was really frightened, and set off like a long dog hurtling over trees in my flight to get away from the irate animal. I recall seeing only a desert ahead of me, flat as a pancake - with not a tree in sight. Now, one needs to have been in the valley to appreciate that those conditions did not actually exist. After covering the quarter mile in less seconds than a dragster with no Postance overtaking me, I became worried and turned back, calling to him. When there was no reply, I assumed he had been trampled to death, and started to backtrack with trepidation wondering how I was going to explain Polly's demise to my superiors. I found Polly very much alive back with the jumbo. By now I was more angry than the elephant and demanded to know why he had not responded to my calls. He replied that, in running away and keeping a wary eye on the elephant, he had run slap-bang into a tree - lights out. - only to come to with the elephant standing over him and chomping from the very same tree. He was in no position to answer my calls for fear of really upsetting the animal.

The moral of the story is: if ever you are charged by a wild bull elephant note the strategy he uses. First, he will stop whatever he is doing then, keeping his head dead still while flapping his ears. He will manoeuvre his body into a straight line facing his unfortunate victim and then suddenly, with trunk raised and trumpet blaring, he will stomp about ten to twenty paces, with the ground heaving like a stormy sea under him. He will then stop, and turn off at right angles, or even turn about. If you survive, you will have experienced an elephant's mock charge. However, in my case I was not prepared to risk standing up to a possible mock charge and ran for my life with my clothing torn to shreds as I sped through the thick mopani bush.

On 11th November 1965 (Armistice Day), I was manning the Operations Room at Kariba at midday when Prime Minister Ian Douglas Smith proclaimed his famous UDI: "Whereas in the course of human affairs history has shown that it may become necessary for a people to resolve the political affiliations which have connected them with another people and to assume amongst other nations the separate and equal status to which they are entitled:

And whereas in such event a respect for the opinions of mankind requires them to declare to other nations the causes which impel them to assume full responsibility for their own affairs.

Now therefore, we, the Government of Rhodesia, do hereby declare.

That it is an indisputable and accepted historic fact that since 1923 the Government of Rhodesia have exercised the powers of self-government and have been responsible for the progress, development and welfare of their people;

That the people of Rhodesia having demonstrated their loyalty to the Crown and to their kith and kin in the United Kingdom and elsewhere through two world wars, and having been prepared to shed their blood and give of their substance in what they believed to be the mutual interests of freedom-loving people, now see all that they have cherished about to be shattered on the rocks of expediency;

That the people of Rhodesia have witnessed a process which is destructive of those very precepts upon which civilisation in a primitive country has been built; they have seen the principles of Western democracy, responsible government and moral standards crumble elsewhere; nevertheless they have remained steadfast;

That the people of Rhodesia fully support the requests of their Government for sovereign independence but have witnessed the consistent refusal of the Government of the United Kingdom to accede to their entreaties;

That the Government of the United Kingdom has thus demonstrated that they are not prepared to grant sovereign independence to Rhodesia on terms acceptable to the people of Rhodesia, thereby persisting in maintaining an unwarrantable jurisdiction over Rhodesia, obstructing laws and treaties with other states and the conduct of affairs with other nations and refusing assent to laws necessary for the public good; all this to the detriment of the future peace, prosperity and good government of Rhodesia;

That the Government of Rhodesia have for a long period patiently and in good faith negotiated with the Government of the United Kingdom for the removal of the remaining limitations placed upon them and for the grant of sovereign independence;

That in the belief that procrastination and delay strike at and injure the very life of the nation, the Government of Rhodesia consider it essential that Rhodesia should attain, without delay, sovereign independence, the justice of which is beyond question;

Now, Therefore, We The Government Of Rhodesia, in humble submission to Almighty God who controls the destinies of nations, conscious that the people of Rhodesia have always shown unswerving loyalty and devotion to Her Majesty the Queen and earnestly praying that we and the people of Rhodesia will not be hindered in our determination to continue exercising our undoubted right to demonstrate the same loyalty and devotion, and seeking to promote the common good so that the dignity and freedom of all men may be assured, Do, By This Proclamation, adopt, enact and give to the people of Rhodesia the Constitution annexed hereto.

God Save The Queen

Given under our hand at Salisbury this Eleventh Day of November in the Year of Our Lord one thousand nine hundred and sixty-five."

Harold Wilson immediately dispatched Royal Air Force Javelin jet fighter bombers to Zambia, and they needed Salisbury air traffic controllers to kindly guide them in. Officially, they had been sent in to defend Zambia's airspace but, according to authoritative journalist Chapman Pincher, their purpose was simply to occupy the airfields to prevent the Russians from doing so. In fact, such was the value of the 'kith and kin' factor, that the Royal Air Force officers toasted Ian Smith's health during their New Year's Eve celebrations in their Lusaka Mess. They even visited Salisbury during their time off and had a few beers with the Rhodesian Air Force pilots. It was also reliably heard that they used to meet the Hunters over the Zambezi and fly formation down the river until they both peeled away to land at their respective bases.

However, the Rhodesians were taking no chances. We continued to occupy Kariba and improve the air defences. That is where I lost respect for the Rhodesian Light Infantry troopies - they promptly bit the crowns off their green beret cap badges and spat on them. I must concede, though, that they were hardened troopies - where else would one come across youngsters breaking pickaxe handle after pickaxe handle digging slit trenches in the rock-hard Kariba earth. They even fell asleep in a standing position, with the tip of the pickaxe resting in the middle of their backs (to give their superiors the impression that they were just resting while digging the slit trenches).

Then, a rather prolonged cat and mouse game started which lasted just under a week, with very little air activity. Finally, on 19th November 1965, I returned to Thornhill with trusty Provost 308. Operation *Wizard* was rather a damp squib from a flying perspective - not discounting the jumbo charge of course which was the highlight of this particular serious operation.

OPERATION NOAH

Kariba and Operation *Noah* are synonymous! The jumbo that charged Polly Postance, Monty Maughan and I was probably a survivor of the operation that rescued all the wild animals. On 13th May 1978 Prime Minister Ian Douglas Smith had a pleasant break from his dealing with the Byron Hove affair, when he had a happy trip to Kariba to unveil a memorial to Operation *Noah*. Smith records in his memoirs *The Great Betrayal* "My heart was in tune with that small, simple dignified ceremony, in keeping with the concept and execution of the operation, which extended over a period of a few years in order to ensure maximum rescue".

Then on 24th November 1965 I reached my first major flying milestone. I clocked 1000 hours. Big deal. The sortie in question was 'pansy' formation, with tail chase. This was a fun sortie, because the tail chase is a loose form of formation flying, following my leader. Loops and barrel rolls can be quite tricky, but steep wing-overs, slow rolls, aileron turns were all fun manoeuvres, where the pilots are able to cut the corners in order to catch up. Conversely, flying slightly wider arcs in order to maintain a constant range from the aircraft in front. I must also admit to the 'spinning' tail chase. This ploy was used in aerial combat, but it was in fact a futile exercise, because the attacker would comfortably 'spiral dive' down onto his prey and wait for the foolish lead aircraft to initiate his spin recovery - then promptly blast his target out of the sky.

The next day I flew down for roller landings on Chiredzi airstrip, as the excuse to 'beat-up' my future wife and father-in-law. Pa Malan was making concrete bricks for S P Burger, with Rina working for N Richards. I would then exercise my flying perk to personally deliver an airmail love-letter via message bag drop. I would like to think it was pranks like this that honed my low-level bombing ability. I was probably lucky to survive this one thousand-hour voodoo but I attribute it to the wise counsel by father who had warned me not to throw caution to the wind when reaching this milestone in my flying career.

At the end of the month I bummed a ride with Flight Lieutenant Mark Smithdorff who was tasked to carry out a Major airtest on Alouette 504. After having done his airtest routine, Mark kindly allowed me to 'pole' the helicopter. The simple task of flying straight and level was no easy matter. One also needed good co-ordination skills to hover, as well as to climb vertically.

NO 4 SQUADRON, ROYAL RHODESIAN AIR FORCE – DECEMBER 1965
Hugh Slatter
Chris Weinmann, Bill Buckle, John Bennie, Mark McLean, Harold Griffiths
Prop Geldenhuys, Pat Meddows-Taylor, Bill Jelley, Sqn Ldr KAS Edwards, Nobby Nightingale, Rob Tasker and Varky Varkevisser

On 8th December 1965, I spent a whole sortie doing just spinning. The limitation was a maximum of eight turns. The Provost spins more easily turning left, as opposed to right spins. I recklessly tried to see how many turns I could achieve, spinning in opposite directions, consecutively. I duly proceeded to the Provost general flying area, climbing to just over eleven thousand feet (jet aircraft pilots check their oxygen flow and connections above 10 000 feet above sea level). There is a long line of blue gum trees running along side the railway line to Somabula. The straight length of railway line is a favourite for pilot orientation purposes when doing aerobatics, because it could represent a runway for low level aerobatics displays. Anyway, after a couple of spins in both directions, I wanted to see, rather foolishly, how many 'complete' spins I could do consecutively. For the record, I managed three. That is, I spun a full 8 turns left, went straight into a right spin for 8 turns, and then immediately left again for 8 turns. I was probably suffering the effects of anoxia - lack of oxygen - and in my over-confident state of mind, got the fright of my life. I had recovered from the last third set of left-hand turns, to find that I had lost so much height that my recovery was below the tops of the blue gum trees. Yes, between the ground level and tree level. Phew - another close shave - too close for comfort. I would have flown into the trees, had my recovery from spinning not been parallel to the tree line. But then, I was so close to the ground that I could have spun straight in. It is those types of sorties where a pilot sobers up instantly, climbs to a safe height, flies straight and level to calm the nerves, abandons the remainder of the sortie, gets down on the ground as soon as possible, and thanks his Maker for His lucky Angels.

That was now foolish, seeing that I had only recently passed the dangerous 1000-hour barrier. Anyway, a sortie on the 11th was a pleasant flag waving mission - I flew with Snr Tech Gipson on a "Magnificent Men and their Flying Machines" leaflet drop promotion exercise - flying No 6 in a formation of Provosts. I recall the recent release of the film attracted a lot of public interest - and was possibly intended as a publicity stunt to stimulate Air Force recruiting efforts.

The three sorties that I flew on December the 22nd, was somewhat unusual. I flew Pilot Officer Barry Roberts to, and dropped him off at, Kyle dam, and returned solo to Gwelo. I then flew a Minor airtest - but my passenger was a certain Aircraftsman Geldenhuys. I didn't think much of it at the time, but now realise, some 34 years later, that he must have been a distant relative. My logbook records that I again flew with the fellow on January the 6th, this time on an engine change airtest. I can thus safely conclude that A C Geldenhuys served as an engine fitter. These are the only clues that I have to follow up on the genealogy research that I had embarked on in the year 2000.

1965 grew to a momentous close, with a night-stop at Salisbury, followed by a round the houses cross-country with roller landings at Que Que, Sinoia, Rusape etc (I can't remember where the etceteras were, most probably Mashonaland and Manicaland towns). Having landed on Christmas Eve, I took a week's leave to visit the fiancé.

The week was disastrous. Rina's bedroom was next to her folks. I was sharing the boys' room at the end of the passage. Then in the middle of the night I twinkle-toed to Rina's room for a spot of hanky-panky. My justification was that tying the knot was only a matter of months away, and I was checking out compatibility. As I bade my 'good'-night, it turned into a 'bad' night - nightmare; because I had stepped on a cat as I slinked out of Rina's bed. The meow raised the dead. I was forced to hotfoot it before all the lights came on. I sheepishly emerged from nowhere to enquire what the commotion was all about at this unholy hour, only to find that the poor cat had departed for its happy hunting grounds.

Let me hasten to add, for the record, that despite all my dirty tricks, I married a virgin. At least one of us was a virgin. I trust the reader won't read anything sinister into what I have just said.

After a couple of routine sorties with Hugh Slatter, the New Year got off to a flying start with our normal ten-day Kutanga Weapons Detachment. The firing of weapons from the air was always special, hence my election to document the detachments separately. Apart from a squadron exercise during February, nothing of particular note occurred during the month. I did fly one low-level reconnaissance sortie with squadron commander KAS Edwards. Wing Commander Mick McLaren was still OCFW.

The Boss kindly granted me six weeks leave to get married and enjoy Operation Paradise - figuratively as well as literally. In those days it was quite a mission to tie the knot. One had to seek official permission to get married "I have the honour to request, Sir, ...Your Obedient Servant ..." Your intended spouse was screened, and the Air Force could withhold permission if they thought your choice of a mate was unsuitable.

OPERATION PARADISE - 5 MARCH 1966 (Ball and Chain)

Sanctions were starting to bite. Fuel rationing had been introduced. Courting long distance was not helping my short circuit. I opted for the 'Ball and Chain' and decided to tie the knot on 5th March 1966 - craftily on Rina's 21st Birthday - so that the anniversary days cum birthdays would mean one day less likely to forget in the future. Rina was by this time living in Chiredzi with her parents and we decided to get married in Fort Victoria. Dominee Jackson of the Dutch Reformed Church officiated. My Dad came up from Pretoria, smartly dressed in Air Force Number Ones, and I reciprocated.

NO 4 SQUADRON GUARD OF HONOUR
LHS – Hugh Slatter, Varky Varkevisser, Mark McLean and Barry Roberts
RHS – Sqn Ldr Ken Edwards, Nobby Nightingale, John Bennie and Harold Griffiths

No 4 Squadron with Ken Edwards in charge of the Guard of Honour at the service performed the memorable ritual of sending the newlyweds off on their honeymoon. Ball and Chain and all.

Rina and I had a brief farewell for family and friends at the local hotel, and made Birchenough Bridge our first stop en route to Hot Springs. Rina was about to proclaim "Not tonight, Darling. I've a headache". Not to be out-manoeuvred, I made a quick pit stop at Birchenough's only hotel, sauntered into the crowded pub nonchalantly, and sheepishly asked the barman whether he had any Aspro for my ailing spouse.

Rina blurted out "I have a headache, and we have just got married." The hotel owner's wife came to my rescue, promptly administered a Grandpa Regmaaker to Rina, and dispatched us off on our long awaited honeymoon night as scheduled to Hot Springs.

Well without letting the cat out of the bag, the deserted Hot Springs pool was the ideal spot for skinny-dipping - and we did not need the hot water to raise our temperatures. Luckily, Grandpa had worked, and the "headache" was a thing of the past. I might add, the previous hanky-panky prior to marriage certainly seemed a lot easier than the real thing.

All Smiles

With such a beautiful bride, it took several months for the smile to be wiped off my face!

Preller Geldenhuys – Junior and Senior – In Air Force No One Blues

The next morning we set off for Beira, boarded the Piper Apache 150 piloted by Joachim Beretta and set course for Inhazorro. Rina was invited by the pilot to sit in front, beside him - while I was left to clamber into the back seat and find a "possie" amongst all the crates of vegetables destined for the Island. At Inhazorro, we boarded a deep-sea fishing vessel for Santa Carolina, popularly called Paradise Island. The idyllic place lived up to its reputation - and although I do not recall seeing much sunlight, I wasn't complaining. The goggle fishing was better than bioscope, and the quiet afternoons and nights were even better. But all good things come to an end. And so it was, that ten days later, Rina and I boarded the 'My Lady' for the mainland where we again met up with our pilot for our return flight to Beira. This time, with the honeymoon over, I helped Rina into the back seat and then took up the front right-hand seat next to Joachim.

We spent a couple of days frequenting all the Chinese shops in Beira, and then set off for Gwelo to establish our first home, albeit a two bed roomed flat. We spent the rest of March getting to really know one another, buy the essentials like plates, a fridge and stove, and just settling down. I rejoined the Squadron just after April Fool's Day (the reader may make what he likes from this coincidence).

No 4 Squadron – Winners of the Jacklin Trophy in 1966 with our Squadron "Secretary Bird"
(Yours truly is seated fifth from the left, with Bill Jelley third from the right)

My first sortie after the honeymoon was flown on 4th April 1966. Pilot Officer Mark McLean was instructed in quarter-attacks, and several sorties on dive-bombing and tear-smoke were also flown during the early stages of the month. Pilots flown with included Flight Lieutenant Rob Tasker, Flying Officer Harold Griffiths and Pilot Officers John Bennie, Derek "Nobby" Nightingale and Bill Buckle.

On 18th April, Flight Technician Gibson and I set course for Binga on Exercise *Armchair*. We arrived at the Army Camp based near the local District Commissioner's offices. After a comfortable night stop, my first sortie was a solo border reconnaissance westward to Deka and return. Navigation along Lake Kariba was relatively easy, and the game, particularly elephant and buffalo was plentiful. Fishing villages along both shores were just starting to be established. Inland from the lake was largely uninhabited. Then on 20th April I flew another sortie, but this time with a Conex (Internal Affairs Conservation and Extension) official named Spiret. Our area covered from Bumi Hills to our east, then along the length of the lake to Deka and return. Despite his obvious discomfort in the Provost, he expressed his gratitude for the opportunity of covering such a large tract of the Rhodesian real estate, which would have taken several weeks had he covered it on the ground. The Browns didn't want to fly the next day, so my Tech and I spent a leisure day at the Binga hot spring. We flew back to Thornhill on 23rd April.

Two days later I was back at Kutanga, doing air-to-ground attacks. Then on the 27th I flew Steve Kesby to the range for RSO duties, while I got in another five gunnery sorties.

INSTRUMENT RATING EXAMINER

It may be recalled that up until now, instrument flying had always been my weakness. I was always rated 'low average' during my Basic Flying Stage and Advanced Flying Stages. I owe it to Tony Smit and especially Squadron Leader KAS Edwards to turn my weakness into a strength. Boss Edwards obviously had a lot of faith in me, so much so that to my own surprise I qualified as an IRE - Instrument Rating Examiner. Although my AFS instructor, Rob Tasker, was the Squadron IRE, I was selected to qualify as well. KAS Edwards forwarded his recommendation to Officer Commanding Flying Wing, Wing Commander Mick McLaren who duly ratified my appointment with effect from 31st May 1966. Boss Edwards duly assessed me "above average" for the twelve month period ending 30 June 1966. My newly acquired qualification was valid for a year, subject to renewal in May 1967.

Now, to jump the gun, if I may. My good fortune continued two years later when I was once again selected on Vampires as a student on No 2 IRE Course, which was run from 7th to 15th May 1968. Flight Lieutenant Eddy Wilkinson was the instructor and the other pupils included Graham Cronshaw, Randy du Rand, Don Northcroft, Guy Jackson, and myself. (See photo, next page).

On May 24th, Squadron Leader Bill Jelley flew as my safety pilot. I was thus able to qualify as an IRE on both the piston Provost and jet Vampire aircraft. This was also in addition to my PAI qualification. Anyway, let me return to the good old Provost days. Exercise Aurora was behind us, 1000 hours on the Provost was looming, Army FAC and Air Force VR training lay ahead.

Then on May the 27th the Leonides engine cut during an Air Test that Chris Weinmann and I were doing on Provost 309. Fortunately it was only a minor glitch, and the wind milling action got the engine going again. This was a somewhat rare occurrence. On landing without any further hassles, the technicians thoroughly ground ran the Leonides before declaring it serviceable. Unfortunately, I can't recall the exact snag, but I flew the same aircraft four days later on my IRE IRT - the day I qualified as an Instrument Rating Examiner.

No 6 SQUADRON
RRAF
No 2 IRE COURSE
MAY 1968

L to R Back Row: Fg.Off. C.Weinmann, Flt.Lt. J.Weir, Flt.Lt. J. DuRand, Fg.Off.G.Cronshaw, Sqn.Ldr. M. Smithdorff (OC 6 Sqn), Flt.Lt. E.Wilkinson (IRE) Front Row: Fg.Off. D. Northcroft, Fg.Off. D. Jones, Fg.Off. P. Geldenhuys.

MASTER GREEN IRONY

Shortly after qualifying as IRE, my Instrument flying ability improved to such an extent that I was rated "Master Green" standard. This was ironical in view of my low or below average flying assessments. This was a classical example of turning a weakness into a strength. By focusing on 'angle of bank, and VSI (vertical speed indicator)', and sub-consciously repeating the saying whilst scanning the instrument panel, one was able to refer to a variety of flight instruments to determine whether the aircraft was either turning (i.e. banking), or descending/climbing. If under partial instrument failure conditions, aircraft attitudes could quite easily be established.

For example, the artificial horizon, turn and slip indicator, as well as the DI or direction indicator (gyrocompass) were three different flight instruments that gave clues to "angle of bank". The VSI, altimeter and ASI (airspeed indicator) were three instruments that gave indications of either climbing or descending attitudes. Should the safety pilot or IRE cover the altimeter during flight, an increase in speed can be interpreted as a descent. Conversely, as speed falls off, the pilot can deduce that the aircraft is in a climbing attitude. For the layman, it may be necessary to explain that it would be normal for the examiner or the safety pilot to hand over control after trying to disorientate the poor guy under the 'hood'. And then invariably only after putting the aircraft in an "unusual attitude" – like up-side-down or a spiral dive. The 'angle of bank/VSI' technique to recover from unusual attitudes helped me immeasurably to overcome my fear of instrument flying.

I owe it to my peers and seniors who passed their skills on to me. It was thus a great sense of achievement to master an inbred inferiority complex, and be doubly rewarded with both a Master Green instruments rating, as well as being selected to qualify as IRE. Hence this short story of Master Green irony. The moral is you can achieve anything as long as you set your mind to it. I consider it a pearl of wisdom worthy of passing on to my descendants.

Then, during the early part of June 1966, No 4 Squadron embarked on a series of maximum range and endurance trials on the Provost. I was very fortunate to get in on the act on at least three occasions. I managed to squeeze four hours twenty out of Provost 302 (at least twice). All this flying resulted in my achieving the magic one thousand hours on type. It came up on June the 8th, which I duly recorded in my pilots flying logbook. Such long sorties did not come around all that often, but it certainly engendered confidence to fly the aircraft to its limits. But pilots also had their limits. Mine was oxygen poisoning. Now that is quite a long time to suppress the nicotine habit, so it did not take long for me to sneak in the odd smoke. I learnt the technique from 'master Provost pilot' P-B - the flying instructor who had taught me to fly. By opening the canopy a fraction, the negative air pressure over the cockpit efficiently sucked all the smoke outside. My Dad had warned me of the 'dangerous over-confidence' stage when 1000 hours is reached, so I took reasonable precautions to ensure there was no fuel vapour in the cockpit whenever I lit-up.

The following day I flew a Pilot Officer Liebenberg to Kariba and return. He was either a South African direct entry pilot because I do not recall a Liebenberg on any of our pilot training courses, or more likely the proverbial wolf in sheep's clothing – in other words a 'smersh' Operation Polo' pilot wearing our uniform as a guise. The latter made more sense because the South Africans were getting their foot in the door with Border Control deployments when SAANC terrorists crossed into Rhodesia in August 1967, and again in March 1968.

ARMY FAC (Forward Air Control)

I wish to reiterate that No 4 Squadron liaison with our Army counterparts was always of the highest order. We regularly mixed business with pleasure, and were streets ahead of any comparable military force anywhere in the world. Our intimate co-operation often meant that we got to now the Browns personally, and this stood us in good stead when the Bush War hotted up. On 10th June 1966 I flew RAR Captain Geoff Atkinson to Gokwe for an Army pow-wow. The return sortie with the Army Captain included a 'flag waving' sortie over the ground troops.

On 16th June 1966 I instructed Bill Buckle in the techniques of FAC - forward air control - whereby troops on the ground can "talk pilots" onto targets during airstrikes.

The School of Infantry in Gwelo was running one of their normal Company Commander's training camps and No 4 Squadron was called upon to demonstrate counter-insurgency (COIN) techniques. My first Brownjob student was Captain Peter Hosking - who later commanded the second Battalion RAR at Fort Victoria. Later the same day, 17th June, I flew Captain Bert Sachse on his FAC air experience sortie. Bert was destined to fly quite a few sorties with me in the years that lay ahead. My last sortie of the day was flown with Captain Engela - whose Christian name escapes me (now thirty-four years ago). Three days later I flew another FAC simulated strikes sortie with Bill Buckle.

Immediately after the Army co-op tasks, on 18th June 1966, I flew to Preston with Flight Sergeant Ken Spoor on another Volunteer

Reserve exercise. Although we only spent the day there, to exercise the Salisbury based squadrons; the day was memorable in that I incurred the wrath of my ex-Boss Ozzie Penton. Boss Os was the current OCFW at New Sarum, the Air Force base that had also deployed a Dakota to Preston as well. Anyway, Preston airstrip was owned by one of the VRs who hosted the exercise on his farm. The VR had kindly lengthened his farm strip to take the larger Air Force aircraft, but the freshly graded area had not been grassed yet. Poor old Ken Spoor had made an excellent spit and polish job on our 'demo' Provost that was on show for all the Volunteer Reservists gathered there. To cut a long story short, the Dak crew did their engine run-up right in front of my gleaming clean Provost and blew the African dustbowl (recently graded runway) right into my cockpit. Ken had to make a dash to close the canopy and hang onto the brakes, just in case the Dak blew my lightweight Provost away. I complained bitterly to my Boss KAS Edwards, who unknowingly, duly bent Ozzie Penton's ear regarding poor airmanship by the Dak crews. Boss Os subsequently gave me a thousand words for squealing like a stuck pig.

I might add that I wondered, many years later, whether Ken Spoor was related to Major Spoor of No 1 EFTS, the Chief Flying Instructor who flew with my Dad and was subsequently killed during World War II. I have my doubts; because Ken was a rooinek and I suspect the Major may well have been a 'slope'.

On 23rd June 1966, I flew Flying Officer Mike Hill from Thornhill to Salisbury in a Provost. Mike was from our Senior Course, and I had last flown Provosts with him on Old Years Eve 1963. Mike was destined to die in a helicopter accident with OC 7 Squadron Gordon Nettleton on 1st July 1970. I think they were on a routine instrument flying sortie when the Alouette pranged on the ring road to New Sarum. Anyway, having returned from Salisbury after dropping Mike off, I was immediately tasked, with Nobby Nightingale, to carry out a reconnaissance in the Hartley area for the terrorists responsible for the cold blooded murder of farmers Johannes and Barbara Viljoen.

OPERATION PAGODA - VILJOEN MURDERS - JUNE 1966

The bush war began when the Viljoens were the first Rhodesians to die at the hands of communist-trained and armed terrorists (CTs). The term "communist terrorist" and its abbreviated form CT owe its origin to the Malaya Campaign of 1951 to 1953. On 24th June 1966 I was tasked to fly a Provost aircraft from Thornhill Air Base on an air reconnaissance mission, and patrol the banks of the Umvuli River which runs into Kariba dam. I intercepted the river bridge along the Hartley - Selous road and followed it downstream for some distance but without being able to observe any sign of the fleeing CTs, for they made a beeline back to Zambia from whence they came.

Rina's brother-in-law Hansie Bezuidenhout, a tobacco farmer in the Tengwe area, was involved with the local BSAP PATU in follow up operations. PATU was made up mainly from farming personnel and most of them often received excellent co-operation from neighbouring farms and even the local citizenry. Hansie recalls that they followed spoor of the fleeing terrorist's right up to Kanyemba, on the border between Rhodesia, Zambia and Portuguese Mozambique. The route taken was along the Angwa valley to the Zambezi Escarpment, then along the Valley floor to a point near Kanyemba.

In February 1967 a captured terrorist Edmund Nyandoro went on trial for the Viljoen murders and was convicted and sentenced to death. Nyandoro told the court that that he had been trained in Egypt, China and Tanzania. The intelligence gleaned from the captures was used by the Security Forces to target the terrorist camps in Tanzania, and later in Mozambique and Zambia. Years later, when I was a Canberra pilot, I carried out several "Z^2" – Zambia, Zaire and Tanzanian – long-range trans-border photo-reconnaissance sorties - like photographing terrorist camps at Itumbi and Mgagao in southern Tanzania and Iringa respectively. But more about that later

June 1966 ended with my carrying out an Instrument Rating Test on Squadron Leader KAS Edwards, and a solo single line flare circuits and landings. I presume that I must have impressed the Boss because Ken Edwards rated me Above Average on Instrument Flying, Gunnery and Bombing. He also rated me High Average on Instructional Ability, Navigation, General Flying and Night Flying. The flying ratings were commendable. The assessments were for the twelve months ended June 1966. Wing Commander Mick McLaren also certified my Special Flying Qualification of Provost IRE. I was indeed very satisfied with such a good periodic summary.

I took two weeks leave to spend some quality time with my growing family. My first sortie in July 1966, on the 13th, was with Major Parker. The sortie was an Army reconnaissance in the hilly and heavily wooded Selukwe area. Parker was destined to be killed with Major-General John Shaw in a Z-Car (SAAF helicopter) flying accident in December 1975. In the past month I had thus flown with three military personnel who would die - the third being Chris Weinmann.

On 17th July 1966 I flew Flight Technician Gibson to Kutanga, with flypast, for our bi-annual Weapons Detachment, which lasted for ten days to 26th July. My only student on this weapons detachment was Flight Lieutenant Bill Jelley. I instructed Bill in gunnery and tear smoke dropping. Together, we fired 200 x ·303 rounds air-to-ground, and dropped sixteen tear smoke.

Chris Weinmann

July 1966 ended with air photography of Provost 310. Should anyone out there ever catch sight of Provost 310, spare a thought that the picture was me flying Corporal Barker from the Photographic Section.

August 1966 started off with OCU instruction for No 19 PTC who had attested into the Air Force on 1st April 1965. My students were Acting Pilot Officers Ken Law, Tudor Thomas and Derrick Rainey. The first week of instruction was temporarily interrupted when I was air tasked to carry out an Army recce along the mountainous Eastern Districts, but concentrating mainly in the Cashel Valley area. A couple of general sorties were also flown with the other No 4 Squadron pilots like Pat Meddows-Taylor, Hugh Slatter and Bill Buckle. A trip to Binga helped to boost my flying hours for the month to forty-seven hours, which was well above the average, in a month, for the Squadron. It was otherwise a rather uneventful month.

August 1966 the RAF Javelin Squadron and British troops in Zambia were returning home. They were given a farewell party by the Rhodesians. Messages of good wishes were conveyed to Ian Smith, including one saying "From one RAF pilot to another - if need be, we would be prepared to come back and help the Rhodesians".

September was slightly more interesting. I carried out 20lb bombing trials successfully, flew a couple of instrument flying rating tests for Chris Weinmann, and Bill Buckle, carried out an air test after an engine change, flew Flight Lieutenant Peter McClurg to Salisbury and prepared for Exercise Armchair to Wankie.

EXERCISE ARMCHAIR - WANKIE 19-24 SEPTEMBER 1966

On 16th September 1966 I had a 'night-stop' at New Sarum. I flew Junior Technician Mick Joss to Salisbury, and returned to Thornhill the following day with Air Traffic Controller Flight Lieutenant Charlie Tubbs. After two nights at home, I flew Flight Sergeant Ken Spoor up to Wankie on Exercise Armchair. Ken was a highly competent all round engineer, in whom I entrusted in keeping my Provost one hundred percent serviceable for the duration of our six-day detachment. The second Provost to accompany us, was Pilot Officer Bill Buckle, who flew up A C Bruce Brislin - a product of Thornhill School.

Exercise *Armchair* got off to a flying start with a morning reconnaissance. One sortie was flown with one of our camp caterers, Senior Aircraftsman Dave Abrahams. Although he enjoyed the ride, Dave remarked that he felt more at home in his hot and sticky kitchen. Then on 23rd September I flew with Bill's technician, Aircraftsman Brislin eastwards for a Lake Kariba recce, landing at Binga. It was good to fly with a fellow scholar from the same school. I was starting to get to know the Lake shore pretty well, with my frequent trips to Binga.

After about a week, we were off again, on another detachment. This time it was to Kutanga for the OCU air-weapons camp that lasted from 3rd to 7th October 1966. Although the duration was only five days, I flew 21 sorties, instructing Chris, Tudor and Ken. Varky Varkevisser and I dropped 2 x 250lb bombs high dive. This size bombing from a Provost can be considered a rarity. I am sure all our spectators, especially the OCU students, appreciated the opportunity to witness the devastating effects of a two hundred and fifty pounder from the Provost. And so ended our Kutanga Range detachment, with the hospitality that we had come to respect from Range Warden John McKenzie.

During October 1966, Varky and I enjoyed ourselves on a night-stop jolly to Beira. We went along to check up on the OCU students - to see to it that they behaved themselves like Officers and Gentlemen. (But also turning a blind eye at the Moulin Rouge happenings - they were entitled to let their hair down), but more importantly, to ensure that their long range cross-countries were flown successfully. I ended the month with IRTs for Varky, John Bennie and instrument flying practice for Ron Vass.

EXERCISE COBRA - WEDZA 19/20 NOVEMBER 1966

Pilot Officers shed their Acting ranks after completing their operational conversion training. Pilot Officer Ken Law and I carried out a low-level squadron navigational exercise to Buhera. Buhera is a small town approximately 80-kilometres south-east of Enkeldoorn (on a secondary road to Birchenough Bridge). We flew over the Sabi

Tribal Trust Land, which was not good country for navigation, but our 1:500,000 scale maps was generally very good. Buhera was not the sort of place that I would enjoy making a livelihood. A couple of other general sorties were also flown. Pilot Officer Terry Jones got in some pre-detachment practice firing 200 x ·303 front gun and dropping eight practice bombs high dive.

I was detailed to deploy to Wedza. This was our third away trip in as many months. Rina and family were getting quite used to me spending a lot of time away from home. However, the VRs could only exercise during weekends and we regulars could only respect and fully support these part-time airmen who so willingly gave of their valuable time and effort. As was customary, we pulled out all the stops. Exercise *Cobra* was the only excitement during the month, and I ended November with another low-level squadron exercise that entailed landing at Kutanga. December 1966, meanwhile, was another relatively uneventful month. I could perhaps mention a partial engine failure while Derrick Rainey was my safety pilot during an instrument flying sortie. These minor emergencies tended to build up confidence between man and machine, and equipped pilots with the necessary skills to handle just about everything. I was doing more and more air tests - in fact the day before my partial engine failure I had done an engine change air test (on a different Provost). It certainly was to the pilots' advantage to handle emergencies calmly, whenever they arose. It also meant that the pilots really got to know their aircraft, could fly them to their extreme limits. I might also add that Flying Officer Pete Woolcock - wolvoël - joined the Squadron for the Specialist Weapons course that got off the ground in the New Year. 1966 ended with Squadron Leader Bill Jelley taking over No 4 Squadron, and Squadron Leader Keith Kemsley standing in for Wing Commander Mick McLaren as Officer Commanding Flying Wing.

SPECIALIST WEAPONS COURSE

Varky Varkevisser and I ran the Specialist Weapons Course in January and February 1967, which was designed to churn out more PAIs. My pupils were Pilot Officers Chris Weinmann and Bill Buckle, and the odd instructional sortie was also given to Pete Woolcock.

Fixed Gun Sighting remained my particular speciality. After giving the students an earful in the lecture halls, I would also put theory into practice by demonstrating air-to-air quarter attack techniques. Ciné film would be taken during the various exercises and these would be scrutinised in the comfort of the classroom to assess the effectiveness of the pupils as budding fighter pilots. Gunnery, rocketing, bombing and tear smoke dropping exercises were also carried out. Some pupils displayed amazingly good aptitudes and they in turn would pass their skills onto others that would follow in the hallowed footsteps of the 'heroes' of the Rhodesian Bush War (that was just round the corner, so to speak).

On 19th January 1967 I few four sorties. The first two were ¼ attacks. The third was a 'pansy' or close formation sortie from Thornhill to Bulawayo with Bill Jelley. This was the first opportunity I had of flying with our new Boss since he took over from Ken Edwards. At Bulawayo, the Boss changed crews (I can't remember who with, but the fact will be found in his pilot's log). Anyway, I exchanged his seat for Aircraftsman Nigel Fotheringham. Nigel had kindly assisted with my aircraft turn round - refuel, kick the tyres and light the fires. And so, Nigel carried out quite a few night flying circuits and roller landings at Bulawayo before returning to Thornhill. This way we could maximise the number of aircraft types scheduled to do night flying - for example, the jets would use Thornhill while the Provosts could keep out of their hair by using Bulawayo.

My last sortie on the Specialist Weapons Course was flown on February the 15th, with Bill Buckle. The day before Bill also came along while I conducted 4 x 60lb rocket projectile trials. The month ended with a Master Green instrument rating test for Rob Tasker (my Vampire instructor).

March 1967 started off with an Army Exercise reconnaissance in the Selukwe area. My passenger on this trip was Flying Officer Derrick Purnell of the VR. The next day, the 3rd, Tudor Thomas and I were scrambled on an air task to Chipinga.

The Squadron was considerate allowing me time off on the 5th to celebrate Rina's birthday and our anniversary date - because our next Kutanga Weapons Detachment started on 6th March 1967. The detachment lasted for five days until March the 10th when I was deployed to Rusape on a Volunteer Reserve weekend exercise code named Liberator. However I did manage to squeeze in frantan instruction for Pilot Officer Terry Jones, and dropped 2 x 250lb bombs with Varky Varkevisser.

After a comfortable night-stop I was again tasked to carry out a recce to the Inyanga area, around Troutbeck and the Inyangani Mountain. It was a rather short sortie, with Flight Lieutenant John Barnes coming along for the ride. My second sortie of the day was with Brian Patton. The next morning I was off again on another Army reconnaissance of the Shabani and Selukwe area with Major Coaton. The Army School of Infantry in Gwelo was running one of their regular counter-insurgency courses. The Army were also using Kutanga Range to fire their 90mm cannon from their Armoured Cars - and I flew Lieutenant Engela to the Range and returned later in the day.

The 29/30th March 1967 was interesting in that a simulated strike was carried out, landing Salisbury, and then proceeding to the Inyangombe Falls in the Eastern Highlands on a low-level cross-country. Then the following afternoon I positioned Kutanga for "Flare Trials" in order for the Canberras to do their thing with night bombing, with the glare of my flares.

The first night sortie I dropped 4 x 4inch Recco flares. With each flare drop a pair of Canberras would need to be at the right place, at the right time, in order to identify the target, do their bomb run-in, and drop their bombs before the flare fizzled out. These flares were equivalent to 600,000-candle power, and they dropped to the ground by parachute. With the low descent rate, wind velocity was a major factor. Timings also needed to be spot on. The onus was on me to find the target at night, drop the flare upwind at the right place, and have the Canberras at the perfect run-in, in order for them to successfully bomb the target. It was a tricky trial. I landed back at Kutanga to await another pair of Canberras from New Sarum. At the appointed time, I got airborne again to drop one more four inch Recco flare, then returned to Thornhill.

While night bombing by flare drop was feasible, its potential usefulness had its limitations. I could only submit my report expressing reservations. Wing Commander Mick McLaren was not that sort of person to accept 'no' for an answer, and ordered everybody concerned back to the drawing board. The Provost pilot needed to 'extractum digit'. Not only was the pilot blinded by the intense light when the flare ignited, he also needed to get the hell out of the way of the jet bombers, as well make sure the Canberra's bombs did not fall on the low flying Provost. I was singled out to conduct further trials in a couple of month's time.

Diverse activities were carried out during April 1967. The first was road reconnaissance from Gwelo to Bulawayo, then down to Beit Bridge and return, with night flying back to Gwelo. The general idea at that time was to identify all stretches of road that could be used as emergency landing areas for light aircraft. While most of the likely sites could be determined by close study of large scaled maps (1 in 5000), visual inspection was necessary to look out for culverts, telephone wires, overhead power lines, presence and condition of farmland fencing. Flight Sergeant Ken Spoor and I duly set off on 4th April to survey the road from Gwelo to Bulawayo. This leg took us slightly over an hour and a half to do. The second leg down to the Beit Bridge border post and return to Bulawayo took one hour longer. On quite a few places I was actually tempted to land, but carried out slow, low approaches - because the greatest hazard was dodging the motor cars, trucks and busses competing for our selected sites. On returning to Bulawayo, Ken kindly refuelled the Provost and we night flew back to Thornhill. We logged five hours for the day - considerably shorter than doing the same survey by road. My next trip was flown with Junior Technician Boet van Schalkwyk to survey the Midlands roads.

As early as 8th April, I had dropped 8 x 20lb fragmentation bombs and fired 100x·303 front gun on an air power weapons demonstration for the Bulawayo PRAW - Police Reserve Air Wing. Now two weeks later, it was a repeat airstrike for the Salisbury PRAW. The three sorties flown on April 2nd were thus somewhat out of the ordinary. It did, however, illustrate the variety of tasks expected from the Air Forces internal security squadron. No two days were really alike - and often the most unexpected was par for the course. I might add that we generally got on well with the civil power in the outlying areas, co-operated equally well with our Army and BSAP counterparts, and spent a fair amount of our time on field deployments.

The other notable sorties during April included a photographic airtask of Loretta Mission, with photographer Corporal Doug Whyte (he was the son of our Station Commander). I eventually got around to instruct my BFS Instructor Flight Lieutenant Pat Meddows-Taylor on bombing and air-to-air. The shoe was on the other foot. If it fits, wear it.

The next day I flew Officer Commanding Flying Wing Mick McLaren to Kutanga Range. The Wing Commander wanted to experience progress on the Recco flare trials with the Canberras bombing at night. I then loaded up with six of the four-inch flares, and with Wing Commander McLaren, dropped the flares while the Canberras carried out their bombing runs. We logged ninety minutes night flying. The rest of the month of May was taken up doing fuel trials on the Provost. I also did a Master Green instrument rating with Bill Jelley (Provost 313, on 26th May 1967). Very little flying was done in June - a mere four sorties with just over three hours flying time. I presume

Rina and I may well have taken leave after I had graduated from the Officer's Administration Course held at New Sarum.

NO 1 GROUND TRAINING SCHOOL

My attendance at No 1 Ground Training School, from 12th to 30th June, on my first Officers' Administration Course, meant that the powers to be considered it fit to give me a break from Internal Security duties. I also needed to focus my attention on career advancement, and passing the requisite Officers Promotion Examinations. The Admin Course thus served as a means to an end.
Although I flew only 18.35 hours during July, the number of sorties totalled 33 with only four being over an hour's duration. That is between the 18th and the 29th of the month. The other interesting statistics include firing one thousand rounds 303, dropping 70 x 20-lb and two frag bombs, 44 tear smoke, searching for a lost Brownjob, night single line flare landings, and flying my first sortie with Acting Pilot Officer Rich Beaver on 19th July 1967. It is perhaps coincidental, that as I write this, Caroline Beaver paid us a courtesy visit just before my departure to America - nearly 33 years later.
August 1967 was rather special in my life, and warrants devoting a separate chapter because it signalled using air power in anger. It was one thing carrying out simulated strikes, or firing live weaponry at pre-positioned ground targets. It was a totally different matter shooting at terrorists. The curtain went up on Operation *Nickel* - and came down on all the exercises that prepared the Rhodesian Air Force to play its full part in the impending Bush War.

OPERATION NICKEL

OPERATION KARIBA (ISOTOPE 2), AND WANKIE (NICKEL)

August 1967 was probably *the* month that created a lasting impression in the whole of my service-flying career. There was hardly a day that passed without my flying on a wide range of duties and operational tasks. Little did I know what lay ahead, and that I would establish an all-time high of logging 105½ hours for the month (as compared with 18.35 hours for the previous month). Operational Conversion Unit weapons instruction for my student Acting Pilot Officer Richard Beaver was imminent, but unbeknown to me at that time, would be rudely interrupted by the demands made on operational pilots. I was also unaware of my pending posting to a jet squadron, and in addition several significant command changes occurred. For one, Flight Lieutenant Varky Varkevisser was Acting Squadron Commander of No 4 Squadron, for Boss Bill Jelley, who in turn was Acting Officer Commanding Flying Wing. By end August, Squadron Leader Peter Cooke had taken over from Bill Jelley as OC 4 Sqn, and Wing Commander Mick McLaren had been appointed Officer Commanding Flying Wing Thornhill.

Bill Sykes happened to remind me of the Kariba power lines episode whilst reviewing my draft biography. He remembered a valuable lesson learnt of 'keeping eyes on path' concepts, especially when trying to be too clever. In this instance, in order to maintain an element of surprise, flying over the Kariba Dam Wall be it down river or up the gorge meant keeping ones eyes peeled for the hazards – gooks as well as man made. It is natural to focus on the Zambian shoreline (especially Siavonga and Sampakruma) for any signs of terrorist presence or activity – often forgetting other "hidden" obstructions. In this case, it was the various cables that span the gorge just downstream of the dam wall. I was more aware of the downdraft over the wall when flying up river, and did not take into consideration the cable hazards. It was only after landing back at base that I realised that it was purely a question of luck, and not skill, that the Provost didn't collide with the telephone or power lines spanning the gorge.

During the next two days, I managed to get in three OCU instructional sorties with Richard Beaver. Having just got home, I was again tasked to get my butt into the air and set off for Wankie for the start of Operation *Nickel*. Beav's operational conversion, after only two days, was once again interrupted by the demands of Internal Security Force operations. Imagine my over-confidence to Rina - "Darling, pack my bags, for a couple of days. Like Makuti, we should wrap up everything in a jiffy - so keep the bed warm."

BATTLE OF INYANTUE

On the 14th August 1967, at the Battle of Inyantue, Flying Officer Prop Geldenhuys with Acting Pilot Officer Richard Beaver, in Provost No 309, put in the first Airstrike of Operation *Nickel*. We fired a total of two hundred and thirty rounds of ·303 from our two Browning machine guns. 1 RAR had pulled out their ambush parties to a safe distance and we would then spray the

Rich Beaver

hilltop with our front guns. Even Richard was given the unique opportunity to squeeze the trigger before his formal OCU gunnery training. However, the experience gained was worth more than many hours of academic instruction. After numerous attacks, we then remained airborne for over 2¼ hours while the ground sweep took place. Two further terrorists had been killed. Nobody laid claims - it could have been the gunfights the night before, or even the airstrikes. In any event, the gooks were gone.

On the 22nd August we had a real ding-dong running battle. It was during a lull in the battle that an AK 47 slug hit Provost 308. I was circling the gook fortification when my port wing opened up right before my eyes. The bullet then struck my side of the canopy, just behind my head, and rattled itself to death inside the cockpit - fortunately without striking either my pupil pilot or myself. On being hit, I banked sharply to starboard. Beaver meanwhile thought that I had been shot and was trying to wrest control during my violent air manoeuvres. I, simultaneously, thought that he had been hit. When we both realised we were okay; we regained our senses and then directed our attention to checking out the aircraft for any other obvious signs of damage. I might add that when one is on the receiving end of ground to air fire, it sounds exactly like the noise of sticking your finger into a fast rotating fan. The tat-tat-rat-a-tat-tat sound of automatic gunfire can be very unnerving. By now our radios went dead and we then lost all contact with Nic Smith. As we were nearing the end of our endurance, we called for Chris Weinmann to relieve us in order to have the aircraft checked out. My concern was that our fuel tank in the port wing had been holed. As the relief Provost passed us, we gave them the contact grid-reference. Five BTs/CTs were killed in this contact between the RAR and the gooks.

On landing, our techs checked out my aircraft, confirmed no vital organs damaged, and applied several strips of masking tape over the bullet holes as a temporary measure. Once refuelled, I set off again and proceeded to the contact scene. By now it was late afternoon. We were saddened to hear that both Lieutenant Nic Smith and Warrant Officer Class II Timitiya had been killed. We made radio contact with Lieutenant Ken Pierson who was in charge of the stop groups and had all his units strung out along the Nata River to ambush the fleeing gooks.

Early next morning, on the 23rd August, I took off before dawn, with Pilot Officer Derrick Rainey. We flew ten minutes in darkness, in order to arrive over the Nata River at first light. It was then that we heard the dreadful news - Ken Pierson had been shot the night before. Our total flight time for this operational mission was a lengthy three hours fifty minutes - maximum endurance for this type of flying. It was primarily to piece together the events leading up to the loss of two commissioned officers and a Warrant Officer - a loss the highly successful RAR could ill afford. Timitiya had been shot in the head, through the fork of a tree, whilst transmitting on the army field radio which he had taken off his dead lieutenant. Ken Pierson had been shot, apparently by one of his own ambush units, while responding to a flanking manoeuvre by the gooks trying to break through the ambush line. When the firing broke out at the dead of night, Ken went crashing through the dense scrub and was mistaken for a terrorist. Terrorist casualties were one BT captured and the gang leader wounded/captured. Derrick Rainey assisted me in relaying the news to Sunray Major - the Brigade Major at Battalion field headquarters. The early morning start had been both tiring and demoralising. Little did I realise that another three sorties lay ahead that day - with another night landing at a strange airfield.

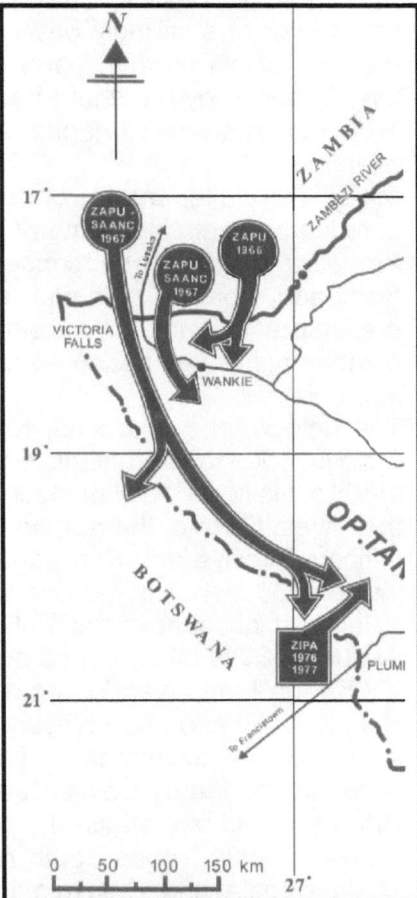

As fate would have it, I met up with Ken's brother John Pierson, 40 years later and willingly gave him a copy of my Operations book, in memory of his brother. John reminded me of the occasion, already long forgotten by me, that I had authorised the parachute jump from a Trojan aircraft when I happened to be OC FAF 5 Mtoko some years later.

Major Terry Hammond, on behalf of the ground forces, made a surprise presentation to me of the Nickel Cross, expertly made by the Army Engineers, from a "condensed milk blikkie". A ribbon of sorts was fashioned from a colourful piece of cloth and the 'medal' duly presented to me at a fairly sombre gathering of really good combatants. I was honoured, and certainly humbled, by this token of appreciation.

The unique, one of a kind, Nickel Cross read: IRAR, Wankie 'Prop' Tjolotjo, 100 Hours. It is this event which convinced me that the title of this story is in no small measure dedicated to those who sacrificed with their lives. For me, the real heroes of this operation had been Warrant Officers Timitiya and Korb, and police Inspector Phillips. I also regret losing good friends in Ken Pierson and Nic Smith.

A terrorist account of the Battle of Inyantue fought on 13th and 14th August 1967 is taken from a book by Bopela and Luthuli, published in 2005. The battle was fought during Operation *Nickel*; after the Chris Hani led infiltration had crossed the Zambezi River at Batonka Gorge, some 35 km downstream of the Victoria Falls. The entire Lupane Detachment, led by David Madzimbamuto alias Jonathan Moyo, was virtually wiped out, effectively putting an end to their brief "to open the Eastern Front". Those South Africans killed at Inyantue according to Thula Bopela and Daluxolo Luthuli, included Gandhi Hlekani from Cradock, Jacques Goniwe and Alfred Sharp – or real name Templeton Mzondeni from Chume near East London, Delmas 'Nsimbi Kayigobi' Sibanyoni, Melane and James Masimini, the commissar. Those captured were Freddy Mninzi, George Mothusi, George Tau, Jonathan Moyo and Bethuel Tamana. Those that managed to escape during the night teamed up with the main group that trekked south-east through the Wankie National Game Reserve – until they either died in battle during Security Forces follow ups, or were captured, or were among the very few who made it to South Africa.

In their excellent book, *Umkhonto we Sizwe*, Bopela and Luthuli had this to say "The first battle between them (the Lupani Detachment) and the Rhodesian Security forces took place on the banks of the Nyatuwe (sic) River between Wankie and Dett and it lasted for ten hours. They had stopped for a rest in a dry river bed and their commander gave orders for them to be fed and watered.

"At 07:00 sentries reported seeing spotter planes (no doubt, the Air Force Provosts) flying low over the area. The commander David Madzimbamuto (alias Jonathan Moyo), didn't think the report significant. At 08:30 the silence of the morning was broken by an outbreak of gunfire and a spotter plane with sky-shout facilities flying overhead. Its loudspeakers boomed out: "Surrender terrorists! You're surrounded!"

"David bawled back that they would never surrender. After that the main business of the day began. For a short time there was confusion and panic amongst the guerrillas, but they soon rallied and returned fire. The commissar James Masimini shouted that he would shoot anybody who tried to run. When we later asked survivors why Masimini had found it necessary to make such a threat, they said it was because most of our ZIPRA allies had shown little stomach for fighting (the Rhodesians). Some had already openly said that they intended to desert at the first sign of trouble.

"During the battle some ZIPRA men hid in the grass and didn't even try to fight, but others resisted bravely. The battle raged well into the afternoon. The Security Forces decided that it would be suicidal to try and dislodge such a determined group by frontal assault, so they called in helicopters to machine-gun them from the air.

"MK's machine gunners like Delmas 'Nsimbi Kayigobi' Sibanyoni and Gandhi Hlekani held the enemy at bay. Guerrillas cannot survive in the way a stand-alone army does. They derive their support from the people they are seeking to liberate. They have to merge with the population to the point where the enemy cannot distinguish between the locals and the guerrillas. The Lupane group, like ourselves, didn't get the opportunity to merge with the people, so they were unable to survive.

"That night some guerrillas managed to slip through the Security Forces' dragnet, leaving four of their number dead on the battlefield. A fifth, James Masimini, also stayed behind. He volunteered to cover the retreat of his comrades and the next morning died in a gun battle with the enemy."

Masimini may well have died from the Provost air strike that went in at first light, because very little resistance was encountered during the early morning sweep. Thula Bopela and Daluxolo Luthuli initially evaded capture and managed to survive the remaining battles. They sought refuge at a village, got dressed as school boys and boarded a bus to Bulawayo. After both travelled to the Eastern Districts, Bopela was captured by the BSAP and tried in the High Court, Salisbury. He was found guilty and sentenced to death. This was later commuted to life imprisonment – but was released from prison after 13 years when Mugabe came to power. Luthuli was arrested in the Plumtree area, handed over to South Africa where he was convicted of terrorism and sentenced to 10 years imprisonment on Robben Island. Both Luthuli and Bopela landed cushy jobs in South Africa's Ministry of Defence – when the ANC government came to power. Surprised? They will probably have streets named after them – before long!

TER(RORIST) SURVIVAL KIT

DEFENCE	De Wire dat goes around de camp
DEFEAT	De ting dat you walk on
DETAIL	De ting dat hangs on de back of de cat
DELAY	De woman dat sleeps around
DIVORCE	De stuff dat you eat with de mealie pap
DESCENT	De money of de White man
DETAIN	De place where de flowers grow
DETOUR	Contact de Sowetan Travel agents
DEFAULT	De de-ter with a gun
DEFINE	De money dat you pay when you break de law
DERIDE	De ting dat you get from delay
DESPISE	De men who look through de windows
DEPART	De piece of something
DESTROY	De ting with what you drink de coca cola
DECOMPOUND	De place where de-ter stays
DENY	De no comment
DEFER	De ting dat covers de cat
DETER	De fault with de uniform
DETERMINE	De bomb of de-ter

DEFECT	De honest-to-goodness truth
DISEASE	De ting dat causes decease
DISTINCT	De word for de smelly ter
DESIGN	De ting dat you show de enemy
DEBUG	De ting dat causes de itch
DECIDE	One of de positions for deride
DELIVER	De enemy of de alcohol
DELETE	De song dat you sing
DELIGHT	De ting dat shines
DERAIL	One of de tings you blow up
DEVINE	De liquor you drink when de mampoer is finished
DECOY	De ting you sleep on

The above insert, for light relief, is a skit on deposed ex Uganda President Idi Amin who spoke the "De" or the De ting language. With such a successful Operation *Nickel*, finding a terrorist survival kit amongst all those gooks would not be an unfair possibility.

On 14th September 1967 I jammied a Vampire ride with Flying Officer Barry Roberts on a 'Border Reconnaissance' sortie, and then proceeded with doing Richard Beaver's operational conversion unit training, pending my posting to the jet squadron. I flew five sorties on the trot with Vulch - the last on 22nd September 1967. I was sad to leave the Squadron that had grounded me in Internal Security operations for the past four years. But then I was equally excited to fly jets again, and looked forward to joining No 2 Vampire Squadron.

As a postscript for No 4 Squadron, the reader is referred to author Rob Thurman's excellent book "*Half a Century in Uniform*", the Story of Group Captain Ozzie D Penton AFC, OLM Rhodesian Air Force Volunteer Reserve (Retd.) – published April 2000. Ozzie is on record as saying that he "had been moved to New Sarum to take over the *troubled* 4 Squadron (in July 1961), a post he held until the end of 1963, the end of the Federation. These two years were probably the most turbulent the young Air Force had had to face until then." The index to Rob Thurman's work reads "Vastly experienced as an Instructor, Pilot and leader Ossie is given the task of sorting out a 'problem Squadron'. It is for this success that he is awarded his Air Force Cross." For the record, I was posted onto No 4 Squadron in July 1963, paraded with the Squadron for the award of the Jacklin Trophy – presented by Chief of Air Staff Air Vice-Marshal A M Bentley – served over four years on the Squadron, and made my own contribution.

Without sounding too modest, No 4 Squadron certainly played its full role with the terrorist onslaught, and I am honoured to have served with such a fine bunch of truly magnificent Rhodesians. Together with No 7 Squadron,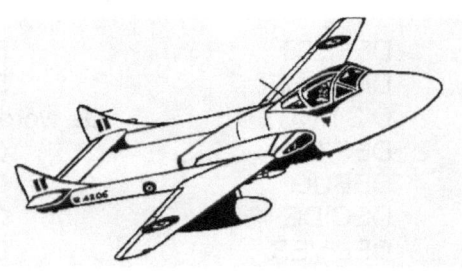
the helicopter crews, No 4 Squadrons record of service speaks for itself, being at the forefront of counter-insurgency operations.

No 2 SQUADRON POSTING

I was posted to No 2 Squadron, Thornhill, which were equipped with Vampire T 11 jet aircraft, on 1st October 1967. Squadron Leader Bill Jelley commanded the squadron. He had been posted from No 4 Provost squadron at the end of June. The squadron was first formed in January 1956 at Salisbury's New Sarum air base with its primary role being one of advanced flying training for the Short Service Unit pupils - such as for Bill Jelley who was on
No 6 SSU (1.3.1954 to 29.2.1956). Bill, by the way, was only one of two pilots who, on completing their course, remained on Medium Service and retired as Wing Commanders (the other being Peter Cooke).

A brief history of No 2 Squadron reads as follows. The squadron was disbanded in June 1957 and the staff pilots posted to No 1 Squadron. In September 1958, the squadron was reformed, this time at Thornhill. At that time, I was a schoolboy at Thornhill High and still remember being fascinated by the twin boomed jet aircraft screaming over our playing fields on joining the circuit at the airbase. Anyway, the squadron was once more disbanded when the staff pilots were posted to attend Canberra conversion courses in England (prior to the formation of No 5 Squadron). Then in March 1960, it was again reformed as a training unit in the RRAF - Royal Rhodesian Air Force. The squadron trained instructors on both the Percival Provost T 1 and the Vampire T 11, before the commencement of the basic and advanced flying training of pupil pilots under the new pilot training course scheme.

Secondary roles allotted to the squadron comprised Internal Security duties for the Provosts, and ground attack/day fighter operations for the Vampire. In December 1961, Vampire pilots were detached to No 1 Squadron, operating from Ndola, at the time of the Katangese crises. In October of that year, the squadron began OCU training courses. Its armaments are relatively formidable: 4 x 20mm cannons and four x three inch rockets, and if the drop tanks are removed, it can carry a fair load of bombs.

My conversion to type was carried our by flight commander Flight Lieutenant Keith Corrans on 9th and 10th October 1967. My solo, also on the 10th was a decent one-hour general with low flying. Three days later I flew with Pilot Officer Mike Mulligan on my first army exercises in the Vampire - we carried out air reconnaissance in the Inyati area. I found that a lot of ground could be covered flying at five miles a minute. After two sorties with the Army, I carried out my first Vampire border recce with Barry Roberts on 14th October.

My first sortie in a Vampire with Boss Bill Jelley was on 18th October 1967 when he was my safety pilot on a simulated instrument flying QGH with GCA sortie. We then next flew together on an internal security border reconnaissance sortie, with night landing on 23rd October. Border recces came around fairly frequently, and I flew the Zambian route on 2nd, 4th, 14th, 22nd and 29th November. Air to ground 20-mm cannon was rather potent – at 650 rounds per minute, the rate of fire of the Hispano cannon was a lot slower than the 1200 rounds per minute rapid fire of the Provost Brownings', but the cannon packed a powerful punch. I fired no less than 540 shells for my conversion during November.

On 8th and 9th November Bill Jelley and I carried out drop tank trials on the Vampire. Although drop tanks were nearly always carried for operational purposes, the success of using Frantans on the Provost warranted the development of a likely 'napalm' type weapons capability for the Vampire as well. The aircraft enjoyed the reputation of being a very stable weapons platform. Also, its gyro-gunsight meant that a lot more accuracy was achievable providing the pilot maintains a steady 'track' for at least four seconds. The technique of adopting a shallow glide dive angle immeasurably improved yardages - as opposed to the low-*level* type of bombing that had hitherto been popular.

On 20th November I was again safety pilot for Boss Jelley - his ground controlled radar approach (GCA) was quite good - above average "Green" standard. Our next sortie together was a night flying circuits and landings on 4th December. The Vampire was a lot easier to land than the Provost, and I imagine my 'arrivals' were just as good as his. The early part of December was devoted mainly to rocket firing - we carried on average 4 x 60lb three-inch rockets, fitted with a concrete head for practice purposes on the Range. For genuine airstrikes we would arm the rockets with armour piercing squashheads. These weapons of war had a soft nose that would crumble on striking the target - say a tank - then the explosive charge would burn through the armour plating and blast the inside of the tank with molten metal - thereby frying the occupants of the tank. Once again, Steve Kesby was the PAI who taught me rocket firing. He did a great job, because I seemed to do particularly well with this weapon. Other squadron pilots that flew with me during this early stage of my weapons conversion included Wally Galloway, Buff Phillips and Brian Meikle. I also flew a couple of border recces and instrument flying practices. Barrel Roberts and I had some fun on a couple of sorties but one in particular dropped us in the dwang with the Boss. The incident, three weeks after my night flying sortie with Bill Jelley, did not charm the Boss.

My episode with Flying Officer Barry Roberts on 27th December did not engender a spirit of good cheer with the Officer Commanding. We were competing against each another to see who could land the Vampire in the shortest distance. Taking turns, and with each landing being shorter than the preceding one, the competition was really hotting-up. With only five minutes to go to the completion of the sortie, Barry was rather harsh on the brakes resulting in us bursting not one but both main wheel tyres. (Not to be outdone, it wouldn't surprise me if he had actually landed with the wheel brakes on before touchdown). Having robbed me of my turn, Barry won the competition hands down - or should I say 'tyres down'. At least this was not as bad as doing a wheels-up landing. Despite the festive season, Boss Jelley was real mad and tore a strip off both of us - me for being the captain, and Barry for all the hassles of blocking the runway pending the ground crews affecting a recovery of the unserviceable Vampire back to the squadron. What counted in our favour was that Officer Commanding Flying Wing, Wing Commander Chris Dams was on Christmas leave, and the very amenable Squadron Leader Ted Brent was standing in for him.

Fortunately, the Boss was not vindictive and I was allowed to proceed the next day with the first of many 'jollies' to Beira. These navex-navigational exercises to the seaside resort in Mozambique meant bypassing all the customs clearance hassles. This was truly mixing pleasure with business - so much so that I have decided to devote a separate section just for all the jollies that the Air Force treated me to.

Early in the New Year, on 4th January 1968, Bill Jelley and I conducted 60 x 20mm air-to-ground trials at Kutanga Range. It was perhaps fortuitous that the squadron was preparing itself for the escalating bush war to support the IS Squadrons in its fight against the infiltrating terrorists, which now were beginning to occur with monotonous regularity. The Security Forces were dealing rapidly with the scourge, but air power was becoming more of a necessity than a luxury. We also owed it to our brilliant technicians who were coping admirably with sanctions, which were starting to have their effect on the supply and availability of essential Air Force infrastructures, especially spares.

Other highlights during January 1968 included Zambian border recces, sorties to Bulawayo with Senior Technician Jim Light (a real character that most pilots can recall his pranks and hilarious incidents), day fighter combat sorties, bombing, radar interception sorties and looping attacks. The latter perhaps need further explanation. This was a technique whereby a pilot either intentionally, or by pure opportunity, flies low level over a ground 'target'. The Vampire is then accelerated to about 250 knots, then, after exactly 30 seconds is pulled vertically into a looping manoeuvre. At the top of the loop, an aileron turn is executed - that is, rolling the aircraft the right side up, and switching on the gunsight while bringing ones guns to bear on the target. This loop placed one at exactly the right height and the right angle of dive for the attack. While this manoeuvre looked quite spectacular from the ground, as well as from the air, it did in fact have its limitations in operations. For one, the element of surprise was lost, and most bush targets in reality invariably depended on some form of FAC target marking. Anyway, it was great fun doing them if only for sharpening up the steely-eyed jet-jock's reactions.

CAPEX WITH CARROTS

On Saturday 20th January 1968, Rina and I loaded up our Ford Taunus motor car and set off for our six weeks leave to the Cape. I had no sooner set course for Chiredzi and Pretoria when Rina started getting violently sick - morning sickness. Well, what a long journey to Cape Town that was. I was forced to stop every few miles so that Rina could spray the roadside with carrots. From Pretoria, our route took us to Port Elizabeth, down along the Garden Route, all the way to Cape Town, terminating at Rhodesia By-the-Sea Hotel in Simonstown.

Rina's folks were still living in the Lowveld. Her father was still working for S P Burger and was engaged in building irrigation canals at Chisumbanje. They had meanwhile befriended Louis and Anna Ferreira of Mayfield Farm in Chipinga, and were contemplating taking up the free offer to farm Knutsford Farm overlooking the Lusitu Valley as well as the southern Chimanimani Mountains. My parents were staying in Gesina in Pretoria; with my father being a 'jam-stealer' (Storeman) at 10 Air Depot, South African Air Force. After brief stops with our respective parents, we headed for the Cape coast.

Our first stop was at Jeffries Bay - but what a disappointment. The sea smelt great, but the wind was howling, the beach was full of blue-bottles and also deserted - and Rina was still manufacturing second hand carrots - where from I don't know. This was not the place for us so we decided to press on. We stopped at Sedgefield and what a nice place that was. From there we made Caledon and spent a couple of days at the Hot Springs. The drive down Sir Lowry's Pass was spectacular, arriving in good time to make the most of our Hotel stay in Simonstown. Rhodesia By-the-Sea Hotel was very popular and home from home for many Rhodesians. Boulders Beach, likewise, was the most popular beach for miles around. Although we also went to Muizenburg and the west coast beaches like Clifton and Camps Bay, the shelter provided by all the boulders at Simonstown gave us the necessary privacy for Rina to feed the sea creatures with all those carrots. In those 'good old days' a family could afford staying in a hotel for several weeks. I might add that the Hotel subsequently became the Officers Mess for the Naval Base at Simonstown.

Our route back took us to a quaint Frederick's hotel in the Cape, and also Keurboomsrivier. We popped in at Knysna and Beacon Island at Plettenberg Bay. The end of February was rapidly drawing to a close and I was itching to get back into the air again - to await the arrival of Askoek who gave us such a hard time all the way to Cape Town and back. I rejoined No 2 Squadron on Monday 4th March, the day before Rina's birthday, and promptly got in two sorties, a solo general with low flying and an instrument flying sortie.

Apart from the "burst both main wheel tyres" episode, my first real emergency on the Vampire occurred on Rina's birthday, 5th March 1968. I was in a formation of Vampires doing stream take-off in pairs. On reaching flying speed, the lead pair would pull up steeply, the next pair would remain low in order to pass through and remain under the lead pair's jet-stream, and the third pair would pull up steeply, and so on. Anyway, during our mass formation take-off, first one then another Vampire aborted their take-off. This placed the aircraft following behind in a predicament - either abort as well so as not to collide with the jet in front of you - or apply full power and pull up steeply. The aircraft that had to abort their take-off knew that the aircraft behind them were accelerating while they decelerated before reaching the end of the runway. In such an emergency, the jet pilot has only a fraction of a second to decide his course of action. In my case, I elected to continue with my take-off run, and fortunately cleared the two aircraft in front of me that over-ran the runway and ended up in the "barrier". Because it was pointless to continue with the exercise, I flew a wide circuit and landed without any further mishap. Nevertheless, it was a close shave - so soon after such a long lay off after my 'honeymoon trip' to the Cape.

The next day I was off again on another border recce, followed with yet another on 12th March 1968. On the latter, I flew with Pilot Officer Rob McGregor, and we landed at Bulawayo. On the return to base leg we were intercepted. Interceptions were the norm on the jet squadrons - one never knew in advance when someone would all of a sudden "jump you". It meant that the jet-jocks needed to keep their wits about them, and expect the unexpected any time. Although the RAF Squadron had been withdrawn from Zambia, they no longer posed any serious threat (in fact, they never did - the majority of the Javelin pilots were rather sympathetic towards our own Prime Minister - and as Ian Smith was an ex-RAF Spitfire pilot during the previous World War). I also don't think the Zambians were feared either - it was our belief they did not have what it takes to be a hotshot 'top-gun'.

I was fortunate, when later in March 1968, No 2 Squadron saw action for the first time. The Squadron was scrambled to New Sarum, and a live air attack was carried out against terrorists during Operation *Cauldron*.

OPERATION CAULDRON

This was the second most major Operation of my Air Force career to-date. Operation *Cauldron* started on 18th March 1968 and wrapped up on 8th April. It is particularly pleasing to the writer to record that as part of the Security Force effort of Operation Cauldron, Hansie Bezuidenhout and his Police Anti-Terrorist Unit - PATU stick was also involved in follow up operations. He got to know this particular area of the Urungwe and Dande Tribal Trust Land very well. In fact, his knowledge of the local rivers – like where the Maura River runs into the Angwa River proved indispensable to the Security Forces. He knew the area like the back of his hand. The Maura and Mkanga rivers bisect the two aforementioned TTLs. Apart from being a fluent linguist, his bush craft skills were also second to none. He was one of the early pioneers who realised that man and animals are creatures of habit – and that when faced with a choice of routes through the bundu, most would opt for game trails and paths. Tell tale signs are that trails often lead from feeding grounds to water, and paths from village to village. Trails and paths follow the easiest route to avoid serious obstacles. It is perhaps fitting, at this juncture, to record the poem composed by Hansie Bezuidenhout, as a tribute to the many PATU call-outs during the bush war. But, perhaps more so, as a tribute to three of his fellow farmer colleagues – Charlie Hay, 'Suffy' Colin Sutcliffe, and, last but no least, Fritzie Fourie who was shot dead in Tengwe.

Being a musician of no mean ability, the ditty he composed, is as follows:-

We've walked in the Valley,
We've been overland
Bitten by Tsetse's
At Chipemberes last stand,

We've walked a thousand miles
Yet a Ter we've never seen
So our next trip will go somewhere
Where we have never been

Chorus: Stride along little Fritzie
Stride along not so slow
As old Charlie and Snuffy
Are a rarin' to go.

But life carried on with numerous continuing border recces, with sorties flown on April 16th and 30th, PAI weapons instruction, FAC strikes and interspersed with No 2 IRE - Instrument Rating Examiner course between May 7th and May 15th 1968. I flew ten sorties with Flight Lieutenants Eddy Wilkinson and Randy du Rand, plus Flying Officers Graham Cronshaw, Don Northcroft and Guy Jackson. My sorties during April with ace photographer Whyte is significant in that air to air pictures were taken of Hunter number 1080 and Vampire 2400. So, watch this space i.e. keep an eye open for the two aircraft that were photographed.

On May 21st Squadron Commander Boss Bill Jelley gave me a Standardisation check on Vampires. Three days later we flew together again on No 2 Instrument Rating Examiner (IRE) Course.

On the Valley RLI continued to have short duration contacts killing and capturing many terrorists, which caused further disintegration of an already scattered force. Many individuals tried to make their way back to Zambia via the line of camps not realising they had become death traps. Many were killed in RLI ambushes at these camps and along the Zambezi River line. One ZAPU terrorist did not go the Chewore River route but set off for Zambia in a north-easterly direction. After more than a week without food, this emaciated man stumbled into an SAS patrol somewhere near Kanyemba. Given normal Army field rations, he gulped these down then dropped dead. When Captain Brian Robinson had recovered from the surprise of the incident, he sent a signal to the Quartermaster General offering SAS congratulations for his unit's first confirmed kill. The QMG was not amused!

Everything was going RLI's way until, on 18th March 1968, contact was made at the Mwaura River with a large group led by Hedebe (ZAPU leader) himself. Under Lieutenant Dumpy Pearce, troops of 3 Commando RLI were pinned down on the north bank by intensive fire coming down on them from heavy bush on the higher south bank. John Barnes with Senior Technician Monty Maughan arrived in their helicopter and put down 600 rounds of MAG fire into the position of the unseen enemy. Their intention was to draw attention to themselves and give the ground commander a chance to move his troops to a safer position. Since this had no effect whatsoever, and the troops remained pinned down, John called for heavy airstrike.

Meanwhile Mark McLean with Corporal Brian Warren came in at lower level to draw terrorist gunfire, which was returned in short measured bursts. Though the helicopter expended only 150 rounds of 7.62mm MAG ammunition, Mark's actions gave Dumpy Pearce the break he needed to move his men to safer ground. Then, under Mark McLean's directions, a pair of Vampires put in accurate strikes with 60 lb. squash-head rockets and 20mm cannon fire before a Canberra checked-in preparatory to making an attack with ninety-six 28 lb. Frag. bombs.

Newly appointed OC of 5 Squadron, Squadron Leader John Rogers, had elected to fly the air task, much to the annoyance of his experienced Canberra crews. When he called one minute out, Mark passed low over the target to place down a phosphorous grenade as a visual marker. The marker was on the terrorists' position but wind carried its white cloud away from target. The bomb-aimer concentrated his aim on this cloud with the consequence that bombs were released off target, some to explode near ground troops waiting in the 'safer ground'. Fortunately no one was seriously hurt.

When the somewhat annoyed troops moved forward, no fire came down on them because the terrorists had pulled out. By the time they had swept through the abandoned area and established the direction of flight, it had become too dark to follow tracks. The following day the tracker-combat callsign was moving on a trail heading straight for the escarpment.

At the same time, a smaller callsign was following frothy pink splatters of blood from a single terrorist who obviously had a serious lung wound. By late afternoon they had not closed on this man but reported that spoor of two hyenas overlaid the tracks of the wounded terrorist. Believing the terrorist would not survive the night, the follow-up troops were uplifted for re-deployment to a more important task.

It was probably five years later when I was asked by Special Branch if I remembered the Operation *Cauldron* terrorist we had given up for dead because hyenas were following him; I certainly did. "Would you like to meet the man?" I was asked. It seemed unbelievable but I met the recently captured terrorist whose beaming face showed he was pleased to be alive following his second brush with our security forces. His story was amazing. No white man would have survived the ordeal he described.

He had been wounded in the attack made by Vampires. He panicked and ran off even before the main group under Hedebe left the contact site. All night and the next day, he struggled for breath as he made his way to the foot of the escarpment. In the late afternoon his attention was drawn to a helicopter coming from behind him. Only then did he see, for the first time, the two hyenas as the helicopter frightened them off. When the aircraft landed it was so close that he could see the rotor blades whirling above low scrub. He tried to get back to it for help but moved too slowly. As the helicopter rose into full view he waved madly trying to attract attention but he was not seen before the helicopter turned and disappeared.

The two hyenas then reappeared and stayed about 30 metres behind him as he commenced his breathless ascent of the steep escarpment. By then it was almost dark and he was too tired and breathless to continue. So he sat down and faced the hyenas as they moved left and right in short runs, each time coming closer. When they were no more than ten metres away he shot one but missed the other and chased it with a long burst from his AK 47 rifle. Overwhelmed by tiredness, he lay down to sleep; surely to die.

He was amazed when he awoke at dawn wheezing and frothing with his clothing covered in freezing-cold caked blood. But he was still alive! All day he struggled slowly up the steep escarpment until evening when he lay exhausted and wanting to die. Again he was amazed at the dawning of the third day. Still wheezing and frothing he struggled to his feet and wobbled on ever higher. By nightfall he had reached the high ground and was about to lie down when he noticed a light shining some way off. He noted its position by reference to a tree and went to sleep; again not believing he would survive the night. But, yet again, he awoke on the fourth day.

Taking a line on the tree and noting the relative position of the sun he plodded off. At around 10 o'clock he came to a farm store that sold goods to the local African people. He was recognised for what he was but told the superstitious storekeeper how he had been unharmed by hyenas; an omen the keeper should know was deadly to anyone reporting his presence.

Using his Rhodesian money he bought a large bottle of Dettol for his wound as well as something to eat and drink. He repeated his warnings of doom to anyone reporting him and returned to the bush. Under shade in good cover he cut a long thin stick and stripped the bark away. He then inserted the stick into the wound in his chest and manoeuvred the stick until it came through the exit hole on his left shoulder blade. Then, moving the stick in and out slowly in long strokes, he poured the undiluted Dettol into the entry point and down his shoulder into the large exit hole of his terrible wound. Having emptied the bottle and removed the stick he knew in his mind that he would heal. He settled down to eat and drink before falling into a deep sleep that lasted for at least two days.

The Special Branch man asked the terrorist to remove his shirt so that I could see his scars. The shiny black puckered scars and the dent caused by the loss of a section of shoulder blade showed how large the chunk of shrapnel from a Vampire rocket must have been. I asked the man, "Was it not very painful when you pushed the stick through your body? Didn't the Dettol burn like crazy?" He said that these were not a problem. "I was choking on neat Dettol blowing out of both holes and into my throat. It was the choking that nearly killed me!"

OPERATION MANSION

Noteworthy sorties during the month included a night stop to Beira in Mozambique and two sorties with Bill Jelley. On 26th June 1968 he was my safety pilot while I flew low-level NDB letdowns on instruments. The second sortie, two days later was interesting in that we carried out low level interceptions, then joined up with the other Vampires and flew No 5 of 8 aircraft for a formation flypast over Thornhill air base.

July 1968 also had its highlights. A healthy 35.15 hours were flown during the month. These included two instrument flying sorties with Bill Jelley, night stop to Waterkloof in South Africa (with SAAF interceptions by Sabres and Mirages, and Hunter and Vampire interceptions on our return leg). Later on, Ted Lunt and I intercepted Canberras and Hunters. We could catch the bombers, but were not very successful against the faster Hunters. We needed to catch them by surprise, but as soon as the Hunters spotted us, they would adopt the Mirage tactic of stuffing their nose down and accelerating away from us. It was nevertheless very valuable day fighter experience. The other highlight included a fair amount of gunnery and rocket firing.

Then on 18th July, I instructed Rich Brand on a 20mm cannon PAI sortie. On landing, I was placed on standby for Operation *Griffin*. (Refer to my Ops book for more detail, including Operation *Mansion* with a successful airstrike with 4 by 60lb squashhead rockets and 280 rounds 20mm HEI cannon). The airstrike was carried out in the Zambezi Valley, upstream from Lake Kariba at Devil Gorge. Although the river crossing was dangerous for the Zapu terrorists, this group believed that they were safe due to the high-rock gully of Devils Gorge and would not be found by the security forces.

BUSINESS AND PLEASURE

JET PILOT ATTACK INSTRUCTOR

During November 1967 Flying Officer Steve Kesby instructed me in Vampire air-to-air ranging and tracking, 20mm air-to-ground gunnery including first run attacks (FRAs), and 60lb rocketry. Flying Officer Wally Galloway gave me a couple of bombing sorties - both shallow glide and high dive. The Vampire proved to be a very stable weapons platform, and I found myself scoring low yardages, especially with rocketry. I should add that the Vampire had a rather complex gyro-gunsight, which computed wind direction and strength, provided the pilot was able to track the target accurately for at least four seconds. The same applied in air-to-air ¼ attacks, with ranging carried out by rotation of the throttle that either increased or decreased the diamond graticule around the target aircraft. The bead, or pipper in the case of the gyro-gunsight, would lag behind the fixed cross, and automatically compute the correct aim-off angle required to ensure the attackers cone of fire enveloped the target.

My first pupil was Flight Lieutenant Rich Brand who had been posted to the squadron from Hunters. I wasn't too impressed with Rich on one particular flying incident. The Vampire was over-stressed during one of our last Kutanga Range sorties after Rich had pulled more than the allowable 6g. As I was just about to point out the G-meter reading to my pupil, he threw the aircraft into a tight low-level starboard turn - ones instinctive action is to cock one's head to maintain eyesight as near to parallel to the horizon as possible. Upon resuming normal flight, I then noticed the G-meter reading 6g. My crafty pupil had reset the meter during the steep turn (in my direction - sitting in the right hand seat), and then pulled exactly 6g during the turn when my eyeballs were focused in the direction of the turn. I didn't have a leg to stand on - the incriminating evidence had been erased and a false max loading now displayed on the meter.

The G-meter is placed in the aircraft for two purposes – one is to inform the pilot how much 'g' he is pulling during a manoeuvre, and the second is to record an overstressed aircraft. The latter is important as the next pilot might well be taking up a damaged aircraft which could fail in flight. This one incident has always made me a bit wary of any aircraft known to be favoured by this pilot. It also needs to be said for the official record - Rich was in fact a pilot who made a name for himself during an otherwise unblemished career.

Anyway, subsequent pupils included a rocketing check-out on Flying Officer Vic Cook in June 1968, Flying Officer Bruce Smith in August (his PAI instruction was interrupted on the 8th, with the birth of our beautiful daughter Renene - but more about this eventful day in my life a little later on). Pilot Officer Rich Beaver's OCU instruction followed in mid-August.

My first full-time OCU students were Acting Pilot Officers Bill Sykes and Chris Wentworth, and the odd weapons instruction for Acting Pilot Officer Ed Potterton. Other squadron pilots who I trust benefited by my techniques included Pilot Officer Ted Lunt, Flying Officer Bill Buckle, and Acting Pilot Officer Ed Paintin. These pleasant experiences continued to the end of the year.

Bill Sykes

Bill Jelley flew two simulated instrument flying sorties with me on 26th June. On the first, he was the Safety Pilot for me - and I completed my NDB plus a LLNDB (low-level) in a mere thirty-five minutes. On the second sortie, I as captain of the aircraft acted as safety pilot for him. The Boss took longer - or perhaps it was a case of hogging the flying so that he could do most of the 'poleing'?

On 28th June I flew with Squadron Leader Bill Jelley on a low-level intercept sortie, then joined up with the other aircraft as number five in a flypast of eight Vampires. The following day I flew an 85-minute low-level navex "GGSR" simulated strike sortie. Bill Jelley promoted the use of GGSR - Gyro-gunsight recorder - following our highly successful Operation *Cauldron* airstrikes. By filming our simulated strikes, we were able to accurately assess the effectiveness of our air-to-ground weapon training exercises, without going actually discharging hellish expensive hard-to-come-by weaponry. This saved the taxpayer thousands of dollars, increased squadron productivity immeasurably, and was as near as dammit to the real thing. Play back could also be done at one's leisure, advancing or rewinding, to iron out faults and improve techniques.

For the year ended June 1968, the squadron commander, Squadron Leader Bill Jelley gave me a particularly good "Assessment of Ability". Flying Officer P M Geldenhuys' annual assessment as a Day

Fighter/Ground Attack, Pilot Attack Instructor pilot on Vampire T 11 aircraft reads "*High Average* in Graduate Pilot, General Flying, Night Flying, Instrument Flying, Instructional Ability, Navigation, Bombing, Gunnery and RP". The Boss's remarks reads as follows "A studious pilot filling the post of Squadron PAI competently". In all modesty, I wonder whether the "Boss" would still have given me one of my best performance appraisals to date had he known that his son Grahame would some day marry my daughter Renene. More careful scrutiny will reveal that Renene had not yet been born. Their marriage would take place exactly 23 years and 11 months, to the day.

The 1st July was another two sortie simulated instrument flying day with Boss Jel. This time I was the safety pilot for him on the first sortie. He reciprocated for the second, during which I carried out an increasingly popular 'Condesc LLNDB' - controlled descent low-level non directional beacon letdown.

Lynx painting by Bill Sykes

EXERCISE "ASKOEK" 8 AUGUST 1968

Exercise "*Askoek*" was both business and pleasure. The event was also not one but two early Christmas presents - an early 1967 Christmas present and an even earlier 1968 Christmas present - resulting in the birth of Renene Delene on all the eighths - 8.8.68.

Rina and I enjoyed another honeymoon after my Operation *Nickel* stint in August 1967. I also guess that I must have had another honeymoon in December as well, most probably celebrating an early Christmas with conception taking place. However, I had no doubts that while Renene may not have been planned too well, our first born was in fact a "love-child". It may sound like an early 1967 Christmas present cum pleasure cruise, but Rina and I were definitely very much in love. When the second Christmas present arrived earlier than intended, my late father remarked that Renene was the most beautiful baby girl he had seen since the birth of Renene's aunt and namesake - Delene Elizabeth in 1945. Askoek's brother, Aspatat, was a 'planned baby'.

Renene was due by normal birth, at Birchenough Maternity Home, with specialist Mr Rodgers in attendance. When the moment arrived, I grabbed two packets of cigarettes to calm my birth pains, or was it anguish realising that I was about to become a father? Mr Rodgers emerged from the labour ward to announce that he would need to perform a caesarean section because of complications. We bundled the long suffering Rina in the back of his Wolsley motor car and rushed off to the Gwelo General operating theatre - advising Rina to relax and not to "push". That was not what Rina wanted to hear and she told the specialist in not so ladylike terms what he could do with his "don't push" advice. Anyway, all's well that ends well. Renene was duly delivered in the Gwelo hospital, with a somewhat elongated skull.

Up until now, my two packets of cigarettes had remained unopened. When I first saw Renene, I counted all the fingers and toes just to make sure that apart from the "long" head, everything else appeared "normal". When Renene moved her head from side to side, the back of her head seemed to remain stationary and only the 'face' moved. I must admit I was a bit worried despite assurances from the specialist that mother and child were all well. As soon as Rina came out off the anaesthetic, she hurled her lunch all over me - it was then that I reached for my first cigarette since rushing her for the delivery. I am pleased to report that despite my concern regarding "swivel" head, 'Askoek' was ready to face the world 'head-on'.

Boss Jelley was also kind to me. I had flown three sorties on the day before Askoek's birth - two on PAI instruction and one solo rocketing sortie. According to my logbook, the Boss gave me time off for the birth - a Thursday. I flew on the 5th, 6th, 7th, and 9th August. The 10th and 11th was a weekend, so Renene will be able to tell her

Grandchildren that she was born just after sunset on that Thursday - 8-8-68.

Sometime after the arrival of Askoek, Rina was admitted to hospital for a check up. Now, I am no mother because I recall having to bottle-feed Askoek. I failed to ensure that the teat was properly screwed onto the bottle, resulting in a sopping wet Askoek, as well as my bed, and a starving daughter content to give her father ulcers. Fortunately, Shirley Smit (Tony's wife) came to my rescue as a much needed day-mother. I would drop Renene off with Shirley on my way to the squadron, and collect her again at cessation of work. I was not very good with nappy changing, dressing Askoek up for visits to her mother in hospital or bedding her down for the night. Being a fast learner, I made sure that the teat was secure whilst rushing around doing all the chores before reporting for duty.

Askoek was only eighteen days old when Bill Jelley took the whole squadron to Bulawayo for the sixteen day Operation *Knuckle* detachment. He did give me a week off to collect Rina from her mother's.

Eight Vampires Lined Up On The Hardstanding

OPERATION KNUCKLE (Bulawayo) - 26 AUGUST TO 11 SEPTEMBER 1968

After some months of careful planning, the No 2 Squadron Detachment to Bulawayo commenced on the 26th August. This was despite my continuing PAI instruction for Richard Brand, and being allocated Pilot Officer Rich Beaver and recently commissioned Acting Pilot Officer's Bill Sykes and Chris Wentworth as OCU students. Squadron Leader Bill Jelley's objective was to test the operational preparedness of his Squadron to operate away from the home comforts of Air Force Base Thornhill. I duly flew to Bulawayo on that noteworthy day with Chief Technician Doug Whyte for the start of 'Operation' *Knuckle*.

Operation Knuckle - Eight Vampire Jets – At Bulawayo Airport

Echelon Formation – Bill Jelley, Bill Buckle, Vic Cook, Bruce Smith, Prop Geldenhuys, Rich Beaver, Ted Lunt and Keith Corrans

Vampire Operational Conversion Unit instructional sorties were somewhat different to the Provost OCUs. The differences included low level battle with looping attacks - whereby the Vampire is flown over a supposedly opportunistic target. Then after a set time, pulling the aircraft into a looping manoeuvre, roll off the top / aileron turn, bring the gyro-gunsight to bear on the target in an air to ground profile - discharging the appropriate air weapon, and recovering at the safety height. From both the ground, and the air, looping attacks are quite spectacular. Whereas flying near or over the target one may lose the element of surprise, the initiative is retained by immediate attack with minimum time lapse to take offensive action. Additionally, Trojan FAC strikes, RP and 20mm FRAs were also part of the training syllabi.

The 8th September was a memorable day. The squadron fielded eight Vampires, led by Boss Jel, and with me as the No 5, we flew various flypast formations over the City of Bulawayo. A ground photographer captured our performances on film and I have a couple of treasured formations in my photo-album. A repeat farewell of eight Vampires was also flown on the day of our return to Thornhill on 11th September 1968.

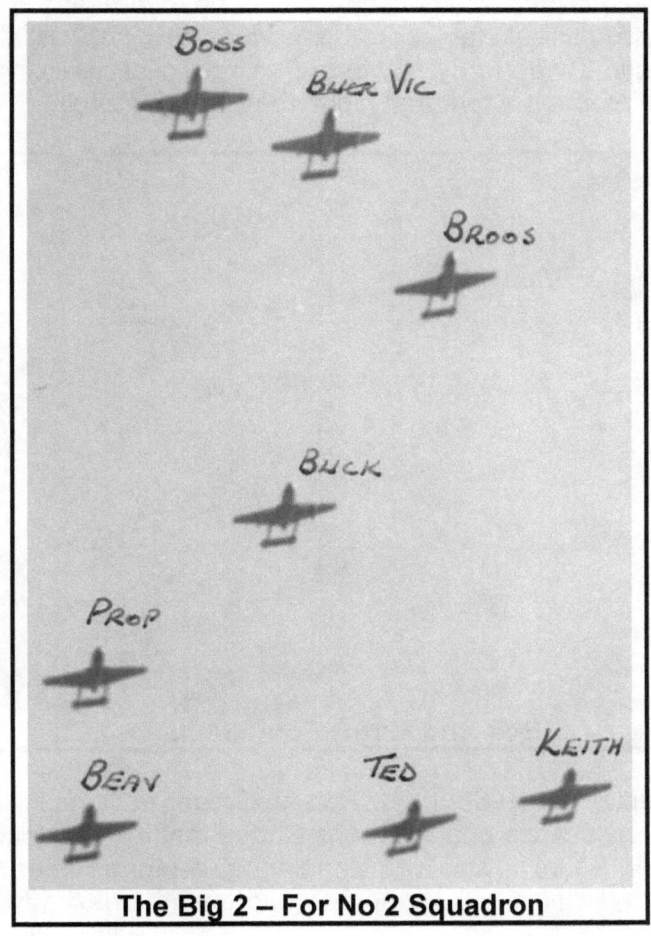

The Big 2 – For No 2 Squadron

At the end of the detachment, a dance was held in the tent across the road from the Control Tower. It was a good evening with many of the local dolly birds coming out to the airfield to join us. Bill Sykes recalls that during the evening he was introduced to a girl called Mary Ann. "What beautiful eyes you have," he said to her through his alcoholic haze. "Especially the left one – the right one can't stop looking at it." He married her six months later…

The Hunters flew down from Thornhill to join us in this social finale, and the aircraft were parked under the lights of the Control Tower. At night the Hunter looks particularly impressive with its beautiful lines and menacing aspect. Many of the pilots impressed their girlfriends by taking them up the tower to show them this wonderful steed that they flew. One genuine pilot (Rob McGregor), about to chat up his girl, was interrupted momentarily when he overheard one of the young technicians explaining to his partner how he was a pilot and how fantastic it was to fly Hunters. The real pilot, realising that the tech would probably score that night, retreated gracefully.

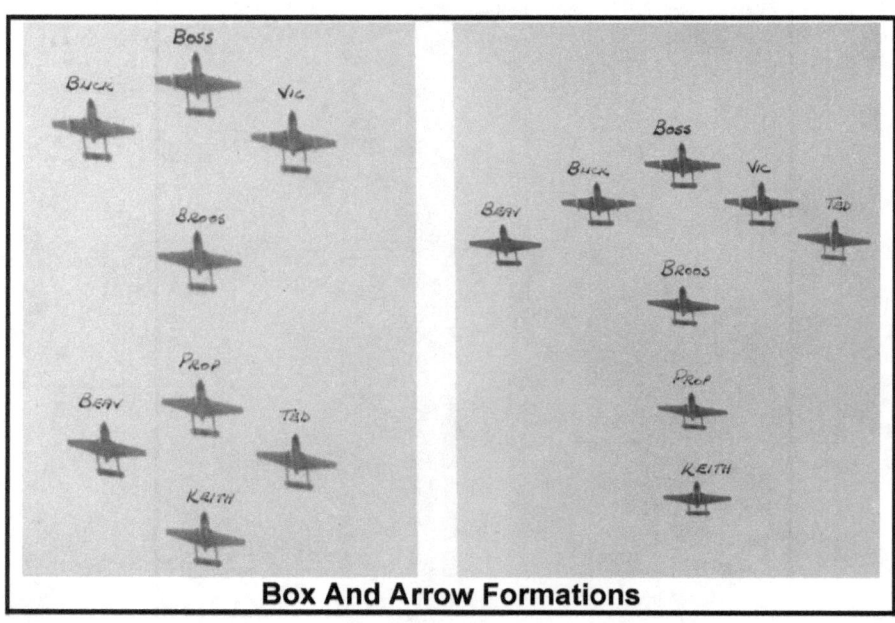

Box And Arrow Formations

On 19th September 1968, I flew Rob McGregor to Bumi Hills to carry out a reconnaissance of a Weapons Range that the Air Headquarters Staff Officer, Strike 1, and was planning to use for an Inter Squadron Competition (for Nos 1, 2, 4 and 5 Squadrons) the next day. Rob and

I thus had the advantage of briefing the other No 2 Squadron pilots regarding our "pre-view" the day before the actual competition took place.

We had no sooner returned from Operation *Knuckle* when, on 20th September we participated in the Inter-Squadron Competition as planned by Strike 1 and Tactical 1 at Air Force Headquarters. This entailed discharging air weaponry at bush targets in a remote area at Bumi Hills. My air-to-ground targets were attacked with four sorties of 2 x 60lb rockets. It was good counter-insurgency operational training to use foreign air-weapon ranges such as at Bumi Hills.

Another interesting incident during September 1968 concerned Pete Woolcock. Pete was flying Canberras and incurred the wrath of OC Flying Wing New Sarum, Wing Commander Ossie Penton. In "*Half a Century in Uniform*" Ossie Penton recalls "Peter Woolcock returned from the Chiredzi area with some high tension cable attached to the tail of his Canberra, a sure sign that he had been low flying. In fact to say that was flying excessively low would be the understatement of the year. It did prove the innate strength of the Canberra. I immediately slapped him under close arrest. His career in the Air Force survived the incident, after due punishment. He went on to become a first class chopper pilot and a valuable member of our team." A double-edged sword? I, for one, could commiserate with Peter, and suspect his promotion prospects were somewhat adversely affected. Many years later, Pete and Miss Ellie proved most enthusiastic leaders of the Natal Branch of the Air Forces Association.

Thereafter, I continued with OCU instruction for my two dedicated students, Bill Sykes and Chris Wentworth. However, other ad hoc students also included Rich Beaver, Bill Buckle and Ed Potterton. The odd normal squadron flying was also carried out with Pilot Officers Ted Lunt and Rob McGregor. On 26th September I carried out high altitude High Speed Stalls, followed by a night-stop jolly to Lourenço Marques (which was with Warrant Officer Johnson).

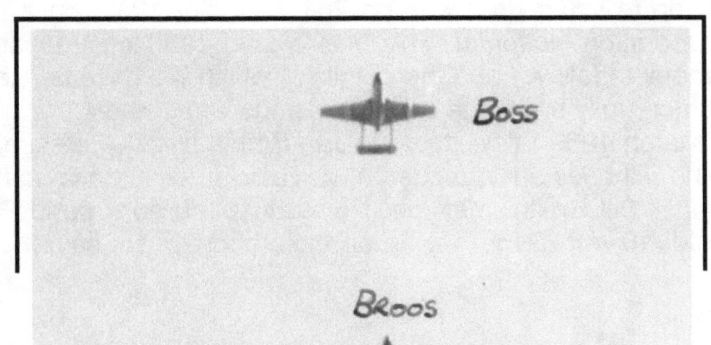

On 9th October 1968, it was my turn to check out Boss Jelley's instrument flying skills. As the IRE, I certified that he passed his Green Rating test with flying colours. IRTs were also flown with Flying Officers Vic Cook and Ed Paintin. October was almost entirely devoted to OCU Instruction.

On Independence Day, 11th November 1968, the new Rhodesian green and white flag was raised for the first time, and the Union Jack was lowered. Rhodesian balladeer John Edmond soon composed a folk song that became very popular, especially amongst the RLI. Although it was a very nostalgic moment in our history, especially with the BSAP band playing 'Abide in Me' when the flag I had served under was lowered for the last time. Had settlement been reached, the Union Jack would still have been displayed in a prominent position in a flag flying in Africa - instead of a Zimbabwe bird superimposed on a Marxist red star. Anyway, for me, it was a time to reflect on all the jollies that came my way, courtesy of the government.

The jollies outside Rhodesia were both business and pleasure. Analysis shows that I enjoyed some 90 days - three months outside the country at government expense. Beira and Waterkloof were the places most frequented - but the trips to Nampula in Northern Mozambique and Luanda in Angola were rather special.

WATERKLOOF - SOUTH AFRICA

One of our first trips to the SAAF base was on 4th and 5th July 1968 when a pair of Vampires 'mixed it' with SAAF Sabres and Mirages in interceptions, and then with our own Hunters on the return trip. I flew down with Flight Lieutenant Keith Corrans, and returned the next day with Rich Brand. We were fairly evenly matched against the Sabres, but had to employ different air-to-air combat tactics against the sub-sonic/super-sonic types. We could not out-turn the Sabres, but adopted 'circle of joy' i.e. maximum rate, minimum radius turn aerial tactics against the Mirages and Hunters.

My next trip to Waterkloof was on 28th February 1969; on a practice run for Operation *Hottentot*. This was a solo effort on Vampires, the start of many to follow - and the details of which will become clearer or covered more fully under the operation of the same name.

On 27th March 1969 I flew down to Jan Smuts by SAA dressed like a civvy. The Rhodesian Attaché in an official diplomatic car, Wing Commander Bill Smith, met me. I was chauffeured around Pretoria, drove into 10 Air Depot at Voortrekkerhoogte (to say 'Hi Dad'), escorted to the OKs to buy tropical fish in a plastic bag, and reported to Waterkloof for our Smersh dusk take-off for Thornhill and New Sarum in a 'no name brand' Vampire. As per prior planning, two Rhodesian Vampires had meanwhile arrived from Thornhill. After they had completed their turn-round, refuel etc, the Rhodesian Vampires started up and taxied out for a stream take-off - just like the routine I had performed a month earlier. I boarded this strange no number South African Vampire, started up in an out of sight hangar and taxied out to latch onto one of the Rhodesian aircraft. They carried out their normal stream take-off - but meanwhile, there were two additional foreign aircraft that remained latched on for close formation take-off. You guessed it. Jan Smuts Radar had witnessed two Vampires approach and land, - then saw two blips depart - whereas there was in fact now a total of *four* Vampires, with yours truly maintaining a tight close formation. More about the drama later on (like failing pressurisation, bloated tropical fish, radios that didn't work, night landings at Thornhill, night flight to New Sarum where the silver Vampires were turned into camouflaged aircraft like a chameleon).

My next trip to Waterkloof was made in Hunters, on 21st and 22nd September 1970. What made this flight interesting was that I was now able to adopt Mirage type techniques against the Sabre interceptions - when they got too close I simply stuffed the nose down and 'ran away to fight another day'. With the Mirages I might add, alas, we were at their mercy. The Air Traffic Controlled approach into Waterkloof, directly over Jan Smuts, meant flying with blinkers on, in view of the congested airspace.

Then it was back to Vampires. I flew into Waterkloof on 10th and 11th February 1971 for a night-stop. A month later, 12th March, was another Operation *Hottentot* visit, where two Rhodesian Vampires became four for the benefit of the initiated, but not for prying eyes.

Then on 7th April 1971, a day stop was carried out, followed by another Operation *Hottentot* mission on 15-16th July. Within a week I was back again, on 21st -22nd July for a proper jolly.

My next visit was a year later, on 13th June 1972, but this time flying Canberras, with my navigator Mike Ronne, on Operation *Junction*. This was followed up on 3rd November in the same year, primarily to uplift passengers Flight Lieutenant Bruce Collocott and Air Lieutenant Ken Burmeister.

Paddy Morgan was my new Navigator for my next Canberra sortie on the night-stop 3rd-4th May 1973. Eleven days later we were back again, this time to drop off pilot Rich Beaver and navigator Bernie Vaughan for the Doppler fit to a Canberra.

I returned to Waterkloof with Bernie Vaughan and Flight Sergeant Mo Houston on 18/19th June 1973 for Doppler trials.

BEIRA - MOCAMBIQUE

My first visit to Beira was with Varky Varkevisser in a Provost night-stop jolly on 20th - 21st October 1966. We took our fartsacks to kip at the beachside Estoril campsite. We were content to spend our allowances frequenting all the night-clubs, especially the notorious Moulin Rouge.

A year later I visited this popular seaside sin bin in a Vampire on 28th December 1967, on a so-called navex - navigational exercise. This, in reality was nothing more that stocking the Messes up with the cheap but necessary 'vino', Portuguese prawns and liqueurs, cashew nuts and other New Year relishes.

June 19th-20th was another enjoyable jolly to Beira with Senior Tech Colin Bedford. The Portuguese had a perfect cure for diarrhoea - a quick visit to the toilet before take-off would ensure instant constipation for days on end. The cause and effect warrants elaboration. 'Gippo-gut' (the self-inflicted type diarrhoea) was invariably the result of too much wine, or oily/greasy peri-peri chicken and /or too many beers. The effect was a running stomach with severe cramps, just before take-off. Somehow, the sanitation systems could not digest paper of any sort; especially the coarse newspaper popularised by non-reflective Portuguese. All forms of 'smudged' newsprint, rocks, leaves etc would litter a smelly corner in the confines of the 'shit-house'. The dreadful odours emanating from these bundles, upon entering Rhodesian nostrils had the effect of sending signals to the rectum to clam up. Instantly, the running stomach turns rock-hard, thus permitting a comfortably safe take-off and return flight for those aircrews whose exhaust valves had failed those only moments before their intended visit to the 'Pork' shit-house.

The next trip was on 6th December 1968 on a Vampire OCU for Acting Pilot Officer Chris Wentworth. This was a navigational jolly, landing Beira, and stocking up with cashew nuts, Bols liqueurs and returning to Thornhill.

The external navex on 18th February 1969 with Senior Technician Ron Janson was special in that the route was Thornhill to Vilanculos, then low level all along the coast, via Paradise Island, up to Beira for refuel, and return Thornhill. It is only the Pungwe River and Save River inlets that spoils and otherwise crystal clear sea shore. Coral appears black in colour when viewed from the air, whereas in reality the rainbow coral can only be appreciated in full when snorkelling. A revisit of my honeymoon stomping grounds brought back pleasant memories. I know that my passenger thoroughly enjoyed the privilege of sightseeing, which he would never have been able to experience otherwise.

The trip on Wednesday and Thursday 8/9th October 1969 was with Acting Pilot Officer Rob Dayton, an introvert back at base, but was a scream of an extrovert when let loose with a couple of Laurentina beers under his belt. Not only that, Rob had to learn the hard way that he was not to taunt the Portuguese police. After much persuasion we managed to spare him a night behind police cell bars, compared with experiencing the attractions that abound in the abundant 'other type bars' along the dockside.

Immediately after the weekend, on Monday 13th October I again visited Beira with my second OCU student, Giles Porter. After a repeat of the week before - except that Giles behaved more like an officer and gentleman - and a more subdued night-club visit, we flew back to Thornhill on the Tuesday.

For 20/21st October 1969 Beira navex night-stop, my third student Acting Pilot Officer Roy Hulley enjoyed his share of the forbidden fruits. The benefit for the PAI is having the pleasure of external jollies in quick succession; whereas squadron pilots could consider themselves fortunate to have just two jollies per year - should they be so lucky. For our ground crews they would only benefit once in a blue moon.

Beira was again visited on 20th April 1970, but this time while flying Hunters on No 1 Squadron. With the much higher speed the one and three-quarter hour solo sortie meant that a far greater length of coastline could be covered. The only snag is that the sights move past so much more quickly and it is not so easy to appreciate the scantily clad beauties sunbathing.

The next trip was in a different aircraft. I flew to Beira on 15th to 16th May 1972 in a Canberra, with Air Sub-Lieutenant 'Starry' Stevens as Navigator and Sergeant McCulloch as the squadron technician. This time our route was along the Zambezi to its delta then south along the coast into Beira. A threesome on a jolly always seem to add courage to do outlandish things, and additionally, the night take-off the following day allows a lot more time for sight-seeing. Our return trip to Salisbury was an Astro-Nav, via Kutanga Range to drop 4 x 130lb medium-level bombs, and landing some three hours twenty minutes from take-off.

The last trip to Beira was on a Forcex code named Black Jack from 5th to 6th June 1972. I flew with my regular navigator at that time, Mike Ronne. We had night-stopped at Kariba, and routed via the South African Roedewal air weapons range to drop one 130lb bomb, and flew all the way up the coast for our night-stop at Beira. The next morning we took off from Beira for one bombing run on Kutanga, landing back at Kariba. That same day we bombed a floating target on the Lake. Air Staff certainly had done their homework well on this Forcex, combining business with pleasure - all at the innocent taxpayer's expense.

LM - LOURENÇO MARQUES

My first jolly to Lourenço Marques (now Maputo) was in a Vampire, routing via Roedewal, on 30th September to 1st October 1968. This was a rather hairy experience. I was flying with Warrant Officer Johnson, with Vic Cook as leader. No sooner had we taken off than we entered cloud and didn't see the ground again until we were on short finals at LM. We were armed with 60lb rockets and had briefed for a standard stream take-off from Thornhill. That meant that I followed my leader about ten

Vic Cook

seconds after he started rolling. When we approached Messina, Vic reported that his radio compass wasn't picking up any beacons, and asked me to take over the lead. I duly complied, although I had only cursorily looked at our 'down' flight, since the plan was for Vic to lead us down, and I was planned to do the leading on the return journey. The weather reports indicated deteriorating conditions along our entire route.

We had climbed through 8/8ths cloud, with the cloud tops increasing in height the further south we flew. Overhead Roedewal, the Range Warden said that he could see gaps, but his 'gaps' and our 'gaps' didn't quite tie up. All I saw was a sea of cloud, and the little ground that flashed passed the odd gap gave no hint as to our exact position. If anything, we were even unsure of our position. The SAAF bombing range did not have any navigational aids, and our most reliable aid was my radio compass. I then elected, foolishly, to press on to Mozambique. This decision was prompted by the desire to make the most of our jolly to Lourenço Marques, and not waste valuable drinking time landing at Pietersburg to refuel.

By this stage the cloud tops had risen to 25,000ft and Vic had no option but to stick close to me for a formation NDB letdown. As we entered the cloud, it started getting dark, with intermittent rain, making formation flying rather challenging for my No 2. When I reached my 'break-off' altitude, I was still in cloud and had no ground visibility. I started to get worried between the outer and inner locator, because I knew I would hardly have sufficient fuel, should Vic lose me in the cloud, to try and find him for another letdown. The thought crossed my mind that both of us could be faced with the distinct possibility of flying out to sea to eject. And so, when I got to the inner locator, I adopted a shallow approach, took my eyes off the instrument panel, and glanced vertically down to where I expected the ground to appear at any moment - even for a forced belly landing on the airfield (if need be).

My gamble paid off. By looking down vertically, I could just see the ground. Unfortunately, I had drifted off the centre line and could not manage a straight in approach. Vic had got such a fright when he saw the ground that neither was he in a position to land straight away. We both peeled left for a low-level circuit and landing. Whilst taxiing in, the rain came down in buckets - so much so that the Control Tower was no longer visible from the ground. We remained in the aircraft for a good fifteen minutes for the rain to subside sufficiently for us to vacate the cockpits. The decision not to descend in the Transvaal was thus a good one, because had we arrived any later at Lourenço Marques, there would have been no ways that we would have made it. On my own it wasn't too bad, because I still had the use of my radio compass. However, Vic with no NDB was not in a position to get his aircraft down. I didn't relish going back to Boss Jelley minus two Vampires, never mind the crews. It was just as well that Vic stuck with me during all that cloud flying. Once safely on the ground, he confided in me that he did not like the idea of ejecting in the shark infested Indian Ocean, and there was no ways that he was going to lose me in all that cloud, with his unserviceable radio compass.

Vic made it up to us by treating the four guys to shellfish - the cheapskate. Having booked into the Polana, we headed downtown to seek the elusive lobster. We settled down to a couple of Laurentinas to whet the appetite. Vic called to the barman to produce his best lobster, who duly flopped down an arms-length specimen on the bar counter. Vic did a quick escudo calculation and didn't fancy the dent in his pocket. He then politely suggested a queen size, followed by a baby

lobster, which the barman also obliged with. Vic then wanted to view all the crayfish sizes, and I could sense the barman's "gat hare" becoming sticky. By now, it was quite a few beers later and we were not making much headway on the choice of either lobster or crayfish. The barman put Vic out of his misery by instructing his dishwasher to serve us with the customary prawn bar lunch. Bringing arms-length lobsters out for us to drool over had come to naught.
Our return journey was uneventful.

CAPE TOWN

Cape Town was visited on numerous occasions, about 14 days in total (including sojourns to Sandy Bay, the nude beach), all at the pleasure of the Air Force. Was this business or *Pleasure*? What a question. My first jolly was on Hunters, on 24th and 25th March 1970. I must admit being a bit nervous flying in at seven to nine miles a minute - not much time to appreciate the Cape beauty when one is approaching the populated southern tip of Africa after having just flown over miles upon miles of featureless Karoo desert.
My Hunter shopping trip with Boss Roy Morris on 9th and 10th December 1970 was somewhat painful. We walked from one end of Cape Town to the other, and back again, haggling over cents for the cheapest balloons, I ask you? My mind was on the pleasures of Sandy Bay, never mind those damned balloons for Mess decorations. To crown it all, we had no sooner stocked up with all the balloons that I could carry, when we found on return to our hotel that a shop round the corner sold balloons even cheaper. I never did hear the end of that story. My arms had grown - no, stretched by several centimetres with all the Cape Wine, crinkle paper, and those balloons that we had trekked all over town with.
The next jolly on 10th and 11th February 1972, in a Canberra with my navigator Mike Ronne and squadron tech Sergeant Ron Flaxman, was a lot more pleasurable than the preceding Hunter trip. For one, I didn't have to navigate, or lug fuel hoses around. The beauty of flying with a navigator also meant visiting more of the countryside - in this case routing via Hopefields bombing range to attack a 'foreign' target. Also, bringing along a squadron technician meant that the poor fellow would carry out most of the after-flight inspections, do the refuelling, and bedding the aircraft down for the night. Whilst the tech was busy, I had the unique opportunity of being shown around a SAAF Shackleton coastal defence aircraft. Its four huge World War II engines with contra-rotating propellers were something to behold. Although the

cockpit was somewhat cramped, the crew had quite a large cabin area to move around in. Once the Canberra was turned-around, we headed for town, Clifton Beach, nightclubs et al, before flying back to Salisbury late the following afternoon.

The 21st to 23rd November 1972 jolly, in a Canberra with Mike Ronne and Sergeant Mike Peake, was different in that our first night was spent in Port Elizabeth before continuing the next day to Cape Town. The highlight of this trip was being entertained by the naval types on SA Donkin, and then flying low-level along the coast all the way from Port Elizabeth to Cape Town. Our flight time to Port Elizabeth was just over three hours, but that included dropping two bombs on the Pietersburg's Roedewal Range. The SA Donkin is steeped in South African history, their Mess walls adorned with portraits of past Admirals, and the role that Coastal Command had contributed to South African defence. Naval traditions are possibly a lot more established than the much younger other arms of the Defence Forces. The other advantage of such a trip was all the free drinks that were dished out - saving our pockets for the pleasures of the Cape. We night-stopped at the posh Hotel Elizabeth, and then flew the one and a half-hours down to Cape Town. We didn't spot any shipwrecks, but marvelled at the beautiful sights en route. We made the most of our three days by returning via Kutanga for night bombing and landing back at Salisbury.

Our next three day jolly, from 29th to 31st May 1973, with Flight Lieutenant Doug 'Glob' Pasea and Senior Aircraftsman Mace in Canberra R 2155, got off to a bad start. We were loaded up with 6 x 130lb bombs which we dropped on three different targets and bombing ranges. After take-off from Salisbury, we headed to the Free State De Wet Range west of Bloemfontein for our first low-level bombing run, then climbed to medium level towards the west coast and dropped two bombs on Hopefields Bombing Range. The weather had started deteriorating with the approach of the Cape Doctor, and we just managed to land at the South African Air Force base at Langebaanweg when the drizzle set in. Glob and I were met by OC Flying Wing and were invited to a nice cup of hot coffee in his office. While enjoying our cuppa, OC Flying Wing pointed out to us that our nose wheeled Canberra was standing on its tail.

The inexperienced technician had started filling up our rear No 3 fuel tank first, instead of our forward fuselage No 1 and wing tanks. The centre of gravity had shifted rearwards causing the nose wheel to lift off the ground, and the tail striking the ground. Here I was, captain of the sinking ship, sipping coffee, while my poor old aircraftsman was dancing a jig, and my ship in a somewhat unusual attitude. Our first priority was to inspect for any structural damage, and then to carry out a balancing act to get the nose wheel back on to the ground, without pounding it into the nose cone. We couldn't decant the fuel from No 3 tank, so slowly started filling those the tech should have started with, and carefully manhandled the Canberra gently back onto its nose wheel. Having accomplished that, we quietly made sex our departure, sheepishly taking off from Langebaanweg with one massive, rather green looking king sized lobster for DF Malan International Airport at Cape Town. OC Flying Wing had kindly gifted me with the monster in order to pacify my embarrassment for my ineptitude in not correctly briefing my tech/cum passenger on the rudiments of Canberra refuelling technique.

Our twenty minute low-level trip down to Cape Town was uneventful. Except perhaps that this was once again at the pleasure of the generous taxpayer. To sight-see to ones heart content (with the navigator doing the entire map reading, leaving the pilot to do his own thing), plus two, not one, night-stops in the Mother City was a pleasure. My only problem was what to do with that large creepy crawly. The shellfish died a slow death in the Hotel's fridge.

Our trip back to Salisbury on 31st May was via the Kutanga Range for three medium-level bombing runs. By this time, the air freighted lobster had turned greener, and smellier. Rina took one look at the thing and chucked it in the dustbin.

My last jolly to the Cape from 6th to 8th November 1973 was a bit of a damp squib. I was flying Canberra R 2516 with my new navigator, Air Sub-Lieutenant Paddy Morgan, and my high powered passenger Air Commodore Dickie Bradshaw. He was one rank below the army equivalent of a 'General', and like three 1/c of the Air Force, reporting to the Air Vice-Marshal. We young bucks were certainly expected to behave like ambassadorial officers and gentleman - and be seen to avoid Clifton and Sandy Bay like the plague. I think the Air Commodore came along for the ride to see first hand what we were up to during the frequent jollies that the hard-pressed sanctioned Government was sponsoring. Anyway, my trip with Paddy went like clockwork. On this trip, Paddy and I dropped four bombs at Hopefields before landing at Langebaanweg. Instead of having a technician with us to do all the donkey work, I was forced to be seen to refuel the Canberra, while the South African Air Force base Station Commander whipped the Air Commodore away for tea and biscuits. I politely declined all offers of crayfish and / or lobster (I did not wish a dustbin burial), but obediently obliged to convey the soon to be 'vrot' fish for my lofty passenger.

After the aircraft turn-round, we got airborne again for the thirty-minute low level coastal flight to DF Malan in Cape Town. This was the start of our two night-stop visit, and we were expected to account for our whereabouts at all times. On our return flight on November the 8th, we were intercepted by SAAF Mirage fighters, - and were sitting ducks smiling for their ciné cameras. I suspect Air Commodore Dickie Bradshaw was impressed, how a plan comes together, with the good co-operation that was evident between the Rhodesian and South African Air Forces. Our return flight was all at high level; landing just after nightfall, so as to ensure his shellfish remained frozen as long as possible.

The memory that I treasure from my Air Force career is the experience of flying the whole coastline from Langebaan on the Atlantic, round Cape Point and then all the way up to the Tanzanian border on the Indian Ocean with most of the route being flown at low-level. The most beautiful beaches are along the northern and central Mozambique coastline. Not many pilots had that opportunity.

LUANDA, ANGOLA

The jolly to Luanda in a Canberra on 17th September 1973 was noteworthy in the sense that our squadron technician mistook a transvestite as a lady of the night. It was only when the poor fellow fondled the lady's goolies that he discovered that the play he was making was a he, and not a she. Our Portuguese host for the night had tipped my navigator, Glob Pasea and myself off to be on the lookout for these funny people - we then schemed that it was perhaps best for Sid Brown to learn the hard way.

Suffice it for me to add that the drive along the Luanda esplanade and the spit of land out to sea that forms the Luanda Bay is perhaps the most spectacular that I had seen along any coastline.

NAMPULA, MOCAMBIQUE

Nampula was a different kettle of fish, compared to Luanda. I visited this inland city in northern Moçambique about four times from 4th July 1973 to 2nd September 1973 on Operation *Polar*, and in view of the fact that these missions were more work than play; I've elected to cover these so-called jollies under Canberra photo-reconnaissance operations.

FORCED LANDING

I was tasked to carry out an Air Test on Vampire T 11 4207 on 28th November 1968. My logbook entry reads "Duty not carried out. Engine failure - forced landed". A filler cap circlip had found its way into the fuel system collector box, resulting in the fuel venting to atmosphere whilst flying inverted. It took me longer than the compulsory four seconds to roll the right side up; convert existing surplus speed to height/gliding speed; orientate myself following a bunting manoeuvre; and establish that the engine failure was not due to white metal bearing failure. And also switch on the FPI - fuel pressure emergency pump switch - within the regulatory four seconds.

Had it been white metal bearing failure, I was not about to chance a mid-air explosion by pumping fuel onto a red-hot turbine shaft. I had just completed the normal air test routine and was in the middle of throwing the aircraft around when the engine failed. I still recall my aerobatics sequence well. Having successfully completed a series of loops - with inverted aileron turns, I then dived down for increased speed. I pulled the Vampire vertically, rolled several times, steep stall turn, vertical dive, pulled the nose through the horizon, rolled inverted and commenced a bunt. A bunt is an inverted loop manoeuvre, all at negative 'g', as opposed to a loop which is positive 'g'.

The collector box holds sufficient fuel for fifteen seconds inverted flight. Before reaching that limitation, it was necessary for the pilot to execute positive 'g' in order to allow the collector box to fill up with fuel again before the next negative 'g' manoeuvre is attempted. Positive 'g' produces a black-out when all the blood drains from the eyeballs. Negative 'g' produces the opposite effect - the blood vessels in the eye distend, causing a red-out. Anyway, whilst pushing the control

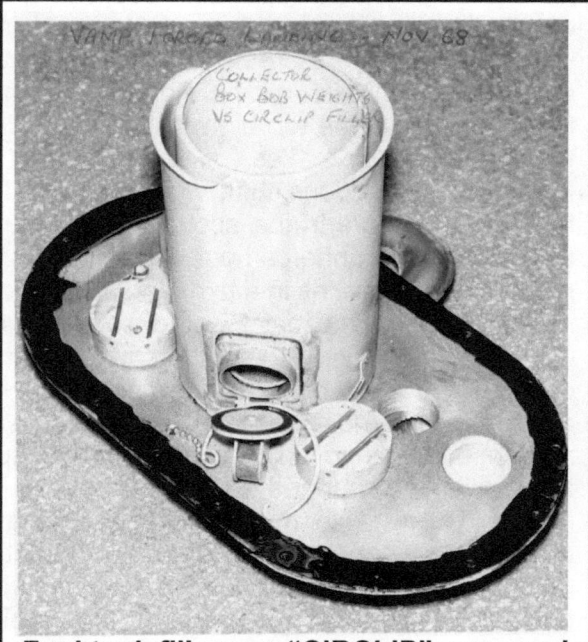

Fuel tank filler cap "CIRCLIP", wrapped around Collector Box bob-weight Valve that caused the jet-engine Flame-out

column forward in my inverted bunt manoeuvre, the Goblin jet engine conked out. I must admit I was somewhat disorientated after my vertical roll, and during the bunt I was pushing as much negative 'g' without redding-out, I didn't know my Arthur from my Martha. My first concern was to roll the Vampire right side up, convert speed to height and get my bearings before I called "Mayday, Mayday - PATCASATNIE." i.e. position and time, course and speed, altitude, type or nature of emergency, intentions and endurance. (Wow - I can still remember the emergency drill 40 years after having gone solo).

As it turned out, Gwenora Dam, which is right in the middle of the Provost general flying area, points in the direction of Thornhill. Because I was flying above the Provost area, I was able to determine rather quickly, that I had sufficient height to glide back to base. Since I wasn't sure of bearing failure, I isolated any fuel supply to the engine by pushing the LP Cock - low pressure fuel supply lever cum cock - to the fully closed position. (The HP Cock houses the re-light button, and is used for starting the Goblin jet engine, as well as for shutting down the engine). Anyway, I felt comfortable carrying out the flamed-out forced landing back at base because we had practised for this eventuality many a time during our pilot training. However, in the real live situation, errors creep in and the mistakes I made were quite embarrassing. Whilst gliding along downwind, I couldn't make up my mind whether I was too high or too low. I decided on the former and popped out my air brakes.

I had no sooner done that, when I realised I would have insufficient hydraulic pressure in the accumulator to pull the air brakes in again, and lower the undercarriage and flaps for landing. I immediately popped the air brakes in again, and started to panic when they failed to retract. This meant that I would now lose altitude more rapidly and would have insufficient height to carry out a copybook forced landing. I delayed lowering my undercarriage, which would also accelerate altitude loss. When the time came to lower my flaps, there was no response. My panic turned to fear - ending up on the ground in a heap. Instinctively, I changed hand and started pumping the emergency hydraulic lever with my right hand (the lever is spring-loaded and situated between the student and instructors ejection seats). This meant I was now flying the Vampire glider with my left, awkward hand, doing a left curved approach to the rapidly rising ground. I just managed to take up the hydraulic pressure slack, when my main wheels made contact with the runway - with wheels down, three greens, flaps down and - would you believe it - air brakes in. This was the classic case of "Where the rubber meets the tar". In other words, a near perfect powerless forced landing. I rolled to a stop with all the base's Fire Engines in tow. The "Well Done, Prop" from the Control Tower was certainly appreciated - but they did not know about the brown stain on my under-pants. I had no sooner got into the crew room than Bill Jelley gave me a grilling.

"Did you try the FPI switch?"
"No, Sir"
"Why not?"
"I was upside down."
"Did you try a re-light?"
"No, the LP Cock was off"
"Why did you turn off the LP?"
"Engine vibration, white metal failure"
"Why did you pop out air-brakes?"
"Kas-sweli - Angazi - Don't know – Khohliwe –Forgot – Foxtrot Uniform!"
"Did you reconsider re-light options?"
"No"

"Why not?"
"And stuff-up the forced landing, Sir?"
"Why is there a hole in your seat?"
"I was nipping straws."
"You must have exceeded inverted flight limitations?"
"I don't think so"
"Your brains were scrambled."
"I wasn't worried about the grey matter. I was more scared about the 'Please explain the skid marks on your underwear' to my wife."
The questions persisted for weeks on end, whereas I only had minutes to get my brown backside back on terra firma in one piece. I must admit, I was commended for not ejecting, (and thereby destroying any evidence). Rina contributed by offering me a spare nappy to supplement my flying kit. Renene was a mere three months old, and soiled nappies were easier options than under-rods with skid marks (Hey, Rina - I'm joking).
Some weeks later, despite the grilling, the technicians found the fuel filler cap spring-circlip wedged in the bob-weights of the fuel collector box. Had it not been for the thorough examination into the circumstances surrounding the flameout, we would never have known what caused the rapid fuel venting to atmosphere when I commenced that bunting manoeuvre. I was vindicated - I had not exceeded the inverted flight limitation of the Vampire. It remains a mystery even today, how such a large circlip found its way from the wing fuel tanks all along the various narrow pipe bends to the collector box. I trust some day, that my grandson Brendan will verify the facts when his other Grandpa, who was my Boss, confirms his having to concur with the investigation findings.
The facts remain, however, that I carried out a successful forced landing back at Thornhill, despite the flameout occurring at about 15,000 feet near Gwenora Dam.
The Vampire OCU instructional sorties for Rich Beaver, Ed Potterton and Chris Wentworth were wrapped up during December 1968. However, I also enjoyed a Trojan ride with Squadron Leader Peter Cooke during the month - on the 15th. I was his passenger on a flight from Thornhill to Filabuzi. It took us fifty minutes to get there - we landed (I can't remember what for), and returned the same day. Two days later Squadron Leader Keith Kemsley also flew me in a Trojan - but this time it was to Salisbury, and I suspect it was for a bush duty stint from 17th to 29th December 1968 - which meant I did not spend my daughter's first Christmas with her. The good news is that I actually

did spend old years eve with my family because I had flown a Vampire to Buffalo Range, landed there, proceeded on to Salisbury, and returned to Thornhill on the 30th. I believe my next bush tour was from 7th January to 5th February 1969.

MIXED TYPES

As a pilot attack instructor, it meant remaining proficient on jets as well as piston-engined aircraft. The Force needed to train pilots meaning that I had

Vampire T11 leading a box formation of Provost Mk 52 aircraft

the unique opportunity to fly with a large cross section of pilots and students. An instructor's reward is the satisfaction of following the fruits of his labours, and to note the career advancements of his students.

Flying mixed types prompted me to review my flying log, and to list alphabetically, those pilots who, I trust benefited from the skills that the Air Force had bestowed upon me. The student that impressed me most was undoubtedly Chris Wentworth. He had near natural flying ability - his rolling manoeuvres, in particular, were better than I was able to execute. It is also perhaps coincidental that my path crossed Richard Beaver's with monotonous regularity. Nay, not monotonous, but a real privilege. In fact so much so, that the Beaver's became life long friends - Rina and I became their son Warrick's godparents. Renene and Pey basically grew up with Warrick and Trish.

The list below tells a story.

Provost

APO John Bennie - Sep 65
Flt Lt Rich Brand - Sep 69

APO Bill Buckle - Oct 65 & Feb 69
Flg Off Vic Cook - Feb 69
Flt Lt Graham Cronshaw - May 69
Flg Off Rick Culpan - May 69
APO Blake Few - Oct 65

Flg Off Harold Griffiths - Aug 65
Sqn Ldr Tol Janeke - Apr 69
Flt Lt Bill Jelley - Jul 66
Plt Off Terry Jones - Mar 67
APO Ken Law - Aug 66
Flt Lt Pat Meddows-Taylor - Aug 65 & Apr 67
Plt Off Mark McLean - Oct 65 to Apr 66
ASL Brian Murdoch - Feb to Mar 71
ASL Dick Paxton - Mar 71
Plt Off Ed Potterton - Feb 69
APO Derrick Rainey - Aug 65
Flg Off Hugh Slatter - Aug 65
Flt Lt Bruce Smith - Mar 69
Plt Off Bill Sykes - Feb 69
Flt Lt Rob Tasker - Aug 65
APO Tudor Thomas - Aug 66
Flt Lt Cyril White - Jun 69
APO Chris Weinmann - Aug 65
Air Lt Alf Wild - Mar 71

Flg Off Pete Woolcock - Dec 66

Vampire

ASL Baldwin- Aug to Nov 71
APO Trevor Baynham -Oct 69
Plt Off Rich Beaver - Aug 68
APO John Blythe-wood- Aug 69
Flt Lt Rich Brand - Apr to Jul 68
Flg Off Bill Buckle - Oct 68 & Feb 69
Air Lt John Carhart - May to Jul 71
Flg Off Vic Cook - Jun 68 & Jun 69
ASL Vic Culpan - Aug to Nov 71
APO Rob Dayton - Aug to Nov 69
APO Spook Geraty - Aug 69 to Aug 71
ASL Barry Heard (†) - Jun to Aug 71
APO Roy Hulley (†) - Aug to Nov 69
Flg Off Guy Jackson - Feb 69
Sqn Ldr Bill Jelley - Sep to Oct 68
Plt Off Ted Lunt - Sep 68
Flt Lt Mark McLean - Mar 71
Flg Off Mike Mulligan -Jun 69
APO Brian Murdoch (†) - Nov 69 & Jul 71
APO Ed Paintin - Oct 68
APO Dick Paxton - Sep to Nov 69
APO Giles Porter - Aug to Nov 69
APO Ed Potterton - Sep 68
Flg Off Bruce Smith - Aug 68 & Mar 69
Air Lt Jim Stagman - Aug 71
ASL Danny Svoboda - Jul to Sep 71
APO Bill Sykes - Aug 68 & Jul 71
ASL Greg Todd - Aug 71
APO Roger Watt - Aug to Oct 69
Air Lt Chris Weinmann (†)- Jan to Apr 71
APO Chris Wentworth - Aug 68

Over four hundred hours were flown on Pilot Attack Instruction. I was thus instrumental in the specialist weapons instruction for quite a few Air Force pilots. Regrettably those with the death cross (†) did not survive the Bush War. Barry was killed in a sports car accident. Roy was killed in a Vampire flying accident on Kutanga Range. Brian was killed on active service whilst on a night casevac in a Trojan and Chris was killed in action, also in a Trojan, whilst flying with Pat Durrett (shot down in Mozambique).

Take note - I even instructed my superior - Flight Lieutenant Jelley on Provosts, and also as a Squadron Leader, on Vampires. Some ex-students that did well were:-

Hugh Slatter - to Air Vice-Marshal (Chief of Staff)
Graham Cronshaw - Group Captain (Director Operations)
Bill Sykes - Group Captain (Director Admin and Director Operations)
Alf Wild – Wing Commander (Officer Commanding Flying Wing, Thornhill)
Ted Lunt and Ed Potterton - Squadron Leaders (both as OC No 7 Squadron)

Additionally, as the Squadron IRE it was my responsibility to carry out the instrument rating tests, and I am pleased to record those pilots that were rated by me, as follows:-

On the Provost:

Master Green Ratings: -Flt Lt Meddows-Taylor '66, Flt Lt Tasker '67 and Sqn Ldr Jelley '67
Green Ratings:- Sqn Ldr Edwards '66; Flt Lt Varkevisser '66, Flt Lt Vass '66; Flg Off Griffiths '67; Flg Off Buckle '69; Plt Off Beaver '69 and Flg Off Jones '69
White Ratings:- APO Law '66, Plt Off Weinmann '66, Plt Off Buckle '66, Plt Off Bennie '66 Plt Off Potterton '69

On the Vampire:

Master Green Ratings: - Flt Lt Brand '69; Flg Off Northcroft '69; Flt Lt Smith '69
Green Ratings:-Sqn Ldr Jelley October '68, Flg Off Cook '68; Flg Off Jackson '69; Flt Lt Brand '69; Flg Off Beaver '69; Flt Lt Smith '69; Flg Off Mulligan '69; Plt Off Sykes '69; Flt Lt Dixon '71; Air Lt Carhart '71; Air Lt Stagman '71; Air Lt Potterton '71; ASL Geraty '71; Air Lt Hulley '71 and Air Lt Murdoch '71.

White Ratings:-APO Sykes '68; APO Geraty '69; APO Murdoch '69, APO Blythe-wood '69; APO Dayton "69, APO Hulley '69; APO Watt '69; APO Paxton '69; APO Baynham '69; APO Porter '69; Air Lt Weinmann '71; ASL Wentworth '71; ASL Heard '71; ASL Oakley '71; ASL Murray '71 ASL Simmonds '71; ASL Litson '71; ASL S Baldwin '71; ASL Culpan '71; ASL Todd '71; ASL Paxton '71 ASL Svoboda '71 and Air Lt Hulley '71

On Canberras

Master Green Ratings: - Flt Lt Donaldson '73 &'74; Sqn Ldr Janeke '73 and Sqn Ldr du Rand '73
Green Ratings: - Flt Lt Bennie '73 &'74; Flt Lt I Donaldson '73; Sqn Ldr du Rand '73; Flt Lt Culpan '73 and ASL Delport '74
White Ratings; - ASL Delport '73

February 1969 was an extremely busy month. I had returned from a month's bush duty on the 5th. Then Bill Jelley checked out my Vampire instrument flying the next day; George Wrigley gave me my Provost re-familiarisation on the 13th, followed by three Provost sorties on the trot with Bill Jelley, a trip to Beira, via Vilanculos in Mozambique and topped off with a Kutanga Weapons Detachment. I flew eight sorties on the 20th (my 26th birthday), led a flypast of five Provosts for the Minister of Defence visit to Thornhill (the next day), and carried out one of many Operation *Hottentot* sorties on the 28th. Having six sorties in one month with the Boss was highly irregular. I logged 35.15 hours for the month - an unusually high amount of flying for a jet-jock.
March 1969, like the month before, was just as busy, split fairly evenly between Provost and Vampire flying. The duties consisted of mainly Vampire frantan profile bombing trials, air test flights, weapons instruction, border reconnaissance, Operation *Hottentot* (Waterkloof, South Africa), and a Barrier Engagement.

BARRIER ENGAGEMENT

I also have the dubious pleasure of running out of runway, to be 'Arrested' by the Arrester Barrier. This is a netted contraption at the end of Runway 13 at Thornhill. My excuse was plausible. I was tasked on 22nd March 1969 to conduct an Air Test on Vampire 4120 - which, if my memory serves me correct, was one of those funny Vampires that we Rhodesians had inherited from the South Africans in our Sanctions

Busting spree. Anyway, on this particular day, I had no option but to call "Barrier. Barrier." to the Air Traffic Controller, who promptly raised the nylon netting. I thus experienced what few pilots can claim, as saving the aircraft from substantial structural damage, by using external means of stopping a jet aircraft on the runway. I presume my need arose as a result of mechanical failure on the test flight when the brakes failed.

OPERATION HOTTENTOT - 28 FEBRUARY 1969 to 16 JULY 1971

Operation *Hottentot* was a classical case of Rhodesian Sanctions Busting of historical significance. On 15th December 1968 Squadron Leader Peter Cooke (my ex-Boss on No 4 Squadron) flew me in Trojan R3248 from Thornhill to Filabusi and return. We landed there, and I was able to enjoy the Trog, albeit as a passenger for the fifty minutes that the trip took. I was impressed with the aircraft's short landing capability, but its long take-off run was somewhat disappointing. A couple of days later, on the 17th, Squadron Leader Keith Kemsley flew me in a Trojan to Salisbury for one of those Field Force Bush Trips, up until just before the new year, 29th December 1968.

After a somewhat long delay, I next flew with Boss Jelley in a Vampire on 6th February 1969. He was my safety pilot for a QGH and four GCAs. Later in the month, on the 13th, we again crewed up, but this time in a Provost R 3609, for an enjoyable fifty-minute general and low-flying sortie. The next day we both flew out to the Range, where I dropped him off to do Range Safety Officer duties. I duly completed my solo 100 x ·303 front gunnery and 4 x 20lb shallow glide bombing (frantan profile). I landed, uplifted the Boss and returned to base. Three days later, on 17th February, Boss Jelley joined me in a Provost for a repeat, except this time it was a dual sortie with us firing our 100 rounds and dropping eight bombs on shallow glide bombing.

On 25th February 1969 Bill Jelley and I carried out low-level bombing trials in a Vampire. We dropped eight bombs and followed this up with another eight on 3rd March. What was significant about this sortie is that the trials were "frantan profile", and secondly, this was the second last time he and I flew together as co-pilots on the same squadron - he was posted shortly thereafter. Just as well, because I had my barrier engagement four weeks later. My next sortie with Bill Jelley would be February 1971.

I had another sortie with Squadron Leader Peter Cooke, ex Operation *Hottentot*, on 29th March, when he returned me to Thornhill in a Trojan, after I had flown another Smersh SAAF acquired Vampire to New Sarum.

By way of general historical interest, it was on 21st July 1969, that American astronaut Neil Armstrong became the first man to walk on the moon. Everybody was glued to his or her television sets to witness this scientific marvel. Neil Armstrong broadcast his historical words "Tranquillity Base here. The Eagle has landed." The headlines flashed throughout the world – "Man Walks On The Moon – A small step for man, a leap for mankind". The event made a lasting impression on me, and I was indeed very fortunate to visit the Kennedy Space Centre in Florida many years later, and relive the experience as played by the Americans, as only they would, in their Saturn IV facility. Masonite sent me to the States in February 2000 on business, and permitted me to visit the Space Centre, as well as the National Warplane Museum in Elmira in New York State.

No 2 Squadron Staff Pilots – March 1969

As a matter of historical interest I also wish to record that Varky Varkevisser brought in two Vampires T.55's on 12/13th December 1972 – and flew another three Operation *Hottentot* sorties between 17th to 21st January 1973. Whilst my own last sanctions busting sortie was on 16thJuly 1971, it will be noted that Op *Hottentot* carried on for quite a while. Winston Brent published his *"Rhodesian Air Force – The Sanctions Busters"* in 2001, with foreword by retired Air Vice Marshal Chris Dams, and does justice to the Sanctions Busting episodes of the Air Force.

Vic Cook was tragically killed in a helicopter flying accident many years after having left the Air Force. He was a hero and the incident that I recall was when he was shot down on Pey's birthday, 22nd December 1976, while flying with Sergeant Mike Upton. Mike was badly injured in the crash and Vic dragged him to safety by which time the terrorists were upon them. Vic rushed the one terrorist, wrestled his AK off the gook and killed him with his own weapon. Vic took up a defensive position until both he and Upton was hoisted to safety. I am not too clear on the circumstances surrounding his subsequent death, but it involved checking and cleaning Eskom power lines. It is believed his tail rotor got snagged on cables and the helicopter crashed to the ground, killing a highly respected airman. Then many years later, Peter Woolcock arranged for me to meet Anne Lindsay, the lady who was Vic's constant companion for something like 14 years. It was a humbling meeting.

THE DEMISE OF PROVOST T Mk 52 R 3036 JULY 1969

My first sortie in R3036, or RRAF 303 as it was earlier numbered, was on 11th May 1962 with Flying Officer Pat Niemand, as my air experience of what lay in store for my flying career. On 23rd July 1962 on commencement of Basic Flying School (BFS) I was allocated to Flying Officer Peter Petter-Bowyer and had my first formal instructional lesson on RRAF 303.

Then exactly seven years later, to the day, on 23rd July 1969, with me as captain, Provost R 3036 died by fire. But a little about this particular sortie later on - first, a little more about its past history. Hunting Percival Provost T Mk 52 had its beginnings in the United Kingdom with a construction number PAC/F/177 and allocated Royal Air Force number WV 648. It started its journey to Rhodesia with three other Provosts among the first batch to be delivered to the Rhodesian Air Force. The aircraft was delivered on 4th November 1954 having been ferried out from the UK - taking 42 flying hours over eleven days, from Benson to Salisbury. Landings were at Dijon, Istres, Cagliari, El Alouina, Tunis, Tripoli, Marble Arch, Benghazi, Benina, Tobruk, El Adem, Cairo, Favid, Luxor, Wadi Halfa, Khartoum, Malakal, Juba, Entebbe, Tabora, Kasama and Ndola. The last leg was to Salisbury.

RAF serial VV 648 was delivered as SR 139 on 4th November 1954 but changed shortly thereafter to RRAF 303 as the title of the Air Force had changed from Southern Rhodesia Air Force to Royal Rhodesian Air Force. In March 1962 a further change in serial number took place, numbering it R 303. A final change occurred in March 1968 to R 3036 - which was an ingenious use of the old RRAF serial with the Squadron number being placed in a certain pattern to give a 4 digit serial - so as to convey a "random" effect and thereby confuse the enemy post UDI.

With the demise of the aircraft, I felt compelled to carry out research into some of the more significant sorties flown with R303 / R3036 - these included: -

R303 was the first aircraft flown on OCU on 15th July 1963, also with Peter Petter-Bowyer. R303 was the first aircraft used as a deadly weapon when 100 x ·303 rounds were fired in my first air-to- ground sortie with Squadron Leader Ted Brent on 9th September 1963 (only 37 rounds hit the target).

Whilst on a Pilot Attack Instructors - PAI - course I sustained a scaiphoid fracture playing rugby on a Natal Tour. Flight Lieutenant Varky Varkevisser had to check me out whether to scrub me from the course with my left hand in plaster. During the tricky level and high quarter attacks old faithful R303 again pulled me through.

I flew Old Faithful on Ex Aurora and Army FAC sorties. Prior to my posting to No 2 Squadron Vampires, my last sortie on No 4 Squadron Provosts was with R303 on 22nd September 1967 with Acting Pilot Officer Rich Beaver, on an OCU instructional sortie.

On 1st April 1969 I instructed Pilot Officer Bill Sykes on night flying single line flares with Provost R 3036 whilst on No 2 Squadron. Other pupils or second pilots included Flight Lieutenants Cyril White, Bruce Smith, Graham Cronshaw, Flying Officer Rick Culpan and Pilot Officer Ed Potterton. It was on my 115th sortie on 23rd July 1969 that the Frantan hang-up exploded beneath the Provost R 3036, destroying the aircraft.

When Renene reads this, I can visualise her saying "Typical Dad - he keeps us in suspense or he tells a story the long way round." - Well Askoek, if you're smart I'll expect you to take the short cut and go straight to the next paragraph.

Anyway, on 23rd July 1969, I was instructing Cyril White on frantan bombing (frantan = frangible tanks = napalm type bombs), but experienced a hang-up with our port frantan. We unsuccessfully tried to jettison the bomb on Kutanga Range and returned to Thornhill air base where we carried out a heavy roller landing to shake off the hang-up. But it was all to no avail. We then taxied back to the hardstanding to carry out the engine run down. As captain and instructor, I was seated on the right and was not aware that the armourers had already started to manually release the hang-up below the port wing.

Bob Breakwell, Steve Stead and Ian Flemming were cradling the frantan, when they either dropped it on the ground or inadvertently set off the detonator. It exploded and Bob took the full force of the lighted gel. "Flamo' and Steve were a little more protected by the position in which they were standing and only suffered minor burns.

My immediate emergency action was to stretch out my arms to switch off the fuel cock and magnetos. The propeller caused the flames to engulf the cockpit and Cyril promptly clambered over me to make good his escape on the starboard side. I was momentarily pinned down and still had to release the aircraft brakes so that the ground crews could wheel the burning aircraft away from other nearby aircraft. The captain abandons the ship last and I was fortunate to escape with only singed eyebrows and a gouge on my knee.

Master Sergeant C J McIntyre kept a cool head and went to Bob's immediate assistance. Bob caught the full force of the frantan explosion, and despite the aircraft catching alight and also burning furiously, had the presence of mind to throw his body over that of Bob, thereby helping to douse the flames from the deadly frantan jelly. He was commended for his actions.

A twist to this whole saga occurred immediately after the explosion – Station Sick Quarters were informed within ten seconds and sent an ambulance straightway to the squadron to attend to Bob. The ambulance did not arrive. Bob was lying on the tarmac, obviously in great pain and all he needed immediately was a hefty pain killer. The squadron phoned Sick Quarters and asked them what the H… they were doing and were told that the situation was in hand and the patient was being attended to. They had actually intercepted Flamo on his way down to SSQ, had picked him up and taken care of him. The ambulance was told to get back to the squadron post haste. When it did not arrive the second time there were angry words. SSQ explained that they had now got it all under control and picked up the real patient, as he too had made his way down to get treatment and had been uplifted. It took nearly twenty minutes for them to finally get to Bob. It was nobody" fault really but tempers were running high.

That evening Rina asked me what the TV news was all about and only then did she notice that I had no eyebrows left. Poor old Bob Breakwell was so badly burnt that he required extensive skin grafts over many months but the medics were not able to replace his missing ears or repair the scar damage to his face. Armourers Steve Stead and Ian Flamo Flemming were much more fortunate (the latter in fact was killed in action as a K-Car Air Gunner on 12th January 1978 - I would like to think that he inherited the nickname Flamo from the demise of Provost R 3036).

At the Board of Inquiry it was established that the detonator had been manufactured incorrectly and the pin that set the whole explosion train in action was too long. It protruded just past the safety mark and had thus set off the charge. All detonators were subsequently examined and a number were found to have the same fault. Also, the Board were interested in exactly how the Tower/Fire Section had been alerted so quickly after the explosion —exactly one second in fact. The answer emerged slowly as they quizzed the people involved. I had parked the Provost right in front of the squadron, literally with the wing tip ten feet from the crew room door. The telephone was positioned at the door and Bill Sykes just happened to be on the phone to the Tower at the time. Don Ogilvy who was on the other end of the phone heard the expletive, looked up and saw a ball of flame and smoke rising from next to No 2 Squadron, and hit the emergency fire button. So the fire section knew within a second and reacted accordingly.

I thus have the dubious honour of featuring in W.A. Brent's 1987 edition 'Rhodesian Air Force, A Brief History 1947 - 1980'. (But according to my logbook it was Provost 3036 and not 3609. I subsequently flew Provost 3609 on 8th February and 17th March 1971).

On 24th July 1969, I dropped 8 x 20lb frag bombs in a Provost high dive bombing demonstration for a Rhodesian Army and South African Defence Force COIN Course. The course was conducted at the School of Infantry, Gwelo - and the Brownjobs went out to Kutanga for the live weapons demonstration. Co-operation between the two countries was excellent, and we Bluejobs were only too willing to cement the bonds between the 'Hairy backs' (also sometimes called 'hairy-legs' or 'Rock spiders'), Browns and the 'Slopes'.

Later that same day I flew Rich Beaver up to Salisbury, dropped him off, and returned to Thornhill.

Mike Mulligan, Bruce Smith, Sqn Ldr Tol Janeke, Rich Brand and Prop Geldenhuys

LLEWELLIN, 6 AUGUST 1969

There is a twist in this tale of Llewellin. The weekend before, my sister Delene and her husband invited Rina and I to a night out at the Jameson Hotel. Several Hartley farmers had received free accommodation at the Hotel for the weekend, and as one couple couldn't make it, we took up the spare reservation. My contribution was a bottle of Portuguese Cherry liqueur but passing the bottle around for sippers got the better of me, resulting in me hurling my second hand carrot supper down the toilet bowl. Unfortunately my false teeth followed suit and I had to fish for the broken pieces amongst all the detritus. Because it was Sunday, there was no chance of a quick repair at a Dentist. And so a 'Boer maak a plan' with glue and sticky-tape.

I used Araldite - a type of super glue commonly used by the Air Force to lock tight any joints subjected to high vibration. I reckoned that if Araldite was good enough for the Air Force, it certainly was good enough for my false teeth. After gluing the pieces together, and waiting for it to set, I sat down and started to read the pamphlet in the box.

The label mentioned that heat treatment would accelerate curing - so I stuck my teeth into the oven, turned up the knob, and sat down to watch TV. After a while I realised that I had forgotten to check up on the heat-treated curing. and duly forgot about them. By the time I retrieved the mess, the plate had sagged and the false teeth were now completely out of shape. In order to try and get the form right again, I stuck the false teeth back into my mouth in an endeavour to regain its original shape. The only thing I achieved was scalded gums - with very loose fitting false teeth that kept on falling down every time I spoke for any length of time.

And so it came to pass that on the 6th August 1969 I was tasked to carry out 'recco flare' demonstrations for a Territorial Force Battalion at Llewellin. I duly flew down to Bulawayo with Senior Technician Cliff Tyson. Then at Llewellin I was required to brief the TF Company on the flare specifications, and its uses at night. When dropped from the aircraft, a parachute deploys and the ignited flare produces 600,000-candle power light as it descends slowly to earth. During my brief, my false teeth kept on falling out, bringing howls of laughter from the assembled Brownjobs. Anyway, Cliff armed up the Provost with the 4 x 4inch recco flares, which I dropped over Llewellin Barracks as planned. I was somewhat relieved to get back to Thornhill, mainly because of my rather embarrassing moments in front of such a large audience.

I still needed to wait a couple of days before the Dentist could fit me with a decent replacement. And all these hassles just because the Portuguese Cherries did not agree with my constitution, or perhaps it was a case of low threshold for cheap liqueurs.

I believe Rina, and even Delene can relate to this story, and do more justice to the juicier parts of the tale. On a different but appropriate tack, Llewellin Barracks was also home to Rina's younger brother Frans Malan who had been called up to do his national service. He wrote me to say he joined A Company, 3 Platoon, No 103 Intake, Llewellin Barracks, Bulawayo from early April 1969 to the beginning of September, then 2 Independent Company, Kariba until 12th December, 1969. His wife

Frans Malan

Kleinding, kept all his love letters to her during the above period and reading through them it is clear that the Government sponsored compulsory Army holiday was approached with great reluctance and trepidation. Looking back on it now the fact that you had someone at home who really cared about you created the best survival mode and Frans remain eternally grateful to her, particularly in the latter stages of the bush war when he was away from home for extended periods.

Frans advanced rapidly, and justifiably so, through the ranks. From Lance Corporal to Sergeant, then to Sergeant Major, followed thereafter to Lieutenant and then to Captain. From the nonchalant days of border control to the deadly serious business of fighting a fully fledged bush war where Frans became, in reality, a soldier and a part time banker without any real say in his preferred "career" choice.

Frans recalls: "Border control days patrolling from near Makuti down the escarpment following the dry river bed of the Shire River. Accompanying our stick of four was a local tracker lent to us by the Police in Kariba who had a very good knowledge of the local conditions but was petrified of elephants and rhinoceros. The first night I chose to sleep on an island in the dry river bed with beautiful big trees providing excellent cover and the surrounding white sand gave a very good field of vision. After eating, a guard roster was set up and it being a full moon that night it was great being in "darkest Africa". I was awoken sometime during the night with the tracker straddling me and violently shaking me, screaming "Nzhou, Nzhou!" and a large elephant bull feeding from the branches above my head. I still do not know who got the biggest fright, me or the elephant but it must have been the elephant because he moved away. Looking across the white sand of the riverbed in full moon light was a herd of at least fifty elephant almost ghostly as they seemed to float across the sand with no noise - a truly magnificent sight.

"At the mouth of the gorge I picked a re-entrant on which to walk up the escarpment from the valley floor and about half way up this steep climb all hell broke loose with a big dagga boy buffalo bull crashing through the undergrowth and stopping no more than five paces directly in front of me. For a tense couple of moments we looked at each other, me over the top of a fully loaded FN with the safety catch off. In the re-entrant with steep sides space was somewhat restricted. The buffalo took off diagonally across the front of me and the rest of the stick and had not run more than five paces when he tripped on the loose rocks in the river bed and went crashing head first into a large boulder. Staggering to his feet with blood pouring from his nose he made a dash for freedom behind us only to trip again going head first into a tree stump so hard that he landed on his back. Struggling to his feet with a lot of blood now pouring from his nose he managed to get away from us up the side of the riverbed. Not a single word was uttered by any one of us during the show which all happened between two and five paces from us, but each guy followed the buffalo's movements over the barrel of his rifle. Close encounters of the wild kind."

RP MASTER CATEGORY

On 24th September 1969 weapons categorisation was determined by carrying out first run attacks. Split over three different sorties and firing a total of 150 x 20mm ball cannon, and eight rockets, I did particularly well. Over the 3 x FRAs and my eight rockets, I managed to score five DHs - Direct Hits. That is, five out of eight rockets being right on target. This achievement earned me a "Master" Category in rocket firing. My gunnery was not quite up to the same standard, but I was very satisfied with my "A" Category. Also, by the same token, as the Squadron PAI, the pressure was always there to perform well. However, as previously mentioned, the Vampire was an excellent weapons platform - and providing the right information was fed into the Gyro-gunsight, good scores would invariably be the just reward.

JOLLY OCTOBER

The Jolly October refers to the perks of the job during Operational Conversion Unit flying training, which permitted three external flights in quick succession. Because I had three students in Rob Dayton, Giles Porter and Roy Hulley, I was able to fly in to Beira on 8th, 13th and 20th October 1969. Although I have told the story under the Beira side heading, it warrants mentioning that these privileges seldom happen with three jollies on the trot - especially all in one month.
Most squadron pilots would expect at least one, possibly two, away trips during the course of a year. A lot of the Squadron Technicians would seldom enjoy the fruits of visiting far off places – and when the spare seat was taken up by an OCU student, their chances diminished further. But being one of the instructors – and especially having three students to boot meant that I could frequent the pleasures of a favourite seaside resort more often than most. In order to get the most out of the jollies; one would visit as many of the haunts as possible. Some were good – others not so good. Being

away from base meant one could really let ones hair down, and really enjoy the night life famous for their popularity for tourists and foreigners.

EXERCISE IRISH STEW 28 OCTOBER - 2 NOVEMBER 1969

See also Bill Sykes and Jim Stagmans reports in my Operations, with Air Strike Log book for fascinating reporting. Bruce Smith and I had also flown to the Range, and landed amidst all the excitement with Jim and Polly having gone down. Trojans were also scrambled in order to get bearings on the Canberra transmissions. On 30th October, the Vampires flew to Bumi Hills and return to Vic Falls. The next day we were tasked to Bulawayo and Thornhill for arming up with live ammunition. And so, on 1st November I carried out an airstrike with 1 x 60lb squashhead rocket and fired 120 x 20mm high explosive incendiary cannon. A second armed sortie was flown, this time with 2 x 60lb squashheads and 60 x 20mm HEI.
Exercise *Irish Stew* ended with my return from Victoria Falls on 2nd November to Thornhill. The rest of November 1969 was spent on OCU training for my regular students Rob Dayton, Roy Hulley and Giles Porter. Other students also included Brian Murdoch and Dick Paxton, plus IRTs for Bill Sykes and Bruce Smith (Bruce died from a heart attack in March 2001).
My last sortie on Vampires before my posting to No 1 Squadron happened to be rocket instruction for Brian Murdoch - who also featured on my 'Pallbearer Theory'.

PALLBEARER THEORY

The following is perhaps a rather morbid story. One thing, amongst many others, that the Air Force did really well, was to organise very decent burials. The playing of the 'Last Post' by bugle is a very traumatic event in itself. Volleys, by the Firing Party, often provided sufficient respite for the odd tear to dry. Whether it was pure coincidence or a strange twist of fate, I will never know - but it took me a while to realise that one's chances of survival were greatly reduced when volunteering for Funeral Party duties.
The strange happenings started in the early 1960s and only by the mid-1970 did I formulate my theory that resulted in my being very wary to perform pall bearing duties
It all started like this:- Bruce McKerron was one of the eight pallbearers when Pilot Officer Terry Ryan of No 14 Course was killed

in a Provost aircraft. Then when Bruce was killed in a flying accident, Henry Elliot (No 15 PTC) and I (No 16 PTC) volunteered as pallbearers.

Six months later, in December 1964, Henry Elliot was killed in a Vampire. Barry Matthews (No 17 PTC) and I were amongst the eight pallbearers. Then in March 1965, Barry Matthews was killed in a Provost. Again I was a pallbearer, together with Mike Hill (also No 14 Course).

On 28 November 1968, I had a narrow escape. Whilst doing an air test on a Vampire, I had total engine failure but managed a successful forced landing back at Thornhill. Nearly nine months later, I had another narrow escape in a Provost after experiencing a frantan (Napalm bomb) hang-up. Whilst doing the rundown in the dispersal area, the bomb exploded under the wing and the aircraft was totally destroyed - I escaped with singed eyebrows and a cut on the right knee. The date - 23rd July 1969.

A year later, Mike Hill was dead. Alec Roughead (same course, No 14 PTC), Barry Heard and I were pallbearers. The jinx had been broken - somehow No 16 PTC was passed by. Then August 1971 Barry Heard was killed in a motor vehicle accident. Guy Munton-Jackson, Alec and I were pallbearers. Alec Roughead died in a Canberra flying accident a month later - 16th November 1971. Guy was killed two months later, in an Alouette.

I had come to my senses. Alec Roughead was the last funeral I volunteered for - because one of the eight pallbearers would surely die.

The first No 16 PTC pilot to be killed was Bruce Collocott in a Dakota in May 1977. I did attend his funeral - he was the first person I met and befriended in the Air Force. Al Bruce, also from No 16 PTC, had a narrow escape on 28th October 1970 when he ejected at very low level from a Hunter, whilst I was leading the Hunter formation at the time. Needless to say, I did not volunteer as a pallbearer at the funerals of Chris Weinmann in April 1974, Brain Murdoch in December 1974, Bill Stevens in September 1976 and Roy Hulley in October 1976.

At the end of the day, there was no scientific basis for my theory. It was most likely pure coincidence. One thing for sure, though, I stayed well clear of the eight coffin bearers.

My Hawker Hunter

SPEED AND COURAGE

NO 1 SQUADRON (HUNTER FGA 9) FLIGHT COMMANDER

I was posted to, and appointed 'B' Flight Commander on No 1 (Hunter FGA 9) Squadron on 1st January 1970. Roy Morris commanded the squadron. This was indeed a double honour for me – firstly, to be entrusted with a command appointment, and secondly, the opportunity to fly the fastest aircraft that the Air Force was equipped with. Permit me to brag that not many Air Force pilots were privileged to have enjoyed the same career opportunity that I had.

My first solo was flown on 15th January 1970, in Hunter R 1817 - but to do so required eleven hours in the flight simulator and one Vampire sortie to do Hunter type circuits. The first fortnight on the Squadron was devoted to studying the pilots' notes and learning everything there was to know about the sub-sonic Hunter. The Hunter was viewed by many airmen as the ultimate that a pilot could fly. It was likened to the Tiger Moth of the by-plane era, the Spitfire of piston engined World War II fame, and the English Electric super-sonic Lightning era.

The Rhodesian Air Force did not have the benefit of the dual-seat Hunter in the Royal Air Force. One did not have the benefit of a flying instructor to hold your hand to show you the ropes. A certain amount of flying maturity was needed to get airborne in the Hunter for the first time – and then to land it safely on terra firma – after a thrill of a lifetime. However, a Hunter pilot did have the box or simulator to practise in. But as many pilots will testify, comparing the two was not quite the same. I should also perhaps mention, that it was only the first simulator exercise that one could "fly" for an hour without being confronted with one or another emergency. The technician in the back of the simulator was able feed the computer controls with all sorts of situations – malfunctioning fuel flows, engine failures, unreal cross-winds, hydraulic failure (for lowering flaps, undercarriage and operating the air brake), etc, etc.

Hawker Hunter FGA Mk 9, number 117, the aircraft the author soloed on, on 15 Jan 1970

The Hunter had a reputation for terrific acceleration and an exceptionally high rate of roll. One's first solo invariably solicited bets on the squadron that soloist would battle to take-off without over correcting aileron movement's and thus waggle the wings while accelerating to climbing speed. This was also because the simulator had by now developed sluggish controls through irreparable wear and tear – while in the real aircraft the Hunter was exceptionally sensitive to even minute movements of the control column. I would like to think that my own first take-off was well under control.

The other surprise with the first solo was that nothing happened. I mean, there was no flight emergency like electrical or hydraulic failure to distract the soloist from a truly memorable experience, lasting forty minutes of pure joy. One was able to thrash the throttle without fear of jet-engine surge, one could pull the aircraft into a vertical climb – and just keep going up, and up, and up. After one or two low approach circuits, touch-down was at 140 knots; and it was something else to pop out the brake parachute on the landing run.

SUPERSONIC, HUNTER 8116; OPS INT OFFICER

Hunter R 8116 was really special. No 1 Squadron was the only unit in the Air Force that allocated specific aircraft to individual pilots. This encouraged the aircrews to take pride in their aircraft, including its servicing and maintenance. It also produced a competitive edge.

Going supersonic is an experience that not many pilots could lay claim to. My opportunities arose on 16th February and 17th December 1970. The Hunter service ceiling was in the region of 48,000ft. Any flight above 40,000ft was very 'wishy-washy' - unlike the Canberra built for high altitude flight; the Hunter tended to wallow at altitude. However, on my second Boom Run, flying a very 'clean' aircraft, I managed to climb into the stratosphere to the giddy height of 55,000ft (being very careful to monitor my health for any signs of anoxia), put the Hunter in a near vertical dive and clocked 1·05 Mach. One is always selective where the sonic boom hits the ground; so as to minimise any shattered windows.

A "clean" Hunter – for Sonic "Booms" - through the sound barrier

For my sins (unrelated to my 'illegal' supersonic runs, I hasten to add) I was appointed the Thornhill Station Intelligence and Operations Officer from 1st April to 16th May 1970. This meant that I was accountable to the Station Commander for all signals and correspondence classified "Secret" and higher - such as "for the eyes of so-and-so only". I was thus the custodian of the Secret Registry and had to account for the keys at all times. It certainly was an eye opener to see what was going on in the Smersh world of espionage, and keeping senior officers informed of events, interpretations and predictions. I treasured the trust and responsibility I was charged with, albeit only lasting some six weeks pending the appointment of a permanent 'Ops Int Officer'.

The 1st July was a tragic day for the Air Force – we lost our first helicopter crew. Squadron Leader Gordon Nettleton and Flight Lieutenant Mike Hill were killed near New Sarum while carrying out Instrument flying. The cause was never established, but the Board of Inquiry did attribute the accident to flicker vertigo.

The new Air Force pilots Wings badge came out, and replaced the old RRAF Wings. After having gone to print, Peter Cooke kindly pointed out the differences in the Kings and the Queens Crown as in the RRAF Wings. These are reproduced for illustrative purposes. For continuity sake, the AFZ Wings are shown as well.

PHOTO-RECONNAISSANCE - PR

Photo-Reconnaissance was not a role that many people associated with the top Day Fighter / Ground Attack capabilities of the Hunter. And yet the F.95 Camera that was carried in one of the 100-gallon drop-tanks fooled many more. The camera was so mounted that film could be taken at an oblique angle when flying over or near targets at low level. Its main advantage was the ability of high speed, semi-surprise intelligence gathering. Because of the high-speed capability, a potential enemy would just not have sufficient time to bring any air-to-ground weaponry to bear.

My Hunter F.95 PR course was carried out from the 5th to the 25th August. It consisted of flying eight sorties, ranging from thirty-five minute sorties and up to seventy minutes, and photographing a variety of targets at low level and high speeds. Good map reading and accurate target acquisition were pre-requisites to completing the course successfully.

On Saturday, 8th August, I celebrated Renene's second birthday – with a loving and very pregnant wife.

FLYPASTS & DIAMOND NINES

Flypasts for ceremonial events and shows formed an important function of the squadron. The shape of the Hunter was particularly suited to fly a "diamond nine" formation. I treasure a photograph of a near perfect diamond - with me in the middle leading the 'box', which only ruler measurements revealing the very slight imperfections. In fact, I would challenge most observers, with normal eyesight, to spot with the naked eye to make judgements. Highlighted flypasts were: -

Bulawayo diamond nine — 5th March 1970.
Salisbury — 10th April
Bulawayo Trade Fair — 16th April
Bulawayo Trade Fair — 2nd May
Rhobrew - Rhodesian Breweries — 20th June
Bulawayo — 27th August
Umtali — 28th August
Gwelo Show — 11th September
Diamond 9 — 5th November
Diamond 9 — 9th November
Independence Day — 11th November
Christmas Card Formations — 16th November 1970.

Hunter P. Geldenhuys – 1970 – The year Pey was born

Close study of the formation below shows that Ed Potterton is ever so slightly forward. Take a straight edge and measure the line-ups. For the layman, it should be realised that this was no mean feat. Consider that the Hunters are flown at three different planes – Steve Kesby at the back was on the lower plane, I with my two wingmen in the middle, with Boss Roy and his "vee" formation on the top plane. With me leading the box four formation, I had to line up with the leader, but also take note of maintaining a line abreast formation with Rikki Culpan and Nobby Nightingale. Steve also had to line up me with the Boss. Not bad, even if I say so myself.

The "Perfect" Diamond Nine – with the author in the middle

The Diamond Nine Pilots – Ed Potterton, Rob McGregor, Rich Brand, Dag Jones, Sqn Ldr Roy Morris, Nobby Nightingale, Steve Kesby, Prop Geldenhuys and Rikki Culpan

I also had the privilege of leading a Diamond Nine formation around the country – but then that would be expected from a Flight Commander on No 1 Squadron.

Smaller echelon, box and line abreast formations were also popular, as the couple of photographs show. The profile and speed of the Hunter makes it an ideal flypast aircraft.

Red Section – Four Hunters in Echelon Starboard Formation

Hunter Box Formation

But not all the flypasts ended successfully. It was thus with regret that it was during my time on the Squadron that I hereby record the loss of a valuable Hawker Hunter during timing runs carried out at Bulawayo.

Line Abreast Formation

HUNTER 1823

The story of Hunter 1823 is rather a sad one. I had flown the aircraft a dozen times, logged 17 hours 35 minutes and was the only eyewitness to see it crash to the ground.

I had had a lucky escape, in that two days earlier, I was the one who had carried out the "Air test, engine performance" on Hunter 1823 following the Squadrons flypast practice for Salisbury and Bulawayo. The practice had gone according to plan and was of one hour twenty duration. That same day, no doubt to get as many Hunters into the air as possible, it was important to ensure as high a serviceability rate as possible. I accordingly flew the aircraft on a rather short thirty-five minute airtest and all appeared well with no serious snags evident. I had had only recently carried out an 'engine change' airtest on Hunter 8122, which took forty minutes.

Anyway, on the 28th, I was tasked to lead a pair, in Hunter 8122, with Al Bruce flying Hunter 1823 as my wingman, on a Bulawayo timing run mission. With me leading, we had just completed our timing runs over Bulawayo, and were climbing to altitude in Battle line-abreast formation, when I noticed that my No 2 was venting fuel from the centre of his fuselage belly. I had just radioed Al "Red two, you seem to be venting excessive fuel from your belly - I am coming across." No sooner had I described the seriousness when Al peeled off, half-rolled and diverted to the nearest airfield, which was Bulawayo. I did a 180, maintaining altitude to conserve my own fuel, and followed my number two back towards the airfield. Al had levelled off from his steep dive, allowing his airspeed to drop to approach/ undercarriage down speed.

As he applied power for flap down and undercarriage down, the Rolls-Royce Avon engine died on him. He radioed his "Mayday" emergency and I responded saying, "Good Luck, Al."

He replied "I don't think I am going to make it." - expressing doubts that he had sufficient height available for a forced landing on the runway.

Meanwhile, Al Bruce had injured his back with the near ground-level ejection and had to wait a while before the Rescue Vehicles reached him. This was despite his landing close to a road track running at right angles to the runway. The rescue teams had wasted time locating the remains of Hunter 1823 instead of reacting to my directions as was voice taped to the Control Tower. The Queen Mary was dispatched to recover the wreckage. Al was hospitalised to recover from his injuries as a result of the ejection and falling through the trees.

Al Bruce Ejection - Bulawayo - 28 October 1970
Hawker Hunter R 1823

The sad moment came on 28th October 1970, when Al Bruce ejected on downwind whilst trying to make Bulawayo airfield.

Al Bruce added his personal touch, when he sent his side of the story to Bill Sykes, and kindly reproduced as follows: "It was a beautiful blue sky day in October when Red leader and I made a touch and go landing at Bulawayo. On the climb I had just transferred from drop tanks when I was informed that my Hunter R1823 was venting fuel.

I immediately turned back for Bulawayo and I could see it was going to be a race against time at the rate the fuel gauges were dropping.

As the gear went down the fuel delivery pipe and the engine parted company and everything went deathly quiet and I reluctantly became glider pilot. At about 200 feet above the trees I put my future in the most capable hands of Sir James Martin. There were three loud bangs. Firstly when the seat exploded, secondly when the parachute erupted and thirdly when I impacted Mother earth, all within a few seconds. The Board of Inquiry found one footprint on the left, the other on the right and a round hole in between which represented my head in one of the more spectacular three pointers.

Bulawayo hospital definitely had the most beautiful nurses and the most efficient red-haired Irish matron. On finding the Board of Inquiry and myself sipping beers, the dear lady summarily evicted the Board and thus saved me many onerous questions. However, unlike the board, who had left in unnatural haste, I was a captive audience and matron explained with much motherly concern the folly of combining beer and morphine. My next two visitors astounded me. The first was a Sergeant from Brady Barracks who presented me with an official envelope containing beers from a school buddy, W/O Dave O'Connor. My second visitor was none other than the Mayor of Bulawayo who also came bearing gifts - beers! Due to the perverse lack of bottle openers in hospitals his Excellency accomplished the deed of bottle opening with a "smack" of the hand against the bottom of my bed rail. I recall with horror watching the top go spinning in slow motion onto the veranda and wondering of the whereabouts of the matron.

Two weeks later I left the hospital with my crutches in my left hand, my clothes in a bundle under my right arm and a suitcase full of little brown bottles."

Hunter highlight sorties during December was 68mm Matra Pod Trials, a jolly to Cape Town, "Boom Runs at Mach 1·05 (i.e. exceeding the speed of sound) and celebrating Exercise Aspatat with a high speed break into the Thornhill circuit at Mach 0·95.

Ministry of Defence VIP Officials visit to
No 1 Squadron - 1970

Dag Jones, MOD Jack Howman, Roy Morris, AVM Archie Wilson, Prop Geldenhuys

EXERCISE "ASPATAT"

Exercise "Aspatat" was a beautiful Christmas gift by Rina who presented me with an heir. Pey Malan was born by caesarean section on 22nd December 1970. Specialist Mr Rodgers had a hassle free operation, and Boss Roy had given me the day off to be with Rina at Birchenough Maternity Home with the birth of our second blessing.

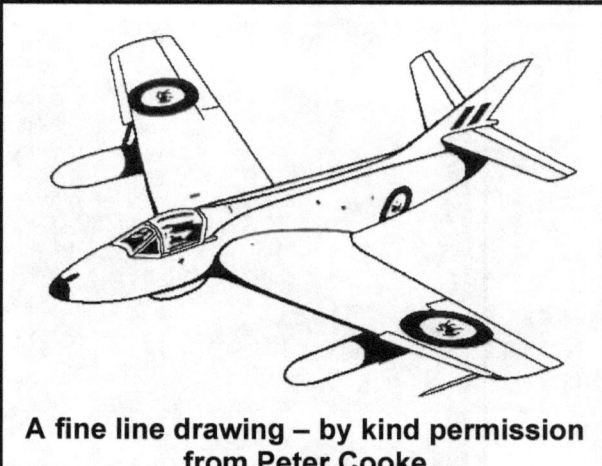

A fine line drawing – by kind permission from Peter Cooke

To celebrate the event, I need to go back to my last sortie on No 1 Squadron, which was on Old Years Eve, 31st December 1970. Roy Morris had kindly agreed for me to have a final fling in a Hunter. Bearing in mind the Christmas break, my previous decent sortie was a rocket and cannon air-to-ground one-hour sortie on the 23rd. As I was about to take up my new posting to No 2 Squadron for OCU instruction, it was a rare honour to be given this opportunity. It was a short twenty-five minute trip, culminating in a high speed beat-up (which is normally frowned upon, because old Mrs Bogey's chickens would have problems passing eggs through their orifices.). Anyway, I relished opening the taps on the Avon, and came 'screaming' into the circuit at max low-level speed, registering 0·95 on the Mach-meter (95% of the speed of sound). What a way to ending a memorable posting on the first Squadron of the Air Force with its long history of aviation in the country.

A Hawker Hunter – with a blotched colouring in job

To cap it all, Squadron Leader Roy Morris certified me as an "Above Average" DF/GA PAI pilot on Hawker Hunter FGA 9 Aircraft.

"It is indeed astonishing that nine of the original twelve (Hunters) delivered before UDI were still flying at the end of the war," said Dudley Cowderoy and Roy Nesbit, in their book *War in the Air. Rhodesian Air Force 1935 – 1980.* I presume that is why they opted to publish their work with a dust cover showing a pair of Hunters flying in close formation. Because it was a good picture, I decided to scan it as shown below.

A Superb painting of a Hunter – by Bill Sykes

Bill Sykes painting of a Hunter – for Ian McKenzie

These photographs were kindly supplied by Eddy Norris (of ORAF's fame), with the aerial photograph taken by Paddy O'Reilly, who was in the chase Canberra, as seen in the bottom left hand corner.

STRIKE FROM ABOVE / FIND AND DESTROY

STRIKE FROM ABOVE

Having been posted back to No 2 Squadron in January 1971 I soon got in to the groove flying the jet-engined Vampire and the piston-engined Provost.

No 2 Squadron 1971
Prop Geldenhuys, Justin Varkevisser, Tol Janeke, Chris Dixon

Roundel changes
Three Federal assegais, One Rhodesia assegai and then

Lion and Tusk – with origins from No 237 RAF (Rhodesia) Squadron

August 1971 was not all that different to the preceding month. I added quite a few more OCU students to my list – these were the new pilots that had been awarded their Wings during July. My new students included Air Sub-Lieutenants Greg Todd, Tony Oakley, Steve Murray, Mike Litson, Steve Baldwin and Pete Simmonds. Pete Simmonds, or Simmo as he was referred to, tells a very interesting story when he was shot in both legs while flying a Provost.

On the 12th August 1971, I tested and passed Air Sub-Lieutenant Barry Heard for his White Instrument rating on Vampires. Ten days later he was killed in an auto accident. What a waste. Barry had just completed his OCU phase, and was now a fully fledged DF/GA – Day Fighter/Ground Attack pilot. I believe he celebrated his achievement by buying a Sunbeam Alpine sports motorcar, and had taken his new car out on the Gwelo to Selukwe road for a spin. He possibly fancied himself as a steely-eyed killer and wanted to see whether he could improve on the world land – speed record. The Alpine did not break the sound barrier. Instead, Barry lost control of his new car, and paid the supreme sacrifice for his foolishness. I say again – what a waste, after spending so much time and resources to train a pilot to this stage, without firing a shot in anger.

On Monday 6th September 1971, it was back to Vampires. My first sortie was a test flight to check out instrumentation with instrument technician Sergeant Johnson. The second sortie of the day was another air test, this time with radio technician Sergeant Pringle in another Vampire. On Tuesday I carried out an OCU White Instrument rating test for Air Sub-Lieutenant Baldy Baldwin. On Wednesday I flew Vampire R 4120 on an enjoyable intercept on three Canberra bombers, with day fighter combat practice. Bearing in mind that our speed envelopes were very similar, radar aids were rather essential with this type of interception to be successful.

No 2 Squadron Crest – Strike from Above

The Canberras could outperform and run circles around us at high altitudes. It was thus essential to position in ideal quarter attack patterns and jump the Canberras at the first opportunity – because with their two pairs of eyes in each bomber, a DFC (day fighter pilot) wouldn't get a second chance in pressing home a successful intercept.

The next day I flew a low-level navex with simulated airstrike sortie. On Friday of that week I carried out two instrument flying rating tests for Air Lieutenant Dick Paxton and Air Sub-Lieutenant Danny Svoboda. It was a Friday, and the start of six weeks annual leave for me, from September the 12th until the end of October. We loaded up our Ford Taunus, with trailer attached, and headed for the Natal South Coast where we had hired a holiday cottage at Mtwalume. The 'Friends of Rhodesia' in South Africa promoted the seaside resort. Preference was given to servicemen, and rentals charged for fully furnished three-bedroomed houses were dirt-cheap. The trailer was taken along in order to load up with all sorts of goodies because of the extra disposable income we had at our disposal.

My first sortie, after my period of leave, was on 2nd November 1971 – I was doing a general flying sortie with Ed Potterton (because of my lengthy six weeks lay-off), but had to curtail the sortie because of experiencing jet pipe temperature failure. The next day was another jolly, flying down to Lourenço Marques for a night-stop – but although this was another holiday at the Mozambique coast, at Government expense, its purpose was the final OCU cross-country. My trip down was flown with OCU student Jim Baldwin and the return the following day with Vic Culpan.

The week after my return from Lourenço Marques, I flew two Green instrument-rating tests on Vampires for Air Lieutenant Ed Potterton and Air Sub-Lieutenant Spook Geraty.

Rina and I had gone up to Salisbury and bought a three-bedroomed house in Washington Avenue, Prospect. I stayed in the Officers' Mess, New Sarum, while Rina waited for the Removals Company to pack up our household goods in Married Quarters for our relocation to our first home ownership in Salisbury.

No 5 SQUADRON - FIND AND DESTROY

Rina's parents were farming at Blackstone, in the Beatrice area, and we spent the Christmas weekend with them.

New Year 1972 was spent in Salisbury. We bought a house in Washington Avenue, enrolled Renene and Pey into Prospect School and commenced immediate plans to convert our garage and storeroom to another bedroom with en-suite bathroom.

The space between the garage and the house was enclosed to form a sewing and general rumpus room. The en-suite bathroom also served as a laundry, and we had a shower, basin and toilet installed. We also built an adjoining garage cum workshop alongside the original garage. Our building alterations took quite a while, and I was able to fly in most of the finishing and fittings from South Africa. When the South African Air Force Canberra No 12 Squadron worked with the Rhodesians, I was able to get stuff in with them as well.

**No 5 Squadron
Find and Destroy**

I was devastated on Sunday 13th February 1972, when my father died in No 1 Military Hospital, Voortrekkerhoogte, Pretoria. Abram Carl Fredrik Preller was my hero and role model, and the inspiration to make flying my career. My Boss, Squadron Leader Tol Janeke, was very understanding and gave me leave of absence – as much as I wanted. I took the initial news calmly, but broke down shortly thereafter. My Mom was living in Gesina, and by the time I arrived my brother Jan was already there. My sister Delene, living in Hartley, was expecting her second child (she gave birth to Rensha two days later) could understandably not make the funeral. The military service was beautiful – and prompted me to formulate my "Pall Bearer Theory". We sold the Pretoria house, and brought my Mom back to Rhodesia. Delene was marvellous and managed to get a job for her in Hartley.

I returned to flying duties in April, carried out a re-familiarisation with Father Dakyns, did some low-level and medium-level bombing, and flew safety pilot for Rich Brand. Then on 12th April 1972 I flew down to Thornhill with my Navigator Mike Ronne and two armourers - Sergeant Craft and Senior Aircraftman Armand. We flew down with a bomb-box and returned with a full load of 96 live fragmentation bombs. The 17th April was also interesting in that I was bombed up with 6 x 1000lb for a full load take off experience. My navigator was Air Sub-Lieutenant "Starry" Bill Stevens. Bill was destined to be the first navigator to qualify as a pilot, but was tragically killed in the Bush War. On 20th April Mike Ronne and I dropped 6 x 130lb low-level bombs on the South African Roedewal bombing range just north of Pietersburg, returning to New Sarum. These exercises demonstrated the long range bombing capabilities of the Canberra bomber.

ASTRO-NAVIGATION

Astro-navigation was an essential part of fine tuning a navigators skills – but was dreaded by most Canberra pilots. These lengthy sorties were flown at great altitudes where the insides of the cock-pit would ice up, despite cabin heat being turned up to full blast. It was not uncommon for the pilots to fly with blankets to keep warm, and some even placed blankets over the rudder pedals in order to prevent the cold being conducted through the soles of the flying boots. One could not chat up the navigator when he was busy shooting the stars in order to establish a fix. These fixes were shot about every 20 minutes during the three-hour sortie.

No 5 Squadron – December 1971 - Paddy Morgan, Prop Geldenhuys, Bill Stevens, Wedge Brown, Rich Brand, Sqn Ldr Tol Janeke

I had the dubious pleasure of flying some thirteen Astro-nav sorties, and endured over thirty-six hours flying in freezing conditions to 'fly perfectly straight and level', while the navigators did their thing. Any pitch or bank would give a false elevation to the star being lined up on the sextant, resulting in our plot being miles off the intended track. A quick glance through my logbook reveals that I flew Astro-nav sorties for Air Sub-Lieutenant Bill Starry Stevens, Flight Lieutenant Phil Schooling, Air Lieutenant Mike Ronne (twice), Flight Lieutenant Doug Pasea (also twice, including one instructional sortie with Paddy Morgan whilst still an Officer Cadet), and then six sorties with Paddy – including one that was aborted after forty minutes flying because of oxygen failure at altitude. Just as well, because of the horror stories where either the pilot had unplugged his pig-tail radio communications lead – only to be assaulted by an 'apparent anoxia suffering' navigator attacking the pilot with the emergency hydraulic lever. Or vice versa for that matter. In this case, unbeknown to the pilot, the navigator intentionally un-plugs his lead to have peace and quiet whist performing his complex calculations. When the navigator doesn't respond to the pilot's call, the pilot extracts the hydraulic lever to prod the navigator with. The navigator assumes the pilot is suffering from a lack of oxygen and tries to take over flying control of the aircraft. The pilot meanwhile assumes the navigator has gone mad, and beats the navigator off with the hydraulic lever. When both come to their senses, the flight can resume – with 'ops normal' reports.

My first Astro-nav sortie was eventful because of a nose cone fracture – but this 'fact-story' has been recorded elsewhere, titled 'Explosive Decompression: 25 April 1972', when the nose cone of the Canberra literally blew off while my navigator was still lying in the bomb-aimers position. Mike Ronne hastily 'extracted' himself from the sharp end while I carried out an emergency descent and was given priority landing clearance to Salisbury airport.

Another interesting sortie was flown on 3rd May 1972 in that Mike Ronne and I carried out a photo-reconnaissance of Blackstone. Blackstone was my father-in-law farm. Oom Frans and Tant Lettie were rather privileged to have their smallholding photographed by the Rhodesian Air Force.

Numerous low-level and medium-level bombing sorties were carried out during the first week in May. I also managed to fly a couple of sorties with Bernie, which included a low level photo bomb exercise, landing Bulawayo, and a night navex with bombing at Kutanga sortie. On 5th May, Mike Ronne and I carried out one of our many northern border recces. These border recces were important for two reasons – firstly to let the gooks know that they infiltrate at their peril; and secondly, to wave the flag for all the South African policemen guarding the border. In this instance, we flew with Sergeant Sid Brown, and also landed at Victoria Falls for refuel (hence the reason for taking one of our ground crew along, to do all the dirty work). We continued with our northern border recce, landing back at New Sarum.

Bill Jelley, my future brother-in-law was appointed OCFW New Sarum in July 1972. He did not show me any special favours – and I sought none either! I doubt very much whether Grahame knew four-year old Renene at this stage – with him chasing high school girls around the playgrounds?

I carried out a repeat IRT for Richard Beaver on the 8th August – Renene's birthday. Because of a night flying sortie that night, with Bill Stevens, Renene was already fast asleep, and it was just a fact of Air Force life that one could not always be at home to share those precious moments with one's family. It may be recalled that Richard Beaver and Murray Hofmeyr were with me during Operation *Nickel* – now five years later. The three of us were indeed lucky to survive the Bush War – a quick glance at the 'Roll of Honour' in my Operations book, - after having been shot three times, nogal, will show just how many of my close colleague didn't make it – and went off to that 'Great Hangar in the Sky'.

Officer's Admin Course October 1972 - with Sqn Ldr Peter Cooke

My highlights in September were the second Operation *Chessman* sortie, providing top cover for the Prime Minister between Cabora Bassa and Salisbury. In October I attended the Officer's Administration Course, the purpose being so that I could equip myself with the necessary knowledge and skills to pass my Squadron Leader examinations. Many competent pilots who did not pass their exams had their Air Force careers seriously stunted. I wrote and passed my exams at the earliest opportunity.

Squadron Leader Peter Cooke ran the course at No 1 Ground Training School, New Sarum. He was my squadron commander during the latter part of Operation *Nickel*, and was also destined to become my Boss as Officer Commanding Volunteer Reserve. As can be seen from the photo, we got on very well together.

On the 20th I flew Richard Airey on his high speed low-level navigational exercise. The next day, Mike Ronne and I had one of those plum jollies to Port Elizabeth and Cape Town. As already mentioned under Jollies, the leg from Port Elizabeth to Cape Town was low level all the way down along the Garden Route of Southern

Africa – What a sortie. We were the envy of a lot of Squadron pilots, navigators and technicians.

On 27th of November I was number three in a formation of five Canberras, rehearsing for our 25th Anniversary Flypast. Richard Brand led the formations. I was extremely proud just being part of it.

However, for continuity sake, I will briefly mention the remainder of noteworthy December 1972 events. I came back from Kotwa late on Saturday evening, 16th December 1972. I de-briefed Squadron Leader Randy du Rand, and departed with my family to Rina's folks for Christmas. Because I had worked two weekends in a row, plus my short notice field deployment, I was allowed the leave I had applied for. Rina's folks were occupying a farm in the Beatrice area, belonging to Louis and Anna Ferreira.

Then on Pey's second birthday, the fertiliser hit the fan. Terrorists attacked outlying white farmers. Altena and Whistlefield farms in the Centenary area were attacked in as many nights. The news headlines flashed across the country. I had fortunately spent some quality time with Pey on his birthday, but was feeling restless by the time Christmas came around. We left the farm on Boxing Day – and my feet did not touch the ground for the next nineteen days. During that period, I flew twenty-one times, only missing two Saturdays in the process.

The armed reconnaissance sortie was a rather short ninety minutes – I can't recall whether it was 'Wedge', or I, that was having hangover effects.

Operation *Tempest*, and Operation *Hurricane*, are major stories on their own.

Christmas Card Photo – Boss, Prop Geldenhuys and Rich Beaver

Rhodesian Markings

1947-53   1953-63   1963-70   1970-79

HURRICANE

When I got back to the Squadron on 5th March 1973 (Rina's birthday), I had a change of navigator. Air Lieutenant Mike Ronne had been my navigator for some fourteen months, up until the end of January 1973 (since I had joined the Canberra Squadron in November 1971). I was then allocated fellow No 16 Course colleague, navigator Flight Lieutenant Doug Pasea with effect from 5th March 1973. On that day, my first day back on the Squadron, we flew my first airstrike, dropping 96 x 20lb bomb-box load on a terrorist target. The Canberra for my first strike in anger, was R 2155.

**No 5 Squadron – March 1973
Paddy Morgan (Nav) & Prop Geldenhuys (pilot)**

April 1973 was noteworthy for my brother-in-law. Frans Malan recalls: "Reality set in with a jolt in April 1973. Our platoon was assigned to Mukumbura as escorts and protection for Special Branch detectives on an intelligence gathering exercise. It was a very relaxing way to spend a call-up. We would accompany the police very early in the morning to certain target areas they had identified where they would gather together locals who they regard as being the best prospects for shedding light on terrorist movements. We would then take them back to our base at Mukumbura where they were made to squeal. We would have the rest of the day off and a guard roster was done each day for the night time. I cannot remember the name of the other SB officer but one was Henry Wolhüter, who in the latter part of the war played a very large role I believe with the Selous Scouts. Henry was a fundi on survival and it was always great to talk to him with numerous funny anecdotes from his police detective days.

"We were due to start our homeward journey the day following the arrival of our relief, however, they were ambushed. The driver was killed and the truck crashed into a tree in the killing zone. On the back of the RL was a drum of petrol which ignited ultimately burning out the truck. A further soldier was killed on the back of the truck. The result of this was that we could not go home until another RL had been provided with additional personnel.

"Our relief arrived and on the last night I asked about six of my guys if they were prepared to go out on a night ambush with me as I had, in discussions with Henry, come to the conclusion that a certain area was really bad news. Amazingly my guys agreed and we were dropped off towards last light. We waited until last light and then walked in some two to four kilometres until we came across a particular foot path that I had previously identified.   The area was pretty flat and cover difficult to come by. Eventually I settled for a large tree with foliage in a dome shape almost touching the ground and facing a reasonable open piece of ground to the pathway.

"It was a reasonably well lit moonlight night. I positioned the guys with the MAG gunner next to me on my right. We had no claymores or any fancy pyrotechniques and I must confess that my orders were not the most detailed. The ambush was to be set off by my tapping the gunner. We had not been in our positions very long when I heard a twig break. I warned the gunner by tapping him on the shoulder. On the footpath out of the darker section of the bush emerged the first of the gooks. It suddenly struck me that I had not taken my safety catch off. I did this as softly as I could but it still made a click noise loud enough for the gooks to hear. They stopped in their tracks and I waited hardly daring to breath. After what seemed like an eternity they began to walk again. I had now used up my ambush initiating signal and I was scared that any further movement or sound would really give our position away so I decided that I would fire first.

RL CRASHED INTO A TREE

23 April 1973
Dave MacIntyre, Sibanda, Henry Wolhuter & Frans Malan

"When sufficient numbers had moved into the killing ground I picked a target and opened fire. All hell broke loose .Machine gun and rifles firing, smoke and dust and as quickly as it had started all was dead quite. I checked that all my guys were alright and asked one to shoot up a flare. In the light I could see one body lying in the pathway. We quickly estimated that there must have been some twenty plus gooks that had disappeared and here we were lying under a tree without any cover. I ordered the guys to move back in our buddy buddy system to where I could select a better defensible position.

"I called the relay and gave a brief sitrep that we had initiated an ambush, we had no casualties but owing to our vulnerable position we were moving back to better defensible ground and that I would shortly provide a full sitrep. We came to a road I knew and I positioned the guys in all round defence and got on the radio only to learn that they had notified base that we were involved in a running contact and that they had scrambled the RLI, who were also in Mukumbura, together with cooks and bottle-washers to come and save us.

"We waited until the 'relief' convoy arrived under command of Lieutenant Pete Heane who was totally pissed off that his drinking had been so rudely interrupted, and naturally I had to lead them back into the contact area which I managed successfully. An Air Force fixed wing dropped flares for us once we were near the ambush site and we found one body with an SKS rifle. Pete showed me that from the pathway the gooks had only to take some three paces then they would fall some two meters into the dry river bed forming the border with Mozambique. I had not been aware of this when selecting the site and this I believe contributed to our low number of only three kills.

"There was a regular Major with the group of cooks and bottle-washers I had to lead back to the vehicles in the now very dark night. I managed to do this by finding a very faint overgrown footpath that led to the road and directly to the vehicles. When we arrived at the convoy the Major came up to me and said "Sarge your leading us so accurately in and out of the ambush site in the middle of the night is some of the best bush craft I have seen". He had been totally unaware that we had been walking on a footpath.

"A comprehensive lecture can be given on everything I did wrong in setting up this ambush , we were naïve but full of enthusiasm a fact which was often overlooked by some of the regulars who could, on occasion be down right derogatory towards us territorial guys. Thirty six hours later I was at home. It had been hell for our wives who originally arrived at the Drill Hall in Gwelo only to be told that we were not with the company, that they did not know where we were or when we would be coming home."

1May 1973
Flt Cdr Prop Geldenhuys, Air Force Cdr Mick McLaren
& Sqn Cdr Tol Janeke

The cherry on the top was winning the Jacklin Trophy for the Squadron – which I believe was achieved with our good showing during the Blackjack Forcex. Air Marshal Mick McLaren presented the award at a parade that was held at New Sarum. The pilots at the time of the award were Squadron Leader Tol Janeke, myself, Flight Lieutenants Ian Donaldson and John Bennie, and Air Lieutenants Rich Beaver and Mick Delport. The navigators were Flight Lieutenants Bernie Vaughan and Doug Pasea, Air Lieutenants John Brown and Bill Stevens, and Air Sub-Lieutenants Paddy Morgan and Rich Airey.

"Strike power vital need says Air Chief", featured in The Rhodesian Herald of Tuesday August 28 1973. The verbatim report read:-

"The Skills, the resources and the time devoted by Rhodesian airmen to the Service must be applied with greater concentration than before – if Rhodesia's true strike capability is to continue to grow against all the pressures that mitigate towards its downfall", the Commander of the Rhodesian Air Force, Air Marshal M.J. McLaren said yesterday.

"He said it is 'ironical but true' that the enemies of Rhodesia realise far more than some of our own countrymen the tremendous importance of Rhodesia maintaining her strike power. Air Marshal McLaren was presenting the Air Force Jacklin Trophy at New Sarum to No. 5 Squadron for a year of outstanding achievement.

"The trophy – given to the Air Force by the Shell Company of Rhodesia – is named after the founder of the Rhodesian Air Force, the late Air Vice-Marshal Ted Jacklin. The trophy is presented to the squadron that achieves the highest aggregate performance in the Air Force taking into account operational preparedness and discipline, training, projects and developments pertaining to aircraft and equipment, the technical record of serviceability, squadron morale, extraneous duties and sport and squadron administration.

"Air Marshal McLaren said: "For a year of outstanding achievement, and for its sound contribution to the balance of the Force and to the overall effectiveness of the Security Forces, No. 5 Squadron has emerged clearly as the winner of the Jacklin Trophy". This is the third occasion the award has been presented to No. 5 Squadron – whose role includes high- and low-level bombing, photographic reconnaissance and survey, and courier and training activities. The Squadron first won the trophy in 1965, then again in 1966. "Since then," said Air Marshal McLaren, "the Squadron has been involved in operational air strikes against terrorists and has effected the introduction of many technical modifications.

"The Squadron has carried out extensive photographic work to provide Rhodesia with up-to-date map coverage, and has managed all along to maintain a high serviceability rate in the face of economic sanctions and steadily ageing equipment. And now, for the third time, the Squadron has won the trophy during a year in which special mention should be made of a large photographic survey operation successfully completed to the highest professional standards. The Squadron has improved its bombing accuracy, and in the field of flight safety it is gratifying to note that there were no accidents, which can be classified as having been caused by aircrew or technical error.

This represents a magnificent achievement by air and ground crews alike. And we do not forget the many officers and airmen in the sporting sections who have worked hard behind the scenes to help the Squadron in its task". He warned that in the years ahead it would be well to adopt the view that the high achievement of the present must become the daily norm. "You who serve in No. 5 Squadron have applied great effort to your work. But if our country's true strike capability is to continue to survive and grow against all pressures that mitigate towards its downfall, the skills, the resources and the time devoted to your Squadron's performance must be applied with greater concentration than before. "It is ironical, but I believe it to be true, that our enemies realise far more than some of our own countrymen the tremendous importance of Rhodesia maintaining her strike power." "I sincerely hope that those of you on parade and every person present will bear in mind that we in Rhodesia cannot allow our country's capability against external aggression to fall behind in any respect. This vital need rests squarely on our shoulders."

Anyway, back to my story (for Renene's benefit). During my March 1974 stint whilst still "A" Flight Commander on No 5 Squadron, our Squadron Commander Randy du Rand was perfecting our offset bombing technique. This method was code named RAMS - Radio Activated Marker Service. RAMS proved a major breakthrough for day and night bombing in insurgency operations. The advantage of pilots undertaking Field Force Unit (FFU) duties such as at Bindura included appreciating ground forces modus operandi and also improve inter-service liaison and co-operation. Dealings with the likes of Brigadier Hickman certainly went a long way to enhance inter-service teamwork.

Whilst serving on the JOC, I was most fortunate to enjoy the comforts of home - the Senior Air Rep was privileged to kip in a caravan. The others had to contend with tented accommodation. Anyway, it came to pass that Rina decided to join me at the front-line and duly took our trusty Taunus motor car and drove up all the way to Mtoko. She was quite brave - because you see, at that time the terrs were just starting to lay landmines in the tar roads as well. You can imagine I was the envy of the others at the JOC to have female company whilst doing bush duty. I must admit it was most probably very boring for Rina because I spent most of my time in the Operations Room - while she spent the her time reading anything and everything she could lay her hands on - being cooped up all alone in the caravan. Perhaps she took such a liking to it because for years thereafter we always caravanned camped and even bus-ed.

Randy du Rand

The mention of Mukumbura "by the Sea", would lack bush humour, had it not been for the likes of Rina's twin brother Phil Malan. I have already mentioned some of Phil's Zambezi Valley TF call-ups. Anyway, on a call-up round about this time, Phil was briefed by his 10th Battalion Company Commander to "shoot anything on two legs." In other words, animals were royal game, but any humans that they came across could be considered 'fair game' and should be shot on sight – because they would be the only friendly forces present in that neck of the woods. They were duly dispatched on a seven-day patrol near the foot of the escarpment and they soon came across terrorist tracks. They immediately initiated follow up action and were soon surprised to establish that the gooks were covering up to no less than an amazing 35 kilometres overnight. The going was tough in the Valley, and it was not long before the patrol ran short of water. Phil did not want to call for an airdrop, for concern that any air activity would only spur the terrorists to make good their escape. Although the speed with which the gooks were moving most probably accounted for some knowledge that they were being tracked – hence the bee-line for the border. The pursuing patrol was fortunate to experience a rain shower one evening, and soon filled their billycans with whatever rainwater they could collect in hollows and game trail depressions. However, imagine their relief to quench their thirst, despite the "water" having a distinct elephant urine smell and taste. It was a question of bush survival, and the right decision to drink whatever 'liquid' they could find in the harsh Zambezi Valley. Some of the troopies found it more palatable to pinch their noses while gulping down gallons of elephant urine, 'contaminated' by the overnight rain shower.

I had then taken three weeks leave - Rina's birthday and our eighth wedding anniversary were on the 5th.

On April the 14th, Flight Lieutenant Chris Weinmann was killed in action whilst flying a Trojan. Chris was a tragic loss to the Air Force. He had been one of my earlier students, and had shared some really hairy moments with me, especially our middle of the night Battle of Inyantue sorties during Operation *Nickel*. Chris was shot down in Trojan R3244, near Rushinga, and had his aircraft cleverly camouflaged by the terrorists. About a week later, on 20th April 1974, while conducting an aerial search for the downed camouflaged wreck, Air Sub-Lieutenant R "Willy". Wilson in Trojan R 3427 was shot down and killed in action by a SAM-7 missile.

Chris and Willy were among the first killed in action. Many were to follow. I had my fare share of successes as well as failures, and was shot three times, the first being a real close shave. Like the proverbial cat, I had survived my eight lives. By the time I was posted off No 5 Squadron, I had dropped nearly one hundred and sixty tons of bombs, made up of 768 fragmentation bombs, 637 by 130lb bombs, 360 by 20lb bombs, 63 by 500lb bombs, 20 by 1000lb 'big bang' bombs and 9 by 250lb bombs.

RTV OP HURRICANE FILMING

On 31st July 1974 Wing Commander Bill Jelley, as Officer Commanding Flying Wing New Sarum, joined Flight Lieutenant Phillips and myself in Canberra 2514 for the trip and night-stop to Thornhill for the Rhodesian Television crews for filming a documentary on Operation *Hurricane*. On landing at Thornhill, we dropped off OCFW, and then got airborne again for RTV to film us dropping 6 x 130lb low-level bombing. After our night-stop at

Thornhill, Bill Jelley again boarded my Canberra for the return flight to New Sarum.

On the 3rd, Mike Ronne and I were tasked to conduct a search and rescue for a Z-Car - South African Alouette helicopter.

ARMY CO-OP COIN

Inter-Service co-operation was the hallmark of the successes that the Rhodesian Security Forces enjoyed during the Bush War. We could, justifiably, claim to be the envy of the whole world. John Mussel wrote me in 2007 to emphasise this very point (it is worth repeating – he said: "something that was probably almost unique in the military world which was that of the remarkably high level of cooperation between the armed services. From what I know of the services of other countries, and the jealousies that build up to prevent the application of armed force in a directed and optimum way, the Rhodesians truly set the benchmark"). This novel, I trust, amply illustrates how well we got on with our sister services. Whilst rivalry remained strong, it was also healthy in that the strengths and weaknesses of each Branch were fully appreciated by the others. I have already mentioned the various FAC and Counter-Insurgency training courses run by the Air Force for the Army (ours, as well for the South Africans, I might add). A couple of others that perhaps warrant mentioning include the following:-

On 24th June 1969, I dropped 8 x 20lb fragmentation bombs by Provost High Dive for a Rhodesian Army and South African Defence Force Coin Course.

On 6th June 1971, I dropped 6 x 20lb Fragmentation bombs by Provost at a Bulawayo Army demonstration.

On 27th July 1971, I carried out 200 x ·303 front gun and 2 x 12-gallon frantan demonstration airstrike at Kutanga in a Provost for a School of Infantry Coin Course. The next day I then positioned at Salisbury for a static display of the range of air weapons that our Army colleagues needed to familiarise themselves with.

On 19th February 1974 I introduced Lieutenants Nick Fawcett and Jenkinson of the RLI to "Army Air Orientation Course, combined with No 2 Squadron Jet Operations". The Brownjobs were my passengers in a Canberra, with Air Sub-Lieutenant Richard Airey as my navigator. These courses were accommodated despite operational requirements as well. In fact, Rich Airey and I had earlier in the morning carried out an Operation *Hurricane* airstrike as well – dropping 96 fragmentation bombs during a mission that lasted an hour and fifty minutes (we could thus demonstrate our skills with actual operational experience). As a side issue, I believe that Lieutenant Nick Fawcett is the same person who successfully established his own Security firm in Zimbabwe after the war.

On 18th September 1974, I flew Army Lieutenants Barlow, Blocker and Nigel Lamb on No 3 Coin Air Ops Course. These sorties were flown with my new navigator – Air Sub-Lieutenant Paddy Morgan, who had replaced Mike Ronne. We flew down from New Sarum to Thornhill, specifically for this Army co-operation exercise. A total of six Canberra sorties were flown during the day – returning back to base after nightfall. The following day Paddy and I dropped 6 x 250lb medium capacity bombs on a low-level first run attack weapons demonstration for our Army counterparts.

The reader is also referred to Peter Petter-Bowyer's (my Provost Instructor, who taught me to fly) excellent "Winds of Destruction" book that was published in 2003. Peter witnessed the Air Strike in which my navigator Rich Airey was killed when his bomb load of 96 frags detonated prematurely below the Canberra.

Three Canberras did not survive the bush war. Two were shot down and the third was lost when the bomb load exploded as soon as they were dropped. One that did survive was nostalgically caressed during an Air Forces Association re-union that was held in the late 1980's. Canberra R 2504 was put on static display at the Zimbabwe Military History Museum in Gweru in 1989. I trust that Courtney and Brendan will recount with a measure of pride one-day that "my Ou Dad flew that aircraft – in fact he dropped ninety-six fragmentation and eighteen 500-pound high explosive bombs on terrorists during Operation *Hurricane*."

Additionally, they could, with authority, quote the following facts about R 2504: -

This Canberra was built by English Electric in 1952.

It served with No 44 Squadron, Royal Air Force Honington (1954 to 1958)

It was ferried to Rhodesia on the 4th May 1959.

Prop Geldenhuys flew this Canberra on 42 sorties (29 December 1971 – 26 June 1974)

It was the first aircraft to drop live Alpha bombs in October 1976.

It was hit by a SAM-7 heat seeking-missile, in the port engine, in October 1978.

STRIKE 1 - NOT-OUT

BLUEJOB - SAAF Col PRETORIA - 13 to 24 JANUARY 1975

I was privileged to be sent to attend the Senior Joint Warfare Course at the South African Air Force College in Pretoria, from the 13th to 24th January 1975.

South African Air Force College, Pretoria - Group Photograph

243

Colonel W Bos commanded the SAAF College. I reported to him on the Monday morning, and after a brief chat he introduced me to Commandant van Niekerk, who commanded the Land/Air Warfare Wing at the College. Commandant van Niekerk then introduced me to the other fifteen participants. I was somewhat surprised to find that I was the most junior officer on the course as well as the only non-SADF participant - everyone else held field rank and I was obliged to call everybody 'Sir' or address them by their ranks. But on the other hand, I held the initiative because of my bush war experience, and I would like to think that my views were listened to. The other common denominator was that nine of the course attendees were from the South African Air Force – the balance being from a cross section from the South African Defence Force.

Our instructors on the Warfare Course were Colonel Bos; Commandant M van Niekerk; Majors J Bouwer, D Nel and J du Preez; and Captain A Jovner.

The students were Commandants J Aveling, P Botha, D Brink, W Schoeman and F Welman; Majors D Badenhorst, A Bekker, Tony Geldenhuys, Jock Kerr, J C Marais, J L Marais, B Olivier, B Pallin and G Roodt; and myself as a Flight Lieutenant (equivalent to Captain).

Fire Force concepts were quite new to the South Africans, but the Air Force types like Tony Geldenhuys and Jock Kerr were quick to employ them in the many exercises we had to plan. The main difference was the South Africans were fundies on classical war techniques, and didn't have to contend with any manpower or equipment shortages. I doubt whether any of them would have coped with the sort of shoestring budget that we Rhodesians were faced with. However, I found their War Exercises most stimulating – and had to refresh my geography knowledge of Southern Africa, and South West Africa/Angola in particular. An interesting finding was that all the South African units tended to operate in vacuums – there wasn't the inter-service co-operation between the various arms of the Defence Force as in Rhodesia. It was pleasing to note, however, that the aims of this Senior Joint Warfare Course was to foster close co-operation and co-ordination of the various arms during joint operations.

I got to know South West Africa, later Namibia, quite well - albeit on paper only. Places like Walvis Bay, Windhoek, Grootfontein, Tsumeb, Ruacana, Ondangwa and even Rundu at the mouth of the Caprivi Strip featured in the battle exercises we had done. I realised subsequently that all that burning of the midnight oil was not in vain - but a very clever strategy by the South Africans. They had at their disposal, the collective brain power of the top candidates at their various military colleges to plan for any eventualities in their trans-border operations - both current and in the near future.

My experiences at the Lanseria Air Show jolly and the South African Air Force College Pretoria (not so jolly) were memorable affairs. Group Captain Len Pink had offered up his seat to me to attend the three day two night-stop visit to Lanseria - and the opportunity to mix freely with our SAAF friends.

There was the three week senior Joint Warfare Course at SAAF College where we figuratively over ran Angola with our mock fire force squadrons from Tsumeb and Grootfontein - burning the midnight oil sometimes till sunrise in order to complete our assignments on time.

But that was just a minute sacrifice for the privilege to utilise play war games with the world's most sophisticated equipment - to ones hearts content. Speaking of jollies - then there were those glorious sorties to Pietersburg, Waterkloof, Bloemfontein, Durban, Port Elizabeth, East London, Langebaanweg and of course Cape Town. What a question.

LANSERIA AIR SHOW

Air Vice-Marshal Len Pink offered his Dakota seat to me to attend the Lanseria Air Show, in South Africa, in an official capacity. As could be imagined, only the top brass with a sprinkling of junior officer's were privileged to attend the top air display in Southern Africa. Spare seats were like hens' teeth. Once selected, there invariably were very few dropouts – to enjoy all the perks associated with a trip of this nature. It included flying from Salisbury, laid-on road transport, hotel accommodation, meal allowances etc, all at government (taxpayer) expense. I certainly wasn't complaining.

One day of the Air Show was restricted to military personnel only. This allowed official guests to witness sights and sounds which ordinary civilians would not be privy to. We were, for example, allowed to clamber inside cockpits, briefed on aircraft weapons loads and armament capabilities. Foreign potential buyers of military hardware also shared this particular day with us – or rather us (the small Rhodesian contingent) sharing the day with many other uniformed and diplomatic personnel. Both the ground displays and the flying, by a whole range of modern aircraft were world class. The general public open days followed subsequently.

The gesture by Len Pink – who was a navigator by mustering – and the highest-ranking one to boot – to offer me his seat, was very generous in the extreme. The offer meant much to me, and raised my respect and loyalty to him several notches. I had witnessed him playing bridge, and soon learnt that as his partner, one would incur verbal and body language chastisement, should one lead the wrong card, or misinterpret his line of play during the card game. Anyway, both Len Pink and Hugh Slatter, in their capacities as Chief of Staff, were destined to play significant roles in the history of the Air Force. I salute both officers, unreservedly.

My cushy SAAF College and Lanseria were short-lived. So also my Strike 1 Squadron Leader appointment – for this then led to more hands on field force deployments to our various FAF's – Forward Air Fields. Of these, I like many others, had my fair share. Some were real holiday camps while others were on the other side of the spectrum – real graphs - and I mean bloody hard work – literally.

FORWARD AIRFIELDS - FAF 5 - BEDOUINS

Forward Airfield 5 - FAF 5 - was established at Mtoko as a strategic base in the middle of the Operation *Hurricane* area. As the most senior Air Force Officer present, one was privileged to live in a caravan - versus roughing it in tent and stretchers. The caravan was equipped with all mod-cons, including gas lighting whenever the electric lights diminished with "lights out", luxury bunks with foam rubber mattresses and minimal creepy-crawlies: The mod-cons where so luxurious that I could not resist the temptation to invite Rina to a tour of bush duty. Rina braved 'landmine alley' (the gooks were just starting to perfect the technique of laying land mines in tar roads), by driving our Ford Taunus motor car, all alone, from Salisbury to Mtoko by herself.

To have one's wife in the bush was the envy of all the other guerrilla fighters, for very few ever experienced home comforts in the bush. Perhaps it was a case of RHIP - rank has its privileges. Anyway, I am indebted to Rina for smuggling herself into the Air Force camp, and to experience our hardships in the bush. I also need to mention tea tray Sally. By this time, the local community at most JOCs and Sub-Jocs had established Forces Canteens. At Mtoko there was one particular kind lady who could literally balance a tea tray on her particularly large posterior. Not only was her backside so large, it also had the right flat topped shape which was capable of balancing an average sized, laden tray.

FAF 2 - KARIBA

I was appointed OC FAF 2 - Officer Commanding Forward Airfield Kariba - on 15th December 1975. Developments in the south-east prompted the Air Force to move me from FAF 2 Kariba to FAF 7 at Chiredzi/Buffalo Range after a mere four months.

FAF 7 - BUFFALO RANGE

I reported for duty on 16th March 1976 as Officer Commanding FAF 7. I had left Rina behind at Kariba to pack our personal belongings, wrap up our affairs and await Air Force removals to cart our effects to the Chiredzi Sugar Estates Research Station across the road from the Buffalo Range airport. My appointment as OC FAF 7 lasted till November, and I was fortunate to witness the rapid development of field operations, as well as some historical external offensive joint-services co-operation.

In August 2001, historian Professor JRT Richard Wood, the author *"The War Diaries of André Dennison"*, gave me a signed copy of his book. He also kindly signed my copy of Ian Smith's memoirs *"The Great Betrayal"* – he had written the Introduction to the book. I had popped round to his home in Glenhills, Durban, where we spent several hours reminiscing about our war experiences. The Professor was in the process of writing and editing his history of Rhodesia, and had only very recently edited Peter Petter-Bowyer's *"The Winds of Destruction"*. Several very interesting exchanges took place during our meeting, and this also resulted in numerous e-mail exchanges. He duly wrote and published his *"So Far and No Further"* – and was collecting material for *"A Matter of Weeks, Rather than Months"* historical account of Rhodesia.

OPERATION MARDON

Chitanga Air Strike – 16 December 1976 – Permission kindly granted by Dr JRT Wood to use this map that he wrote about in his War Diaries book.

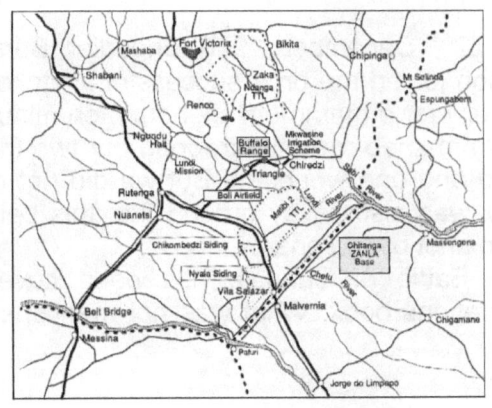

On 16th December 1976, whilst flying in Lynx R 3154, I marked the Chitanga terrorist camp with two frantans for the Canberra airstrike by my 16 PTC colleague Al Bruce and his navigator Jim Russell. They dropped their bomb load of 100 Mk2 Alpha bombs. My involvement in Operation *Mardon* is significant, in that this was the second time that I was shot – fortunately only the aircraft was hit by small arms fire.

The next day, after a Lynx change, I carried out an armed reconnaissance sortie of the Operation *Repulse* Sengwe area. Then on December 19th, I had another lengthy sortie with SAS Captain Graham Wilson, and an AMJ - African male juvenile, for casevac. We had a contact at Tshiturapadzi in the Matsai area, fired one 37mm sneb rocket, and recorded a casevac in Mashoko. Then on the 21st I flew with Major Pat Hill on an Operation *Repulse* HDF - high-density force reconnaissance sortie in the Nyajena area.

Lynx Aircraft – No 4 Squadron – Operation Mardon

On 22nd December 1976 Brigadier Barnard and Captain Graham Wilson joined me on a successful airstrike. On this particular mission, we flew for a mammoth six hours ten minutes in Lynx R 3407, fired 33 x 37mm sneb rockets, dropped our two frantans, and claimed five CT killed and one wounded. But we did not come away unscathed - the Lynx was also hit by ground fire, this being the third time that I had been shot by the enemy.

This Battle of Bangala has been covered in great detail in my Operations book. What was not mentioned was Rina's brother Frans

Malan's account. He says "I served in all major Operational Areas, Hurricane, Repulse, Thrasher, Grapple and Tangent Names that come to mind are Kariba, Kanyemba, Mushumbi Pools, Centenary, Mount Darwin, Mukumbura, Mtoko, Hot Springs, Sabi River, Boli, Mbizi, Mabalahuta, Wedza ,Enkeldoorn, Shabani, Vic Falls, Gokwe, Nkai, but the one that really sticks in my mind is the Nyajena TTL. I remember the very first patrol I took out in the area. As we were dropped off and the trucks left I got an extremely uncomfortable feeling-the hair stood up on the back of my neck and because of the terrain you knew that you were in gook country.

"To make matters worse our stint in the Nyajena co-incided with a tropical cyclone that had hit Mozambique and we had thirty six inches of rain during our five weeks in the area. I remember getting home and Kleinding throwing the contents of my trunk out the house, the stench was unbearable, and telling our domestic to wash my kit outside first before she would put my clothes in our wash machine. Sweat and virtually permanently wet clothes don't go together so well.

"We were based at Renco Mine. I had broken a front tooth (probably on a army dog biscuit) and had come into base to catch the ration run to Fort Victoria from where I could hike to Gwelo to have my tooth repaired. Late afternoon one of our company sections made contact and Fire Force from Buffalo Range was called in. Sticks were dropped off and the K-Car commander radioed in that he required an additional stop group. We being the closest base the company 2I/C, Dave Brockelhurst, two cooks and bottle-washers and myself were uplifted. Circling the contact area was frustrating as I had no clue what was happening on the ground

"We were eventually dropped off in a slight clearing on the side of a kopje. As we hit the ground gunfire was heard and we were radioed to make our way as quickly as possible to a small stream to cut off any escape. We did this running through the open veld and set up our stop. Nothing happened. Light was fading fast and a massive thunderstorm courtesy of the cyclone was brewing.

"Fire Force was uplifted and we received instructions to wait until last light then to ambush the gook base camp from which our troops had flushed them earlier in the day resulting in the contact. We moved very slowly up a small re-entrant of the stream and took cover in amongst some rocks and tall trees to wait for darkness. The storm started with a vengeance, rain pouring down, lightning flashing every few seconds and the massive claps of thunder reverberating amongst the granite kopjes we were lying in. A flash of lightning, gun fire starting from the cook and bottle-washer followed by a massive clap of thunder and a gook screaming. Two gooks watching the area to which we had run when we were dropped off by the helicopter, walked backwards into our position on the side which the cook and bottle-washer were lying. Some excellent firing from them in the light of the lightning flash had downed both of them. Dave and myself moved in next to the cook and bottle-washer and at the next lightning flash we all fired together in an attempt to silence the one gook. Everything went quite only to start up again after a few moments, and the process would repeat itself.

"Being frightened of a grenade being lobbed at us, he was that close, I told the guys to cover me so that I could move to the flank in order to see what the problem was. I moved round to the right and waited for the next lightning flash, fired and everything went quite. He had been hit and had fallen behind a small ant hill and every time we fired this protected him. We spend an extremely uncomfortable night in the wet and were uplifted the following morning.

"One of my platoon sections successfully ambushed a gook camp from which we had, if I remember correctly, a further two kills but my biggest regret was that whist on OP in the farm land bordering the TTL I had a sighting of a large bunch of gooks. I called out Fire Force and requested that the Lynx approach from behind the mountain range so that it could initiate contact on the rocky outcrop on which they were hold up. Target descriptions and identification proved to be difficult and by the time that they had identified the target the gooks were well on their way towards making their escape. Sticks were put down by the G-Cars and on doing a sweep towards the rocky outcrop a gook opened fire with an RPD killing a Rifleman Little, without any kills on our part.

"From high density ops, to cattle drives, to a Roman Catholic priest being brutally murdered despite a life time of serving the local community, to talking in a night time casevac from the top of a kopje with the aid of the sticks gas cookers as flares, to being choppered in to a young farmer and his wife who had sighted some locals on his farm who he believed were gooks to us standing guard for him and his wife that night so that they could get a decent nights rest and always the never ending rain and more rain.

Once you had operated in the Nyajena it certainly was not a place you could easily put out of your mind."

My own near miss made the history books, albeit just a one liner. Refer page 560 of Beryl Salt's *"A Pride of Eagles"*. The next morning, while my aircraft was being patched up, I got airborne again, with Colonel Peter Hosking for a Nyajena high-density operational reconnaissance. I re-united with Peter 31 years later at the Dickie Fritz Shellhole Lunch Club in November 2007 (but unfortunately I could not interest him in my book promotion. In fact, our association goes back much further to 1967, 40 years, which is well documented in the excellent RAR book, Masodja – The history of the RAR, by Alexandre Binda, 2007).

Then on Christmas day, I was tasked on a transborder telstar mission and relayed that three terrorists had been killed. On Boxing day the Selous Scouts called for a night telstar in the nearby Matsai area. My next sortie was also a night mission, but this time for three SF casevac that nearly cost me my life.

Three civilian soldiers from D Company, 5 Rhodesia Regiment had been injured in a landmine explosion in Matibi 2 TTL and were being taken to the nearest airfield which was Boli in the Gonarezhou area where Joshua Nkomo had been interned. When I landed at Boli, the petrol that the ground forces had thrown on the ground for my night landing ran out before I could bring the Lynx to a stop. I was not very charmed - Christmas and all - with my wife and children in Gwelo. And here I was, in the middle of the night, with no runway lights, no gooseneck flares, and only a bunch of Territorial Force soldiers trying to siphon fuel from their vehicles so that I could casevac their mates out of this hellhole.

I duly loaded stretcher cases Captain Irvine and Rifleman Johnson, with Rifleman Erasmus, an enormous overweight Boer sitting on the floor. Despite my appeal to the Brownjobs for a decent flare path for take-off, I found to my horror running out of lights with the overloaded Lynx just managing to scrape the trees on the far end of the runway. I was barely able to climb, and any attempt at turning 180 degrees for Buffalo Range, meant losing precious height. Anyway, I survived the trip, otherwise I wouldn't be telling the story now.

MAHOGANY BOMBER / SEEK AND STRIKE

MAHOGANY BOMBER – OC Admin Wing Thornhill

My appointment as OCAW Thornhill on 17th January 1977 came through whilst still at FAF 7 as a No 4 Squadron Lynx pilot. I reported to the Base Commander, Group Captain Tol Janeke. OC Thornhill briefed me on my duties that I would be accountable to him for all the administrative functions.

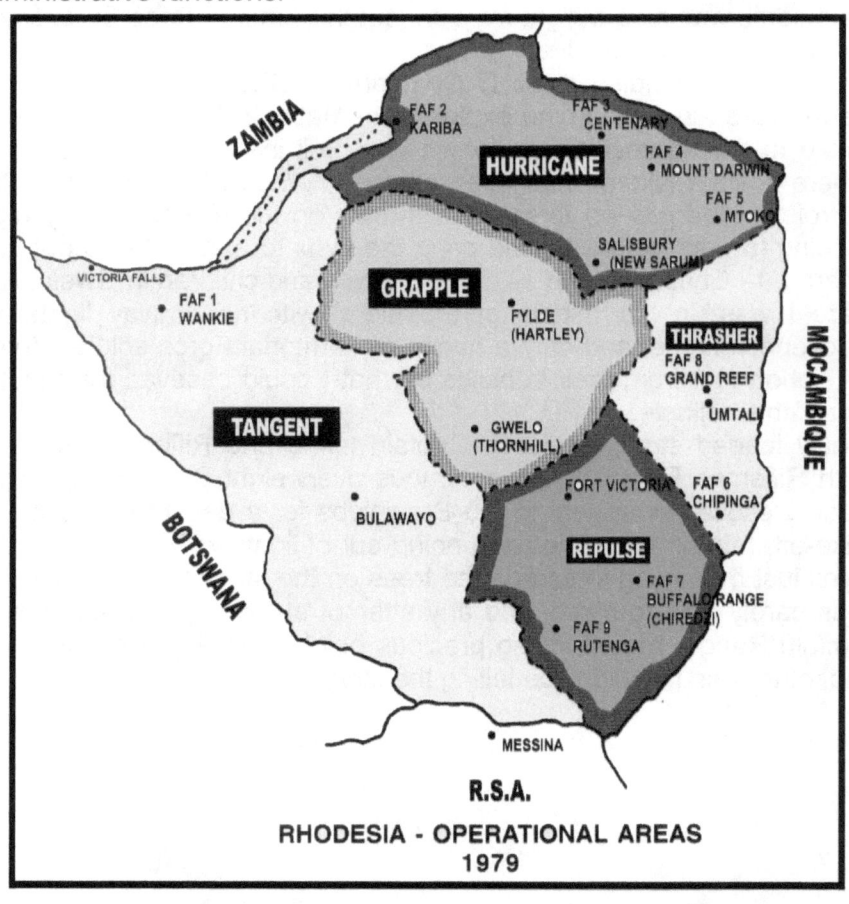

Map of the Rhodesian Operational Areas

Rina packed my bags for the four-day detachment to FAF 1 for Operation *Tangent/Ranger* duties. I uplifted Sergeant Kevin Nelson from Thornhill and positioned Wankie late on 4th November 1977 - having flown six sorties for the day, and logging a total of six flying hours for the day. Allow me to add that Kevin's younger brother Rob had been killed in action earlier in the year - on 8th May, and as fate would have it, his turn would come a mere seven months after my sortie with him. Kevin was killed in action in Mozambique in a South African Z-Car (on 28th July 1978. A tragic sequel was that his mother, who had now lost two sons killed in action, committed suicide).

ELIM MISSION - 23 JUNE 1978

This one incident, on 23rd June, had done the cause of détente with the Patriotic Front more damage than anything had before it.
A terrorist gang attacked the Elim Mission in the Vumba Mountains on the Mozambique border. Elim one of the few mission stations that had stayed open in the face of the war. Eight British missionaries and four children - one of them just a month old - were massacred. A ninth died later in hospital. Missions had been attacked before but the savagery of this particular incident drew world-wide condemnation. The women victims were raped. When the SF arrived they found one lady bludgeoned and bayoneted to death with her arm reaching out towards her baby murdered beside her. Another child, in her pyjamas, carried the imprints of a boot on her shattered head.
In Britain, crowded congregations at Elim Pentecostal churches prayed for forgiveness for those responsible. But elsewhere, notably the British parliament, there were calls for the immediate cessation of any talks with Mugabe - and the immediate recognition of Ian Smith's internal settlement initiatives. As expected, murderer Mugabe tried to shift responsibility to the Selous Scouts.
In August, Ian Smith met Joshua Nkomo, in absolute secrecy, in Lusaka. Not even Muzorewa, Sithole, or Mugabe for that matter, knew of the overtures by the Nigerians, who were in cahoots with Kaunda.
During the same month, August 1978, my erstwhile brother-in-law, Hansie Bezuidenhout was again involved in one of his many PATU call-outs. On about the 14th August, there was a contact with terrorist at Nunedon Mine in the Urungwe, which was well known to Hansie. His PATU stick was detailed to follow up on tracks, which they duly did. Having chosen an ideal spot, they set themselves up in ambush positions that only had a restricted killing ground – a large bush

obstructed their view, just prior to the enemy being caught by complete surprise. Whilst laying in wait, the ambush's presence was compromised when the machine gunners tripod slipped, and thereby made sufficient noise to alert the gang as they approached the bush obstruction. Hansie had no option to fire off the first shot – dropping one floppy in his tracks. As soon as the first gunshot rang out, the terrorists bombshelled, scattering and merging with the surrounding bush with amazing speed. As a result the compromise, and forced premature springing of the ambush, this action accounted for the one floppy shot by Hansie.

As a matter of interest, Hansie confided in the writer of the high regard that the ground forces held the Air Force. He recalled one particularly long 'leap-frogging follow-up', with helicopter support – and paid tribute to pilot Nick Meikle who attended to every need which the PATU came up with.

I did not do any flying during August. I next flew on 5th September 1978. Air Lieutenant Guiness was detailed to be my safety pilot for an hour's formal instrument flying with VOR and NDB letdowns. This single sortie was sufficient to restore my flying currency - flying the 1¼ hours in 10 weeks was hardly good enough to keep a pilot sharp and alert. Operational pilots were flying 50 hours a month - notwithstanding my own 105½ hours on Operation Nickel in August 1967 and even my 89¼ hours during December 1976. Anyway, to round off my current inadequacies, I carried out solo night continuation flying with single line flare landings on 7th September 1978.

VISCOUNT HUNYANI - 3 SEPTEMBER 1978

On 3rd September 1978 Viscount Hunyani of Air Rhodesia, VP-WAS, was struck by a Russian *Strela* SAM-7 surface to air missile shortly after take-off on an internal flight from Kariba, on the country's border with Zambia. The pilot managed to retain some control and crash-landed in the bush. Eighteen of the fifty-three passengers and crew on board survived the crash. Eight of the less seriously injured survivors set off to seek help. When they returned with rescuers, they found that Zipra terrorists had massacred the other ten remaining survivors, including women and children.

Zipra insurgents, whose base was in Zambia, had fired the missile. Their leader Joshua Nkomo, publicly exulted the success of his forces in carrying out this action. The Rhodesians were speechless, they were real mad. To avenge the Hunyani, the Rhodesian Air Force planned three attacks, timed to take place simultaneously commencing on 18th October 1978 against Freedom Camp (Westlands Farm/Green Leader), Mkushi and Rufunsa.

Rhodesian Intelligence estimated that one thousand five hundred guerrillas were killed in these three attacks, but the British International Institute for Strategic Studies reports that their estimates were usually on the conservative side. Many more were maimed, wounded and made limbless for life. I doubt whether Joshua Nkomo laughed, like he did on British TV with the downing of Viscount Hunyani.

On 13th September 1978 I again traded in my Mahogany Bomber for a Lynx.

LAST OPERATIONAL SORTIE

Rina once again packed my night-stop bags - she was an expert in cramming all my home comforts in the Air Force issue Carry-all. In fact, my IS-kit had a permanent home in it. She just needed to add the toothbrush and paste, plus the shaving kit. Because of my early start, I did not bid my children farewell - 10 year old Renene and nearly eight-year-old Pey was still fast asleep when Rina drove me to the Air Base. I also knew that my good next door neighbours, Vic and Shirley Wightman would keep an eye on my family. The beauty for the No 1 Squadron pilots meant less bush trips; they would carry out their air tasks and return to base, every time a coconut. Having reported to No 4 Squadron the courier Lynx was already fuelled up and waiting for me.

We hit the jackpot on 19th September 1978. We accounted for two CTs during a contact in the Wankie National Park. I was still airborne during my two-hour flight in the Lynx when I was asked to relay to the Special Branch chaps that the gook Sectorial Commander had been captured. The SB had their ways and means of making uncooperative terrorists squeal. My detachment was nearing its end and to account for such a big fish was like the cherry on the top to end an otherwise very productive spell at the sharp end. Later in the day I provided top cover for the Spiders who were trooping the SAS. Lynx R 3094 had performed well on every day since my bush deployment. As fate would have it, the fifty five-minute top cover mission for the SAS and Alouette helicopters would in fact prove to be my last operational flying duty (as a retread pilot) for the remainder of the Rhodesian bush war. I thank my Maker for having spared me the ravages and horrors of the bush war. While I could count myself fortunate indeed as having survived – there were many airmen who hadn't. How true those immortal words of my late father who uttered "there are bold pilots, and there are old pilots – but there are few old bold pilots". Thanks OuDad. I count my Blessings, for now having lived my length of days.

Rina's nephew, Johan Bezuidenhout, known amongst his SAS colleagues as Sergeant Small Bez, was on a mission of his own. Actually, he was part of 12-man SAS group in position along the road to Tete with the mission to stop enemy munitions getting into Rhodesia. Johan was waiting for the arrival of a Zanla munitions truck, because his colleagues had blown up the rail-bridge at Mecito.

At five o'clock in the morning on 20th December 1978, Small Bez heard a rumble in the distance and called to an OP on a nearby hill to verify his suspicions of approaching vehicles. This was duly confirmed – a large convoy of about 20 assorted trucks appeared through the early morning rain half an hour later. The ambush was sprung when the SAS fired an RPG-7 rocket at a troop carrier, while the mission commander remotely detonated a landmine under a Land Rover. The explosions brought the assorted trucks following the convoy to an abrupt halt – they U-turned and sped off in the direction they had come. The convoy sought shelter in an orchard, but was spotted by an eagle eyed Lynx pilot. By 08h30 the low cloud cover had cleared sufficiently for the Lynx pilot to talk a pair of Hunters onto the target. Airstrikes accounted for the remaining vehicles, with the cherry on the top being a Zanla petrol bowser.

The huge mushroom that billowed into the sky as the explosion went off when the petrol ignited was clearly visible to Johan Bezuidenhout and his SAS ambush mates on their hill ten kilometres away. Comops could, once again, chalk up another very successful airstrike, convoy and bridge demolition operation – Operation Shovel (15 December 1978).

Lynx – effectively used by the Rhodesian Air Force during the Bush War

PART TIME FLYER i.e. The "Retreads"

My flying logbook records that I had flown a grand total of 3,713 hours 55 minutes during my Air Force flying career. My end of year summary read:-

For two years, 1977-1978 = 152.05   Aircraft Types   1. Lynx - 146.50
                                                      2. Trojan -   5.15

My part time flyer days had come to an end. It was back to a desk job grindstone for me, and a posting to the glass palace. I was no longer a re-tread.

Aircraft	Types	S.E. Acft	M.E.Acft	Engine
Percival	**Provost TMk 52**	1601.15	-	Leonides
De Havilland	**Vampire T 11**	817.50	-	Goblin
English Electric	**Canberra T 4 / B 2**	-	796.05	RR Avon
Hawker	**Hunter FGA 9**	220.00	-	RR Avon
Cessna	**Lynx MB633**	-	238.30	Continental
Aermacchi Lockheed	**Trojan Al-60c**	40.15	-	Continental
Grand Total 3714 Hours				

TROOPER GELDENHUYS – 18 APRIL 1979

Trooper Ronald Olwen Geldenhuys, serving in Four Troop of 1 Commando, Rhodesian Light Infantry, paid the supreme sacrifice when he was killed in action against terrorists on 18th April 1979. His contribution is recorded for history in the Rhodesian Roll of Honour, and features in this biography as the "Unknown Soldier". Ronald, I salute you. At the going down of the sun, let us remember him – lest we forget.
The Roll of Honour, which runs to no less than 157 pages, makes for sombre reading. It lists 55 Airmen killed or died, out of some 1873 Security Force casualties during the period 11 November 1965 and 30 March 1980.

URIC AND BOOTLACE LESSONS LEARNT: 2 - 8 SEPTEMBER 1979

The Mozambique land-mining programme had gone fairly well, despite the loss of two helicopters with its programme re-adjustments, and by D-Day plus two, most of the roads had been mined and enemy transport had begun to hit the landmines. The landmines had been planted along all the roads where airstrikes had taken place, no fewer than about 15 different places.

The wash-up revealed several lessons learnt, namely::-

Enemy resistance, weaponry and Russian designed trench systems were under-estimated.

With limited resources, the Security Forces were virtually helpless when the aircraft returned to base to re-arm and refuel.

Demolition of the Barragem Bridge was not 100% effective. They should have gone back. Also, although damaged, the Aldeia da Barragem dam was not breached.

The adverse weather was bad luck. Changing plans were not thought through adequately (contingency plans were too rushed).

As already mentioned, South African involvement was code named Operation Bootlace, and the successes achieved would not have been possible without the external air and ground power.

OPERATION MIRACLE – 1 OCTOBER 1979

See separate Lulu.com publication "***Operation Miracle***"

Operation *Miracle* consisted of attacking five camps which formed the core of the Chimoio Circle - well defended by revetments, linked by trenches and spread over sixty-four square kilometres. Chimoio Circle was Russian planned and was dominated by a granite kopje called Maingue but dubbed Monte Cassino, complete with Russian 12,7mm and 37mm guns. The operation is remembered for the loss of a Hunter and Canberra on day 5 (3rd October 1979) – and more so because the bodies of Air Lieutenant Brian Gordon and Flight Lieutenants Kevin Peinke and J J Strydom were never recovered.

As fate would have it, Kevin Peinke was not meant to be on that air strike - Keith Spence did a refamil flight to the Range with navigator Paul Perioli on 1st October – having just returned from his honeymoon, in the UK. Sqn Ldr Ted Brent briefed Keith and his normal navigator to JJ Strydom to fly number two to Sqn Ldr Dave Rowe and Perioli for the airstrike on the 3rd, but Kevin asked Keith if he could do the sortie in his stead. Ted Brent agreed to Kevin's request. The rest is fact-story.

However, Bob Manser and his co-searcher performed a miracle 28 years later by discovering both crash sites.

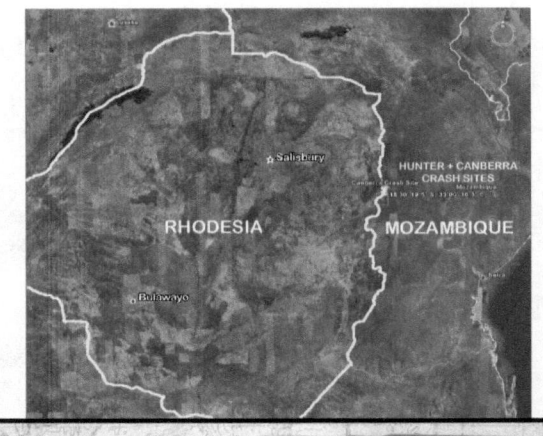

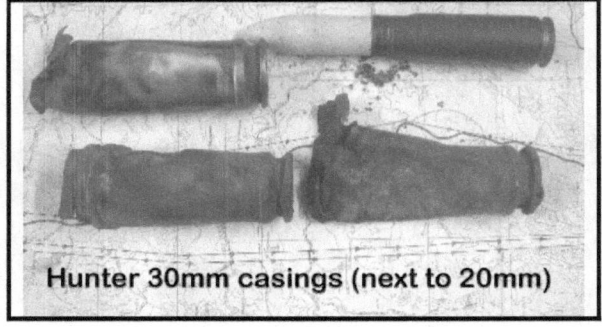

Hunter 30mm casings (next to 20mm)

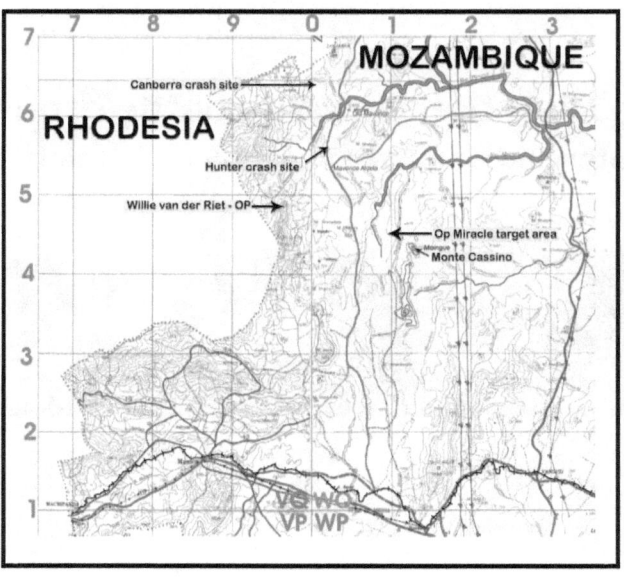

Maingue / Monte Cassino Defences

Dug out Gun-pits (left) and Covered Hide-outs (right)

. . . .At the going down of the sun, and in the morning, we will remember
gallant Brian Gordon, Kevin Peinke, J J Strydom, Paddy Bate and Garry Carter

OPERATION DICE – 16-20 NOVEMBER 1979

This four-day SAS operation demolished nine bridges, all surrounding the Zambian capital of Lusaka. It is mentioned again because Rina's nephew, Johan Bezuidenhout, was mentioned in dispatches on numerous occasions. A brief repetition would not do justice to his heroic exploits. I'm sure his parents, Hansie and Gerta, are very proud that *Sergeant Small Bez* served his country so well. On 13th November 1969, Johan was in a group of 15 SAS 'B' Squadron that was flown into Zambia to lay an ambush on a road south-east of Lusaka on the Kafue-Chirundu road. Johan manned a 60 millimetre mortar observation position and it was he who first noted the approach of a Zambian Army Land Rover on 15th November. Unfortunately, the claymore mines failed to detonate, and the two RPG-7 rockets that were fired missed their intended target. The next day, the 16th, when Operation Dice clearance was given to blow the bridges, Johan was joined by a 20 millimetre gun crew, who had been flown in by four Bell 205s of No 8 Squadron. The reinforcements had been helicoptered in from FAF 2.

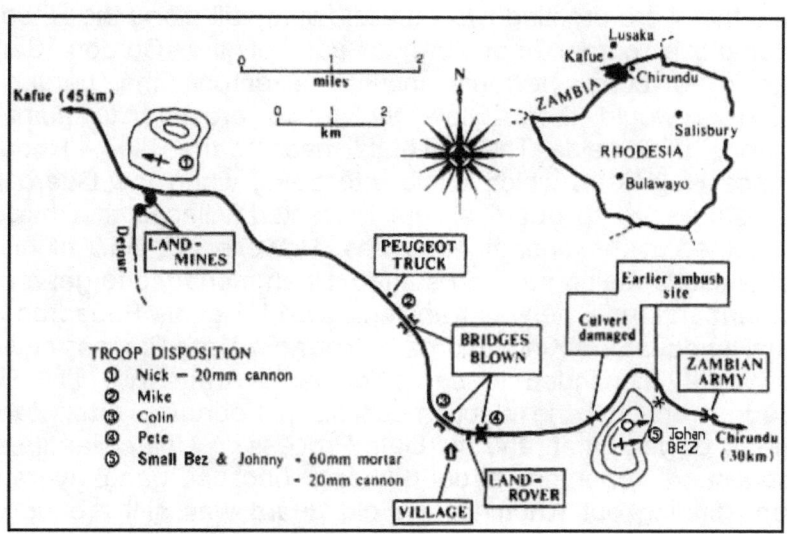

Operation Dice – Johan Bezuidenhout manning his 60mm mortar on an OP

One stick of SAS who had remained behind was able to destroy two out of three armoured vehicles, as well as the lead Zambian Land Rover. This 20 millimetre gun crew was also recovered to Kariba some nine hours after having been brought in. The Zambian Army came off second best in this clash with the Rhodesians.

The Rhodesians were victors in all these encounters although the cost in men and material increased steadily. The intense offensives against the lines of communications had reduced Zambia's economy and administration to chaos; and so the general mobilisation ordered by Zambia was but an act of despair and empty gesture.

Also of historical interest, especially for the Jelley's, is one Leonard William Jelley, who was killed in action on 14th December 1979. He was a Field Reservist in the British South African Police, and killed a mere seven days before the Lancaster House cease-fire agreement date. Not much is known about this fellow, or whether he was related to Brendan and Courtney Jelley. However, his second name, William, does raise sufficient curiosity to one-day further research whether there is any family connections. Speaking of which, a certain Brian Jelley warrants special mention - - Brian Jelley was called up in 1973 for Dad's Army, and did two stints in the RHU – Rhodesian Holding

Unit – at Mukumbura. Brian guarded Internal Affairs construction teams that were erecting two parallel fences all along the Rhodesian Mozambique border that formed part of the Cordon Sanitaire program to curtail terrorist incursions across the border. The Engineers would then follow the fence erectors to plant anti-personnel mine fields. The RHU later became the RDR – Rhodesian Defence Regiment, which came into being when the Guard Force was established to guard all the Protected Villages that had been constructed in the operational areas. However, in view of his firm, Mitchell Cotts, being so short staffed, Brian managed to get a couple of deferments until he was transferred to 11 Signals Squadron at the Army Headquarters King George VI Barracks Data Processing Unit.

Brian Jelley continued to serve in Dad's Army with 11th Signals Squadron up until the election results in February. After Zanu PF came to power, Brian and his Data Processing Unit colleagues "just discontinued" reporting for duty. In fact, because gangs were going around finding out whom of the old guard was still around, Brian opted to burn his military uniform. Nobody ever came around for 'destroying government property'.

STAFF OFFICER RESERVES / VOLUNTEER RESERVE

I was appointed SO Res / VR on 15th May 1980, accountable to Wing Commander Peter Cooke for Air Force Territorial Force members, for their call-up, and Volunteer Reserve liaison. This was a rewarding posting in that the Reserves as civilians were a fine bunch of fellows, plus the dedication of the Volunteer Reserve Squadrons that played such a vital role in the smooth functioning of Air Power aspect of the Rhodesian War effort. The job necessitated keeping tabs on 8 VR Squadrons and 2 500 General Reservists. My posting lasted till 18th January 1981.

Wing Commander PDC was an exceptional administrator, could juggle several balls in the air at the same time, and always had all his ducks in a row. He was particularly empathetic towards genuine TF deferment needs, was well respected by Dads Air Force, and was always very welcomed at the various VR Squadrons. My posting in effect replaced him, when he took over from Ozzie Penton as OCVR.

VR Headquarters was situated in the dungeon of Milton Buildings, which was in fact the ideal location in view of the vast amount of records and archiving that needed to be maintained. I recall a staff of four, Boss Peter, myself, Warrant Officer Moore and at least one Bluebird - uniformed Rhodesian Women's Services female. Air Force

Headquarters and the Prime Minister's Office was in the same building.

All Camp Commandants of the Forward Airfields were members of the VR, and it was Boss Peter's responsibility to ensure that all the FAFs were administered with the highest degree of efficiency, administrative acumen, strength of character, tact, stamina and a sense of humour, combined with compassion. The VR also manned the field Operations Rooms and some even took on active flying duties with the regulars. Their main function, however, was to provide an additional source of manpower to support and release more regular members for operational duties. It was a tall order - and not once did I encounter a disgruntled volunteer. They certainly acquitted themselves as invaluable and worthy of wearing the uniform of the elitist branch of the Security Forces.

The Volunteer Reserve was formed in 1961 and expanded to eight squadrons: -
1-Bulawayo, 2-Gwelo, 3-Salisbury, 4-Umtali, 5-Air Movements, 6-Chipinga, 7-Lowveld and 8-Field. Each Squadron was commanded by a Squadron Leader, of equivalent regular force rank, and structured on normal chain of command levels. VR parades were held weekly on Thursdays, with a monthly Saturday parade and long weekend training every second month. They served mainly in four categories: security, administration, operations and intelligence, and air movements.

101 (Bulawayo) Sqn – Brady Barracks
    Sqn Ldr Ted Strever
    Sqn Ldr Al Westwood
    Sqn Ldr Peter Corbishley
102 (Gwelo) Sqn - Thornhill
    Sqn Ldr Alan Brown
Sqn Ldr John Eadie
    Sqn Ldr Tommy Robinson
103 (Salisbury) Sqn – Cranborne Barracks
    Sqn Ldr Molly Maltas – till 1964/65
Sqn Ldr Graham Smith – till 1967/68
Sqn Ldr Percy Newton – till 1970
    Sqn Ldr Marshal Robinson – till the end
104 (Umtali) Sqn - Umtali
    Sqn Ldr Bob Annan
    Sqn Ldr Don Howe
    Sqn Ldr Pete Genari

Sqn Ldr Tony Chisnall (Chipinga Flt)
105 (Lomagundi) Sqn – Preston Farm, Banket
    Sqn Ldr Abbey Williams-Wynn
    Sqn Ldr Harry Turner
106 (Air Movements) Sqn – Cranborne Barracks
Sqn Ldr Gordon Leitch – till 1968
Sqn Ldr Clive Littlewood – till 1970
Sqn Ldr John Cramp – till 1977
Sqn Ldr Alan Shires – till the end
107 (Lowveld) Sqn – Buffalo Range Airport
    Sqn Ldr Colin Saunders
    Sqn Ldr Steve Fenton-Wells – till 1975/76
    Sqn Ldr Dave Sinclair – till the end
108 (Field) Sqn – Cranborne Barracks
    Sqn Ldr Geoff Fenn – died ?
    Sqn Ldr Stan Wilson – retired after a heart attack
Sqn Ldr Ron Blackmore

I was able to renew many of the friendships I had made during the course of my military career. I particularly enjoyed visiting Nos 101, 102, 106, 107 and 108 Squadrons. Ted Strever and Peter Corbishley commanded 101 in Bulawayo. John Eadie and Tommy Robinson were in Gwelo. John was also the Headmaster of Thornhill High School, so I had a lot of common interests. Pete Genari in Umtali, with Tony Chisnall in Chipinga, were always so helpful – and 106 also affiliated my old No 4 Squadron (a special soft spot in my heart). 107 down in the Lowveld, commanded respectively by sugar cane farmer Steve Fenton-Wells and pharmacist Dave Sinclair, endured and shared all those eventful months during my OC FAF 7 stint. 108 was just everywhere – wherever the invaluable expertise of the Volunteer Reservists were needed.

After a mere nine months in the job, I was transferred and took up a new posting challenge as Officer Commanding (Headquarters) Unit/Personnel 1.

NIBMAR

TIGER AND FEARLESS

The failed *HMS Tiger* Talks in 1966 was essentially over a return to legality, which was totally unacceptable to the Rhodesians. Harold Wilson wanted Ian Smith to capitulate, hand over the reins of government to Sir Humphrey Gibbs (despite our self-government status since 1921 and that Britain had never in our history been governed from London). Although much progress had been made regarding the first moves to settle, while the constitutional proposals could be accepted (some with great difficulty), the terms for a return to legality were completely out of contact with reality. The Cabinet findings were unanimous.

There was much evidence indicating that British public opinion was strongly on our side. Not only did 672 of the 674 souls on board Tiger side with Ian Smith, the Conservatives lambasted Wilson in the Commons. Sir Alec Douglas Home made the telling point that, if Britain believed it necessary to invoke mandatory sanctions "because the constitution of a country falls short of the standards of democracy that we require, we should be at war with half the world today." The drift towards double standards continued to accelerate year after year, and it reached a state where it can truly be said that the Commonwealth is the biggest fraud in the world. Its charter underlines parliamentary democracy and the freedom and justice associated with it, but the majority of its members have become one party dictatorships, where there is no freedom and justice.

Then, nearly two years later on, there were renewed settlement efforts in 1968 aboard HMS Fearless. Ian Smith and his team flew to Gibraltar again and were quartered on the warship Kent. Wilson and his cronies stayed on Fearless. Both warships were moored alongside one another in the harbour. The talks commenced in October 1968, but floundered over the main stumbling block of the return to legality. The British insisted that we renounce our current constitution, abandon power and virtually drift in space until a test of acceptability had indicated an acceptance of a new constitution. The situation worsened when Wilson introduced more vindictive restrictive conditions concerning British Privy Council interventions. Additionally, the British wanted the Zanu and Zapu terrorist organisations, which had received their training in Russia, China, Cuba and Libya to regroup and participate in the test of acceptability. Ian Smith addressed the Rhodesian nation on 19th November 1968 and said:

"After listening to what I have told you I am sure you will accept the validity of my claim that this alternative proposal is infinitely worse than the original one. I find it difficult to believe that the offer was made seriously. It was clear to us throughout the talks that the British were obsessed with the question of black majority rule and that this dominated all their thinking. They are prepared to accept that the white man in Rhodesia is expendable. We Rhodesians believe that there is a place and a future for all Rhodesians, black and white. Any other suggestion is unacceptable for us."

It is significant to record that on our Independence Day celebrations of 11 November 1968, the new Rhodesian green and white flag was raised for the first time, and the Union Jack lowered for the last time while the BSAP band played "Abide with Me."

The quote in Ian Smith's biography is good enough for me. He mentioned what historian Kenneth Young said in his book "*Rhodesia and Independence*:"

"After four years of struggle it appeared that Britain had come off worse in her war against her tiny adversary with its puny budget, its midget exports and its miniature army, civil service, police and air force. But the spirit and courage that made Britain great were not extinct; they had emigrated."

The moral of this story was NIBMAR - No Independence Before African Majority Rule. Were we farting against thunder?

AFZ - AIR FORCE OF ZIMBABWE

Fire Force operations, airstrikes and external raids continued for a time until the Lancaster House agreement between the warring parties led to a cease-fire.

The Lancaster House cease-fire agreement allocated the Rhodesian forces 47 operational bases - and the Patriotic Front 14 Assembly Points. The greatest fear that Mugabe had, was that the Assembly Points were vulnerable to being bombed by the Rhodesian Air Force. The peace agreement was signed in the great hall of Lancaster House on 21st December 1979.

Josiah Tongogara was killed in very mysterious circumstances. His Mercedes had crashed into the back of a truck while it was trying to overtake a lorry on a road near the town of Palmeira about 100 miles north of Maputo. It was pitch dark at the time of the accident and the truck did not have its lights on (unlikely, being pitch dark and in the process of over taking). Tongogara, who was sitting in the front passenger seat, was decapitated as he was hurled through the windscreen on impact. His driver was injured. Mugabe's attempts to get the body back to Maputo quickly turned into a fiasco that served only to fuel the suspicion and rumours that Tongogara had been murdered. A member of one of the local Salisbury funeral parlours was tasked to get to Maputo to inspect the body – he came back with dubious evidence that there were no bullet wounds.

The monitoring force comprising many nations arrived in the country to oversee the new elections. Vast Assembly areas were set up to accommodate the estimated 50,000 guerrillas expected to flood into the country from Mozambique and Zambia. In terms of the Lancaster House Agreement, both the Zanla and Zipra forces, for the time being united under the Patriotic Front banner, were supposed to be confined to these points until after the elections on March 3, 1980. The British Government believed it had the perfect plan to establish a stable coalition government in an internationally recognised Zimbabwe. And it didn't include the ultimate winner – Robert Mugabe.

The belief was that Joshua Nkomo's Zapu faction would win enough seats in the new 100-seat parliament to warrant the senior position in a coalition which would also contain 20 constitutionally-entrenched white seats and several dozen for Bishop Abel Muzorewa's Uanc party.

The cease-fire was very fragile indeed. Notable breaches included:-
Three days after the Soames/Mugabe meeting, 15 black civilians were killed and more than 20 injured when a bus was ambushed about 100 miles east of Salisbury on the road to Umtali. The rockets and small arms used suggested that Zanla was responsible.

February 10th, Enos Nkala intimidated and incited Matabeleland crowds with the statement that the war would resume if Mugabe did not win the election. February 11th, a bomb exploded underneath the motorcade taking Mugabe to the Fort Victoria airfield. Five guards in the car behind him were injured. Mugabe falsely accused the Rhodesian Air Force of bombing two villages in the north-east on the Mozambique border. Lord Soames ignored it.

February 17th, Comops HQ communiqué stated two churches in the city centre damaged by bombs - the blast from one damaging the Monomotapa Hotel That same night, an explosion occurred near a church in Harare Township. It occurred in the back of a car, and killed the two black occupants - Selous Scouts operatives Lieutenant

Pirigongo and Corporal Moyo. The Mambo printing press in Gwelo, publisher of Moto, was blown up.

Some 207 breaches were reported by the cease fire commission - the vast majority attributed to Zanla.

The number of contacts between the Rhodesian forces and bandits (the so-called guerrillas who had not gone into the assembly points) was now running at nine or ten a day, twice the level of a few weeks earlier and mainly in the Eastern Highlands. British observers concluded a systematic and calculated campaign of violence and intimidation by Zanu (PF).

Neither the British nor, ironically, the Rhodesians for all their knowledge of Africa, had the basic concept of African rule. While the Rhodesian authorities complained bitterly, they were unable to convince the newly installed temporary British governor, Lord Soames, that wholesale intimidation was being conducted by Mugabe's gooks in the rural areas where eighty percent of the voters lived (the *unable to convince* is putting it mildly – Ian Douglas Smith did not mince his words – he called it *The Great Betrayal*).

This intimidation was brutal, widespread and very, very effective. It was later estimated, and corroborated by several Zanla officers, that up to sixty percent of all guerrillas in the Assembly Points were, in fact, *mujibas* – local youths armed with rusting, unworkable weapons. This gave the impression that PF forces were abiding by the rules, while in reality the hardened men of the terrorist ranks were in the field doing what they knew best – coercing simple peasants into voting the right way. By permitting the intimidation to continue, the British lost control of events and out-smarted themselves. When the results were announced, Mugabe had swept the board with 57 of the available 80 unreserved seats.

As one German observer put it: "If that was a fair and free election, I am a Chinaman."

17th April 1980, at midnight, Rhodesia became Zimbabwe. The violence that followed included:-

At Assembly Point X-ray, near the town of Mtoko, the guerrillas took the law into their own hands, seizing control of the main roads around the town and arbitrarily ambushing civilian and military vehicles. Police and farmers in the town were killed.

At Chitungwiza, 15 miles from the centre of Salisbury. Nkomo's men were fighting Mugabe's units. Open warfare broke out on the streets of Bulawayo in November – the Battle of Entumbane, when at least 55 people died and more than 200 were wounded in street battles between the two rival armies for control.

A New Sarum K-Car was stolen on the eve of the election results being announced.

Chaos reined, a flood of emigration followed; and both General Peter Walls, for the economically active whites, and Edgar Tekere were victims of the New Zimbabwe. In Tekere's case, he was tried for murder, having personally led an attack on a farmhouse whilst being a cabinet minister in Mugabe's regime.

The people who really lost out were not the whites, but the Africans themselves. At no time were they ever given a real say in what they wanted; rather, they were told what they would get. True, they were given the right to vote, but that one vote put them under a much harsher yoke than the white men ever did. "One man, one vote is what the people want," the slogan went. One man, one vote is all the majority of the population has really received since that day in March 1980. In the 20 years since Zimbabwe was born, the country has still been a de facto One Party state; and with the President listed as the 11th richest man in the word. And, in a country whose economy is shot to hell – I might add.

STOLEN K-CAR

"In the week leading up to the March 1980 elections, 1 Commando 1 RLI were manning the then Salisbury Fire Force operating out of New Sarum." Rick van Malsen related to the author. He continued: "Our task was fairly mundane and consisted of two, 40-minute sorties a day over Salisbury, dropping troops off at key points and then picking them up later, and with the aim of boosting flagging civilian moral more than anything else.

"At last light each day the troops returned to their Cranborne barracks and then they re-positioned at first light the following day to take up the waiting game at Sarum. On the evening of 3rd March 1980, the CO of 1 RLI, Lt Col Charlie Aust, summoned all officers to a briefing at the Battalion HQ. In the briefing he stated that preliminary counts of the ballots had indicated a landslide victory for Mugabe and that all military options to prevent this had been scuppered! Fundamentally it was the end! We were then given our detailed tasks for the following day – the 4th March. Election result day

"One Commando's task was to be at Sarum by first light on the 4th March, and to take off at 0845, so we were airborne and over Highfields High density suburb when the election results were announced at 0900 hours. The task of the Fire Force was to enforce law and order and to react to any "victory" celebrations by the way of looting, arson etc that the winning party and their supporters may have planned.

"Early on the morning of the 4th we arrived at Sarum, to find a very confused K-Car tech who couldn't find his K-Car! All of the Fire Force helicopters had been parked on the hard standing outside the hangars overnight, as was standard operating procedure and now it was nowhere! At first, it was thought that techs from another Squadron were responsible for taking and hiding it, as some sort of prank, but by 0830, a thorough search of the whole of Sarum had revealed nothing, and indeed the K-Car was still missing, together with my flying helmet which I had left in the aircraft.

"As our task had do continue, with or without a gunship, Ian Harvey the K-Car pilot commandeered a G-Car and off to war we went somewhat concerned as a K-Car in the wrong hands was a frightening thought!

"The sortie was a non-event excepting for about halfway through it 'Harvs' noticed a lone K-Car circling over the city center. We were unable to establish comms with the stranger, and as Sarum Ops didn't know who it was either, 'Harvs' decided then it was time to go and have a look! So here I was, sitting in a Perspex bubble, on the last day of the war, about to get involved in a potential air-to-air combat with a "dissident" – him armed with a 20 mm cannon and us with a .303 Brownings!! To say I was unhappy was a major understatement! As we started to approach this "target" Sarum Ops came up and confirmed it was a legitimate K-Car covering an SAS operation and not the missing aircraft. Panic over, and with one very relieved Brown Job, we then returned to our task.

"By the end of the day we had still had not found the missing aircraft, nor had it come to light anywhere else. It was however found, two days later, abandoned and undamaged on the side of the main Glendale - Centenary road.

"About a year later I met the pilot responsible, who told me the full story of when and how he had stolen it. The "thief" was a reserve pilot, who had retired from the Air Force, and was then a farmer in the Centenary area. All the farmers in the area had been called to a meeting on the evening of the 3rd March at the local Farmers Hall. There, some Special Branch idiot had got up on the stage, and told them that the war was over, that Mugabe had won, and that mayhem, revenge rape and pillage, such as had been seen in the Congo in the early 60's, was about to erupt throughout Rhodesia. The farmers, now thoroughly alarmed at these statements from someone "in the know," then tried to contact Salisbury to see what was happening there but were unable to get through on the phone. With 2000 bad guys sitting in an Assembly Point only 30 kms down the road, they felt threatened and totally isolated from the main centers. They firmly believed it was now "everyman for himself" and isolated communities, such as theirs, would have to fight their own way into the main centres, and then join the rest of the populace in a mass exodus south. They also believed that the Rhodesian military machine would become totally splintered with a million calls for help and so decided to make suitable retreat plans of their own! As they had an active Air Force pilot in their midst, air support was centre to all of the plans they conjured up that night. Initially, they thought the easiest thing would be to steal a Dak, load all the woman and children on board and fly them out to safety. The men would then form a convoy, and fight their way South via Salisbury. However, as there were too many pax for the Dak, they opted for the next plan, which was to steal a K-Car and for this to ride "top cover" over "their" convoy heading south, refueling from diesel on the back of a truck.

"So later that night, the pilot and a friend drove to Salisbury. The pilot was dressed in his uniform so he had no problem getting into Sarum air base. Once inside the perimeter, he found the K-Car unguarded, fully fuelled up ready for the next day's operations. His main fear was that the noise and time it took for the start up might alert someone, so he just sat and waited until a heavy jet came into land at Salisbury International, then started up under cover of the noise of the big jet, and ducked off over the Sarum revetments.

"Initially the flight went fine. However in the darkness he became disorientated (Lost in Army parlance!) and so landed on a high rock dome, (all done without a tech to assist) and waited for first light so he could see where he was. At first light, he then flew to the bottom end of his farm, and hid the K-Car in a grove of trees.

"As we all know, nothing really happened on the 4th March 1980 and all the fears of revenge and mass murder never occurred. The pilot, however, now had a problem - a stolen K-Car at the bottom end of his farm! Two days later, he flew it out and parked it on the side of the road, where it could be found, and a friend then picked him up and returned him home.

"It didn't take CID, police etc very long to work out who had stolen the aircraft, and the pilot was picked up and placed in Centenary jail, where, from all accounts he was treated like visiting Royalty!! From Centenary he was taken to Air Force Headquarters where the

Commander of the Air Force interviewed him. Because of the sensitivities of the time, the Air Force declined to prosecute but did ask him to resign his Commission, which he gladly did!
Rick van Malsen never did get his flying helmet back! Air Force recovered it from the K-Car, but told him that as he no longer had a need for it, they were keeping it!

OFFICER COMMANDING (HQ) UNIT / PERSONNEL 1

Command of the Headquarters Unit was assumed on 19th January 1981. Little did I know that this challenge would only last for slightly over four months, until 31st May 1981. I fancied the OC Unit (Air Force HQ nogal.) title but found responsibility for the general personnel administration for all the other ranks in the Air Force – totalling some 1200 permanent members somewhat daunting. Tutoring by Peter Cooke paid dividends. My duties and responsibilities are summarised as follows:-

Appointments in respect of regular airmen – to specific established posts.
Promotion Boards – for Flt Sergeant, WO II, Master Technicians and WO Is.
Routine Promotions – on time qualification and Trade Test Board certification.
Promotion Examinations – Officers (was secretary to the Promotion Board).
Postings and Attachments
Changes of Engagements
Minor Works – liaison between MOW – Ministry of Works, Defence Ministry and the APU – Accommodation Planning Unit
Issuing of Unit Orders – on a weekly basis.

Air Force Headquarters were in the planning phase of relocating from Milton Buildings in Jameson Street, to King George Barracks. With the groundwork done, I was replaced by Paddy Morgan as the new P1, and took up the next challenge of Staff Officer Personnel on 1st June 1981.

STAFF OFFICER PERSONNEL

With my promotion to Wing Commander (the Army equivalent of Lieutenant-Colonel) came the appointment as Staff Officer Personnel, reporting to Director Administration, Group Captain Pete Nicholls. This responsibility entailed administrating all the Officer affairs, and having P1 or Personnel 1 reporting to me and being responsible for all the Other Ranks i.e. all the NCOs - Non Commissioned Officers. Having previously held that post of P1/Officer Commanding Headquarters Unit, I was fully au fait with my subordinate's duties.

Staff Officer Personnel needed to keep tabs on the Air Force Establishment, and submit monthly reports with progress made to fill the various vacancies. Whilst scratching among some old papers, I came across a copy of one of my old lists:

Air Force Strengths

Officers	Estab.	Str,	Vacancies	Tech.Branch	Estab	Str	Vacan
GD	190	101	89	Engineers	148	74	74
ATC	12	5	7	Airframes	160	78	62
Admin	8	15	0	Armament	93	62	31
Computer	3	0	3	Elect Air	69	51	18
Medical	9	4	5	Elect Grd	9	7	2
Equip	12	8	4	Instruments	63	33	30
Education	6	6	0	Metal Wkr	7	3	4
Legal	1	1	0	MTSO	7	3	4
PJI	3	2	1	Radio	103	48	55
Catering	1	0	1	Telep	50	26	24
Tech	43	35	8	Line Telep	7	1	6
TOTALS	**288**	**177**	**111**	Photo	13	7	6
				Carp	7	5	2
				Draughtsmen	5	0	5
				Safety Equip	39	16	23
				Gen Fitter	8	4	4
				MT	35	12	23
				Range Wdn	3	1	2
				Pool	24	0	24
				TOTALS	**850**	**431**	**419**

Airmen: Other Trades

Airmen	Estab	Str	Vac	Regiment	Estab	Str	Vac

275

Airmen	Estab	Str	Vac	Regiment	Estab	Str	Vac
Med Assist	26	19	7	Officers Regt	29	22	7
Handyman	4	3	1	Cadets	0	6	0
Clk GD	64	44	20	Officers AA	12	12	0
Clk Canteen	2	1	1	Instructors	83	74	9
Fire Fighter	17	8	9	Storemen	8	7	1
Cat/Stwd	23	23	0	Clerks	20	20	0
Supplier	83	64	19	Cooks	30	27	3
PJI	14	9	5	Tailors	4	4	0
Drill Instr	2	2	0	Range Wdns	3	3	0
Groundsman	2	1	1	Fire Fighters	72	71	1
Tailor	2	1	1	MT	62	54	8
PJI/DI	6	4	2	Provost	128	115	13
Tech Assist	1	0	1	D/Handlers	50	50	0
Dental Assist	2	1	1	Infantry	256	240	16
No Trade	0	52	0	Sqn WOs	4	2	2
TOTALS	**250**	**231**	**19**	HQ Staff	15	15	0
				AA Gunners	272	0	272
				Regt Amin	54	35	19
				TOTALS	**1126**	**779**	**347**

It doesn't take a rocket scientist to conclude that the Air Force faced critical skills shortages. The Officers Gradation List also reflected serious doubts in the confidence of the hierarchy forced integration of the warring forces could maintain standards. The Air Force Regiment was the exception to the rule – the ex-gooks could be slotted in much easier, but technical-skills were still in short supply. The loss in confidence in the new government resulted in daily retirements. Those remaining would be frustrated by accelerated 'affirmative action' – and possibly only stayed on to enhance their pensions.

In 1979, long before the cessation of hostilities, Zanu signed pilot training deals with Romania, North Korea, Red China and Libya. Zanla did not have the slightest inkling of what qualifications were required for pilot trainees, with the result that most of those sent for training were totally unsuitable. When Zanu-PF came to power they called for volunteers from the Assembly Points for the Air Force – and they were duly dispatched overseas to those countries where pilot training deals had been signed – but without preliminary suitability checks. This resulted in a wholesale failure rate. The white command element of the Air Force only became aware of this dismal situation when the so-called 'pilots' began drifting back to Zimbabwe in mid-1981 – when I held the post of SO Pers. The Air Force faced a political difficult situation, as recognition of the 'flying qualifications' of the Communist Bloc and other states was impossible. To solve the problem each returnee was given full pilot retraining with 'three chances' before wastage. Despite this generous modicodling, only about 10% ultimately received their pilot's wings with the Air Force of Zimbabwe. That the white core of the Air Force was not expendable did not endear the elite service to Zanu-PF. Standards were dropped alarmingly to accommodate the new political masters. The Piper plays the Tune. (See also Operation *Sausage Machine*, which follows).

By July 1982, two years after independence, the overall composition of the Air Force of Zimbabwe was still predominantly white. The aircraft strength of the force was:-

No 1 Squadron – 11 Hunters (ten FGA 9 and one T 8 trainer).
No 2 Squadron – 4 Hawks (with four more Mk 60 on order).
No 3 Squadron – 8 Dakotas and 5 Islanders.
No 4 Squadron – 5 Lynxes
No 5 Squadron – 1 Canberra
No 6 Squadron – 31 Genets
No 7 Squadron – 8 Alouette and 4 Bell helicopters

Not all of these aircraft were serviceable, owing to a lack of technicians and in the event, there were insufficient pilots to fly all the machines. Other aircraft were mothballed, although one Provost and two Vampires were maintained in flying condition as museum pieces. No 5 Squadron was effectively disbanded, apart from one Canberra retained for photographic reconnaissance work. Besides, there was a critical shortage of navigators.

If I thought the Air Force was going down the tubes, the Rhodesian Army was indeed a lot worse off. The SAS and the RLI struck their colours and sent them down to South Africa. The two units ceased to exist. The Selous Scouts had become extinct a few months earlier. Its members had been badged to other regiments to avoid the violent recriminations that would follow. These magnificent units, and I include the old order of the Air Force, simply vanished into the air. Gone – with the winds of change.

I expect Harold Macmillan to turn in his grave.

The first page of the Officers Gradation List dated December 1980 resembled the following:

Rank Name	No	D.o.B	Joined	Left	Remarks
AIR MARSHAL					
N Walsh	242	5/1933	6/1956	4/1983	Retired to Australia
AIR VICE-MARSHAL					
GL Pink	4026	2/1932	10/1958	2/1982	Retired to Pretoria
AIR COMMODORE					
MRHD Grier	4000	9/1934	9/1956	3/1982	
HCS Slatter	4115	4/1942	3/1962	7/1983	Deported to UK – Treason charges
GROUP CAPTAIN					
HG Griffiths	4099	5/1943	6/1961	10/1981	
PV Pile	1014	12/1939	3/1956	7/1983	Promoted Air Commodore - Deported
JF Barnes	4043	10/1939	1/1959		Promoted to Air Commodore
PJ Nicholls	4140	3/1931	11/1962	4/1983	OC NS
GV Wright	4051	1/1938	1/1959	4/1983	
DAG Jones	4149	5/1943	3/1963		
WING COMMANDER					
LAS Taylor	4006	10/1931	1/1957		Retired Kariba
RAB Tasker	4109	9/1937	1/1962	2/1982	
SP Kesby	4171	1/1945	4/1964		Group Captain, Retired
PD Cooke	230	3/1932	4/1976		
BW Vaughan	4132	12/1943	6/1962	5/1982	
JD Annan	4288	9/1944	4/1971	?/1982	
PM Geldenhuys	4117	2/1943	3/1962	6/1982	

Name	Number	Date 1	Date 2	Date 3	Notes
PR Briscoe	4239	6/1946	1/1969	7/1983	Wing Commander, Deported
TN Bennett	4129	1/1941	5/1962		London
DR Thorne	4352	5/1936	2/1974		
RWJ Sykes	4216	8/1943	4/1967		D.Admin
AW Wild	4252	8/1949	4/1969		

SQUADRON LEADER

Name	Number	Date 1	Date 2	Date 3	Notes
DW Pasea	4133	3/1943	6/1962	5/1982	
SW Baldwin	4267	7/1951	3/1970	12/1981	
AD Oakley	4171	12/1951	7/1970	?	
MJ Litson	4263	3/1950	3/1970	1982	Pietermaritzburg
CP Dickinson	4276	3/1948	2/1971		Withdrew resignation
SP Morgan	4282	4/1949	2/1971	?	
L Webb	4480	3/1949	3/1978		
CP James	4490	11/1946	6/1978	?	Withdrew resignation
CG Ward	4286	11/1948	2/1971		

ACTING SQUADRON LEADER

Name	Number	Date 1	Date 2	Notes
IM Harvey	4062	11/1940	2/1978	

FLIGHT LIEUTENANT

Name	Number	Date 1	Date 2	Date 3	Notes
MR D'Hotman	4174	12/1929	11/1964		
JG Russell	4320	7/1954	3/1973		
NDE Maasdorp	4318	3/1954	2/1973		
KW Blain	4451	11/1946	1/1978	10/1981	
DP Squance	4341	5/1955	1/1974		
DM Vernon	4346	11/1955	1/1974	?	Left ?
NHM Meikle	4349	4/1953	1/1974		OC 6 Sqn, wef 1st January 1982
GA Osborne	4371	2/1956	2/1975		
JD Kitson	4367	2/1956	2/1975		Withdrew – for Air Zimbabwe
RH Griffiths	4362	8/1957	2/1975	1/1982	
M Cappuccitti	6871	6/1952	10/1976		'A' Flt Cdr
BW Cockcroft	4392	10/1957	3/1976		
RT Skinner	4406	12/1957	3/1976		
ANJ Thorogood	4407	12/1956	3/1976		
DG Bryson	4391	7/1956	3/1976		
JH Ludgator	4435	11/1956	1/1976	12/1981	
MM Pingo	4430	6/1957	2/1977		
JFD Skeeles	4434	10/1955	2/1977		Withdrew resignation 12/1981
DS Shirley	4405	2/1953	3/1976	10/1981	
ET Jackman	4420	4/1958	2/1977		

ACTING FLIGHT LIEUTENANT
M Orbell   4428   7/1957 2/1977
IMW Wallis   4437   4/1957 2/1977
MJ Seegmuller   4433   11/1958   2/1977
AR Middelton 4426   2/1958 2/1977 12/1981
AIR LIEUTENANT
TJM Ernst   4446   1/1954 7/1977 10/1981

Quite a while after retiring from the Air Force, I carried out a brief survey of those Rhodesians that were killed or died between 11th November 1965 and 30th March 1980. A total of 1 873 Security Force personnel paid the supreme sacrifice. This figure of 1873 was made up of 55 Air Force, 933 Army, 506 Internal Affairs and 379 BSAP members. The majority of the airmen were aircrew, and bearing in mind that the General Duties establishment of the Air Force was but 190 officers (with actual strengths normally way below establishment), it will be noted that a high percentage of airmen did not survive the Rhodesian bush war.

Conversely, Security Forces accounted for a much higher ratio of enemy killed during the war. Crack Units like the SAS and RLI claimed ratios in the order of 10 enemy for every one Security Force casualty. I presume that in some time in the future a reasonably accurate figure will emerge.

My CV on retiring from the Force, in respect of my SO Pers duties read "Primarily responsible for the personnel administration for all the Officers in the Force. Duties included recruiting, postings, appointments, engagements, commissioning, promotions, retirements and discharges. Other specific secondary duties included the direction and control of the Personnel section of the Administrative Branch: Implementation of Officers Promotion Examination Policy: Administrative action in respect of civilian employees: Processing Honours and Awards: Injury Reports and notification action in respect of casualties: and the issue of Air Force Orders and Officers Confidential Orders."

Quite a mouth full. During the latter stages of the war, the most painful aspect of the job was the notification of next-of-kin that husbands and fathers had been killed in action.

OPERATION QUARTZ

Operation *Quartz* called for the bombing of all the assembly points. Special Force personnel would assist in directing the jets onto targets.

The SASs mission involved the assassination of Robert Mugabe, Simon Muzenda; plus Zanla commander Rex Nhongo and Zipra's Dumiso Dabengwa and Lookout Masuku. Other targets included hundreds of Zanla in separate buildings around the capital, another hundred or so Zanla at the Medical Arts Centre, and several hundred at the University of Rhodesia's audio-visual centre. Intensive and thorough rehearsals for the operation was carried out – with top secret sanctions-busting 106 millimetre recoilless anti-tank rifles that were to be used for the first time. The SAS even had eight Russian T 55 tanks at their disposal, never mind the Eland 90 armoured cars and a wide selection of heavy artillery and weaponry. Exhaustive battle preparations and house-clearing drills for all the targets were carried out at Kabrit Barracks. The tanks were pre-positioned at KG V1 Barracks, the Armoured Car Regiment moved to the SAS barracks, all waiting for the "Go" code-word. The mission was one of the most-detailed and well-planned operations of the war. The Security Forces waited, and waited ....and waited.

Time was running out. By Sunday, 2nd March 1980, two days before the election results were to be announced, a false sense of security prevailed. A feeling spread that that Mugabe had indeed lost the election and there would be no need to activate Operation *Quartz*. Rumours circulated that the South Africans were already secretly inside the country, ready to react whatever the election result. At 09h00 on 4th March, the results were out. The reaction among the Security Forces and the country's whites was one of paralysing shock, then disbelief, and then dismay. A mass exodus followed overnight.

The Nat JOC, and Comops in particular, floundered. A rift between Peter Walls and Air Marshal Mick McLaren widened. Ian Smith was hoping that daring action, reminiscent of the transborder operations when the chips were down, should be forthcoming from the military leaders. Mick McLaren had confided in Ian Smith that he was at logger heads with Peter Walls. On Friday 7th March 1980, with time rapidly running out, Air Marshal Mick McLaren met with Rhodesian Prime Minister Ian Smith. Mick McLaren explained how things had gone wrong. The Nat JOC had three options. The first was to eliminate intimidation, but that had not succeeded. The second was to proscribe certain areas (declare known areas as not complying with the spirit of the election process) – but Lord Soames had changed their minds. The third was disclosing the truth about intimidation and declaring the election null and void. Mick McLaren is quoted as saying, in response to the query whether to force an issue: "...Some of us have been trying to get this moving over the past week, but it's a case of flogging a dead horse." After many years of thought, I chose to interpret this discussion between Air Marshal McLaren and Mr Ian Smith that General Walls was the stumbling block, and the reason why the "fingers on trigger" faithful lost confidence in the discredited Comops.

This finding, to my mind, seems to be borne out by Ian Smith's *"The Great Betrayal"* that on Tuesday afternoon 11th March 1980, he (Ian Smith) saw "..a pretty depressed Mick McLaren. He was collecting much flak because the Nat JOC had failed to deliver the goods they had promised to all and sundry, including their own security forces. He had his time cut out explaining that the decision had not been his and, if it had been, things might have been very different."

My finding, is perhaps, further justified when Air Marshal McLaren resigned on the 10th April. Again, I quote Ian Smith's words:- "...an interesting discussion with McLaren, who came to inform me the next day that he had handed in his resignation, not only because of his belief that Comops had served its purpose but, into the bargain, was completely discredited. He wished to disassociate himself from the duplicity associated with Comops and the resultant total contempt in which it was held by every serviceman."

The Selous Scouts faded into oblivion, the Special Air Service disbanded, as did the Rhodesian Light Infantry. With dignity and a great sense of pride, the latter two units were formally paraded and stood down. Many men from these regiments drifted to South Africa and joined that country's defence forces; broken in spirit, but sticking as far as possible to each other in the brotherhood.

OPERATION SAUSAGE MACHINE – ZNA –1980s

At Lancaster House, the three parties – the Rhodesians, Zapu and Zanu – agreed that a new army would be formed by amalgamating the Rhodesian Security Forces, Zipra and Zanla into the ZNA – Zimbabwe National Army. The British provided BMATT – The British Military Advisory and Training Team.

The integration exercise, according to *Soldiers in Zimbabwe's Liberation War*, was coded Operation Sausage Machine. General Peter Walls, however, doubts such a derogatory term officially given, particularly considering the sensitivity of the times, and suggests it might have been a nickname given by someone involved, probably BMATT. Anyway, the barriers to commissioned rank were lifted, Zanla's Rex Nhongo and Zipra's Lookout Masuku became Lieutenant Generals, and Josiah Tungumirai was made a Major General.

Despite the rapid promotions to senior ranks, serious problems arose integrating the lower ranks, or cannon fodder into the ZNA. Mutiny, desertions, banditry, lawlessness, in-discipline and in fighting amongst Zanla and Zipra became the order of the day. There was also widespread non-surrender of terrorist weapons from the Assembly Points to the ZNA. Zipra in particular cashed a lot of their conventional war weapons, and were known to have massive stockpiles at Gwaai River Mine in north-east Matabeleland. They even shipped in trainloads from Zambia, across the Victoria Falls bridge.

By the end of 1980 less than 15,000 out of a total of 65,000 ex Zanla and Zipra had been trained and integrated into the National Army.

To keep the feuding elements occupied and gainfully employed, instead of twiddling their thumbs in the Assembly Points, Operation *Seed* was launched – short for Soldiers Employed in Economic Development.

OPERATION WINTER

The SADF liaison officer in Salisbury Commandant Andre Bestbier was aware of the overtures that the Selous Scouts, and particularly the SAS, Lieutenant-Colonel Garth Barrett's, visits down south.

During the post election period, while Lord Soames governed Zimbabwe before handing over to Zanu PF, and while the new ZNA was being phased in, the Rhodesian Army used low loaders to move much of the sensitive equipment to South Africa. A lot of equipment was also flown out from New Sarum, Thornhill and Fylde Air base by SAAF C-130 Hercules and C-160 Transall transport aircraft.

Major Mike Curtain's first job was to sort out the problems of the SAS move to South Africa. His experience made him a useful man to have around at the Diplomatic Mission, because he had gained a wide personal knowledge of personnel serving in the Rhodesian Security Forces. Applications by civilians anxious to obtain residence permits went to the bottom of the pile, and priority was given to the military personnel wishing to relocate. Volunteers for the SADF were dealt with expeditiously. Preference was initially given to all the Special Forces. The SADF's net by this time had widened beyond restricting recruitment to members of the SAS and Selous Scouts for the Recces. They began taking every experienced man who came along for placement in the wider SADF. The only difference was that they retained their offer to take complete units, while everyone else joined as individuals. Men from the Rhodesian Air Force, the Rhodesian Light Infantry, the British South African Police and whatever, were offered identical contracts.

During February / March 1980, 100 SAS members arrived at 1 Reconnaissance Commando in Durban and formed 6 Recce Commando. This unit, as well as the Reconnaissance Commando Base unit, was absorbed into 1 Reconnaissance Regiment (on 1st January 1981). 3 Recce Commando was activated in April 1980 when the Selous Scouts from Rhodesia arrived in South Africa. In this month, 120 former Rhodesian soldiers and their families were accommodated at a new base on the farm Schiettocht, outside Phalaborwa. Garth Barrett commanded 6 Reconnaissance Commando during 1980 – with the unit boasting about the fact that 17 Honoris Crux medals were awarded to its members – no other unit has achieved this feat. Ex Selous Scout 'Commandant' Bert Sachse commanded 5 Reconnaissance Commando during 1983 (and again from February 1990 to December 1993).

Major Curtain also recruited some thirty blacks with military experience, but to his surprise, none were particularly desperate or regarded themselves as political refugees. They were merely looking for jobs and were more interested in the higher SADF pay than anything else.

Then in July 1980, the Zimbabwe Government announced it was downgrading the South African Diplomatic Mission in Harare to the status of trade mission. The reason given was that the South African diplomats had been recruiting spies and mercenaries.

My brother-in-law Frans Malan also had an opinion to express as the sun set with the demise of Rhodesia. This is what he said: "Regarding the Rhodesian bush war I have often asked myself the question why? In the words of some author whose name I cannot now recall "It was the best of times and it was the worst of times". The legacy it has left with me which will not change in my life time is an utter distrust and dare I say it, a loathing of all politicians."

Peter Petter-Bowyer wrote "Please God, (note pause) Save the Queen." I concluded, perhaps it was all in vain, but I don't think so.

PROJECT BARNACLE

Project Barnacle had its origins as the *Section of Pseudo Operations* of the South African Special Forces. The Commanding General Special Forces Fritz Loots was interested in recruiting a team of professional clandestine operators from the Rhodesian Security

Forces. The South African Special Forces obtained Renosterspruit Farm, south of Hartbeespoort Dam and north of Johannesburg, as a base from which D40 operated. Rhodesian recruits started arriving there in June and July 1980 – including one particularly notorious ex BSAP Special Branch operator known only presently as "Brian" – and referred to as *Major Brian* in *Cry Zimbabwe* (and as KD in *The Kevin Woods Story* – and subsequently identified as Gray Branfield – who was killed in Iraq in 2005). During the following twelve months, Brian's team expanded to 40 as former regular policemen, turned Zipra as well as ex-Zanla terrorists, filtered down south.

Brian had been stationed in Bulawayo, with the rank of Detective Inspector, and had commanded a Special Branch pseudo team of regular detectives, both black and white, as well as captured terrorists converted to the Rhodesian cause. These were the turned or tame terrs of Security Forces parlance. They were used mainly on external operations to pinpoint terrorist camps and establish infiltration routes. Brian's area of expertise lay in Rhodesia, Botswana and Zambia.

On 9th January 1981, Major-General Fritz Loots issued a Top Secret directive formalising *Project Barnacle's* operational tasks as follows:-

Purpose: To manage extremely sensitive operations
Functions:
Elimination's
Ambuscades against individuals of strategic importance
Operativeness as instructed in super sensitive operations
Gathering of combat information regarding the above mentioned operations
Gathering of information as assigned in cases where other sources could not be utilised
The conducting of special security tasks, such as observation of sources/agents and the performance of certain special tasks, such as observation of at random security experiments as instructed for Spec Forces.

Project Barnacle consisted of three wings:-
Operational Wing, commanded by Major Brian (Gray Branfield – a particularly deadly ex BSAP SB operator) and responsible for urban operations in Zimbabwe, Botswana and Zambia.
Intelligence Wing, commanded by Major Winston (Hart – authors guess), charged with gathering intelligence from their own and other sources – and were also fed information by the operational wing.

Long Range Reconnaissance Wing, commanded by Major Boet Swart (an ex-Rhodesian Air Force officer, and former Selous Scout), operating in Angola. Initially only two ex-Rhodesians, Tim and Chris, were involved, but were later joined by Lieutenant André Diedricks of the Recces.

CSI – Chief of Staff (Intelligence), was headed by a Major Pete (*nom de guerre*) and specialised in operational intelligence. Major 'P' was also an expert on cross-border activities into Zimbabwe. CSI also absorbed intelligence officers not involved in Project Barnacle. This tended to create a rift and some jealousies between the former Special Branch (BSAP) officers doing their own thing with the Rhodesians of Project Barnacle and those absorbed by the greater SADF. The Barnacle posts were considered plum jobs. (I beg to differ. I also held an Int. Officer appointment while flying Hunters. I preferred flying than trying to interpret intelligence.).

The single black operators were accommodated at Renosterspruit and in Hillbrow, and the whites were dispersed to the Fourways area in northern Johannesburg. Their pay cheques came from Armscor. A pseudo front company, NKTF Properties was established, and later changed to President Security Consultants (Pty) Ltd – with a head office listed in Verwoerdburg. The Managing Director was Colonel Rautenbach of Special Forces. President Security was funded entirely by the SADF. Renosterspruit was expanded with the construction of office blocks, mechanical workshops and armouries. Much money was spent.

Project Barnacle operatives were involved with, and implicated in, several closely guarded events in Zimbabwe. These included the sabotage of, and discovery of explosive devices found in Zimbabwe Armoured Regiment vehicles at KGVI Barracks in December 1980; a car bomb blast at Second Street and Central Avenue, Salisbury on old years eve 1980; the elimination of Gqabi on 31st July 1981; Operation Gericke in November 1981; support for and armament supplies to Zipra dissidents and with covert activities associated with CSI. Project Barnacle ultimately became the BSB – Burgerlike Samewerking Bureau – whose activities were partially made public during the Doctor Wouter Basson testimonies in the Truth and Reconciliation Commission (TRC) hearings. Ex-Recce operator Douw Steyn assured the writer many years later, that we "have heard nothing yet." It will be interesting what unfolds in the future – but that is presently outside the scope of this story.

Last, but by no means least of Project Barnacle's covert activities – was the sabotage of Hawk and Hunter aircraft at the Air Force base at Thornhill.

A certain Project Barnacle *'Team Oscar'* operator, responsible for gathering intelligence in the Midlands, passed on vital information about the Air Force whilst on leave in South Africa. The report on the current strengths of Hunter, Canberra and Lynx aircraft was passed on to Major Brian (Gray Branfield)– as well as the imminent arrival of the British Aerospace Hawk Mk 60 fighter/strike aircraft. The plan, formulated by Major Brian, and which included using the Air Force contact and the ex-Selous Scout operator, was approved by Major-General Kat Liebenberg. EMLC –Electrical, Magnetic, Logistical Component Technical Consult (Pty) Ltd at Speskop put together the custom made demolition explosive devices. These consisted of a wooden box packet with TNT slabs taken from a Soviet tank mine and used in combination with ex-Rhodesian white phosphorous grenade.

But more about this story later.

"Major Brian" (nom de guerre - real name Gray Branfield – revealed by former MK member Thula Bopela who infiltrated Rhodesia with Chris Hani in 1967 during Op Nickel), of SADF Special Forces. Four teams were selected, varying in numbers from one to three people, and included CSI (Chief of Staff Intelligence – SADF) operatives as well as contacts within Zimbabwe ex-Special Branch officials who were in positions to conduct surveillance and monitoring observations.

Project Barnacle established their base at Renosterspruit Farm, south of Hartbeespoort Dam and north of Johannesburg. A safe forward base was sited at Messina, from where teams were flown to Induna airfield (between Cement Siding and Ntabazinduna, outside Bulawayo). A chartered aircraft flew Major Brian from Induna to Charles Prince airport at Mount Hampden on Sunday 18th July 1981. A safe house was set up in Greendale suburb and the various teams were able to monitor and track their quarries movements.

Major Brian / Gray Branfield could not fit on board, so he drove a further 300 km south to a second airfield that had been nominated in case of emergencies, and was picked up by a Seneca late that same afternoon.

Fred Varkevisser and his family stayed at a safe house in Pretoria's Waterkloof suburb, where they met with Foreign Minister Pik Botha,

General Fritz Loots and General Kat Liebenberg – the latter was in the process of taking over as GOC Special Forces from Loots. The Varkevissers were moved to Cape Town and compensated for the loss of their belongings in Zimbabwe. Despite being a reluctant accomplice to the escape, it remained impossible for them to return to Zimbabwe. Fred Varkevisser was listed as a deserter with the BSAP Regimental Association. However, he was exonerated in a report to the President following an official enquiry that lasted two years. Fred died of cancer in May 1999, at the age of 49.
However – take note of Major Brian / Gray Branfield / KD – his name features predominantly with other Project Barnacle operations – as well as the Hawk / Hunter sabotage saga.

A ONCE JUSTIFIABLY PROUD AIR FORCE

MEDICAL FIASCO - RSA SOJOURN

The drop in medical standards at the Andrew Flemming hospital was appalling. Renene developed stomach pains in the middle of the night and we rushed her to the nearest hospital from our home in Meredith Drive, Eastlea. On arrival, we filled in the necessary forms and waited - and waited. Four hours later, when the sun came up, I'd had enough and phoned the Air Force Medical Officer, Squadron Leader Ben Masimbe. He reacted immediately and diagnosed a burst appendix. Renene was admitted for an emergency operation - with the prognosis that her ability to have children was in serious jeopardy. That was the straw that broke the camel's back.

I was furious when I reported in to Air Headquarters. They were sympathetic and I confided to Director Admin Group Captain Pete Nicholls that I wished to seek my fortunes elsewhere. Although he was not surprised at my outburst, I sensed that he was perturbed at the brain drain that was occurring in the Force.

However, at the end of the day, Pete Nicholls was sympathetic and granted me leave of absence. I guess he was privy to a lot of intelligence concerning the frustrating integration process – and had already seen the writing on the wall.

By the time I retired, the Air Force of Zimbabwe could field only 53 aircraft, and had just 43 pilots left serving on five squadrons. My diary entry records the following alarming sad state of affairs.

No 1 Squadron	6 aircraft	7 pilots
No 2 Squadron	2 aircraft	2 pilots
No 3 Squadron	6 Dakotas	
	6 Cessna	12 pilots
No 6 Squadron	20 aircraft	8 pilots
No 7 Squadron	8 Alouette	
	5 Bell 205s	14 pilots
total	53 aircraft	43 pilots

OPERATION OCTOPUS – JULY TO OCTOBER 1982

Operation *Octopus* was mounted to locate and seize weapons following the upsurge of Zipra activities in Matabeleland – and the kidnap of ten young tourists at the 70km peg on the Bulawayo-Victoria Falls road. The arrests of Zapu officials, including Dumiso Dabengwa and Lookout Masuku, triggered the defection of thousands of Zipra guerrillas who went back to the bush, concealing their arms.

Skyshouts called for armed people to surrender their weapons. Houses were searched without warrants and without prior warning. Roadblocks were set up, people were frisked, a curfew was imposed and the general public was subjected to manhandling in a most unpleasant manner.

The clampdown in Matabeleland did result in the seizing of many weapons, but failed in its objective of reducing escalating criminal activity – and locating the whereabouts of the young tour group led by Bruce Watkins (who were travelling overland down Africa).

RETIREMENT AND EMIGRATION

My retirement from the Air Force, according to my Certificate of Service, read as follows: -

AIR FORCE OF ZIMBABWE

Certificate of Service
(OFFICER)

Preller Matt Geldenhuys
on the 15th day of June 1982 completed 20 Yrs 93 Days Service with the Air Force of Zimbabwe. His rank on leaving the Service was Wing Commander

                      Date   *15 June 1982*   N. WALSH
                                                                   Air Marshal
                                                  Commander of the Air Force

FLYING RECORD

Assessment
1. Basic Training   *99.55* hrs   *(F.414A-AV)*
2. Advanced Training   *117.35* hrs   *(F.414A-AV)*
3. Operational Training *82.50* hrs   *AVERAGE*
4. Service Flying   *3413.35* hrs   *HIGH AVERAGE*
5. Total Flying *3713.55* hrs
6. Authorised to wear Air Force Flying Badge from *29th JUNE 1963*
Instrument Rating: *MASTER GREEN (Lapsed)*

APPOINTMENTS HELD

1. *Staff Officer Personnel*
Officer Commanding (HQ)(Unit) / Personnel 1
Staff Officer Volunteer Reserves / Reserves 1
Officer Commanding Administrative Wing A.F.S. Thornhill
OC FAF 7 Buffalo Range

Snr Air Rep F.F.C.
OC FAF 2 Kariba
Strike 1
'A' Flt Cdr No 5 Sqn
'B' Flt Cdr No 1 Sqn

SPECIAL QUALIFICATIONS

2. *Instrument Rating Examiner (IRE)*
DF/GA/IS Pilot Attack Instructor
F95 Photo Reconnaissance Pilot
Graduate Senior Joint Warfare
and Joint Service Coin Course

DECORATIONS, MEDALS AND AWARDS

3. *Rhodesia General Service Medal*
Zimbabwe Independence Medal
Exemplary Service Medal
Service Medal

AUTHORITY TO RETAIN RANK

4. In terms of Section 12 (3) of the Defence Act (Chapter94), the holder of this certificate is authorised to retain his rank of *Wing Commander* and wear the uniform on appropriate occasions

Date *16 June 1982*   R.OBORNE
Group Captain
Director Administration

With my length of service and retirement, I was entitled to, and took six months leave pending, and was thus able to take up the Masonite's offer of employment on 4th January 1982. On leaving my Air Force career, it may be of interest to reflect on what happened to the other members of No 16 Pilot Training Course who attested over 20 years earlier. In alphabetical order: -
Ian B. Bester-Bond   Completed course and left at the break up of Federation 6.12.1963. Became a Salesman with Rothmans and later branched into photography at Victoria Falls.

Al R. Bruce   Left the force on 31.8.1965 and joined Qantas, Australia. Rejoined the force some years later. Was awarded DCD 13.4.1979. Ultimately left the force and joined Air Zimbabwe. Left to join BOP Air. Now in Gauteng, flying B727s with BA (COMAIR).
Bruce I. Collocott   Completed flying training. Had various medical problems but continued to fly in restricted category. Killed in action at Mapai, Mozambique, May 1977.
W. Graham Cronshaw Completed course and served through to 1980. Commanded No 7 Sqn and retired as Group Captain. Flew with the Ciskei Air Wing, then with Coin Security, based Pretoria. Currently running the Aviation side of Fidelity Guards in Johannesburg.
Harwood J.G.de Kock Suspended from flying training 18.12.1962. Joined Mashaba Mines as Chief Surveyor under ground. Retired as Mine Manager, and settled in Masvingo.
Chris J.T. Dixon   Completed flying training and served through to 1980, when he retired as Squadron Leader. Was awarded DCD 13.4.1979. (Green Leader). Commanded No 5 Sqn. Has flown for Tabex, Afretair, and MK Mike Kruger Airlines.
André P. du Toit   Suspended from flying training 29.4.1963. Remustered to Navigator 14.8.1964. Trained in the UK and served on No 5 Sqn.
Prop M. Geldenhuys As per above certificate of service. Joined Masonite (Africa) Ltd, and retired to Natal South Coast.
Roy D. Hopkins   Suspended from flying training and returned to the Technical Branch. Served as Station Signals Officer Thornhill and held Staff Signals Posts. Retired as Sqn Ldr. Ended up in Australia, where he died of cancer August 1988.
Trevor Mc Roberts   Suspended from flying training 15.8.1963. Left the force 30.9.63. Worked for SA Rubber Co and was killed in a motor accident November 1968.
Hugh C.S. Slatter   Completed course and served through to 1983. Retired as Air Vice-Marshal in the post of Chief of Staff, was awarded the DMM 13.4.1979. Was imprisoned and charged with the Thornhill sabotage fiasco. Deported to Britain, immigrated to the States, currently marketing General Electric GE90 engines on the Boeing 777 in Seattle.
John F.R. Strnad   Suspended from flying training. Awarded Sword of Honour at Wings, Left during OCU - got married without permission, beat up Al Bruce and Hugh Slatter - Pooftah suspect.

SECRET POLICE

The speed with which the South African secret police latched onto me was quite frightening. To this day I suspect the aviation officials that I had visited Virginia Airport during my sojourn. Or it could have been the various Personnel Employment Agencies that I had interviews with – and had left copies of my CV with. Although I had left Zimbabwe, I still owed allegiance to the Air Force. I was technically still a member, on six months leave pending retirement, when the Security Police came a-knocking. They looked like ordinary fellows. Their introductions were somewhat muffled but it did not take me long to realise their fishy business. Their questioning was incisive and in depth. They wanted to know what the Air Force strengths were, who was who in the zoo, and whether I was prepared to divulge sensitive information. I courteously suggested that they check in again after June and I would then feel more at ease turning over any documents that they would be welcome to scrutinise. I subsequently escaped by the skin of my teeth, passing south through Beit Bridge immediately before the Hawk and Hunter aircraft were sabotaged at Thornhill.

The Secret Police disappeared in the night – just as quickly as they had come a knocking. What happened to them, I don't know. They never came back, and I don't know what happened to them. I suspect they returned to Durban and realised I wasn't about to squeal on the Air Force mates that had remained behind. Just as well – the confrontation was scary and I would have felt very wary spilling my guts to total strangers. In the end, I was relieved to be spared the frightening experience.

OPERATION MUTE – 198

Operation *Mute* was SADF assistance to Zimbabwe's Zipra in 1982 – and the SADF's Project Barnacle raid on the Air Force of Zimbabwe Thornhill Air Base in July 1982. Ex BSAP Special Branch Mac Callaway, disenchanted with the Zanu-PF government, joined the South African Special Forces, and became synonymous with the SADF re-supplying of Zipra forces with arms and ammunition. He was also involved with the training of dissidents. His escapades, however, are outside the scope of this autobiography.

Peter Stiff concluded in *Cry Zimbabwe*, that "There was a widespread fear of the Air Force of Zimbabwe, Not only could it mount air strikes, but it was the key factor in the deployment of Fire Forces against Zipra. The Air Force's capabilities remained virtually undiminished since the days of the Bush War and posed the main threat to Zipra's activities." Further down, on page 106 of *Cry Zimbabwe*, Stiff added "unbeknown to Jan Brytenbach and Dunning who had no 'need to know', Barnacle and Special Forces were even then engaging in planning a major strike against the Air Force of Zimbabwe". However, before I jump the gun too far ahead, allow me to recap on the events immediately prior to and leading up to Operation *Mute*.

Operation *Mute* ended 1984 with South African support for Zipra dwindling following the murder of white farmers in the Kezi district, slaughter of other innocent white civilians (all by South African supplied '20-80' AK-47 cartridges), disappearance from the scene of Captain Mac Callaway, and the embarrassment to South Africa – and in particular to CSIs Major General H Roux.

MASONITE [AFRICA] LIMITED

On 5th January 1982 I joined the Masonite brand hardboard manufacturing company in Estcourt, Natal. The Company owes its origins to American William H. Mason who in the mid-twenties developed a unique explosion process by accident. One day, he turned off the steam and went to lunch; upon his return, he found the press still hot because the steam valve had sprung a leak. His piece of wetlap had become a hard, dense, dry board. It wouldn't split, splinter, crack, dent or snag. This was the word's first piece of hardboard. The corporation formed in 1925 was named Mason Fibre Company, but changed to Masonite Corporation in 1928.

MAL, as the South African company has become known, had its beginnings in 1939, but interrupted by the war years, only really got off the ground in 1949. The Company expanded gradually over the years, and was producing hardboard, softboard and mineral fibreboard on five lines - and employing some 1,000 employees - by the time I joined the Company as their Personnel Superintendent. The grounding that I received in the Air Force helped me to cope with the challenges in civilian street, with most of the demands being Selection, Recruitment, Job Descriptions, Performance appraisals, Disciplinary Enquiries and personnel administration. After about a year at the Estcourt Mill, an opportunity arose to move with the Forestry Division to

Pietermaritzburg – in order to be more central to the seven forestry plantations that supplies the Mill with its raw material.

The Forestry employed more people than the manufacturing plant. Labour totalled some 1161 employees, with a two million Rand payroll. Rina and I soon found a very comfortable house at 27 Christie Road, equidistant from the University, Girls High, Maritzburg College and Alexandra High Schools. Unfortunately, we couldn't find places at Girls High or Maritzburg College, so enrolled Renene at Russell and Pey at Alexandra. The Forestry Office rented offices in Longmarket Street and I commenced my transfer officially on 1st February 1983. The nature of the job was such that a company car was a requirement and I took delivery of a brand new Toyota Cressida sedan – the first of many brand new cars during the course of my 20-year career with the Company.

My stay with the Forestry Division lasted some seven years – with just as many changes in job title. From Personnel Superintendent-Forestry, I became Personnel and Administration Superintendent on 1st May 1984, then reverted to plain Personnel Supt. on 1st February 1985 following rationalisation. Further restructuring occurred on the 1st August 1986, assuming responsibility for the Safety portfolio, as Personnel Safety Superintendent. I had recruited trainee forester Paul Wainwright, who made a better Safety Officer than a forester, and he landed the cushy Safety vacancy at the Estcourt Mill. It was during this time that Forestry was outsourcing a lot of their silviculture and harvesting operations, with retrenchments reducing the staff compliment to some 700 odd people. The retrenchment exercise was quite a major challenge for me, and taking over the Safety function as well added to greater responsibility.

FINALLY GROUNDED

Fire Season, from July to the first rains in November, is a particularly stressful period for the Forestry Industry. Imagine for a moment, witnessing ones crop going up in smoke that has taken anything from ten to fifteen years to grow. Saw logs can take an additional ten years. It makes sense that the industry spares no effort to protect themselves from the ravages that forest fires can inflict to producers, small and large alike. When the opportunity arose to fly on forest fire spotting missions, I jumped at the prospect to exchange my Masonite bomber for the controls of a light aircraft. The spotter flights were co-ordinated from the Natal Midlands Forest Protection Association, or NMFPA Offices at Oribi airfield, Pietermaritzburg.

I was indeed fortunate to have flown on several such missions. These covered plantations in the Kranskop area north of Greytown, to afforested areas in the Harding and Kokstad towns on the Transkei border. Popular turning points also included Bulwer, Creighton, Ixopo, Eston, Crammond and Howick. My first sortie with Johann van Niekerk, in Cessna 182, ZS-RMC was on the 21st August 1988. It took us sixty-five minutes to fly the northern round route to Kranskop and Howick. After a breather at Oribi, we took off again for an eighty-minute fire patrol of the Southern plantations.

I need to mention that Renene had befriended the Stott's from Port Shepstone, who also owned a Cessna hangared at Margate. Jo Stott was an honorary civilian pilot in the Air Force - and I was thus also able to get my bum in the air on at least three occasions. One in particular that I recall was with Pey as a passenger - I believe Pey was not all that keen on my steep turns over Albert Falls dam. I have often wondered whether Pey recalls that particular sortie. Anyway, the Stott's son was a privileged scholar at the upper crust Hilton College - he had eyes for Renene, or was it the other way round? Who was I to complain, as long as I could enjoy "The wild blue yonder" once again. Renene no doubt has her own story to tell, concerning her affair - and it is perhaps best to leave that side up to her.

On 9th September I had another memorable sortie which lasted three hours, spotting eleven fires, and giving a good olde Air Force beat-up at Masonite Rockvale plantation situated between Ixopo and Highflats. Unbeknown to me at the time, Area Manager Richard Guy was on the telephone to my Boss, Jack Hubble, in Maritzburg. The aircraft noise on the very low flypast drowned any coherent discussion between the foresters. When my Boss enquired what all the racket was about, Richard casually replied that it was only "Prop's normal antics on Fire Patrol". Needless to say, the message was received on the other end of the phone went down like a lead balloon. Accordingly, my sorties on the following day were regrettably my last. I was duly grounded, because the Company was not prepared to take the risk of having to notify next of kin of misadventure in the line of duty.

For the record, I had managed to get my bum off the ground at least nine times before my final 'wheels-up'. The last ten odd hours did not feature in my logbook - I was truly *grounded* once for all.

During this time, Renene completed her high schooling and commenced a nursing career at respectable Greys Hospital. Pey, meanwhile, also did well at Alex, and enrolled at Technikon Natal to pursue a National Diploma in Computer Data Processing. I might add that Masonite generously subsidised their higher education. With our offspring vacating the coup, we sold the Christie house and bought a two bedrooms duplex right in town – Murrayfield in Burger Street. The Forestry Office also relocated to Church Street, and the office was thus within walking distance from home.

In 1990 I transferred from the Forestry Division, in Pietermaritzburg, to the Manufacturing Division in Estcourt.

As Loss Control Manager in charge of security at the Estcourt mill, I met up with Commandant Douw Steyn who had served in the South African Recces during the Rhodesian bush war. Some of his exploits included: -

Operation Coolith – the reconnaissance and partial demolition of the bridge at Cuito Cuanavale, Angola on the 25-26th August 1987. As an operator with 4 Reconnaissance Regiment Douw conducted the first phase to reconnoitre the bridge. They paddled down the river, destroyed their boats, hid them under water about three kilometres from the bridge and swam on the surface to the bridge. After that, they swam down stream to be picked up. Douw planned the whole operation, for Major Fred Wilkie to destroy the well-defended enemy target.

Reconnoitre of the Vianna base in Angola.

SAAF Canberra airstrike on the Bengo River bridge at Quifangondo in Angola on 11th November 1975 during Operation Savannah. He was a signals officer at that time, with the South Africans fighting alongside the non-communist FNLA against the MPLA and Cuban forces.

The Recces' final reconnaissance against the FAPLA's headquarters at Calai in the Angolan Cuando-Cubango area two years later, November 1977. Douw also conducted intensive demolition training with Unita troops.

Blowing up the Humbi railway tunnel on 28th October 1979. They were flown to their target in two Puma helicopters.

Para drop by Dakota into Mapai, with the SAS, escorted by Lynx from FAF 7, during early 1978. As the team engineer, their team accounted for 20 Frelimo terrorists after the gooks truck hit a makeshift vehicle mine and the gooks dashed straight into Douw's South African *Rimi* anti-personnel mines.

It is also of historical interest that the South Africans were involved in many different aspects of the Rhodesian bush war. Many of their exploits only came to my notice as units were disbanded, or my stumbling on facts during the many years it has taken me to document this record. Examples include the specific development of the "rose mine" by Dr Jan Coetzee. This anti-personnel mine was virtually lift proof in that it had a photoelectric cell on top of the mine, which when uncovered and exposed to any day or night light, the cell activated and would then trigger the detonator. The mine was issued to the Rhodesian Special Forces to create havoc in Mozambique, and knock-off their engineering specialists who tried to lift them. The South African Special Forces, under General Fritz Loots, and particularly legendary Jan Breytenbach, had their forces operate side by side with their Rhodesian colleagues – often without the knowledge or sanction of the South African government. Admittedly, they used us as guinea pigs to hone their own brand of bush warfare expertise. On the other hand, I would like to think that they were envious of the Rhodesian reputation as being one of the finest fighting forces in the world. They copied our successes, and used their unlimited resources to increase their troops' survival rate when confronted at the sharp end. The South Africans were thus a source of weaponry, equipment and expertise supply that was far beyond the research and development capability of the Rhodesians. However, let the record show that whatever the gadget, it was only as good as could humanly be made to work. It was thus only as good as the Rhodesian operator could make it work.

When the Rhodesian Special Forces were forced to disband, the South Africans built complete replacement barracks to accommodate them – lock, stock and barrel. And, they were not shy to recruit the cream of the crop.

One of many highlight – twice awarded

Masonite MD's, Alan Wilson and his successor, Mike Slater humbled me with the Excellence Award. The company also has an Honours Board in their Head Office reception, displaying the names of the recipients.

I was also nominated and awarded the NOSA 'Safety Practitioner of the Year' for two years, the awards being made at the Annual Banquets – once in Pietermaritzburg and the second in Durban. They also count as career highlights - - but not as highly treasured as my first trip overseas to America. To say that Masonite was good to me is an understatement. Rina and I were truly blessed with having two complete careers – first in the Air Force, followed by a second twenty years with Masonite. Seems everything happens in two's? We will need to break the cycle, because we have also had two trips to New Zealand – and that definitely won't be our last.

USA TRIP

My trip to the States was the highlight of my twenty years service with Masonite. 1999 was our best safety year ever when we broke our previous record of 3,3 million hours without a disabling injury. All employees were rewarded with the issue of specially logo-ed umbrellas. We had also celebrated our 50th Anniversary earlier in the year. For my 57th Birthday present I was given a fortnight's notice to attend a safety conference to be held at Disney World - and to include a visit to two of Masonite Corporation mills in the States. I chose the Towanda Mill situated close to the Canadian border, and Laurel mill in Mississippi, in the south.

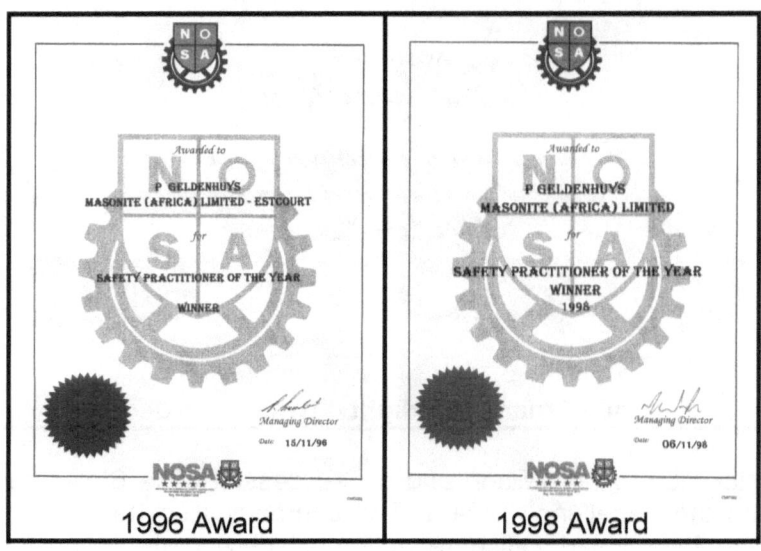

1996 Award   1998 Award

SAFETY MATTERS
MASONITE AFRICA SCORES STAR STATUS

Masonite Africa Limited (MAL) was a star at a January 25 awards banquet that paid tribute to top performers in the field of occupational safety, health and environmental risk management.

Masonite International's Forestry Operations (at Pietermaritzburg) and Estcourt Mill (200km inland from Durban) won FiveStar status, the highest possible ranking, for the 14th year in succession, from NOSA (the National Occupational Safety Association, a private agency which is South Africa's counterpart to OSHA, the U.S. Occupational Safety and Health Administration).

This year, both divisions also scooped "Special Recognition" awards for their proactive approach in implementing NOSA's comprehensive system of best practices in workplace occupational safety, health and environmental risk management.

"The Estcourt and Forestry operations continue to be leaders in the field of safety, health and environment in South Africa," said **Bob Woods**, Masonite International Safety Manager.

Accepting Masonite's awards at the banquet in Durban, South Africa, are (left to right) **Brian Griffiths**, *Safety, Health and Environment Consultant,* **Grant Rowe**, *Divisional Manager, Forestry, and* **Prop Geldenhuys**, *Loss Control Manager.*

"Awards such as this again recognize the ongoing efforts of all our employees to provide and maintain a safe and healthy work place," Woods added.

My flight schedule took me to Atlanta, Pittsburgh and Elmira in order to reach Towanda. I flew SAA to Atlanta, routed via Cape Town and Fort Lauderdale, but then the wheels came off. My flight by US Air to Pittsburgh was cancelled because of sleet and ice, and I was then routed via Philadelphia instead. At Philadelphia I was faced with a further two cancellations by US Air, one because of deteriorating weather conditions, and the other because of aircraft unserviceability (I eventually arrived at Elmira six and a half hours late). Then from Towanda I flew to New Orleans, routing via Pittsburgh as planned, to reach Laurel. Then it was on to Orlando and a twenty-minute shuttle-bus ride to Disney World. I returned to Johannesburg via Orlando and Atlanta.

The highlight of this USA trip was visits to the National Warplane Museum in New York State, and the Kennedy Space Centre in Florida. Rina opted to spend the fortnight with her sister Lettie at Tweeling in the Free State. After dropping Rina off, I motored to Atlasville where the Beaver's kindly took me to Johannesburg International. And so, on Sunday 13th February 2000, I boarded SAA Boeing B747-400 for the twenty-one hours to Atlanta. I had a window seat and enjoyed the views as we flew the 1.45-hour, 1272km (687 nautical mile) flight to

Cape Town. We climbed to 35,000 feet, cruised at 584 mph or 940 kph and encountered mild turbulence en route - with stratus cloud about. We spent 90 minutes on the ground, but were not allowed off the Boeing - even for a quick smoke. Our cruise to Fort Lauderdale was at 39,000 feet, skirting South America and with a top of descent over Nassau. At that altitude I had a bird's eye view of the Bahamas and Cuba.

SAA served a magnificent dinner and breakfast. Dinner consisted of smoked peppered mackerel, sliced beef fillet Peking with Chinese noodles, honey and nut mousse, cheese and biscuits, coffee and an after-dinner chocolate. For breakfast we were served fruit juices,
Freshly sliced fruit, fruit yoghurt, Muesli, scrambled eggs with grilled bacon, grilled chicken sausage and sautéed mushroom rusty, bread rolls with butter and strawberry jam, plus coffee. At Fort Lauderdale we spent another 75 minutes on the ground for refuelling and then off again to Atlanta. For this short hop we climbed to 37,000 feet and I was able to make out Cape Canaveral and Daytona.

However, as we approached Atlanta, we entered cloud, with turbulence. The pilot climbed to FL 410 where the outside air temperature was minus 67°C. Distance covered so far, according to the global positioning system - GPS - as relayed on the monitors, was 12,500 kilometres. After landing, we set our watches back the seven hours difference in the time zones - making it a rather long night as we followed the sun. Then the fun and games began - with me needing a smoke desperately and discovering my flight to Pittsburgh having been cancelled. This meant running between Concourses 'C' - where there was a smoking room and Concourse "B" - my revised departure point - and having arrived at Concourse 'E'. There was an underground train shuttle between the various Concourses and I found myself lugging my cabin baggage to and fro, trying to emerge at Concourse 'C' every now and then to draw on a fag. Anyway, as luck would have it, I was able to arrange an alternative flight to my Elmira destination, but this meant routing via Philadelphia instead of Pittsburgh.

I departed Atlanta with US Air at 11 o'clock and arrived at Philadelphia at 12h33. The flight was in 8/8thscloud cover as we climbed to 33,000 feet. I was able to make out Washington DC through gaps in the cloud. What initially appeared as sandy soils from the air turned out to be snow covering the fringes of fields and along the roadways. Having been pre-briefed, I rushed over to boarding point B12C and found out that the connecting flight to Elmira was again cancelled due to aircraft unserviceability. I was then booked for a departure at 17h05 but was turned away because the flight had been oversold by one passenger.

A flight via a place called Itacha was offered but I declined because I did not know where I would end up. I passed up a shoeshine - for 5 US Dollars (equivalent to R30), and settled for a beer and chips instead.

The hour was getting late, and as I now found myself all alone, in a strange place, a long way from home, and I was getting concerned that the people from Towanda picking me up, would be waiting in vain. As it turned out I eventually got airborne in a 50-seater Dash 8 liner, landing at Elmira six and a half hours late at 21h23.

Joe Ritsko and Mike Chatburn were still waiting for me - thank goodness. And to my surprise my baggage arrived at the same time. Much to my relief, I was dropped off at the Comfort Inn - within sight of the Masonite Mill. Joe's safety team kindly showed me around their Mill the next day. It was cold, with snow everywhere, a pretty place, but not the sort I would choose to settle in. The highlight of this trip was the visit to the National Warplane Museum.

NATIONAL WARPLANE MUSEUM

What do you know - the Museum displayed a Canberra - called a B 57 in the States. Or Martin RB-57A to be exact. The Canberra was one of 26 aircraft included in the Museum's collection.

The National Warplane Museum, established in 1983, is dedicated to preserving the history and heritage of military aviation, from 1914 to today. The exhibits honour the development and sacrifices made in military flight from pre-World War II years through to the present day. One of its primary aims is the preservation of vintage aircraft in flying condition and is also host to the annual *Wings of Eagles®* Air Show - which has been described in the Air Classics magazine as one of the best all-military shows in the States. The Museum maintains a fleet of several flying 'planes', including one of the last airworthy B-17 Flying Fortresses in existence, one of the last three McDonnell FH-1 Phantom fighters and the last surviving Douglas BTD-1 Destroyer. Other rare examples are the first C-45H Expediter and a prototype Pratt-Read XLNE-1 glider. Then of course, the Canberra.

They also had a Piper Cub in their restoration hanger - the same type of aircraft that my father had given my brother Jan his first air experience way back in September 1957. Other notables on display included the flying boat Catalina, F-14 Tomcat, F-15 Eagle, Grumman Avenger, Corsair and the North American T-6D Texan (the SAAF Harvard - equivalent of the RRAF Provost). But for me, the Canberra stole the show.

National Warplane Museum at Elmira, New York State, and Space Shuttle Explorer – Kennedy Space Centre, Florida

Despite signs saying "No touching the aircraft", I could not resist opening the hatch and peering inside the Canberra - looking at the navigator station, bomb aimers couch, and of course the pilots cockpit. My hosts were somewhat surprised that I knew my way round the cockpit and could share in my delight in caressing an aircraft that held so many fond memories for me.

MASONITE USA MILLS

I visited Towanda Mill in picturesque Pennsylvania where the rivers were iced up and the hills were covered in snow. Road signs read "Speed Limit 55 mph" and "Ice on Bridges in Cold Weather". The golf courses were spectacular, with the 'pin' flags on the greens protruding through the snow blankets along the fairways. I considered the houses 'cute', invariably double-storied and of wood construction. There were no frontage walling or hedges, and one erf seemed to merge with the property next door without any visible intervening separation. Shovelling snow away from the driveways leading from the road to the garages seemed to be the only popular outdoor activity. The mainly white population was estimated at about 6,000 souls. The countryside was slightly hilly, with undulating high points only rising to about 500 feet high. All the people were rather large and thick set in stature - possibly as insulation against the wintry cold. Although pretty to the eye, it was not the sort of environment that I would like to live in. I spent two nights and three days in Towanda, and then took a US Air flight to Pittsburgh (by DC-9), and then on to New Orleans by B737-300. Captain Feltcott flew the latter leg - and he had a true 'greaser' on landing at New Orleans.

The Mississippi River estuary enters the sea at New Orleans - and the area along the river is steeped in American history. I was met at the Airport by DJ Shuttle services from Hattiesburg and driven the 120 odd miles to Laurel. En route we crossed over the impressive Lake Ponchetrain on a bridge 5½ miles long. Dan, my driver, mentioned that the road bridge that was to our left was 7½ miles long and a third bridge across the Lake was in fact 26 miles long. I must say it felt quite unusual driving a motor car in the middle of a lake where the shores could hardly be seen. The countryside was very flat and marshy - with the marshy areas called creeks. The one that caught my fancy was named Hobolochitty Creek. For the first time I saw racoons - but they were all dead - struck by oversized American cars and trucks travelling on the Interstate freeways - at 70 mph - which is the speed limit on the Louisiana roads. Another New Orleans observation was that all the tombstones were massive above ground structures - apparently because of water seepage in the low-lying area on which New Orleans was established.

Laurel was somewhat larger than Towanda. The Mill is a massive place, the home of Masonite, and where Masonite was first manufactured in the 1925s. The Mill itself is sited on 600 acres, with 64 acres under roof. The factory is so large that the staff drive battery powered golf-cart type buggies. Within the factory, select employees get around riding tricycles. I spent three days and two nights at Laurel and was fascinated to see timber-chip lorries raised bodily to about 40° from the horizontal, in order to discharge their load of wood chips in a matter of seconds. The press floors were also fully automated and the factory as a whole was exceptionally clean. Laurel fully justified itself as the flagship of Masonite Corporation.

I returned to New Orleans via Hattiesburg (to pick up a couple of free training videos), and booked into the Holiday Inn situated close to the airport. After dumping my kit in the room, I caught a lift with DJ Shuttle into the city centre. Dan, my driver, dropped me off in Bourbon street - because no visit to Louisiana would be complete without visiting the Hillbrow type highlights of the city. A Mardi Gras was in progress, so I seated myself at a pavement café to witness the spectacle of an odd procession winding their way through the narrow streets. I then went on a shopping trip to the Mississippi River Walk where paddle steamers were plying the river. I had no joy locating the specific computer software that Pey wanted, and settled on buying a scanner for myself in order to digitise the selection of pictures for my autobiography.

Early the next morning I boarded a Delta Airlines flight to Orlando in Florida. We got airborne in a Comair Canadair CL68, which seats about 50 passengers. We took off at 07h57, climbed to flight level 33,000 feet, flew past nice sounding Tallahassee, and landed at Orlando, Florida at 10h25. The co-pilot put down an absolute greaser and I complimented him on his landing. The Captain mentioned to me that the CL68, being a low wing airliner, was generally easy to land. I familiarised myself with the airport layout and established that I needed to get to the 'B' Concourse for my return flight for Atlanta. Having done that, I then boarded Mears Shuttle for the 26-minute minibus ride to the Double Tree Guest Suite hotel at Disney World. It seemed to me that everybody in the States not only expected to be tipped, but actually demanded some form of gratuity. I had paid the New Orleans airport porter $5.00 to check me in, $2.00 for the Mears Shuttle driver just to off-load my bags from his bus, and the hotel porter was somewhat indignant at the $1.00 I paid him to show me the nearest room to reception. As the bus ride cost $15.00, this little exercise came to 23 x 6.4 = R 147,20.

The hotel room was also quite pricey, but then it had a separate lounge, with microwave oven, fridge, coffee maker, - and three televisions - including one in the bathroom. Everything in the States was big, real big. The king-size bed, the motor cars, the people, the shopping centres, the factories - just about everything.

DISNEY WORLD

Talking of big - Disney World was spread over something like half a dozen sites over ten to fifteen square miles. Downtown Disney and Pleasure Island at about two miles was within walking distance. Epcot Centre was about ten miles away, Magic Kingdom about fifteen miles, Sea World, MGM Studios and Animal Kingdom like distances. Buses ran frequently between all the pleasure resorts. Although I spent one week at Disney World, the time waster was queuing up at the various popular shows - some taking as long as an hour to gain admission. While I wish not to list all the various attractions, I intend only to elaborate on those that were memorable. But before doing so, permit me to summarise some of the attractions at the many Disney resorts:

Planet Hollywood – at Disney World, Florida, USA
Downtown Disney Area

Planet Hollywood – a landmark at Downtown Disney. The structure is global shaped with the inner spiral staircase lined with portraits of current and past 'stars'. The exhibits glamorised the world of film and television, with its celebrity-style dining amid Hollywood's greatest memories. Unfortunately the pictures I took inside the building did not come out and I was unable to show Rina some of the suspended cars, sailing ships and aircraft.

Rainforest Café – with its animations and column aquariums. The volcano erupted periodically, spewing clouds of steam and thundering waterfalls. The restaurant was always full, with the diners being able to marvel at the tropical fish swimming up the glass pillars and along inter-linking tubular aquariums. There were also a large variety of animated tropical robotic reptiles and animals suspended amongst artificial foliage.

Marketplace Shops – these were just too numerous to mention, with shopping hours from 9:30 in the morning till midnight.

Lego Imagination Centre – this was a mammoth array of constructions, all made out of Lego pieces. Every kind of Lego toy you can imagine of is here, so you can build anything your imagination can create.

World of Disney – Smoking is prohibited in most restaurants, all merchandise shops, waiting areas and rest rooms. I pitied all like habitude oxygen poisoning Homo sapiens.

PLANET HOLLYWOOD – possibly the most photographed background At Disney World

KENNEDY SPACE CENTRE

The visit to the Space Centre was the highlight of my USA trip. I joined a bus shuttle tour to travel the sixty odd miles from Orlando to the east coast of Florida. We travelled on the Bee Line Inter-State (USA terminology for Freeway), so called because of the Bee and Honey industries as a result of all the pine trees growing in the flat lands which Florida is renown for. As the bus approached the Kennedy Space Centre, we spotted the odd alligator lazing in the water courses along the freeway. Nearer our destination a couple of real monsters were around – like about three to nearly four metres in length, with girths that I wouldn't be able to put my arms around.

After going through the turnstiles I made a beeline to the Space Shuttle Explorer that had been pensioned off and now stands on sturdy frames to permit tourists access to the cockpit. It was awesome to think that here I was, in a space ship that had actually been in space and landed successfully back on earth. Other space shuttles included Discovery, Endeavour and Atlantis.

I walked around the static display of the various rockets that were the forerunners of landing man on the moon. Seeing the Mercury and Gemini rockets just blew ones mind. Right at the back was a Saturn 1 rocket, which launched man around the moon. It made the other displays pale into insignificance. From there, visitors could board busses to visit other areas of interest.

From there, I visited Launch Control LC-39, from where the shuttles are propelled into space. After clambering all over the gantry, I jumped the long queues that was a feature of my visit to the States. I was pleased that I did so, in order to inspect the Saturn V hangar. Well, if one thought that the Model 1 was enormous, there was just no comparison to Saturn V. I stopped to ponder the achievements of Apollo 11 – from 16th to 24th July 1969, when Commander Neil Armstrong broadcast his historical words "Tranquillity Base here. The Eagle has landed." The headlines flashed throughout the world – "Man Walks On The Moon – A small step for man, a leap for mankind". The space crew on Apollo 11 were Commander: Neil Armstrong, aged 38, a veteran of Gemini 8. Command Module 'Columbia' Pilot: Michael Collins, also aged 38, and flew on Gemini 10. The Lunar Module 'Eagle' pilot was Edwin Buzz Aldrin, aged 39, and commander of Gemini 12.

Apollo 11 achieved President Kennedy's goal of landing on the Moon with only 30 seconds of fuel remaining, astronauts Armstrong and Aldrin planted the American flag and collected the first samples of lunar soil. A sample of lunar rock was appropriately mounted on display, and visitors were able to touch the surface of a foreign planet.

There is a memorial for all the astronauts that died in space. Most people will recall the horrific visuals when the Space shuttle Challenger exploded whilst launching in February 1986. During my walkabout I was also able to sit in one of the Lunar Buggies on which the astronauts practised their routines on the moon.

x – 0 – x

The year 2000 was eventful for the family. Apart from my good lady Rina, we all did some Globetrotting. Shortly after I returned from America, Grahame, Renene, Courtney and Brendan went to New Zealand, and Pey had an envious trip to Israel. Dr Jelley landed a locum position at Westport, South Island. Having time to enjoy some of the sights and sounds such as the Frans Josef and Fox Glaciers, skiing in the Alps, visiting the hot springs, doing crazy things like bungy jumping, the KiwiJels soon found job offers in Hokitika and Westport. Zimbabwe land invasions by the so-called war veterans, with its breakdown in law and order, enticed the KiwiJels to seek their fortunes elsewhere. Then Pey and his lady friend Marcelle joined a tour group to the Holy Land. They visited Cairo, went to the biggest under-water observatory in Eilat, toured Tel-Aviv, Bethlehem, Nazareth, Jerusalem, the Dead Sea, Galilee and all the Mounts that are so popular in the Bible. Rina was green with envy, but relived the stories and pictures via the Internet.

My dear sister Delene went on an extended holiday to North Island, New Zealand in late 1999, ostensibly to be with daughter Chanli who was expecting their third Kiwi, and stayed there, waiting for her husband Stu McColl to sell up shop in Kloof, to join her in their new homeland. That left my brother Jan and I to make the most of the last British outpost – on the Natal south coast.

The Rocket Garden – Kennedy Space Centre

Many rockets were built for manned and unmanned space flight. The size of Saturn ♦ was awesome, but the Saturn ⊗ Rocket at the Apollo Centre just blew my mind

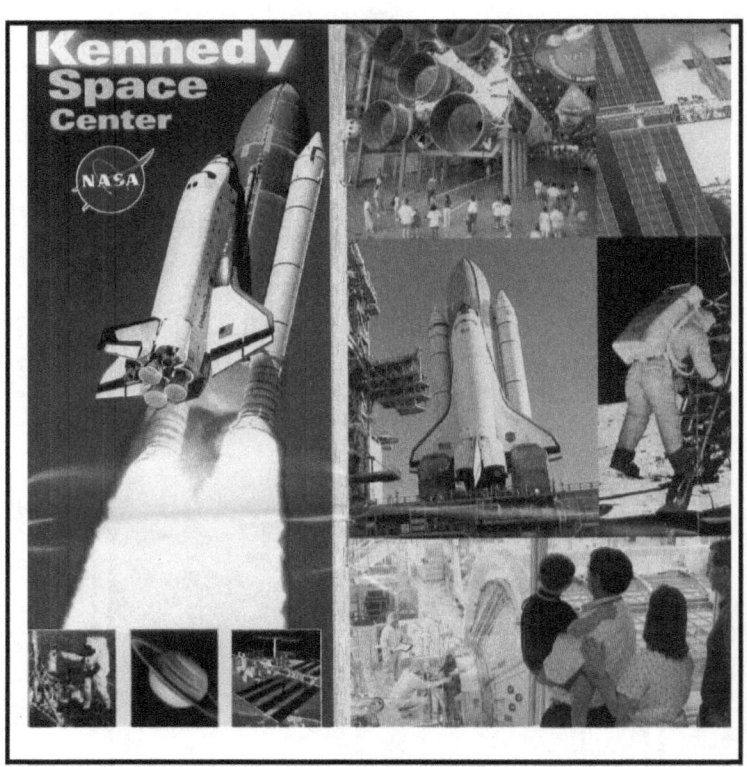

COMRADES 2000

Living in Pietermaritzburg for seven years would be incomplete if no mention is made of the 87-kilometre marathon run between that city and Durban. Over 24,000 runners from all over the world took part in the Millennium Comrades on 16th June 2000. Although the Russian runners have dominated the marathon in the latter years, I can record that I witnessed the greatest of them all – Bruce Fordyce.
We lived in Christie Road, virtually a stones throw from the route into Jan Smuts Stadium – and well placed to watch the men separating themselves from the boys after conquering the dreadful Polly Shorts. It was this particular hill that enabled Bruce Fordyce to leave his challengers in his dust. Bruce won the Comrades a record eight times in succession – a record unlikely to be equalled or bettered during my lifetime. I was at the finish to see Bruce make history. It

took many years for his 'down' run record to be broken, but his 'up' run record stood for decades.

Our Christie Road home allowed Rina and I to take our camp chairs, cooler box, picnic goodies and beach umbrella and plonk them alongside Jesmond Road – to lend our crowd support to the thousands of runners. For the down run into Durban, we would watch the start from the Maritzburg City Hall, return home for a good breakfast, and then set off for Kings Stadium to see the finish. I might add that Tony Venton, the Masonite Estcourt Mill Manager, was also an athlete of no mean ability – having not only completed some 25 Comrades marathons, but who also rowed the Duzi race a like number of times. Very few athletes can boast of doing both the Comrades and the Duzi for over a quarter of a century. One of the great names of the Comrades will always be Wally Haywood, who ran regularly even up to his eightieth birthday, and even my sister Delene can boast of sporting a Comrades Bronze medal.

Flags – BSA Company, Rhodesian, Green and White, Zimbabwe-Rhodesia and Zimbabwe

The Comrades was traditionally run on Republic Day, 31st May, every year. The ANC Regime abolished that public holiday, substituted 16th June, Sharpeville Day and then re-named it Youth Day instead. The Comrades 2000 race was won by novice 42 year old Vladimore Kotov from Poland in a record time of five hours twenty-six minutes. German Maria Bakwon the women's race. Abie Geldenhuys, probably a distant relative, came in twelfth position in a very credible five hours forty five minutes – not bad when one considers that there were about 24,505 starters. For those that know the Comrades, the tune that is broadcast at the start, and the finish for the first ten men as well as the first ten women, is Chariots of Fire. As any marathon runner will tell you, Chariots of Fire is one of those tunes that brings a lump to the throats of spectators and athletes alike – in recognising human endeavour.

SABOTAGE – THORNHILL

I retired from the Air Force of Zimbabwe on 15th June 1982, after 20 years and 93 days service. My first pension payment failed to arrive at the end of the month, June 1982, as expected. My new employer, Masonite, granted me a week's leave to visit Zimbabwe, with the purpose of stirring the inefficient civil service into action.
I duly reported to Air Force Headquarters in the third week of July and satisfied myself that all their formalities had been complied with and the delay was attributed to the Government Pensions Office. While at Air Headquarters, I collected my Certificate of Service, was presented with my Retirement Silver Tray by the Director of Administration – Group Captain Bill Sykes – and then enjoyed a cuppa and friendly chat with my ex-Boss, Wing Commander Peter Cooke, who was still Officer Commanding VR/Senior Staff Officer Reserves. Group Captain Pete Nicholls, the current Officer Commanding New Sarum Air Force base, mentioned that I had just missed the arrival of the Hawk aircraft.
Pete Nicholls invited me to have tea with him at New Sarum. However, my limited time did not allow me to take up his offer. In many ways, it subsequently proved to be a blessing in disguise. Pete, as my ex-Boss immediately prior to my retirement, had given me Zimbabwe dollars to invest in South Africa. With the very favourable exchange rate of one dollar worth two South African Rands, it had enabled me to tie us over until I received my first pay cheque from Masonite. Pete was obviously interested to know how his investments were performing – and hence his invitation to me for tea at New Sarum. However, more significantly, I had no sooner crossed the border into South Africa when "Air Force Crippled – Sabotage" headlines hit the newspapers.
Realisation hit me immediately. So that is why the South African Secret Service was on my case so soon after arriving in Estcourt. Also, more sinister – I had no doubt that I would be considered a prime suspect.

SUNDAY, 25 JULY 1982

Sunday 25th July 1982 will be remembered when seven Hawker Hunter FGA 9, one British Aerospace Hawk Mk 60 and a Lynx Riems/Cessna F 337 were totally destroyed at Thornhill Air Force base.

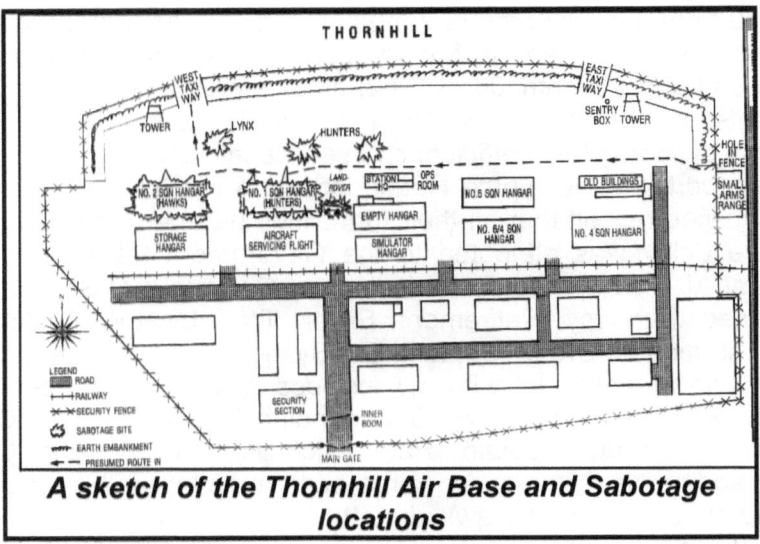

A sketch of the Thornhill Air Base and Sabotage locations

The first timing device went off at about 03h15 on the quiet, overcast, guti winter's Sunday morning – when everybody was fast asleep – more than likely including the one security guard that was supposed to be on duty. I would hazard a guess that only the guard dog was awake, but was most likely snuggled up to his untrained guard – for extra body warmth.

Hunter cockpit – destroyed – 25 July 1982

316

THORNHILL Sabotage – photos kindly supplied by Al Thorogood

AVM HUGH SLATTER

Air Vice-Marshal Hugh Slatter was arrested on Tuesday 31st August 1982. He was interned at Mkoba (Gwelo), moved to Umvuma on 9th September, then taken to Mtoko on Sunday 12th September and tortured. He had a heavy blue-coloured cloth bag pulled over his head, and handcuffed – minus shoes, socks, belt and jacket. He was then taken to a remote area and tortured with electric shocks – needle electrodes were inserted into the top of his back and the base of his spine. His body was racked by spasms as the current was increased – his back arched violently and he gasped involuntarily. He felt as though hundreds of burning fishhooks were tearing his muscles in every direction. So excruciating and frightening was the pain that all his efforts were directed at staying conscious.

He was then subjected to intense interrogation, still hooded and handcuffed. Any denials of complicity resulted in further electric shock treatment. In spite of the late night chill, he felt damp with perspiration and was having difficulty breathing. He felt he was suffocating. The interrogation was hostile in the extreme, calling the Air Vice-Marshal "you white bastard", "all lies and bullshit", and other expletives and abusive language. Hugh Slatter was then subjected to a second torture session, and he realised how the confessions had been extracted from the other airmen. In his false statement, he wrote the following: -

"The previous Chief of Staff, Air Vice-Marshal Len Pink, had told him the demise of the Air Force would embarrass the government and they should have cancelled the Hawk order. When Slatter disagreed, Pink told him his feelings were immaterial. He claimed that Pink had already put in motion actions that Slatter would have to follow. Slatter's job was to see that certain people performed their tasks, otherwise unnamed people would act against them and their families. When Slatter remonstrated, Pink said he should not jeopardise his family's lives. Someone who would identify himself by using the word BOSS would contact him. Slatter was under the impression that Cox was the main man in putting the plan into action, whereas his own responsibility was to keep pressure on and to lend his weight if problems arose. Weir was useful because of his knowledge of Thornhill; Lloyd and Lewis-Walker were necessary from the security aspect; Briscoe's job enabled him to cover for Cox where any courses and exercises were planned, while

Pile had to cover for Slatter in his absence and give assistance when necessary.

"He falsely alleged that a man named Swanepoel had visited him at Air Headquarters, using the word 'BOSS'. Swanepoel saw Cox about the detailed arrangements and Cox reported to Slatter that they were to provide trained South African-based saboteurs with explosive devices, transport, accommodation and access to Thornhill. The Board of Inquiry included Pile, Briscoe and Lewis-Walker to divert suspicion away from the Air Force. Slatter was fearful about the planned actions but more fearful about what would happen if they were unsuccessful as several families would suffer dreadful consequences."

The next to be broken was Phil Pile.

Pile falsely claimed "That former Chief of Staff, Air Vice-Marshal Len Pink had told him that if he resisted helping destroy the Hawks, his family would meet with an accident. He claimed that he was scared when Pink said the plan had the support of BOSS. Later, he asked Slatter if he should comply with John Cox's request to withdraw security from Air Force Stations and Slatter agreed. He believed Cox helped the saboteurs, with their devices, to Thornhill. Lloyd and Briscoe were also involved. After the sabotage, Commander Walsh – who was not involved – suggested Briscoe serve on the Board of Inquiry and Pile agreed. Lloyd, who had allowed the three specialists into Thornhill, said Neville Weir had helped them leave the Station."

Meanwhile, retired Air Vice-Marshal Len Pink had written to the Prime Minister (from South Africa), expressing his dismay at the arrest of Slatter and Pile.

"From this distance, I can only assume the detention of these two officers will have done irreparable harm to the Air Force. If your trust cannot be placed in two men of such high integrity then I suggest there is little hope of building a truly multiracial and harmonious Air Force, let alone a country. Once again, I urge you to reconsider your decision and to examine not only the possible motives of the officers concerned but the source and reliability of the information or misinformation that may have been passed to you."

Len Pink's letter had no effect whatsoever – and the airmen remained in prison. It soon dawned that the dictatorial black government was gambling on a plan to rid the Air Force of its white leadership. No black airman had the ability or capacity to replace the arrested white Air Force hierarchy. World pressure mounted against Zimbabwe for a fair, open trial. American Vice President George Bush extracted a promise from deputy premier Simon Muzenda that the trial would be in open court. A year after the arrests, the trial opened on Monday, 23rd May

1983 – and lasted till mid June. The court was adjourned for six weeks, with judgement being given Wednesday, 31st August 1983.

Respect for the rule of law deteriorated rapidly amongst the rank and file. More and more Air Force people were emigrating. Even the Thornhill CO, Dag Jones took the gap. To fill the gap, Pakistanis arrived on contract in the wake of the white exodus.

Major-General John Hickman, the ex-Commander of the Rhodesian Army, was detained for several months in the maximum security prison on trumped-up allegations that he would have lent himself to an invasion by South African forces - the last thing he was likely to do. (In the opinion of Ken Flower, head of the Rhodesian CIO). Air Vice-Marshal Hugh Slatter and Air Commodore Phil Pile were detained on scant evidence. They were acquitted before the Chief Justice, Dumbutshena, who bravely censured the Government, only to see the Airmen he had discharged immediately re-detained with no further evidence being led, illustrating open contempt for the rule of law. Even Bishop Abel Muzorewa was committed to prison after Independence on charges that were never disclosed.

It is worthy to record that tragedy struck General Hickman when his son, Trooper Richard Hickman, was killed on 7th June 1979 whilst serving with the Special Air Service. It will be recalled that I rated the General highly; having him as my passenger when I flew him to the School of Infantry in January 1977, and prior to that, working closely with him at Bindura when he was a Brigadier.

The trial took 44 days; Judge Enoch Dumbutshena, Zimbabwe's first black judge and later Chief Justice, presiding. He castigated the State for withholding legal counsel from the accused airmen, found that their confessions had been obtained under extreme duress (torture), and acquitted them. As the Air Force Officers walked from the court as free men, they were re-arrested for indefinite detention, and taken back into custody on the same charges that they had just been acquitted. An immediate hue and cry followed from civilised society – and within days Air Vice-Marshal Hugh Slatter and Air Commodore Phil Pile was placed on an Air Zimbabwe flight and deported to London on 9th September 1983. The Air Zimbabwe Captain welcomed them aboard over the intercom and was soundly castigated afterwards by government.

Nigel Lewis-Walker had been set free earlier on 16th November 1983. Peter Briscoe, John Cox, Barry Lloyd and Neville Weir were released just before Christmas.

Air Marshal Norman Walsh – pictured here - retired when the trial of all the airmen commenced. Boss Norman was replaced by Pakistani Daudpota, who duly handed over the reins to Josiah Tungumirai. The latter had no air experience – not even a pilot training crash course.

CULPRITS AT LARGE

The culprits of the Thornhill sabotage are still at large. Special Forces operatives Barry Bawden (aged 43, in June 2000), Philip Conjwayo (68), Mike Smith (46) and Kevin Woods (48), were, for more than 20 years, thought to have been the prime-suspects – and I thus owe them a public apology. It will be recalled that the Air Force Board of Inquiry had established that South African Air Force aircraft were identified before the senseless arrests of Air Vice-Marshal Hugh Slatter and Air Commodore Phil Pile. A Canberra had carried out a photo reconnaissance directly over Thornhill, and a large Puma type helicopter was seen in the vicinity of Guinea Fowl shortly after the Hunters and Hawks blew up. At an early stage, the Air Force had concluded that a South African based organisation was responsible for the Thornhill sabotage.
In 1989 the perpetrators were mistakenly identified. My source, John Cox, believed the reasons for the lengthy detention of those involved was because Mugabe did not want the double-agents to make any revelations to the South African Truth and Reconciliation Commission and thus cause him further embarrassment. I met Kevin Woods at the Shamwari Club in Durban in 2007 – and then again at his book launch late November. By this time, Peter Stiff, in an exchange of e-mails, convinced me that Woods was not involved in the Thornhill sabotage. Stiff confirmed to me that Major-General Fritz Loots made the 'Go" decision – and that Major Brian was in fact ex-BSAP Gray Branfield (killed in Iraq in 2005.
MK operatives Thula Bopela and Daluxolo Luthuli, in their book "*Umkonto We Siswe*" revealed Major Brian's true identity as ex SB Gray Branfield who was killed while working for a security company in Iraq in 2005 – branding Branfield as a particularly deadly operator.
Zanu PF inherited the Air Force of Ruins.

Australian Hawk – colour picture, for the record

AIR FORCE OF RUINS

He merely joined a flood of white resignations that had been triggered by the whole unsavoury affair.

His tour lasted much longer than anticipated and the whites that wanted to stay on and make something of the force were eventually worn down. The blacks and whites actually got on well together, just as they have always done in Rhodesia, (with exceptions) bonded by a mutual distaste for the interlopers.

Despite Red China supplying twelve MiG-21 aircraft, efficiency plummeted. In May 1988 the Air Force was tasked to carry out the traditional Bulawayo Trade Fair flypast. They took off from Thornhill, but despite the long and straight road unmistakably pointing like an arrow from Gweru to Bulawayo as an aid to navigation, they lost their way and never showed up over the stadium.

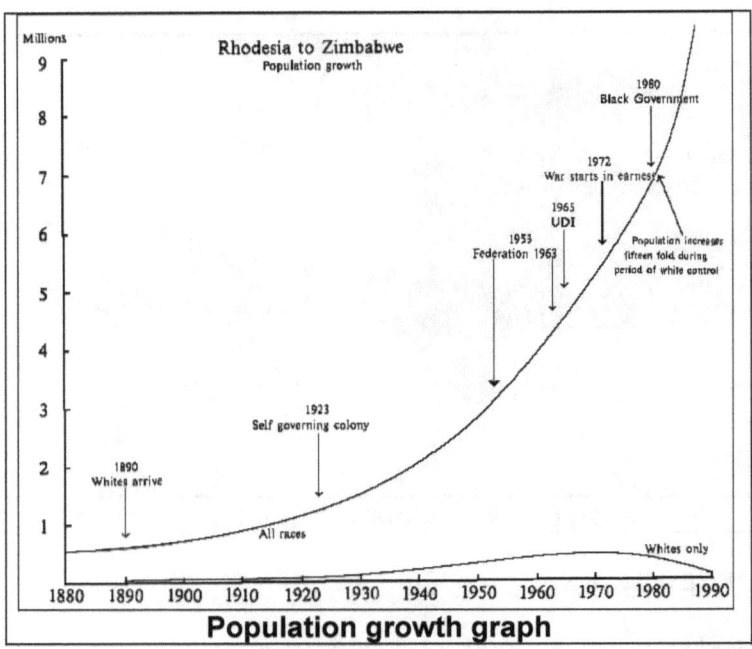
Population growth graph

The graph dramatically illustrates the ultimate dominant factor in the history of why the war was lost – a fifteen fold explosion of the black population (during the ninety year period of white rule). The battles were won, yet the war was lost. Many of the old die-hards attributed the inability of blacks to achieve military successes on the battlefields – and to govern themselves for that matter, to the K-Factor.

A status quo can only be maintained in a totalitarian state. Rhodesians were not totalitarians, no matter what the world may say about them. Indeed, many had fought and given their lives in either a world war or a bush war against such political systems. They were a people with rather old fashioned virtues, who placed honesty, decency, honour, courage and compassion high on the list of qualities they admired most.

I had occasion to revisit both my old forward airfields - FAF 1 and FAF 7 - in January 2001. Whilst at Kariba with Courtney and Brendan Jelley on a game viewing drive, Rina and I diverted into the old Air Force base. The place looked deserted and after hooting several times at the boom gate, a scraggily dressed civilian emerged from the old operations room. He apologetically explained that he and the only two other occupants of the now ZNDF base were having a drinking session and had not heard the car approaching. He had no objections to me driving around the base, which I hastily did before he could change his mind. I stopped near the old pub watering hole, with its now derelict building and disused swimming pool. The pool showed signs of elephant spoor leading down to the mosquito infested puddle of stagnant water, plus heaps of elephant droppings. The glitter-stone pathways that I had so painstakingly laid some twenty-five years earlier were now succumbing to the encroaching African bundu. The Mess hall was in ruins. Only the Ops Room, Barrack block and Ablution block (all brick built) was left standing. An old broken down Bedford RL truck lay abandoned in the cantonment area. There were massive gaps in the old rocket box perimeter security wall – no doubt helped in its collapse by elephants getting to whatever little water remained in the swimming pool. The grass was literally knee-high everywhere and the whole place had been allowed to go to rack and ruin. The corner gunpits that had been constructed from empty ammunition boxes were also in a poor state of disuse and abandonment. While the visit was very nostalgic for me, after so many pleasant memories so very long ago, it was tragic to realise that the Air Force of Ruins was indeed an apt description of my findings.

Buffalo Range was a different kettle of fish.

Rina and I had just bade farewell to the Young Jells (who were wisely packing up for New Zealand) and needed a diversion to dry tearful eyes. Saying bye-bye to our adorable grandchildren was heart wrenching. Anyway, en route to Beit Bridge, we stopped at my old FAF 7, where we were ushered to a shady parking spot. The Guardroom orderly summoned the ZNDF base commander, a recent veteran from the DRC. Lieutenant Mashumba appeared, and  kindly escorted me though the old "Prop Stop" pub that Tom Preston had built from bar profits and friendly donations a quarter century ago. The fifty by fifty foot building is still in good shape. 'Our' bar counter is still being put to good use, spoilt only by pictures of all the recent gook ZNA ex-commanders adorning the bar walls – and the barman's sleeping quarters being in one of the booze stock rooms. I was shown around the office buildings and also saw the accommodation buildings from a distance. The Army was using the base, with a large military type sign calling it the ZNA "Buffalo Range Training Centre – Section Commanders Training Course". There was no air activity, and no aircraft in sight. The aircraft revetments were still standing, but looked disused and in need of maintenance. Overall, it was a one hundred percent improvement on the Kariba base.

What was the Jewel of Africa was no more. Mugabe had tainted Nyerere's jewel.

Is there any light at the end of the tunnel? I for one have always maintained that Zimbabwe indeed has the potential of being the true jewel of Africa. That there has been a setback, let nobody fool him or herself. The time will come when "Responsible Government" will turn full circle to like-times of the 1923s when a person of the likes of Solomon emerge to lead the country to greatness once again. Let's hope that Zimbabwe becomes world renown for the Ruins that it is (i.e. in the Fort Victoria district) and that the once Great Rhodesia will re-emerge.

CANCER - 24 SEPTEMBER 1992 & 27 MARCH 1993

Rina was admitted to Medic-clinic hospital in Pietermaritzburg and was diagnosed with breast cancer. She had no option but to have her left breast removed and be subjected to chemotherapy and some radiation treatment. A wig hid her crowning glory when all her hair started falling out. To take her mind off matters, Masonite kindly allocated us another house and we then moved from Short Street to Robert Morrison Avenue.

On 27th March 1993 Rina suffered a massive stroke which left the right side of her body paralysed, unable to speak and the loss of vision in her left eye. She was still unable to utter a sound when the doctors discharged her from hospital.

One day, while motoring to Estcourt after spending time with my sister Delene, I was astonished to realise that Rina was singing "You are my Sunshine" along with me. I stopped the car in a state of shock - I could not believe my ears. Tears of joy flooded my eyes and I had great difficulty driving the short distance back home. We phoned everybody and Rina sang "Happy Birthday and You are my Sunshine" to all our relatives and friends. Despite Speech Therapy, Rina remained inflicted with a speech impediment - she could not utter high frequency sounds - words used most often.

The Physiotherapist did get Rina to walk in a fashion, but after two years kindly informed us that while she was quite happy to charge for her services, there would be very little further gain. Should stroke victims not make a full recovery within two years, regaining use of limbs would remain remote. We decided to discontinue the speech and physiotherapy. At that time I was studying part time at Technikon Natal and had completed 10 out of my 14 subjects to qualify for my Diploma in Personnel Management. I became a fifty-year-old dropout. I needed to spend quality time with my spouse – "until death us do part."

After a couple of falls at Robert Morrison, Masonite did not hesitate to re-allocate us a very large four-bedroom house in Percy Sperryn Drive.

CRIME AND VIOLENCE

Our family also experienced our fair share of crime and violence. We lived through and endured turbulent times. Rina had her car stolen whilst shopping, Renene was attacked and stabbed four times, my sister Delene was accosted and held hostage in her own home and my brother Jan had his Microbus hijacked at gunpoint. All these events were subsequent to the loss of my youngest sister Dawn who died when an arsonist set fire to our thatched cottage on the Copperbelt many years before.

The incident regarding the car theft was fortunately only a material loss and no personal injury occurred. I had just bought the Toyota Cressida from Masonite, and Rina had popped into the Checkers Supermarket in Estcourt for a couple of minutes. When she came out of the shop, the car was gone. The Branch manager was very helpful - he called me at work, notified the police and gave Rina a cup of black tea while I rushed over to comfort her. We completed all the necessary police dockets, but that was the last of our loss - the car was not insured.

I mentioned that Renene was attacked a couple of days before her wedding. I was in Pietermaritzburg at that time (studying at Technikon Natal), Rina's elder sister Gerta was staying with us pending the wedding, and Renene was in the Drakensberg, having spent the afternoon with Bill and Margaret Jelley who had just arrived prior to the wedding. On her way back to Estcourt her car broke down near the Draycott turn-off. A black guy who had drunk one matriculation celebration drink too many took his apartheid hatred out on Renene. He chased her, stabbed her twice in her chest, and then commenced slashing the Renault's tyres. Renene had managed to escape his grasp and sought refuge in her car. She locked all the doors. The black male, having slashed the tyres, then forced his way into the back seat by smashing in the rear window with a brick sized rock. He then stabbed her twice more in the back before she could get out the immobilised car. A passing motorist happened to frighten off her assailant and she was picked up by a good Samaritan who brought her to the hospital and notified Rina. Through sheer guts and determination my brave baby heroine made her wedding day a day to remember. Renene was scarred for life.

The incident concerning my sister was just as traumatic. Her husband had gone outside their posh Kloof house to lock the driveway gate. Two armed assailants demanding money beat him up. Delene got worried when Stu had not returned and went outside to investigate why he was taking such a long time, only to be confronted and frog-marched back into the house. Stu and Delene were severely assaulted and terrorised in their own home. Both were tied up while their home was ransacked. By pure coincidence, Chanli and Charles arrived in the early hours of the following morning and frightened off the terrorists. It took nearly three weeks for Stu and Delene's wounds to heal. The scars remained a lot longer.

My brother Jan had just delivered SAFA juice and collected cash from his telephone card franchise in Umlazi when he drove off into a set-up. The ambush was cleverly planned - a red VW blocked his exit, and as he was bypassing the obstruction one guy yanked at his door while another entered his Microbus by the side door. As he sped off, trying to dislodge his assailants, the one in the back of the Kombi threatened him with a gun to the head. Jan had no option but to heed the warning

- and in a matter of seconds the highjackers sped off with his delivery vehicle. He was indeed lucky to escape with his life.

We have also had our privacy invaded on numerous occasions - theft of property, car break-ins, handbag snatching, and forced entry into homes and pick pocketing. It explains, perhaps, why Renene and Grahame, Grahame's brother Keith and Delene seeking their fortunes in Australia, Canada and New Zealand. At this late stage in our lives, Rina and I remain contented with our current quality of life, and plan to spend the remainder of our days gazing at the sea on the East Coast.

COASTAL RETIREMENT PLANS

My Zimbabwe pension permitted me to invest in coastal property. We started by buying a three bedroom flat in Bryanston Heights, which also served as digs for Pey whilst studying Computer Data Processing at Technikon Natal. During this time, interest rates escalated and the Dollar Rand exchange rate deteriorated to such an extent that we were obliged to sell the property. Pey then moved into a two bedroom flat and shortly thereafter, into a rented bachelor pad in Willern Court, Esplanade.

When I retired from the Air Force, the Zimbabwe dollar exchanged for two hundred South African cents - or R2.00. By end 1998. $1.00 paid only R 0.20, or one twentieth of the original pension worth. At the time of writing this chapter, the exchange rate has further deteriorated to only fourteen cents. By the 2007's, any conversion attempts became futile.

When a one bedroom flat came up for sale in the grand Gables, Pey persuaded us, rather wisely, to once again make retirement plans and invest in property. This we duly did. Pey had meanwhile got married and moved into 813 The Gables.

By this time, Rina contracted breast cancer and suffered a disabling stoke. Shortly thereafter, No 2 Anchors Aweigh at Illovo Beach came on the market, we snapped it up because it was a ground floor garden flat near my brother who was in No 4. With its view of the Illovo lagoon and sea views, it was just the right size as a retirement prospect. It must be said in all honesty, that Robert Mugabe's government has funded both the Esplanade and Illovo properties. Rina and I spent many a happy weekend, and most of our leave, at the 'Huisie by the Sea'. After my brother Jan moved out of Anchors Aweigh, the attraction to retire in Illovo Beach gradually diminished. An unexpected offer on our seaside resort materialised late December 2000, and we reluctantly decided to sell. This meant that we modified our retirement plans, and we both decided that we would settle on the Gables, with its ever-changing scenery over the Durban harbour. Our original thought was for Renene to inherit Anchors Aweigh, and Pey to inherit the grand Gables. But this is not to be.

Whilst not formally willed, let the record show that in the event of my dear wife Rina predeceasing me, being of sound mind it is our 'will' that Renene inherits her fair share of The Gables. Pey will receive his fair share for all the improvements like tiling the floors. However, Rina and I have every intention of spending many a happy year gazing at all the shipping, sailing and boating which graces the waterfront.

The flat is within wheelchair distance of Durban Bay and Ferry Services – partly owned but managed by my brother Jan and his good lady Julia. They also have an interest in the daily charter of the massive Hakuna Mutata, so I should be able to bum the odd jolly. Sea trips are not Rina's scene – she is apt to feed the creatures with second hand carrots. However, there is always something to do on the waterfront, albeit just a change of scenery. It is thus that we look forward to spending quality time together during our twilight years. With this in mind, we decided on October 2002 as the retirement date from Masonite (Africa) Limited. My service with the board manufacturer would thus equal the time we spent in the Air Force – over twenty years with each – and what a great period that has been for us. We have been truly blessed. We can stand on His Word "There is a right time for everything". Praise the Lord.

Roll on, November 2002. It did – but the Hakuna Mutata sank near Maputo, and Jan with son Paul (plus Karen) embarked on a massive property development project in Amanzimtoti. At age 67 he must have rocks in his head!

The time is right to mention reunions.

REUNIONS

THORNHILL

1996 was a memorable year when past pupils gathered at a Goodwood Sports Club in Durban north. The function was organised professionally, with radio, TV and press announcements. On arrival, we were name tagged with colours according to the year one left school, issued braai packs and joined like-minded groups at the various braais or in the sports club pub.

Age had certainly taken its toll - the familiar names often did not match the odd bald head, sunken chest cum potbelly or otherwise person who appeared a total stranger who would normally not warrant a second glance. There were possibly more ex-pupils, some 600 odd, than one could recall being at school at any one time. However, what could one expect when eyes had not been set on one another during the past 35 to 40 odd years.

Old Miss Nuttal did a roaring trade selling coffee mugs and numerous other mementoes to commemorate the occasion. She was the old girls hostel hag that many a time caught Rina and me in various stages of undress or in compromising poses. Fortunately, she did not seem to recall past indiscretions - or perhaps was just very diplomatic not to broach the subject.

GORDONS PRAWN - UMHLANGA

The get-to-gether in Umhlanga was the first formal function that Rina and I attended that was organised by the Natal Branch of the Air Forces Association. The function was a Rhodesian Air Force reunion

Rhodesian Air Force
Reunion Dinner
GORDON'S PRAWN
Lagoon Drive   Umhlanga Rocks
Saturday   4th May 1985   8.00 pm
R25 DOUBLE

dinner held at Gordon's Prawn on Saturday 4th May 1985. We motored down from Estcourt to attend. Whilst the venue was renown for its delicious prawns (and reminiscent of our jollies to Lourenço Marques), the prawns were no match to the pleasure we enjoyed with meeting up with so many past Air Force colleagues. The event started at 8.00pm and no time was lost drinking and chatting into the wee hours. Most found settling down in Natal traumatic and difficult. We were not alone, and being amongst life-long friends made the adjustments that little bit easier. I couldn't afford to get too drunk, because Estcourt was a good two hours drive home. The early hours contributed to a quick sobering up experience, and we fortunately arrived home safe and sound.

AFAZ – AIR FORCE'S ASSOCIATION OF ZIMBABWE

Peter and Anne Cooke warrant special mention for the sterling work done in compiling the bi-annual Bateleur newsletter, for organising Air Force get-togethers and for keeping all members of the Air Forces' Association of Zimbabwe informed of common interests. I believe, they more than anybody else, maintained the esprit de corp that was the hallmark of all the airmen that served, or were connected with the Rhodesian Air Force. Many of the activities and highlights of events have already been mentioned elsewhere, and it is just not possible to do justice to all their good work. Suffice it to say that they have been a significant source of material for this biography.

SAAF 75 ANNIVERSARY

Wow – What an experience to witness the biggest International Military Air Show on the African continent that was held at the SAAF Air Force base Waterkloof in 1995. At least a dozen Air Force's participated with truly magnificent static and flying displays. I was told that no less than Chiefs of Air Forces of 36 countries were present – amongst the 380,000 people that visited the show daily – more than the total white population of Rhodesia in its heyday. I possibly spent more time navigating through all the road traffic jams than at the actual show itself – but was still able to catch sight of the flying displays, albeit some miles away from Waterkloof. I rated the Russians tops, followed by the Americans, then the British, and of course the South Africans.
The most impressive was the Russian pilot in his SU - 35 flying level at about 200 knots. The aircraft is pulled nose up, pointing skywards at about 90 degrees, whilst still maintaining level flight. The SU virtually stands on its tail. The pilot then lowers the nose and continues his

level flight manoeuvre – pointing the right way. I would not have believed it possible had I not seen it with my own eyes. The Russian MiG-29 was just as polished, with its aerobatics sequence right in front of the spectator's field of vision.

The American F-16 display was awesome power – all verticals – so much so that the aircraft paled out of sight as it disappeared in the wild blue yonder. The SAAF Mirage air display was all speed – all horizontal. Also disappearing out of sight as it streaked across the sky. The British Red Arrows aerobatics team put on a very professional display – and stole the show with their tight formation flying. Also impressive was the Rooivalk helicopter, which performs a loop as well as a slow roll. The Rooivalk is the most advanced gun-ship in the world – developed and built in South Africa. Another impressive SAAF manoeuvre was performed by a CASA – 212 transport aircraft that does a loop. I am sure that many a pilot present marvelled what modern aircraft nowadays were capable of.

I summed up the displays thus: Americans – all power, with spectators nodding heads, more often than not craning necks skywards. South Africans – all high speed, with spectators shaking heads from side to side. Russians – perfect, combing speed and power to confine spectators gazing in awe right in front of them – and within a comfortable field of vision.

Then there was also a nostalgic flight by a Vampire. My heart was pumping a lot of lumpy custard.

But the highlight was undoubtedly meeting up again with all the old Air Force colleagues. To name but a few would include Peter and Anne Cooke, PB and Beryl Petter-Bowyer, Ozzie and June Penton, Di Brent and Babs White, Bill Sykes, Johnny and Noelene Green, Pete and Ellie Woolcock, Dennis Spence, Tony and Shirley Smit, Gordon Wright, Nobby Nightingale, Les Authers, John and Elaine Childs, plus many others whose names now escape me.

The SAAF certainly did itself proud, to have organised such a terrific 75 Anniversary air show. Also hats off to the organisers of the Veterans tent – where shelter and good company was enjoyed when the weather turned somewhat foul.

1998 - HARARE

The Air Forces' Association arranged a humdinger of a reunion at the Mount Pleasant Sports Club, followed by a four-day jolly at Kariba. What made this event rather special was having Renene and Pey meet all the old fogies. A really special guest was Ian Douglas Smith, who kindly signed the first edition of Bush Horizons, which was launched at the function.

To Prop & Pey Geldenhuis
My best wishes
I. Douglas Smith

My proud possession – despite the duplication below

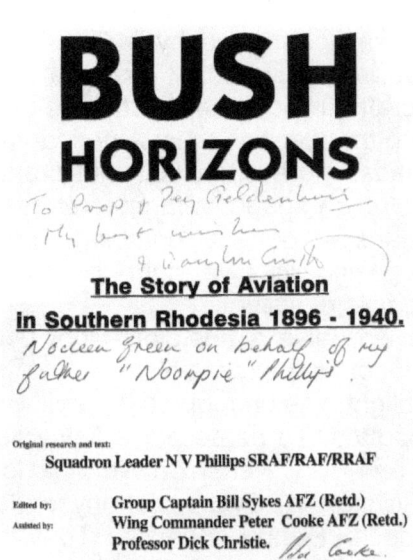

Bill Sykes, Peter Cooke and Noelene Green – who signed on behalf of her late father – also autographed my edition of the book – and I trust will one day become a collectors item.

Pey came up from Durban on the Friday afternoon, 15th May 1998, and we immediately set off for Beit Bridge. We met up with Grahame and Renene in Gweru, and after lunch, visited the Air Force Museum. On display were a Canberra, Hunter, Vampire and a Provost – actual aircraft that I had flown during the Bush War. The Museum visit was a real thrill, to experience the smells and sights that were part of my life for so many years. It was a real privilege to have my whole descendants with me, especially Pey and Renene. Courtney and Brendan were still too young to appreciate the significance of the event – but being Zimbabwean born and bred, will, I trust, one day revisit the actual aircraft that Granpa Jelley commanded, and Oudad also flown. In all modesty, I was the No 1 Squadron (Hunters) and No 5 Squadron (Canberra) Flight Commander during the war. I flew the Provost for the full duration of Operation Nickel (hence the title of this novel), and both Bill Jelley and I were in the same pair of Vampires that carried out pinpoint accurate airstrikes during Operation Cauldron.

Rina and I then proceeded to Thornhill High School and were fortunate to meet the Headmistress and deputy head who kindly showed off all the old sporting team photographs as well as past school prefects which is displayed in the school hall. The Headmistress appreciated the fact that an 'old boy' had married an 'old girl', and had taken time out to revisit their "alma mater" nearly forty years later.

A quick visit to the Air Force base did not meet with much success - the guardroom orderly eyed my South African car number plate suspiciously - and only allowed a trip around Married Quarters with an uniformed orderly. The next morning, a Sunday, we set off in convoy for Harare to join the reunion at the Mount Pleasant Sports Club. This certainly was the Gathering of the Century – there were more ex-Force personnel at one place than at any other time in the history of the Rhodesian Air Force. The expected number of people – 450, rose to over 700 as the day progressed.

The only other 16 PTC member there was Chris Dixon whom I had last set eyes on some 18 years earlier. We were both really thrilled to catch up on the past - as well as renewing old acquaintances. Several of the 750 odd ex-Air Force members had arrived from afar - like Australia, UK and the States. I was really proud to brag about my grandchildren, and spent a memorable time with Joe Cameron while Courtney was enjoying the jumping castle. I was also thrilled that both Pey and I were able to spend a couple of minutes with the Guest of Honour ex-Prime Minister Ian Douglas Smith. I relayed that his son Alec had served at FAF 1 (Wankie) with me; and I conveyed my condolences with the passing of his wife Janet. Unfortunately, I did not have the copy of *The Great Betrayal*, (which Heather Rider kindly gave me), for IDS to autograph.

We spent the night with Bill and Margaret Jelley, and set off for Kariba on Monday morning 18th May 1998. Grahame had to return to Chipinge, but Renene, Courtney and Brendan came with us. Rina was able to spend some quality time with her elder sister Gerta and brother-in-law Hansie, while Pey and I joined the 100 or so ex-Air Force types that could make the three day gathering at Charara. The trips on the houseboats were really enjoyable, and afforded the opportunity to reminisce at one's heart content.

Hansie and Gerta took us around for sight seeing and we were pleasantly surprised with all the changes that had occurred since Rina and I had lived in Kariba during the war years. Hansie and Gerta had built a magnificent home on Mica Point, and we marvelled at all the kapenta fishing fleets that put out to 'sea' at night – recovering early every morning to beach there overnight catches. But all good things come to and end and before the week was over, we headed back to Natal. The others went back to all the four corners of the earth – America, Australia, the Far East and Britain.

JOHN KUTANGA McKENZIE: 13 NOVEMBER 1999

John and June McKenzie organised a re-union gathering at their Swaziland home for: -
    Justice (Varky) and Amy Varkevisser   No 8 SSU
    Vic and Shirley Wightman   No 11 SSU
    (Prop) Preller and Rina Geldenhuys   No 16 PTC
    Ken Eva, ex Army School of Infantry, and
    June McKenzie's Mom and Dad.

Mac hosted an elaborate Dining-In type function, with a magnificent spread laid on by June. As PMC, or simply Master of Ceremonies, Mac excelled at the speeches and then surprised his guests by presenting to the couples an inlaid genuine Rhodesian Teak cheese-boards. If this was not enough, Mac crowned this by presenting each person with personalised sand blasted inscribed glass tankard.

The inscription read: -

An
Evening of
Green and White
11th November 1999
(Zimbabwe Bird)
(Rhodesian Coat of Arms)
The Mac's & The Millennium
Swaziland

Even the coin that was inlaid in the Teak cheese-board bore the Rhodesian Coat of Arms.

Rina and I had left Estcourt early on Saturday and motored up to Mbabane, routing via Newcastle, Volksrust and Ermelo, arriving at midday. Varky and Amy came through from Johannesburg, and arrived somewhat before us. Vic and Shirley arrived the night before, having come from Nelspruit. The Brownjob arrived in time for Sundowners, and came from Big Bend. The afternoon was spent reminiscing, telling war-stories, and abusing the free flowing liquid refreshments and kind hospitality. I might add that John and June have built up a mansion in Swaziland where John owns and manages his Buffalo Soldiers security business. June is a keen gardener and was recognised for the magnificence of their garden by winning the Best Garden Competition in Mbabane. Past and present connections will reveal the significance of this particular reunion. I'll start off with the date and Mac.

11th November 1999 - UDI, 34 years earlier. The thirteenth was the nearest weekend, and 1999 was just weeks away from the new millennium.

John McKenzie - Kutanga Bombing Range Warden, and most likely the only Air Force person that interacted with every pilot in the force, one way or another. Mac featured at all the Kutanga Range detachments when I was on No 4 Squadron. At his Dining-In Night, I took the opportunity to rag Mac about the one-eyed Grimmie that he used to bring out to the Range during those long ago detachments. She was a certain Miss Rose Nicholson - who had the habit of taking out her glass eye in order to 'eye-ball' the randy goings on from misbehaving aircrews. As the Range Safety Officer - RSO - it was Mac's responsibility to control and direct all aircraft movements on the Range. Mac first flew with me on 14th March 1965, during a Police Reserve Air Wing Operation that was held at the Range. We also travelled together down to South Africa for the Air Force Rugby tour in the same year. John also featured prominently when Hugh Slatter, Phil Pile and Co were tortured when the Hawk and Hunter aircraft were blown up in 1981 (as a supporter for the plight of the detained airmen). Mac then also attended my daughter's wedding to Graham Jelley in 1992. And now this super gesture to honour Rina and me as his guests at this very special function in Swaziland in November 1999.

June also was a star in her own right. She played Squash at National level. Together with John, June has built up a magnificent R 750,000 home in Swaziland. June is very proud of her boys - Darryl and Duncan - and they dwarf her in the photos that she cherishes - and quite rightly so.

Varky J.E. Varkevisser was one of 14 student pilots of No 8 SSU (Short Service Unit) that joined the Air Force on 1st March 1955, but only one of seven that received their Wings on 28th February 1957. Some of his fellow course Officers that impacted on my own career included Randy du Rand, Eddy Wilkinson, and Peter McClurg. Basil Green was a notable rugby player, who seemed to clash with Randy on the rugby field (Basil was described as having more ass than class). Two of Varky's course mates were killed - Garrett in a Vampire accident and Scott in a motoring accident.

Varky was my PAI instructor way back in 1965; we won the Police Commissioners Trophy in same year, toured together to South Africa for rugby and were masters at bombing and gunnery. He and I competed fiercely for the No 4 Squadron Low Level bombing trophy. Varky retired from the Force in the late 1970s to go farming in the White Waters Dam area outside Gwelo. He served as a Reserve Pilot and then rejoined the Force and finally retired to farming. In 1988 he emigrated to RSA, and established a cosmetics business with his wife Amy. They import the oils and acids from France. Their bottling techniques are state of the art - unique according to market and customer demands. They presented John and June with a special, personalised and labelled cosmetic set.

Vic Wightman was a member of 11 SSU, then left to join the Royal Air Force, flew the Lightning supersonic jet and then rejoined the Rhodesian Air Force. Vic features prominently on No 1 Squadron, flying Hawker Hunters. He was also amongst the chosen few to ferry out the Lynx sanctions busting aircraft acquisitions during January 1976. When we were at Thornhill, Vic and Shirley were our next door neighbours. They lived in MQ 5 and we were in MQ 6. Our children used to play with one another. Renene loved it, because they had three sons and a daughter. Pey didn't have a choice, not that I think he minded. He was not as fussy like Renene. It was pleasing to note that all the Wightman boys have qualified as engineers - in the Cape, Johannesburg and Pretoria. One of the children is about to go to the States and UK. Vic is still flying, cloud seeding in the Nelspruit area.

Vic is one of those keen sense of humour people who has a very nice way of saying things. I enjoyed his theory of why people turn 'grey' in their old age. We all know that hair keeps on growing. Vic maintains so do the roots - only at a slower rate. Once the roots penetrate the 'grey matter', ones hair then turns grey. However, if there is no grey matter for the hair roots, then ones hair falls out. That no doubt explains why half the old folks are grey, and the other half are bald? Shirley chips in to comment that all women have 'grey matter', because a bald condition amongst females is very rare.

Chatting to the third quest couple was also enlightening. Ken Eva served a lot of time at the School of Infantry. He was involved in quite a few punch-ups with the gooks, spooks and Bezuidenhout. He mentioned the only time he was in an aircraft prang, it was during trooping into a tight LZ by helicopter pilot Giles Porter. Now Giles was one of my first Vampire OCU students that I rated highly - in fact Giles was considered a natural. But it goes to show what a small world we live in. The Eva's also farmed in the Tengwe area near Karoi and knew Hansie and Gerta Bezuidenhout - Rina's sister, and brother-in-law. They currently farm citrus on Tambuti Estates, in the Big Bend area of Swaziland. As such, they also know Stuart and Joy Geldenhuys who are citrus growers on Crooks Estates, Big Bend.

As can be imagined, the Mac's *Green and White* affair was a shot in the arm, with much *Whenwe* story telling.

KUTANGA RANGE FACT-STORY BY JOHN MCKENZIE:

Kutanga Bombing Range is situated to the South of the Midlands town called Que Que in the district area commonly known as the Bemberzaan / Sebakwe (named after the two rivers in that area) farming community called Rosedale. This geographically placed the Range north of Thornhill some 50 miles. The history of the Range was originally part of a much larger Air Weapon Range called KUBANGA allocated to the Royal Air Force / Southern Rhodesian Air Force of the day. Kubanga range was 75, 0000 acres; Kutanga took over 30, 0000 acres, being the top northern section of the defunct Kubanga range area. The remainder of Kubanga had been closed down and sold to farming.

McKenzie joined Kutanga Range staff in 1960, which consisted of: Sgt Nobby Clarke, Cpl Mitty Immelmann, three askari's of no rank, Mursheri, Joseph, Takawia, yet mighty fine troops, the best. There were three kitchen boys, Bennie the cook, a John, the cook's side hand, who had a sudden name change to Jack and Michael the waiter who ferried tea and toast all day, every day; a labour force of some twenty prisoners clad in white garb, which amazingly seemed to tie in with all the targets were painted white!

The range was a composite range allowing for all types of air-weapons and consisted of the numerous targets: Two gunnery ranges of 10x10 Hessian targets, six on each range, a Vampire and

Provost high-dive target, a high level bombing target for Canberra and a rocket dump, all in a cleared area called 'the danger area' of 1,000 acres

The range had a main-tower and two plotting huts. A grass runway 130/310, 1500yds long with two 'helva' bumps in it. Then there was a small mess/come house, so sweet and cosy having two bedrooms, heaven knows why as we were not allowed to night-stop. The danger area had only two internal roads leading to the targets and they were named Kirk and Barber. Jock Barber dropping the first bomb on Kutanga, and Kirk being the Armament Officer of the day. That was Kutanga Range 1960.

Mac's first Range improvement was to remove the one plotting hut that was constructed inside the danger area by the RAF-pommies who designed the Range. Heaven knows what they were thinking at the time, but it sure was hell watching Vamps turning live with rockets or high-dive bombs from behind your back and only brick, mortar and a tin roof protecting the guy plotting -The rocket dump was situated some 500 yards to the right of the hut. Also, once in the hut there was no-way the plotter was able to get tea delivered or to relieve himself until the end of the flying programme (This would have entailed a vehicle moving in and out of the danger area thus contravening Range safety laws).

Mac recalls: "Hell the poms are wasters. Sgt Nobby Clarke was more than in agreement as he could see the problem and demolishment commenced soon after we had burnt our own clay- bricks from anthills on the Range. On the Northern boundary of the Range was a small koppie of stone, ideally situated to allow us to rebuild the plotting hut on top of it and also create a new rocket dump allowing proper safety - and tea deliveries to the guys plotting!

"Thereafter it was called the 'Koppie Tower', all aircraft turning live attacks did so after passing the tower position, no more having the tower ahead of the aircraft. What remained of the old hut was eventually blown to bits during One and Two Squadron dusk-strikes. The Koppie Tower has many a tale to tell and one of its main events was during the break up of the Federation, where many Parliamentarians and Top Brass sat their ass with a thousand others evaluating the might of our Air force, a display of fire-power and air superiority.

"Having just finished building the Koppie Tower, Nobby and I started to build the mess extension so as to house and dine detachments proper. The notorious jail-bird, Adrian Diggaden, who by the way was able to and did escape from any prison in the country, was one of the white clad prisoners working on the Range. Being a brick-layer, he built the mess extension. A brother of mine made the .M. pattern breeze block mould which was used in the construction of the new mess hall so as to get fresh air, cooling down on the heat. Adrian Diggaden, for his part in building our mess, was a recipient of the famous Kutanga Star deck chair medal, and got the privilege to dine the first meal served in our new mess. We ate venison, reedbuck roast and fresh veggies grown on the Range, the venison came from, hell I've forgotten. He was a very nice guy to work with and gave no problems as a prisoner.

"However as a Range Warden, I had land for 'Afrika' and the lay-out of the Range, its targets and access to them made our job unbearable. We were forever working full tilt simply because the targets were damaged on every attack and pilots were so keen on shooting the place up that there was no time for tea! I immediately set about expanding the danger area to accommodate more target facility and area for weapon firing. The white clad labour force of prisoners, under duress, cut down trees and stumped out another 1,000 acres, thus increasing the danger area to about 2,000 plus acres. It was fun working with them; the land and soil being virgin looked and smelt for real. I fuelled the prisoners on guinea-fowl, and they not having meat in their daily ration of beans and dried 'sudza,' the bird got them working like Trojans. The range soon had a danger area big enough to treble the target requirement.

"Round about 1965, Ben Pretorius re-mustered from Airframes Thornhill to the Range, thank goodness for that as we worked jolly well together. Soon to follow was Boo-Boo Milne from the armoury at Thornhill, round about 1968. Ben and I worked our butts off developing new targets, roads and gunnery ranges. The job was made easy as each time a grader from the roads department arrived to grade fire-breaks we commandeered it and its crew, diverting them to new target projects. As well known we flew till lunch time and because of that we were able to grade all afternoon, sometimes late after dusk by means of the goose-neck flares normally used for night flying, lighting our way.

Early 1970 saw the loss of Nobby Clarke to early retirement causing me to take over full management of the Range and to conduct the duties of Range Safety Officer for all squadrons and all flying exercises, not just for Five Squadron the Canberra bombers. O.C. Flying and the squadrons were happy with the discipline shown by me in carrying out the RSO duties. My rank at the time was Cpl/Tech,

I say this because before the RSO/duty was only carried out by the aircrew who were qualified in the type of weapon being fired on the Range that day. What a waste of manpower and money, and many officers who did arrive at the Range to conduct RSO/duties were seen to be less disciplined in sustaining range safety regulation. Due to the shortage of range manpower, I requested for one more Range Warden and was given Guy White, who didn't stay too long with us as he missed the bright lights and opted to return to Thornhill.

Morgan Lanham re-mustered from safety equipment at Thornhill filling the gap and proved to be more than a wild Welshman of great value, thank goodness for that. Before leaving, Nobby had started cutting out a new runaway 090/270 but within its first year it degenerated and we ate much dust due to propeller erosion. O.C. Flying, Boss Tol Janeke was able to get the runway tarred. At this stage the Range now consisted of the following staff and facilities:

Snr Tech John McKenzie; Cpl Ben Pretorius; Jnr Tech Morgan Lanham; Three GSU members (i) Cpl Moyo ii) SAC Joseph iii) SAC Takawia); Three kitchen boys - i) Bennie the cook ii) Michael the tea and toast waiter. iii) Shadrick the guy who always stole the sugar

Mac continues: "Re-placing the prisoners, we employed civvies who ate guinea-fowl and worked just as hard as the previous guys. The danger area now consisted of 2,000 plus cleared acres and the following targets:

i) 4 gunnery ranges; A, B, C, D, each having six 15 x 15 Hessian targets, for 30/20mm

ii) A bigger Canberra bombing target, a triangle made of stone laying flat on the ground and a 25ft dome of steel, ex gold mine crusher from Que Que Mines

iii) Bomb/dumps, E, F, H, used for high-dive bombing, a rockets/dump and low level bombing and frantan attacks dump.

iv) Two, 303/bub range of six targets each for gunnery and bubs.

v) Reserved 30mm gunnery range for H.E. rounds consisting of another four sets of six targets scribed on the ground in white-wash positioned on sloping ground, just short of the main gunnery ranges called A, B, C, D.

vi) 7sqn gunnery target placed on the bub range, having 12 cardboard targets 15 x 15 targets on drums.

vii) A new tarred runway 090/270 some 1600 yards long.

Putting up tents for Squadron detachments was always the worst job in my life so we once again burnt clay bricks and built the barrack hut to house thirty techs' while the officer took abode in the mess. Thornhill saw the reason to provide a well needed ablution block of showers and toilets, we lived like kings. That was Kutanga Range 1970

However as Range Wardens, Ben, Morgan and myself were more than sons of the soil and just couldn't keep out of development work and having the grader come our way by virtue of demand for fire protection, we graded our requirement with ease.

We developed several more roads and increased the boundary firebreak all the way around the Range perimeter fence-line giving us access all the way around non stop 47 miles, and it was three grader blades wide. A road was made down the centre of the Range from North to South, which once again was cut out of virgin land, giving great moments of satisfaction and surprises in the amount of wild game seen in numbers; it was worth its sweat.

I was promoted to Warrant Officer Two. ZIMBABWE-RHODESIA came and Ben Pretorius left. Young Ian Myburg, ex/RLI joined the range about this period. He was a mighty fine soldier and proved to be a mighty fine warden. The danger area got its own internal firebreak a great saving in fire control, as most fires started inside the danger area and burnt outwards toward the boundary.

Having developed the required amount of targets and bomb/dumps the range for the first time was able to conduct Range flying programmes properly, practice weapon on their own target and live deliveries on live target areas. Live 68mm/Matra and 37mm Sneb rockets were fired on target dump just for live rockets or bombs. Live 20mm and 30mm guns were fired at the H.E. gunnery range which was positioned on sloping ground below and about 100 yards before the practice gunnery ranges A, B, C, D. This took the danger out of having U.X.B's all over the place. U.X.B. means unexploded bomb, and instantly a U.B.X. was dropped the law forbids the continuation of the flying program and therefore the range was closed for safety reasons. However having live weapons dropped on their own targets allowed deliveries of practise weapons to progress.

Kutanga Range being the vast area it was encouraged the other members of the defence force to request the use of the range for purpose of their weapon training. Permission was granted as long as they did not damage the air force facilities and the range as a whole. The Range up until then only allowed the School Of Infantry from Gwelo training rights.

By about 1975, I received Warrant Officer One status and the following defence force units commence their weapon training and camps at Kutanga Range. They were the following units:-

1) School of Infantry = soldier boys tools/toys
2) 90mm Armoured Cars - eland, tank/weapons
3) Artillery 25lb guns, howitzer
4) RLI = jungle ranges, lanes and soldier boys tools/toys
5) Selous Scouts = smirch/sabotage
6) Grey Scouts = horse drill/tracking and battle simulation
7) SAS = sabotage/jungle lanes
8) Police Air wing = booze/tell-star air observing, if they got airborne !!!
9) Police Reserve = weapon training/jungle lanes
10) Prime Minister's Office = Chuck/Danny/Ken Flowers/smersh
11) The Range Staff were: i) W/O1 John McKenzie ii) Sgt Morgan Lanham iii) Sac Ian Myburg iv) Three GSU members, Cpl Moyo, Sac Joseph, Sac Takawia
12) The same old kitchen staff, Bennie, Michael and still stealing the sugar, Shadrick, Jack changed his name back too John and vanished !!!

That was Kutanga Range 1980

"During my career of twenty-three years on the Range I was able to establish the BIG FIVE, which catalogue as the Top Gun Weaponeers of the Rhodesian Air Force. I saw them, I heard them, and I marked their targets that time with them was good enough to declare them ace pilots, on all aircraft they flew, with all types of weapons sustaining master/cats.

However there were many, many greats who, I can assure you probably just missed out by one round or a yard short of a D/H. They know for themselves, and I salute them.
The word weaponeer is not found in the Queens English, but rather Kutanga Range jargon, a word or expression developed for use within a particular group, hard for outsiders to understand.!!!!!!

TOP GUN WEAPONEERS OF THE RHODESIAN AIR FORCE
1) VIC WIGHTMAN
2) JUSTIN VARKEVISSER
3) PROP GELDENHUYS
4) STEVE KESBY
5) ALF WILD

Zimbabwe got its independence tools of credentials and we, the Range staff, got to see the integrated forces at work, thank-goodness the war was over, with this bunch we would have lost our boots.

Late in 1981 I was commissioned and retired in 1983 as an Air Lt, but the best rank I ever held was Warrant Officer One, a very powerful chevron and position, I loved it. My career was wonderful and I would never trade a day of the 8395 Range days, in fact if I had it all over again, I would work harder and more dedicated to the men and our Air Force. We, the Scatters of the Soil, they in power scattered, us The Sons of the Soil. That was Kutanga Range 1983

KUTANGA HONOURS AND AWARDS

John's unique Honours and Awards are legendry. It was John's way in a very humorous but respectful manner that these austere occasions were conducted - - more often than not on the spur of the moment. I treasure the awards Big Mac has bestowed on me - - starting with the Shield on which he mounted my Nickel Cross, which even today has pride of place in my home after 40 years (1967-2007) and as readers will note, forms the back drop to this my autobiography. He has honoured me as the third Top Gun in the Air Force, presented me with the Kutanga Star, made Rina a 'Sash' award

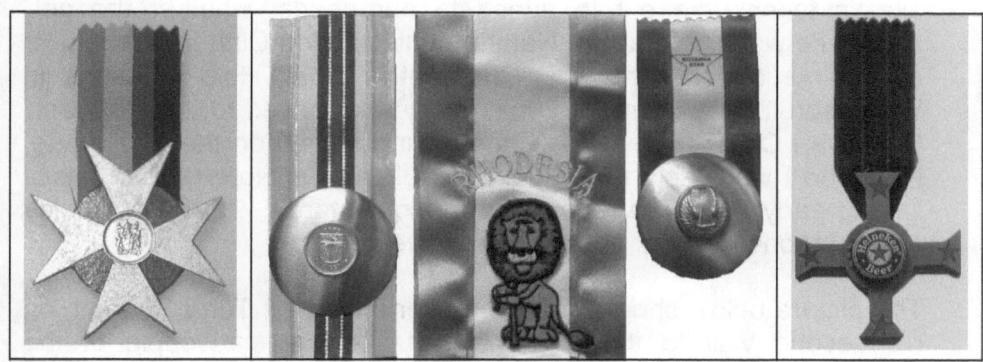

GENTLE ANNIE – NEW ZEALAND

A really special reunion was arranged and organised by my daughter Renene, for the Geldenhuys "clan", for Christmas 2002. I had just retired from Masonite, relocated to Durban, and boarded the Qantas flight to Christchurch towards the latter part of November. We were met by Doug and Yvonne Pasea and had a good old chinwag to the wee hours. Doug took some leave for a couple of days and showed us around all the highlights. Then after taking the Trans-Alpine express to Greymouth, we spent awhile on the West Coast, plus a week-end retreat to the popular north coast – also spent with my son Pey – who had flown in from South Africa, via Kuala Lumpur – for the reunion. My sister Delene, living in Whangaparoa, Auckland, joined us at Mokihunui, Gentle Annie holiday resort. Interestingly, her entire family, like mine, were able to make the reunion (of a lifetime – six relatives having flown out from South Africa).

Rina and I spend three months getting to know and see all in Kiwiland. The memories that linger are Sandflies and needing jackets during summer to keep the chill out. After all is said and done, we remain content that our grandchildren are raised in a beautiful, and peaceful, part of God's creation.

AFA NATAL BRANCH

Pete and Ellie Woolcock warrant special mention, together with a vote of thanks, for the normally thank-less job of keeping the Natal Branch alive and well. Although Rina and I were separated by distance from attending the regular functions, those that we did attend were thoroughly enjoyed. Unc (Dave) and Joan Stone have always taken time out to attend to our needs, whether the get-together's were held at the Natal Mounted Rifles Club in Durban, or at Virginia airport, and even the Moth's Shell Hole meetings in Winklespruit. At the end of 2002, the venue moved to the German / Shamwari Club in Westville. Once having settled on the Esplanade, Rina and I were able to frequent the Club on a more regular basis. During early 2003, we renewed our acquaintance with Peter Scales of Operations *Phoenix* and Nickel involvement.

The picture below shows T the B, better known as Terry Bennett, on his second visit to the Shamwari club – were a couple of the 'regulars' would meet to welcome the overseas visitors to our neck of the woods. Those present are Johnny and Noelene Green, Bruce and Erica Edward, Neville Mare, and the writer with Rina. Other regulars not shown include Dave "Unc" and Joan Stone, Fynn Marcussen, Alec Scott, Pat Lockhart and a couple of others whose names currently escapes me!

ORAFs

The *ORAFs – Old Rhodesian Air Force Sods* – owes its origin to the Cape Branch of Peter and Anne Cooke's Air Forces' Association. Eddy Norris started to build up a database of electronic mail of willing ex-Air Force members. By March 2001, Eddy was sending his weekly ORAFs newsletter to no less than some 276 Internet and E-mail users. I owe Eddy a debt of gratitude for helping to obtain permission from countless mates throughout the world to use their stories in this amateur novel.

ORAFs also facilitated last minute additions to an otherwise one sided war story, and also kept me posted on what was happening in the rest of the world. Examples included first hand accounts of noteworthy events, and letting everybody know when ex-members of the Force departed for that Big Hangar in the Sky. The passing on of Jerry Dunn and Basil Moss, and my good mates John Bennie, Ted Lunt, Bruce Smith and Pete Briscoe immediately come to mind.

Thanks, Eddy Norris, for the magnificent opportunity to source facts and figures the world over. I might add that the e-mail medium

contributed immeasurably in relaying input to Peter and Anne Cooke as well as William (Bill) Sykes as the go-between to author Beryl Salt and publishers Covos Day Books in the production *A Pride of Eagles*.
Peter Cooke passed away the day I completed this second edition review – Wednesday 28th March 2001. Solomon said:
"There is a right time for everything."

As one chapter or phase in our lives ended, so another started. Up and until now, relevant subject matter was inserted in the most appropriate place. However, as time progressed, a story line was being lost and a change in direction was taken, to once again, continue this biography as time unfolded chronologically. Significant milestones that warrant elaboration are very varied and includes but a low sampling of the following (new "Contents"):

- New Zealand trip 2006
- Pey's marriage to Eloise Howard
- Renene, Courtney and Brendan's SA visit / Attend wedding.
- Delene and Stu / Brinks visit to Africa.
- Finding Oudad Jannie Geldenhuys's Anglo-Boer War diaries at Bloemfontein
- Courtney and Brendan performing at the Tauranga Arts Festival
- Eventual book launch
- A Miracle: Once was Lost, But now am Found

MUGABE IS A THIEF – HE STOLE MY PENSION

Yes, I can say it, without fear or favour. Mugabe is a thief. May he rot in hell for all the human suffering and human right abuses he and his cronies are responsible for. I was commissioned by the Flame Lily Foundation to help compile a database of Zimbabwe pensioners who had their remittances stopped by the Mugabe regime. This list expanded rapidly to over 1750 pensioners who have been robbed of their livelihood. What I found as heartbreaking, was the increasing number of pensioners who were dying on a monthly basis – many in abject poverty. At the last count, this tragic number stood at over 87 deaths. Let their blood be on Mugabe's hands.

OPERATIONS BOOK LAUNCHED – 14 JUNE 2007

This significant, life-changing date was shared with Rina at Virginia Air Show, which was the launch of my 'third' book but the first one that was done professionally. Pey had very kindly used his influence at Virginia to have a charming lady, named Helen, arrange free access, umbrella, table and two chairs for the Saturday and Sunday that the Air Show was staged.

Just Done Productions Publishing would like to announce the release of a new book *Rhodesian Air Force Operations with Airstrike Log* by *Prop Geldenhuys*.

This book records the operations of the Rhodesian Air Force. It includes a complete log of all the airstrikes carried out as well as maps where these strikes have been meticulously plotted. The maps are printed in full colour. There are numerous black and white photographs that illustrate the text.

The first copies of this book were on sale at the Virginia Air Show in Durban and the first copy was sold with the sound of a Mirage's engine rumbling overhead as it performed aerobatics. An entirely appropriate occasion.

The initial feedback reports were very encouraging. From Denise – daughter to Eddy Norris – "Dear Mr. Geldenhuys, Just a short note to congratulate you on the release of your book. I know from talking to my Dad that it will be a terrific book and that much time and dedication went into your writing it. On a personal note from a young Rhodesian, I would like to extend my thanks to you for making more history available to us, and for sharing your experiences. Take good care and God Bless. Denise."

From Hugh Bomford, Tauranga, New Zealand – "Publishing books is not a way to great wealth unless you come up with a Harry Potter or Wilbur Smith book. So please - look after yourself first. Just getting these records down is important and you have done bloody well. Excellent book - well done and thanks for doing it."

"Just a little story for you.............I managed to find #538 (referring to the air strike number in the Log) which I was part of the ground troops - all 4 of us. There was a sighting on an island in the Zambezi. Why I remember it was that we set ourselves up to be picked up as we had been trained (and done before) with the wind to our backs. The G-Car landed with its tail to us so round we went and emplaned. The chopper could not take off so we were deplaned and had our gear checked - we only had webbing - no packs as we expected to be in and out. Back in and we did these bunny hops until we were facing into the wind, then off we went. The pilot had a picture of a nude woman in a rather welcoming posture on the back of his helmet. I wondered to myself as to how many stick leaders this was the last woman's fanny they ever saw and why the pilot seemed to my non flying expertise to have made such a tadza of the landing and take off. My stick leader did actually get killed but that was 6 months later.

"Anyway this all stuck in the memories until I came across Joe Syslo who said that he had a helmet like that. I told him my story but could not recall the exact date which did not help Joe with his recollections.

"You have no result on your record. The result was un-ignited napalm all over the reeds which we had to pick our way through and no sign of the gooks although we suspected they may have been a couple of very frightened fishermen. We shot the bottom up on the dugout which we found to destroy it."

Rina at book launch – Virginia Air Show – July 2007

Peter Petter-Bowyer wrote "Considering the political turmoil that brought about hurried separation and destruction of Air Force records in March 1980, Prop's attempt to save whatever could be recovered for this work is highly commendable. Certainly there are errors and omissions that arise from late searches and faded memories. Nonetheless these records will prove most useful to historical researchers."

And the review I valued came from a complete stranger – Dr Tim Lovering – Research Fellow at the University of the West of England, who said "Geldenhuys has produced a comprehensive account of the Rhodesian Air Force role in the war in Rhodesia. The work includes one of the most detailed summaries of Rhodesian military operations to have been published, and in this respect serves as an excellent work of reference. However, the book is much more than this, as the author's personal experience leaps from every page, producing a fascinating combination of memoir and historical account."

Peter Petter - Bowyer

CONTROVERSY

Controversy abounds as to how or who was responsible for removing RSF records and archives, initially to SA and then to the UK.

The collection of RAA documents with the BECM is common knowledge, especially since it was published on the Internet by the UWE. What has NOT been publicised is how they came to be in the UK - something that was known to a few individuals, including PB and Dave Heppenstall. The location of the documents in South Africa could result in litigation to gain access, or even to attach them. These documents are now in the UK (but not yet in the BECM), having left SA at the end of 2006. A certain body, known to the author, could be accused of acting unlawfully, knowing that an application had been made to gain access to them in terms of the PAIO - Promotion of Access to Information Act.

Publishing information relating to how the documents were obtained could open a can of worms. It could even result in court action. Legal advice on this subject is to "say nothing".

Pretoria News court reporter Zelda Venter's headline "History archive trust set for war with Defense Ministry – Organisation seeks court order to obtain military intelligence files" on Monday 3 September 2007 set the cat amongst the pigeons. My revelations in the first edition concerning P-B and Chris Dams' e-mails to me had all sorts of people jumping up and down. I reluctantly agreed to delete the offending passages. Whose versions are more plausible – two collaborated feedback reports from ones own Bluejob colleagues rather than from one Brownjob? Despite umbrellas going up, focus is on the SANDF as evidenced by a news release in the 'Tswane' newspaper. Extracts are as follows: I don't have issue with South Africa History Archive's director, Piers Pigou, saying in papers before the court that the archive was dedicated to recapturing the country's lost and neglected history and recording history in the making. Siviwe Nijkela, of the SANDF's legal services, stated that the documents were official Rhodesian Security Force records from 1964 to 1979. They had been obtained unofficially by the SADF'S military intelligence division in 1980 and kept in the archives for safekeeping. 'At the time the provenance of the Rhodesian files was not realised ...and ... embarrassment to South Africa should their provenance become known," he said. Njikela said no court can order the SANDF to have them returned from Zimbabwe (he had claimed, earlier that the records had been returned to Zimbabwe - - however, these records are now all in the UK).

Once again I was knee deep in the fertiliser - - I had Brownjobs rattling my cage, telling me that the verbatim reports I quoted from two very highly officered and respected Bluejobs was all wrong! I couldn't believe, or credit what I was hearing – because I still believe, as this manuscript is going to the printers, that there is more to my 'fact-story' than my accusers are prepared to admit. There is more concern for putting umbrellas up so that the fertiliser can be re-distributed to protect ones' own skin. Surely, the time is right to cut out all the bull and for the truth to be known? I even had one Brownjob, Terry Leaver (who had written to say that he was a friend of Chris Weinmann and had been at school with Graham Cronshaw) approach me to sign his copy of my 'limited' first edition as a collectors item because "all was revealed on page 8"!!! Tol Janeke hit the nail on the head, once again, by saying "Well, that can only be good for sales".

351

SAS MEMORIAL SERVICE / REUNION 2007

Johnny Green persuaded me to stand in his stead for the SAS Memorial Service that took place at the Flame Lily Park, Durban and followed by their SAS Regimental Association of Southern Africa Reunion Dinner held at the Beachwood Club on Saturday 3 November 2007. It did not take much to twist my arm.

I was rather humbled when General Walls came up to me when he recognised me at the Shamwari Club on the Friday night, before the service. Then later in the evening his wife Eunice brought the General over to our table to introduce him to Rina! Hobnobbing, nogal êk sê!

George Galbraith, Chairman of the Special Air Service Regimental

Association of South Africa officiated. The KwaSizabantu Mission School Band played Amazing Grace beautifully. Rina and I have always associated this moving hymn with Renene – on her wedding day after having been so savagely attacked and stabbed four days before her wedding day to Grahame Jelley (on 6th June 1992). Our AFA Branch Chairman Pete Woolcock laid an Air Force wreath, followed by a very moving ceremony when the bugler sounded the Last Post. Then it was my turn to cry! I was most impressed with the brochure for the service – depicting the SAS plinth superimposed on the Zimbabwe Ruins.

Pete Woolcock being photographed – about to lay the wreath

Lieutenant General Peter Walls, Prop Geldenhuys and Judge Hilary Squires
SAS REUNION - 3 November 2007

The picture, taken at the Beachwood Club (SAS Reunion) - with Judge Hilary Squires, is rather interesting, or so I thought. It was he who put multi-millionaire Shabbier Shaik in prison - and ruled that his 'relationship with Jacob Zuma' was generally corrupt. As a result thereof, Jacob Zuma lost his job as the country's Deputy President (but not of the ANC hierarchy!). Interesting times we live in!!!

General Walls requires no introduction. He was our Military Supremo during the Bush War and considered by many as the next most powerful man to the Prime Minister. Bill Jelley remembers playing rugby against him in the 1950's! George Galbriath and his SAS Association did a great job of organising a grand affair. I also need to mention the main organiser - Pete Maunder of Glenashley – and the fund raising auction that was held of a grotty / very old No 8 Springbok rugby jersey. During the course of the dinner, an anonymous bidder put a reserve price of R10 000.00 for the shirt! But that is not all – perhaps spurned on by the Amabokke winning the World Rugby Cup in 2007, seemed to make the grotty old jersey some sort of prized possession. The bidding advanced rapidly over double the initial 'reserve' price and was eventually auctioned for over R25 000.00!! Well done, Mr Maunder, Sir (Pete wasn't too interested in my Operations book, and said he would buy it if his name is mentioned – I trust he will be satisfied with Nickel Cross instead, especially with all that lolly in the SAS kitty)!

When we got back, Pete Woolcock sent me the sad news to report that Wally Jeffries died that Friday of a heart attack. Our most sincere condolences go out to his family from all of us, especially those of us in Natal who knew him so well. He will be sadly missed. Readers may well recall that Wally was 'my' SWO at Thornhill. Although he reported to me on the official chain of command, many considered him as the next 'powerful' man to the Station Commander! I attended his Stellawood Chapel cremation service, saying my farewells to a much respected 76 year-old military colleague, and conveying my condolences to Ann, his cancer suffering wife, and their sons and daughters present. David and I exchanged e-mail addresses, for being an RLI man we seemed to speak the same Troopie language.

With funerals and memorials very much on our minds I followed up who Balgair Print-in-Time Publications were, and was not too surprised to find that it was George's wife, Lynn Galbraith who specialises in artwork design. I was after the Zimbabwe Ruins photograph that she used for the SAS Memorial Service – for a Nickel Cross insert. Despite being fully booked-up for four months in advance, Lynn kindly made / manufactured time in keeping with their corporate reputation. What about the Nickel Cross superimposed with the Zimbabwe Ruins as a backdrop? Now we're talking – with both Renene and Pey having forsaken their land of birth – leaving what little Ruin-ous country is left after Marxists / Socialists terrorists have plundered a once beautiful piece of God's country. Just like the good old saying – We made Rhodesia great, They made Zimbabwe Ruins!

RFMP P.O.Box 95474
Waterkloof0145
South Africa

31

October 2007
Dear Prop and Rina,

RHODESIAN FORCES MEMORIAL PROJECT

On behalf of the RFMP Committee, thank you most sincerely for your kind contribution to the fund. A concept which has been discussed for many years is now becoming a reality, and your gift has materially contributed to this. We anticipate that the Memorial will be commissioned on 11 November this year at the Annual Remembrance Service.

Attached for your interest is an artist's impression of the Memorial as it will look when deployed for Remembrance Services. Manufacture of the Force Badges is in hand and Rolls of Honour have been checked and updated in readiness for printing.

Should donations exceed the cost of the Memorial, we intend to use the excess to establish a "Living Memorial" Fund to be used for the benefit of former members of the Forces in need, or their widows and dependants. We believe that this is a fitting way to perpetuate the memory of those who made the supreme sacrifice for their country, Rhodesia.

Yours sincerely,

Pat Hill
Chairman, RFMP

Pat Hill – jou doring! We sure had some good times together. I still have fond memories of flying with one another - specifically that May 1974 Special Joint Services Coin Course where we honed our battle skills and subsequently when we fought the "Battle of Bangala" in the Nyajena in December 1976.

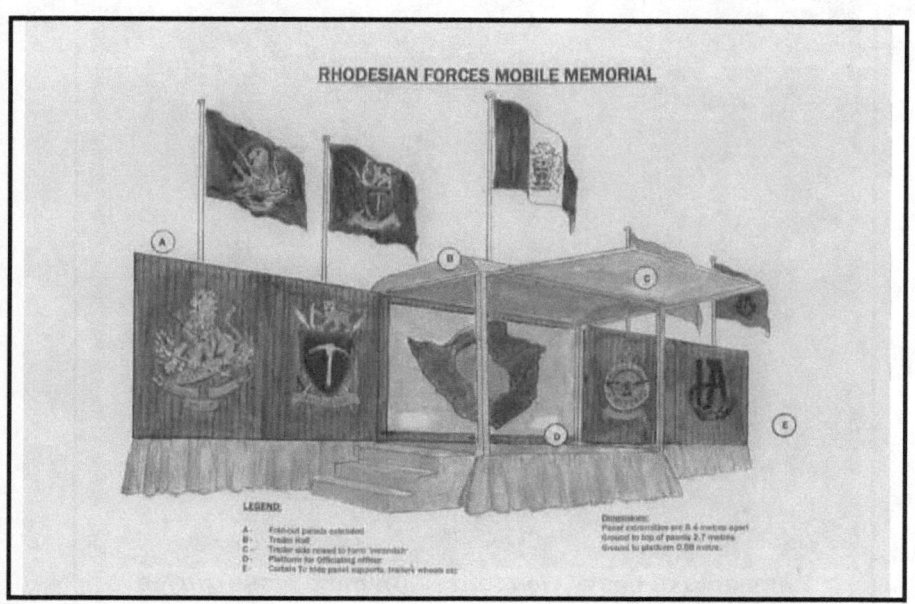

FLF National Management Committee of the Flame Lily Foundation met and suggested that John Mac be asked whose bodies he has in mind. Natmancom appreciates that John Mac is looking for someone to do the ground work, if there are any bodies to be reburied, but this is not within the scope of the FLF. The best they could do is ask the Commonwealth War Graves Commission to investigate what became of the bodies that have been identified (there were also three bodies of soldiers who were killed on a clandestine operation into Zimbabwe in 1982).

Bruce Harrison is the Air Force representative on the Committee, who kept me informed of progress, and motivated me to do my bit. In addition to cash donations I also donated an Operations Book to be raffled / auctioned at the November Ladies Lunch function that followed after the Annual Remembrance Service 2007. This inspired me to join forces with my soul buddy, Big Mac John Kutanga McKenzie to do something meaningful about those airmen whose lives were sacrificed in Moçambique. This was also prompted by Bob Manser's magnificent achievement in locating the remains of the Hunter and Canberra shot down in Moçambique.

Remnants of heavy weapons – Chimoio mass graves

Monte Cassino fortifications
Wooded shelter   A cave, of sorts?

CHIMOIO

Chimoio Circle Operations
Vila Pery was a popular stop-over for Beira bound Rhodesians. When Portugal abandoned Mozambique, Frelimo garrisoned the Chimoio renamed-town and provided safe haven bases for Zanla. Aerial photography soon identified the various camps and a series of hot-pursuit and cross-border strikes were carried out. The more noteworthy strikes included:
Operation Eland – 8 to 12 August 1976 (base camp known as Nyadzonia/Pungwe). ZANLA casualty figure was determined as 1,028 killed, 309 wounded and a 1,000 missing – 14 were captured and 200 believed drowned.
Operation Dingo – 23 to 26 November 1977. Casualty numbers were estimated at 800 Zanla killed and 750 wounded (some sources says it varies from 2000 to 3000). In addition to airman Phil Haigh killed, Trooper GJ Nel was also killed and 6 RLI wounded.
Convoy – 20 December 1978. Hunter airstrike on a ZANLA convoy of six vehicles including a petrol bowser off the Chimoio to Tete road.
Operation Neutron – 15 February to March 1979 and 12 September 1979 (Airstrikes carried out 17 to 19th March).
Operation Miracle – 21 September to 6 October 1979. This Operation will be remembered for the target fixation loss of a Hunter (Brian Gordon) and the shooting down of Canberra crews Kevin Peinke and JJ Strydom. Trooper Gert O'Neill was also killed.
Over thirty cross-border strikes were carried out against Chimoio and surrounds, before the end of the war.
This memorial essentially commemorates the Rhodesian Operation *Dingo* airstrikes and para-troop assault of 23rd November 1977. It was the biggest attack so far mounted in the war, involving virtually every serviceable aircraft in the Air Force. The huge Chimoio Base complex was situated three hundred and twenty kilometres from New Sarum, to the north of the town of like name, it housed eight thousand inhabitants, and had become the official headquarters for all the ZANLA forces. Its administrative core was well established with offices, great stores of arms and ammunition, vast stocks of food, a hospital, two schools and several substantial buildings roofed with corrugated iron, and concrete floors. It was a military base

heavily defended with 12.7mm and 14.4mm anti-aircraft batteries. War refugees, numbering about twenty thousand at the time, were concentrated at Doeroi, some fifty-five kilometres further east.

Chimoio memorial at Tembwe, Mozambique

The success of Operation *Dingo* has attracted USA military interest, and is believed studied for its strategic planning and brilliant execution in cost effectiveness.

Operation *Miracle*, as documented elsewhere, followed nearly two years after Operation *Dingo*. However, this time it was a different story altogether and three Airmen were killed in action, with the loss of an invincible Hunter and a Canberra, all on the same day. The bodies of the downed crews were never recovered. Only the Canberra crash site was 'inspected' very briefly immediately it crashed, but no bodies as such was found. For all intents and purposes, they were "lost" for a very long time.

A MIRACLE

This section has been added as a post script because so many last minute additions kept on coming up, resulting in delaying the publication process. So in order to find a home for these, and hoping for Bob Manser to come up with the 'Canberra find', this section will start off with Google maps that Pey kindly supplied. The first factstory is the Hunter find!

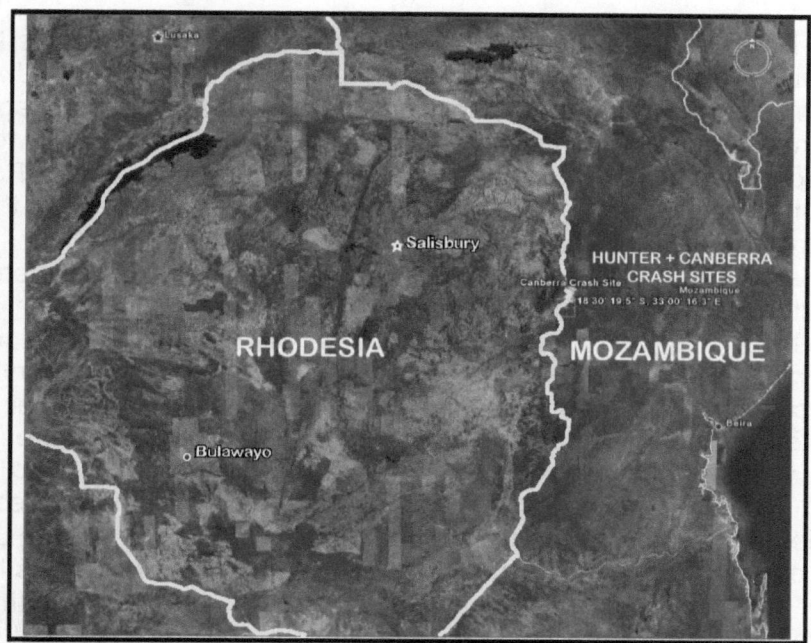

Google maps – Operation Miracle

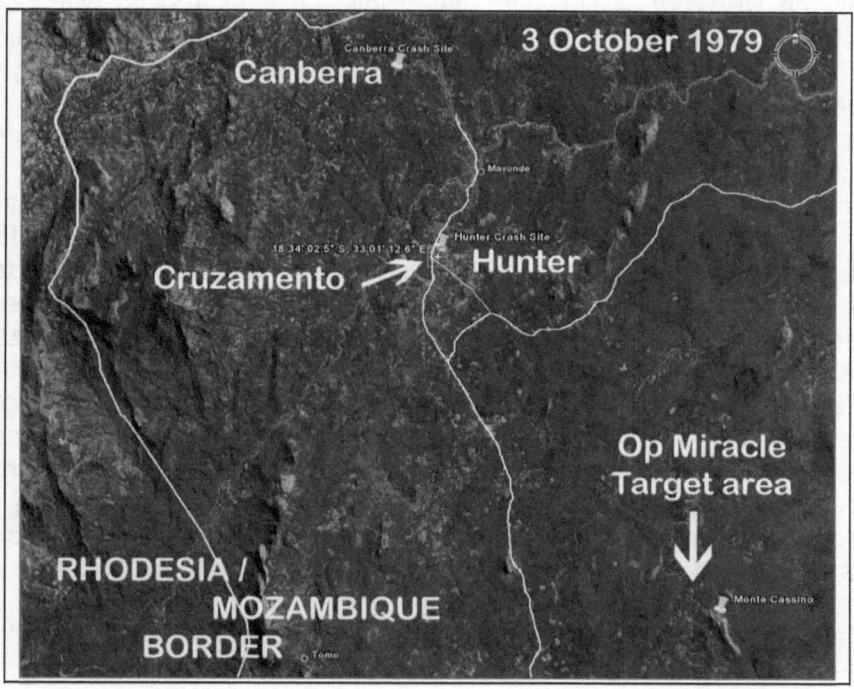

Guy Dixon sent me his factstory in November 2007 and recalls the events of 3 October 1979 as follows: "I was flying with Baldy Baldwin, my wing leader. We were flying a pair of Hunters and were engaged in an interdiction run in Mozambique after Op *Miracle*. We were called out on standby by the Brown Jobs (Scout Willie van der Riet) who had spotted a target over the boarder in Mozambique, and they thought it required investigation.

"Unbeknown to us, the SAS/Scouts had left "observers" in the area to monitor the possible resupply of the camps by the gooks after our ground and air assault during Operation *Miracle* (targeting Monte Casino in Mozambique) the previous week. So, on observing vehicular activity in the area, the Brown Jobs called out a pair of Hunters to check out a convoy of vehicles returning to the area. It was October with shocking bush fire haze and very poor visibility. From Thornhill, Baldy and I routed via Umtali to initiate our "recon sortie" to the north. It was futile trying to spot anything at altitude due to the haze. To try and locate the target Baldy elected to take us low level in a loose battle formation at about 400 knots just north of Umtali, following the main Tete dirt road north. Baldy chose "fast" so as to give any ground fire some problems in tracking us. Good thinking Red 1 !! ☺ However, even low level, at 400kts, with poor visibility and no horizon due to the bush fire haze and big mountains all around, spotting the convoy was all but impossible. Just trying to keep separation from each other and the ground was challenging enough while trying to look for ground targets. It was hot and also viciously turbulent, a rough ride low level.

"The Brown Jobs on the ground could hear the convoy opening fire on us each time we patrolled up and down the target area. So the way we finally isolated the ground fire was to ask the spotters to tell us when the ground fire was starting, and when it had stopped, during our patrols. We then marked this on out maps and localized the search. On our third pass, finally, I sported the tracer fire directed at Baldy's aircraft. I told him he was being shot at and I had the target area visual. He handed me the lead and I then maneuvered to attack the target with 30mm cannon. Changing battle formation at that speed, in the haze while pitching up to perch height and trying to keep the target in sight was just about as challenging as the attack was itself. Not to mention we were surrounded by gomos (mountains) that were hiding in the think haze.

"Baldie spotted my strike, and went in and delivered his own strike. We continued to attack the convoy in sequence. The convoys vehicles had now pulled off the road, split up and were scattered in the bush along side the road. So it was a case of 'spread em around' with our cannon fire in the dive as the convoy was now quite dispersed. The vehicles were only really vaguely identifiable by the tracer fire coming out of the bush and the haze. This really was the fog of war. It was all happening so fast, cannon fire from us, tracer from them, explosions from the ground, fear, adrenaline, burning vehicles, severe heat turbulence, constant uncomfortable G in a turn to keep the area in sight, radio jammed with chatter and thick haze. Just total overload and confusion as one tries to assimilate everything that is happening.

"All this done from the relative silence of a jet. What you see on the ground, you invariably don't hear in the cockpit. Bizarre. This was my 22nd Hunter strike of the war and in truth I was still very light in the pants as combat goes. No previous strike had even been vaguely similar so I was just winging it, as I had no previous similar experience to draw on. As you can see by the date, 3 October 1979, I was 20. I got my wings a year earlier on 29 August 1978. As I put in my first strike on the target I can clearly remember Baldy's words to me during my training on the Hunter: "Remember Dixburger, its not the bullet with your name on you must worry about, it's all those bullets with "to whom it may concern on," those are the ones that you have to worry about!!" ....Fine advice indeed.

"Ostensibly the convoy looked like (and was designed to look like) a resupply convoy but in reality, when the vehicles pulled off the road and the tarps were pulled off, we realized this was an air ambush with heavy anti aircraft artillery, 12.7, 14.5 and possibly some 23 mm. Very little resupply under the covers at all. We have been suckered in to this engagement and this was certainly the first "air ambush" of the war. The Brown jobs had almost completely withdrawn after Operation *Miracle* so there was no ground back up apart from the SAS/Scout observation posts. After 2 attacks each Baldie and I were very short of fuel and had to make a plan to start heading home. The low level work trying to isolate the target had burnt much of our fuel.

"At this stage 2 more Hunters flown by Brian Gordon and Ziggy Seegmuller arrived overhead to relieve us. Baldie had to leave immediately as he was on minimum fuel for Thornhill, but Brian couldn't identify the target so I said I would go in and mark the target for him so we could get some continuity with the fresh pair of Hunters. Otherwise he would never find it in that haze with just a map. Baldy was just leaving the target area, and told me to "let rip" with all the cannon fire I had left, as well as ripple fire on my remaining 68mm matra rockets - and then break for home.

"I released all my remaining armaments in the final attack to mark the target for Brian and turned for home. Brian confirmed that he had spotted my strike and that was my "green light" to leave, fast. (However, the final strike was one pass too many for me and by this stage I was critically sort of fuel for Thornhill, so I immediately diverted to New Sarum, landed and refueled there).

"Brian turned in live and initiated the strike on the convoy and according to Ziggy, who was number 2 to Brian, 'There was a huge explosion when Brian was in the dive'. The confusion was such Ziggy wasn't even sure if a fuel or armaments truck hadn't been hit. He didn't think that it could have been Brian's Hunter, the invincible Hunter – never!

"Bottom line, Brian never came out of the dive. Whether Brian was shot, the aircraft shot down or had target fixation, we will never know, but he went in. That we do know. My own opinion is that ground fire was the more likely cause. Why do I say that? Firstly because the amount of ground fire. (As Baldy would always say post op when asked how things went on the squadron, "well the flak was so thick we could walk on it" and chuckle ....) Secondly, the resistance was so fierce they sent a Canberra to bomb the target into "submission" in the afternoon.

"Kevin Peinke and JJ Strydom were the crew. They too were shot down by convoy's ground fire, (23mm?) and sadly both were killed. Heaviest Air Force losses of the war were that day. It was a very sad day for all of us. I only found out of Brian's demise when I got back to Thornhill after refueling in New Sarum. Baldy met me as I got out my aircraft and broke me the news. His exact words which I will never forget: "Brian has gone to the great big beer drink in the sky"

"That was just over 28 years ago, and the Brains wreckage has now finally been located. Great work indeed. History in the making – totally fascinating, and it sure brings back unbelievably vivid and indelible memories. As for war – look at Zimbabwe today and ask yourself was it worth it and what did they all die for? Oh the futility of it all. War is the ultimate tool of politicians – pity it never has any real winners".

Ziggy Seegmuller was Brian's wingman, and this is his recollection when ORAF's broke the 'Hunter Find' factstory. It brings further closure to the tragedy of 3rd October 1979.

"Politically, it seems the writing is on the wall; the Western powers have assembled against Rhodesia to find a quick fix to this thorn in their collective side. There is a definite feeling, especially amongst the civilian population, that time is now very limited for the present government. Many are already "taking the gap" (emigrating), and many more are starting to make plans to do so, most to South Africa, but some to UK and even further.

"On the military side, the war has taken on a new more intense phase; fighting is ferocious, almost in a conventional style at times, and whilst the kill ratio still remains at 20:1 in our favour, the numbers have increased dramatically – there is not a week that goes by without the loss of a dear one or a friend or acquaintance. The mood is one of concern, with many beginning to wonder where this is all leading to. As a result, although morale is not low, it is certainly more serious and business-like, and much of the bravado that always characterized the forces' behaviour in the past is now wearing thin, hardly veiling the macabre reality lying beneath."

"In September 1979, security forces launched an almost conventional infantry attack upon the town of Mapai in Moçambique. A small town along the railway link to Maputo, Mapai was used by the terrorists as a staging point to launch cross-border raids into Rhodesia against farmers in the south-east, and then scurry back to the relative safety of Moçambique. Reliable intelligence backed up by photo-reconnaissance showed that the terrorists were amassing there, preparing for a major offensive. So, in September 1979, a large scale combined forces pre-emptive strike was launched against the enemy. Although mainly a ground force conventional style operation, the Air Force was very active in the support role using Lynx a/c and Alouette helicopters ("G"-cars to ferry troops around the battle zone, and "K"-car gunships to soften hard targets with their superior 20mm cannon firepower).

"The enemy was very well dug-in indeed, and their fortifications and trench system network were well planned and defended with dozens of heavy machine gun emplacements – we were fighting terrorists who had been trained to expect such an attack, and were prepared for it. Not the norm at all, where resistance would be fairly ineffective and short in duration, these guys meant business!

"On a number of occasions, we (No 1 Squadron Hunters) were called in to support troops that had been pinned down by enemy fire. On one such occasion, I recall being wingman to Sqn Ldr John Annan (one of the Squadron's reserve pilots called in to help in times of high activity) when we had been called out to put in an accurate strike onto the pinnacle of a 300 feet high piece of granite we nicknamed "Monte Cassino", from where an array of heavy machine-gun fire was taking its toll on our troops on the ground. When White Leader's bombs went one above and one below the target, affected by the intervelometer arrangement we had on the 1000-pound "Golf bombs", there was some pressure on me to produce the goods! I steepened my dive angle a few extra notches to 65 degrees (the steeper the dive angle, the less gravity affects the trajectory of the bomb), and luckily my bombs landed plum on target! What happened next remains a blur in my memory: The Lynx spotter aircraft frantically reported that the gooks had broken ranks and had started scurrying in all directions along the top of the hill after the bomb attack many of them still dazed and confused from the huge concussions of those big bombs. The Lynx pilot urgently called us back into the target area as we were pulling out of the bombing attack profile, and we turned tightly to commence a 30mm cannon attack on them.

"This weapon can only be described as either totally exhilarating, or totally terrifying, depending on which side of it you happen to be on! The Hunter is equipped with 4 Aden 30mm cannons mounted within the fuselage, and each cannon has a rate of fire of 1200 rounds per minute. Each round has the explosive capacity of a small hand grenade. The pilot can select either two or four guns to fire, although the latter selection is specifically designed for air-air combat. On this day I selected all four guns to fire (that's 80 rounds per second!), and the effect of those High Explosive rounds on granite against a swarm of ant-like targets was devastating, oblivion for many.

"Some weeks later in Salisbury, I met up with a good friend of mine who had left his home in France to come and join the RLI to help fight our war. A mountain of a man, he saw me from a distance at the Oasis Motel, and he rushed up and picked me up and threw me into the pool, showering me with hugs and embraces (as the French are prone to do), shouting that I had saved his life on that terrible day – Mon Dieu, I couldn't have asked for more!"

**Trenches visible on Maingue – Monte Cassino
(kind favour Bob Manser)**

"This attack on convoy story does not have a silver lining
"A few days later whilst the battle for Mapai raged on, we were once again called out, this time to attack a convoy of trucks proceeding to the battle zone. On this day I was paired with Flt Lt Brian Gordon, a great guy with awesome flying ability and with whom I shared the same birth date. The Lynx pilot, Flt Lt Mike Huson, had given us the target description on our way to the area, and when we got there, Brian instructed me to remain at 15 000 feet (above the range of small arms fire), whilst he delivered a rocket attack onto the target. This was not standard procedure, and I shall forever wonder if…
"Anyway, the convoy was not readily visible – they had heard us and had camouflaged themselves in amongst all the trees. As Brian entered the attack profile I was positioned exactly in his 6 o'clock, which enabled me to see the rockets ignite in their rocket pods as he squeezed the firing button, very shortly followed by a huge fireball and explosion, as if he had hit a fuel truck in the convoy. Exuberantly, I recall shouting over the radio frequency in use, 'Good rockets, Brian!'

"I continued circling overhead at 15 000 feet, waiting for Brian to join up, but he never did. I called him on the emergency radio frequency repeatedly to no avail, eventually coming to the realization that maybe the explosion I had seen was not what I originally thought it was, and that maybe he had taken a hit.

"Eventually, approaching minimum fuel to return to base, and after brief discussion with the Lynx pilot, I put in an attack into the same area, delivering all my rockets in the hope of rustling out the enemy. I was also looking out for any signs of Brian's Hunter, but nothing was evident. Even stranger, there was no fire on the ground, as one would expect from an aircraft crash such as this. We never did recover Brian's body or the wreckage. However, months later, a photo was published in a terrorist paper showing what could well have been a piece of Brian's Hunter, claiming it had been shot down by 37mm anti-aircraft fire. The terrorists had planned this and had been lying in wait – it was a classic textbook ambush.

"Upon my return to Thornhill Air Base, still quite shell-shocked from the event, I was de-briefed by the Station Commander, asked if I was ok to continue, and then ordered to return to the same area to carry out another strike against the same convoy.

"Tragically, whilst we were re-arming and re-fuelling on the ground, one of our precious Canberras, piloted by my good friend Flt Lt Kevin Peinke with Flt Lt JJ Strydom as navigator/bomb aimer, had attempted a low-level bombing run against the very same target that had already claimed one life, and had themselves been shot down with no survivors. I think that this was the worst day ever in the history of post WW2 Rhodesian Air Force.

"More importantly, it heralded the coming of a new type of war – one where the enemy was far more committed, better equipped, and better trained that we had ever seen before. Ironically, the politicians would put an end to it all just five months later."

The search for the crash sites of the Hunter and Canberra lost during Op Miracle, Oct 1979
.By Bob Manser

As I now live in Chimoio, Manica Province, Mozambique, I have been keen for some time to locate the exact crash sites of the Hunter of Brian Gordon and the Canberra of Kevin Peinke and JJ Strydom (killed in action on 3 October 1979).

I was not sure where to start but having had chats with various ex-Scouts friends plus many chats with Prop and also help from PB and other ORAFs members I had a fair idea where to look, give or take a few hundred square kilometres! Feedback from local farmers and other folks resident in Manica helped, plus also intrigued by vague stories that local tribesmen knew of the incidents that occurred nearly thirty years ago and had varied ideas as to where the remains of the aircraft were.

Luckily a few weeks back my two friends – Pedro Swanepoel and Richard Quinell - who work for a SA based forestry company offered to take myself and co-searcher, Barry Meikle on a tour around Monte Casino as it was all part of their forestry area. We started off from near Manica town and headed up the old Tete, Mavonde road looking for the elusive crossroads and the village called "Cruzamento" which translated means crossroads, all a bit confusing. After some hours of working our way up to the Pungue and back down the power line tracks on the east side of Monte Casino we drew blanks. Every indigenous we spoke to had not heard of any crashed planes: especially all those years ago.

We backtracked to the old Tete road again and stopped at various crossroads and hailed any bystander we could find seeking information. Mick Hamence will chuckle at this as I always carried the book on Canberras by him and Winston Brent and showed the cover to any local we chatted to, hoping we may find one who may have had seen something similar in years gone by.

Anyhow eventually our luck was in; one chap knew of a site and pointed us in the right direction. It was to a small village cum growth point about 3kms past a crossroads. There we spoke to two officious looking gents who immediately knew what we were after. When asked as to the name of the small village, they replied "Cruzamento"

About 50 metres east of the road virtually in the centre of the village we came across a smallish depression in the ground and the remains of a turbine. The crash site was very close to the road, maybe 40 or 50 metres in, just behind some small shops.

We scrabbled around under the turbine and discovered about ten 30mm Aden gun "doppies" and a few rusty 30mm H/E heads. Many of the doppies still had un-burnt black cordite like granules in them. I reckon the 30mm shells certified the crash site as the one of the Hunter.

Barry Meikle and Bob Manser with a 30mm case and Hunter turbine disc's

We were disappointed in the lack of wreckage but it must be remembered that most of it was taken away by Frelimo and put on display in Maputo.

The GPS co-ordinates are South 18degrees 34' and East 33 degrees 01'.
Another interesting fact is that the officious gents had heard of another crash site to the northwest, and said an aircraft was supposed to be in the foothills just on the border with Zimbabwe near a village called Ndanga, this must be the Canberra site.
We had run out of time that day but my forestry mates have promised us a jaunt in their sturdy Toyota Landcruiser next month when they visit that area to pay wages so hopefully we will eventually discover the Canberra wreckage.
It is a small world as a few weekends ago I trekked up to the Zambezi to see Mary Moffat's grave, wife of David Livingstone and on the way back popped into the bush camp and sawmill of Ant Whites and chatted to him about our planned search. He could not help though, as he was not involved in Operation Miracle. However a

day later into my office comes my mate of old, John Barnes who was returning from a brief holiday to the coast. He was actively involved in Miracle and was busy extracting his team from Cruzamento when the aircraft incidents occurred, so I got some first hand info from him.

The Gordon Hunter crash site and remains of the turbine

All in all it was a great team effort and many thanks go to my Chimoio mates Pedro, Barry, Richard and all at ORAFs who helped in this search.
Many years ago my wife taught at the Sir Roy Welensky Junior School in Dete and one of her young pupils was a Brian Gordon (this was subsequently confirmed as correct)?
B Manser
Chimoio 27/10/07

I remarked that all credit goes to Bob for this terrific achievement, for the resolute tenacity and drive to persevere in order reach the objective. Well done Bob, I am sure we all salute you. I also need to acknowledge all the fine photographs (that in themselves speak a thousand words) and many maps which helped one to appreciate the enormity of the task.

I believe some special words of thanks are in order. To Eddy Norris for putting many interested bodies in touch with one another. To Kevin Tidy (the engineer who constructed the Chimoio Memorial) who flew Bob around Maingue / Monte Cassino in his Cessna 182 aircraft. Thanks to local historian James 'Tackie' Bannerman who supplied maps of the areas. To Barry Meikle for his enthusiastic support for Bob. Pedro Swanepoel, who speaks Portuguese fluently, an essential team-member together with fellow forester Richard Quinell. Peter Petter-Bowyer was particularly helpful for pointers to Cruzamento village in his e-mails and his descriptions in *Winds of Destruction*. Willie van der Riet's reminisces was riveting – he was sitting on a gomo at the time! Tony Oakley gave first hand accounts of the appalling weather conditions prevailing – plus a good write-up in Pride of Eagles. Big Kutanga Mac John McKenzie for edging everyone on, especially me! Thanks also to Bruce Harrison for his evaluations, and particularly his influence and involvement in the Rhodesian Forces Memorial Project.

Readers may well be interested in the comments received so far. Tony wrote: "What a marvellous achievement, thank you for your fortitude and perseverance. The loss of Brian, on what was a very troublesome target, was a sad loss indeed. I have written to Prop before on this incident; Beryl also has some material in her book, for up until this point, the Squadron had achieved remarkable successes against very hostile targets without loss of life. It was an accepted fact that the Hunter was invincible, how could this have happened? I am pleased there can now be some closure on this sad event and would also appreciate pictures or maps as they become available. Thank you all once again for your sterling efforts and I look forward to hearing that you have been as lucky with finding the Can".

Willie wrote: "Fantastic news, a moment in time brought back, well done Bob and team, please keep me in mind when you have the photos. Pamwe Chete".

Bill Sykes added: "I have read all the letters of praise for your efforts, and cannot better those sentiments. Congratulations indeed. Wouldn't it be great if you have as much success with the Canberra? And what a story for the next Bateleur ..."

PB wrote: "Amazing after 28 years to see Brian Gordon's unfortunate death site. Copied to Vic Wightman who was his OC. No doubt you will pass this to Eddy Norris when he returns to RSA. He will pass it on to many who will be very interested."

Graham Patterson, in Australia, wrote: "I have maintained a motivation to seek something further for these people, apart from being Bluejobs; it is also that they deserve some form of memorial. I am incredibly proud of their sacrifice and that we all served together. I do know Bruce (Harrison) and would make some form of donation to the project, but would wish to see if any other groups would wish to take something further on and try to obtain the info of their resting place and if possible erect a memorial".

Al Thorogood wrote: "I still remember the day well even after all these years and it was of my personal low points. Especially as it occurred exactly a week after a K Car crashed killing Paddy Bate, Gary Carter and Bruce Snelgar - I saw them go in and had a medic on board so went to land and assist only to fly under the wires he hit(without seeing them either!). A week later after a fairly busy time! We had word at Grand Reef that Brian had gone in and were scrambled with Willy (?) Joubert as my tech. We went to a Rebro just on the border to learn of the loss of the Canberra as well - we were tasked with S&R. We were unable to locate Brian's crash site as things were a tad warm around the area still and there was still a reception committee waiting, however we did locate the second site at OS map coordinate WQ 008543. . We landed at the site and sadly could confirm no survivors - Kevin still had a load of Alphas on board when he went down. A tragic loss of all I too still salute you all as well. Gone but certainly not forgotten."

-o-O-o-

Eddy Norris also complimented Bob Manser - "Stand Tall" my Friend. You are "True Blue." Sincere thanks for your wonderful achievement and for your friendship. Thanks also must go to all that were involved on this project.

Michel (Ziggy) Seegmuller: "I took great interest in the story of how you succeeded in discovering the crash site of Brian's Hunter - true perseverance indeed - well done!!! I was Brian's wingman on that dreaded 3rd October in 1979, and I have included a recounting of the events of that day out of my memories for your info. Funnily enough,

Brian and I shared a birthday on November 15th, he being a year older than me, and we were good drinking buddies! About 10 years ago, I spoke with his parents who moved to Sedgefield in SA"

I asked Bob to recover the bits of engine turbine compressor discs because I just knew that John would perform more Jesus inspired miracles with his famous Kutanga Stars.

Two poems, by kind favour of Matthew Blackley

A HUNTER WAS LOST

In a Rhodesian sky
Hunters flew
High above
In the blue

With speed and courage
Down, they streaked
Unleashing
All of its' fury
On the enemy

A masterpiece of design
Flown by the chosen few
A Hunter was lost....
In seventy nine

We could not effect..
A recovery...
All that did belong
To a family
To a squadron

So many years
Have passed
Since that terrible day
So many tears

Never again will we hear
That special Hunter sound
Flown by Brian

It does not matter
For now...
He is found

CANBERRAS ONCE FLEW

In a Rhodesian sky
Canberra's once flew
Like eagles
In to the blue

That wide wing
Like a Bateleur
...rising

Of the men
Who flew such machines
Of the skill,
and courage instead

Seek and destroy
Canberra's once flew
Like eagles
In the blue

Two lost Eagles
In a foreign land
One has been found
The other,
still lost

How fitting...

That an Eagle found
By ones' fellow airman
No longer downed

One more Eagle
To find...
For somewhere
Over there
Lies two Bateleur's
and a soldier
Never far from our minds

That special day
Will come
When we can honour them
In our way
Then...
Duty is done

Matthew Blackley
November   200

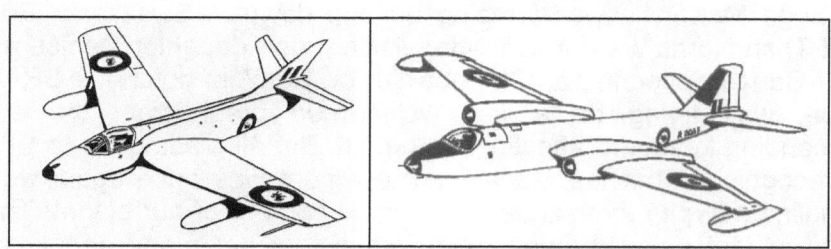

ONCE WAS LOST BUT NOW AM FOUND

Amazing Grace. . . . . Indeed!

Bob Manser found the Brian Gordon Hunter that crashed in Moçambique twenty eight years ago, just as my second edition Operations book went to the printers, in November 2007. This phenomenal news was just too late to make deadlines already set for a Forces promotion in Johannesburg that coincided with the Annual Memorial service held 11th November every year – a date which is so sacred to most Rhodesians.
There is indeed a right time for everything (Solomon, Eccl 3:1). John Kutanga McKenzie was jumping up and down in Swaziland. Eddy and Trish Norris were in Canada, visiting their daughter Denise and ex-7 Squadron technician Shumba Taylor. Eddy, of notorious ORAFs fame, was trying to take a well-earned break from the ever demanding keyboard affecting his health. But all credit goes to Eddy in recognising that the Manser achievement was once again world headline news to thousands of folk in all corners of our planet. They were in fact going through tough times that not many people are aware of; that Eddy was gasping for breath and was actually being wheeled to world heritage sites by Shumba. Mark my words – it was not the right time for Eddy to kick the bucket. Readers of my Operations book will have noted that Bob's original aim was to try and find the Canberra because of the connection Bob enjoyed with his close friend Kevin Peinke.
With Eddy's news flashes congesting cyberspace, reports from all over came flooding in. Eye-witnesses of the Hunter and Canberra crashes came to the fore. I even got a fascinating report from well-respected RLI Fire Force Commander Rick van Malsen who not only was with the Peinke crash search and rescue attempt, but also came across the Ian Donaldson Canberra crash site (with navigator David Hawkes and Selous Scout / ex SAS Rob Warracker) in the Malvernia area. Readers must realise that the remains of our heroes here mentioned and killed in action were never recovered. Close relatives may not forgive me for digging up old bones - - but for many more others it will at long last bring closure so that souls may rest in peace – on this 11th Day of November 2007 – the very day I now write this but more so a day very worthy to commemorate the unveiling of the Rhodesian Forces Memorial at the Dickie Fritz Shellhole in Edenvale.

Then the miracle happened – Bob Manser and his very good friend Barry Meikle (cousin of Brian Meikle) found the remains of the crashed Kevin Peinke Canberra exactly 7.05 kilometres (only 3 odd nautical miles) north of the Hunter crash site – three days after the eleventh hour, of the eleventh day, of the eleventh month – 2007. May our fallen heroes without decent, identifiable graves, now have a final resting place.

The following report and pictures speak volumes. The maps set the scenes, Bobs spiel follows and captions to Bobs photographs tells the "fact-story".

KEVIN PEINKE CANBERRA CRASH SITE FOUND – BY BOB MANSER – 14 NOV 2007

Bob wrote: "Most ORAFs members will have read recently of our discovery of Brian Gordon's Hunter crash site.

"My next objective was to locate the site of the Canberra, so on the morning of Wednesday 14th of November, my co-searcher Barry Meikle and I set off for the village of Cruzamento which is about 120km from Chimoio. We hoped to find one or other of the chaps that had helped us on the previous (Hunter) search, so on reaching the village we asked around. We headed for a likely bunch of villagers but we could not get much sense out of them as they had imbibed vast quantities of some potent beverage and were like the proverbial newts. However our luck was in as nearby we found one of our previous helpers who thankfully was an apostolic member and sober. He agreed to lead us to the village further on called Nenhanga where he had heard rumours that the villagers there knew of another downed aircraft. We travelled about 14kms further on and the road became more of a scotch cart track but Barry's Isuzu handled it well.

"Here we encountered the first brick wall, the locals had also been on the hops and were loud, unfriendly and suspicious of our intentions. I take my hat off to Barry, for here he used all his tact, diplomacy and patience for nearly an hour to get permission granted. They were a bureaucratic bunch and wanted paperwork from various authorities granting us permission to seek out the wreck. Eventually a lone policeman arrived complete with an antique looking AK rifle. He calmed the crowd and eventually we had permission granted as long as he came along plus the young guide and his cantankerous drunken father who had nearly scuttled the whole trip with his obstructionist attitude.

"We travelled a few Kms further on in the bakkie but eventually reached a small village where the road ran petered out. Here we debussed and contemplated the rest of the search on foot, the guide said it would take about an hour but sometimes their hour is different to ours! We had come so far so no turning back. We grabbed cameras and the GPS and headed off. Only after a few minutes we encountered the first obstacle, the Honde River which was about 30 metres across and flowing swiftly. Our guide laughed at our concern and casually strolled into the river which was less than half a metre deep so no problem. We trekked on, up and down small hills and now and again caught sight of that jagged well known outcrop of rocks on the Zimbabwe border commonly known as "Eve's Toes".

Crossing Honde River | **30 x 60 metres**

"We also cursed and cussed, as we had left the drinking water behind in our rush, it was midday and the sun pretty hot and we got mighty thirsty. Our guides timing was fairly accurate, after approximately one hour and 15 minutes we came across a rather scenic Msasa / Mnondo woodland and there in a large depression in the ground, was a very squashed Canberra turbine and jet pipe. We were about to skirmish for wreckage and take photographs but the locals told us to wait. They seemed to revere this site and we had to crouch down whilst clapping loudly, one chap said a few words in Shona and again more hand clapping. This they said was to advise the spirits that we were there.

OLEO

Avon Turbine

"The wreckage was scattered over an area of approx 30 metres wide by 60 metres long. There was a ravine running through the centre of the site with the main depression on the south east bank where we found the one turbine, an oleo leg (undercarriage) and some alpha bombs that appeared to have burst open rather than exploded. Also a sad piece of someone's bone dome (helmet).

"On the other side of the ravine were bits of the other turbine and the other oleo leg, plus scattered around small unidentifiable bits and pieces. I think most folk know that the Canberra is a rather largish bomber and constructed mainly of aluminium. Amazingly at this site there was not one scrap of aluminium, not a piece of fuselage, main spar, wing, tailplane or anything in aluminium could be found. Someone in years gone by must have had a mammoth job of extracting this lot on a scotch cart or whatever, as there were no roads anywhere near.

"We took various photographs and got the GPS co-ordinates of the site but before we left Barry held a small service. He spoke a few words of prayer for Kevin and J.J and I placed a small cross and remembrance Poppy by the turbine.

<u>These were Barry's words.</u> " With thanksgiving let us remember Kevin Peinke and J.J. Strydom who sacrificed their lives so that we may live on in peace, and in appreciation we now dedicate this cross to their memories. Help us to keep them in our thoughts and never to forget what they gave for us". We then recited together that well known First World War poem (Robert Graves / Wilfred Owen?)

They shall not grow old as we that are left grow old
Age shall not weary them, nor the years condemn
At the going down of the sun and in the morning
We will remember them.

"The locals then asked us to crouch whilst they repeated their ceremony; they said it was to tell the spirits we were now leaving. Again a hot weary trek back to the bakkie but we had achieved our objective. We said cheers to the policeman and the others and gave the police chappy some money to dish out to the guide and his subdued father who was looking decidedly seedy after his longish trek in the midday sun, his previous heavy intake of hooch couldn't have helped!

"Don't know if they got a fair share of the handout, who argues with a cop with an AK? We then returned to Cruzamento and the Hunter site where Barry carried out a similar service to the one he had recited at the Canberra. We did not leave the cross behind here as it would have been taken away in no time. The people here did not seem to have the same respect or reverence as the villagers at the previous site. , I suppose because it was in the middle of a busy village shopping centre.

"Many thanks must go to Barry Meikle as his input into this search was immense, without his help I doubt if I could have made it happen. We had attained what we had set out to do right in the beginning, located the two sites and also obtained accurate GPS co-ordinates for future reference.

Canberra 183019.5 330016.3.
Hunter 183402.5 330112.6

"Thanks must also go to Eddy Norris, Prop Geldenhuys and Tackie Bannerman for all their help, advice, and prodding to get the job done and to other members of ORAFs who helped in anyway. I personally think that we can now close the chapters on these two tragic events

of 28 years ago. I also feel that Barry's few words of prayer at both sites brought a touch of spiritual peace to these rather sad places.
"What about the Canberra that went in down Malvernia way? Well, maybe a search next year."
Bob Manser, Chimoio

Rick van Malsen writes:- The story on the search for the two aircraft lost post Op Miracle brought back a few memories as 1 Commando RLI were very involved in this second phase of the operation.

I concluded: "With respectful thanks to James 'Tackie' Bannerman for pasting the maps together, and marking the sites where Kevin Peinke's Canberra and Brian Gordon's Hunter went down on the 3rd October 1979, this Chapter to our downed crews is now complete. We now know for a fact the exact spot where our Air Force colleagues were so honourably killed in action.
"Bob Manser has given much credit to Barry Meikle (and justifiably so) in locating the Canberra remains, this in no small measure detracts from Bob's original stated intention right at the onset of these phenomenal expeditions to find his mate Kevin's final resting place (and of course, Brian's as well).
"I am not ashamed to admit the deep emotional impression it made on me to read Bob's "fact-story', and also being privileged to be one of the first to absorb the many photographs Bob sent Eddy Norris and I. The Hunter find came just too late for inclusion in my Operations Book, but with Bobs permission I wish to include most of them in an abridged version of my Nickel Cross - which I am now motivated to follow as a supplement to the Operations book. I have headed the chapter by what I consider a most appropriate and moving 'Once was Lost, But now am Found' heading."
Bob and I have already discussed the publication of a 40 to 60 page novel covering the Chimoio Monument (constructed by Kevin Tidy). I believe this can still be a very real possibility. The matter has been raised with my publisher, and he is very much in agreement. Time will tell which course of action we should pursue depending on the sort of reaction we get from the current two books which mention the Chimoio Circle operations. Bob and Barry tried to get the full ranks and names of the airmen who perished - - - unfortunately I was en-route to Gauteng by car and was too late to respond in time. But in matters of the heart, it is never too late. I can, but with content, quote

my favourite scripture (Eccl 3:1): There is a right time for everything. It is thus fitting for me to say, Amazing Grace:

Once was Lost - But now am Found

Air Lieutenant   Brian Kevin Gordon   KIA 3 October 1979
No 1 Squadron
Flight Lieutenant Kevin Leslie Peinke   KIA 3 October 1979
No 5 Squadron
Flight Lieutenant Johannes Jacobus Strydom KIA 3 October 1979
No 5 Squadron

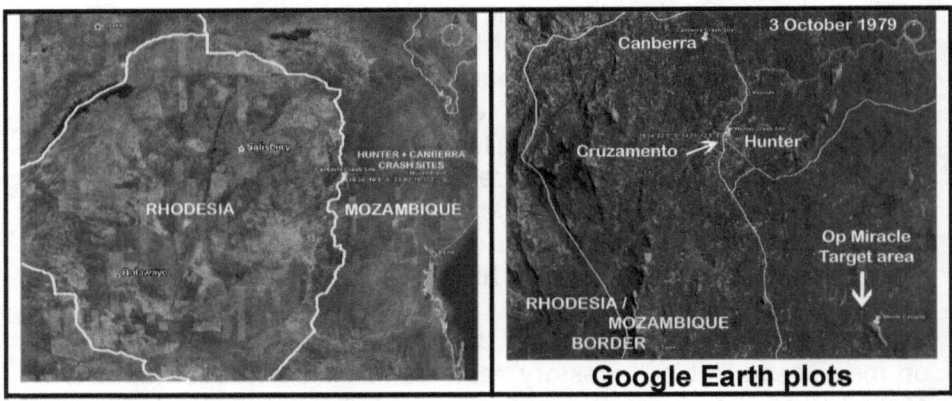

Google Earth plots

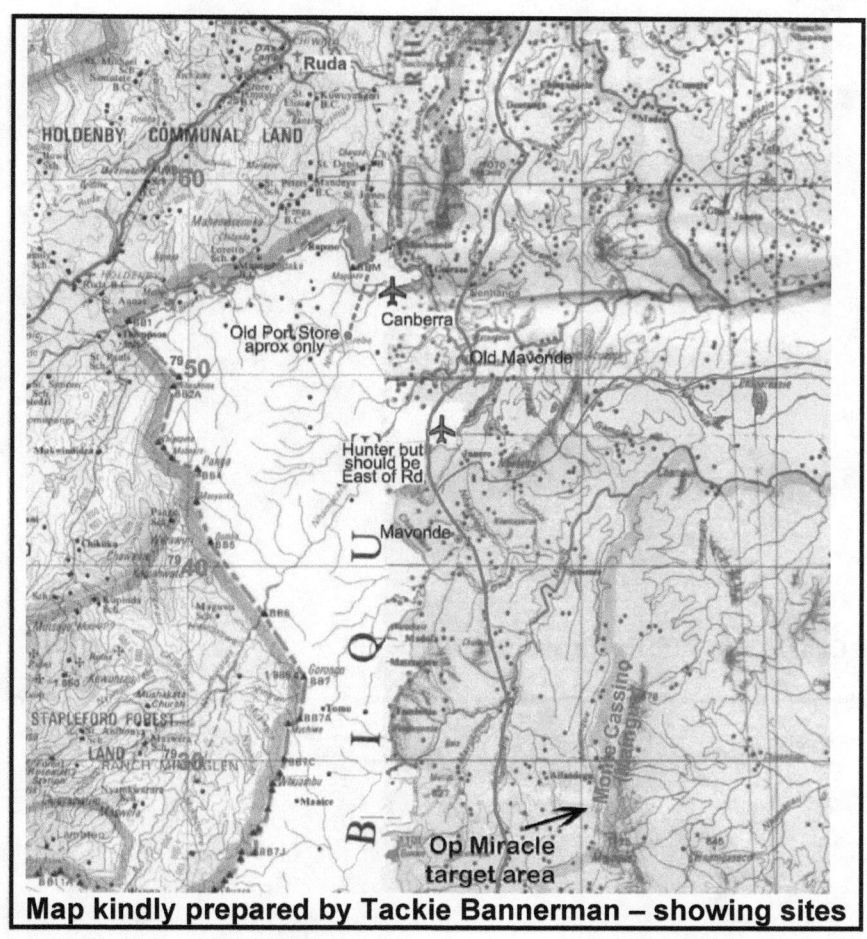
Map kindly prepared by Tackie Bannerman – showing sites

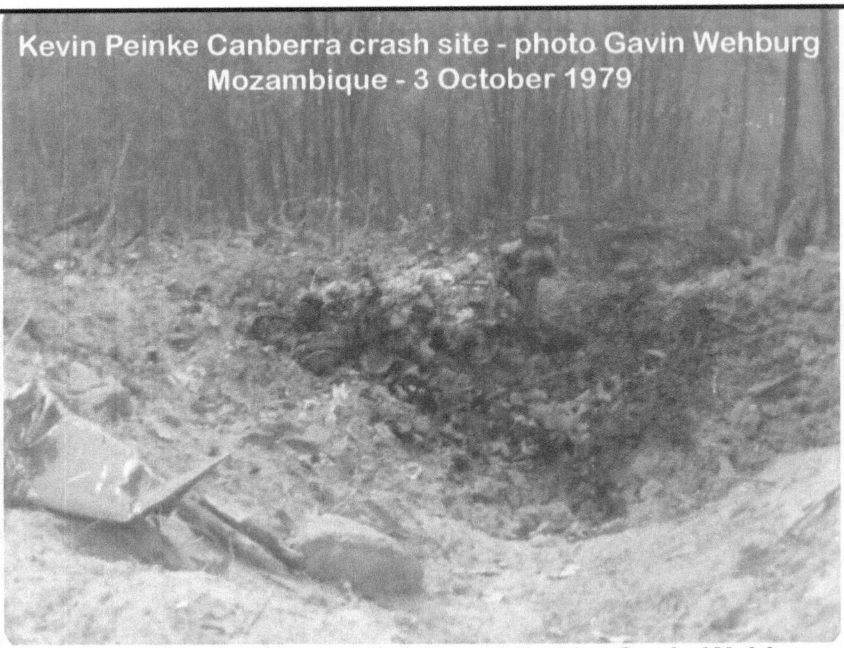

Crash site photographs kindly supplied by Gavin Wehburg – 1CDO RLI

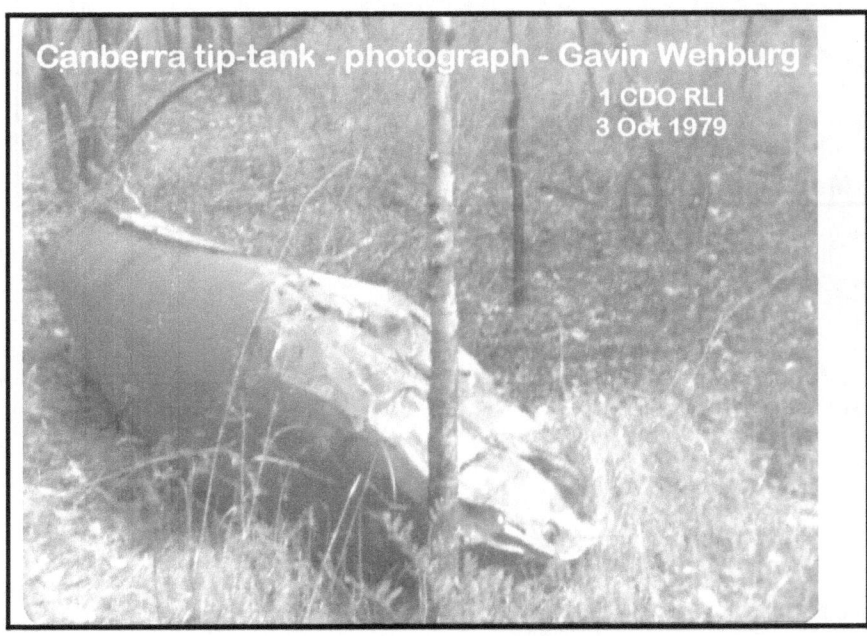

Wreckage remains

Credit for these last four photographs is given to Gavin Wehburg, his 1CDO Saint colleague Rick van Malsen, and with tip-offs by Pamwe Chete Willie van der Riet.

Operation *Miracle* produced another Miracle 28 years later, when our living heroes Bob Manser and Barry Meikle found the remains of Rhodesians in Mozambique – November 2007.

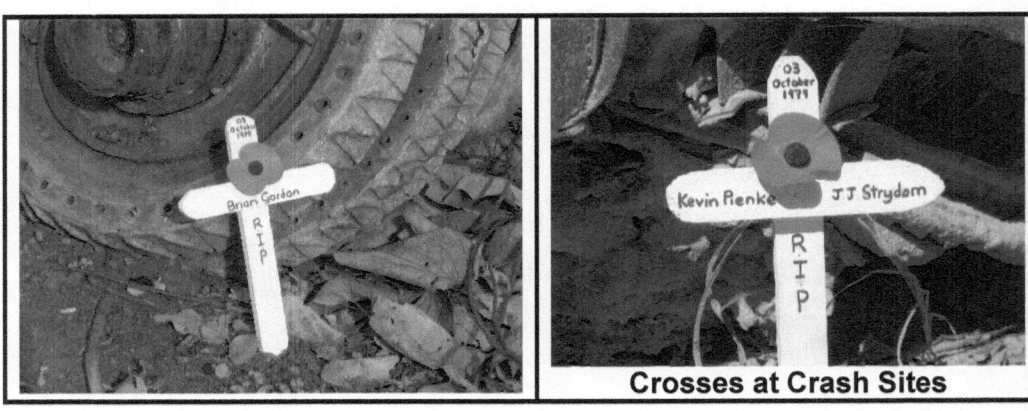

Crosses at Crash Sites

It is the right time, God Willing, to say once again:

At the going down of the sun, and in the morning, We will remember them.

And let us not forget:

> Rise O voices of Rhodesia,
> God may we thy bounty share,
> Give us strength to face all danger,
> And where challenge is, to dare.
>
> Guide us, Lord, to wise decision,
> Ever of thy grace aware.
> Oh, let our hearts beat bravely always
> For this land within thy care.
>
> Rise O voices of Rhodesia,
> Bringing her your proud acclaim,
> Grandly echoing through the mountains
> Rolling over far flung plain
>
> Roaring in the mighty rivers
> Joining in one grand refrain
> Ascending to the sunlit heavens
> Telling of her honoured name.

Ian Douglas and Janet Smith

November 2007 proved quite momentous. After the joyous news of Bob's Canberra and Hunter finds, our Rhodesian war leader, Ian Douglas Smith, has passed to higher service. The airways are going to be congested with condolences, with reminisces from friends and enemies world wide.
For me, he was our 'Winston Churchill", the right man at the right time when Britain convinced the world to shut all doors. We lived through historic times - - Rest in Peace, at last, Mr Smith.
Smith made Rhodesia Great - - Mugabe made Zimbabwe Ruins.

December 2007 caped it all – with the birth of our last grandchild – Jake Geldenhuys.

EPILOGUE

Dedicated to all our grandchildren, Courtney and Brendan Jelley, Matthew, Lucy, Mia and to the memory of Jake Pey Geldenhuys.

I started on this project for my children many years ago. As time went on, I realised that Renene and Pey had outgrown my desire to impress them, and that I should instead write this life story for the benefit of our very dear grandchildren. But I then changed my mind and came to the conclusion that I need to honour not my offspring, but to acknowledge that Rina was the person who shared my life and should be honoured. This I did when Nickel Cross was superseded by the Operations book that was published in July 2007.

In my old age, and like an old woman, I again changed my mind! I was lying on Oumie's lap, and crying that is my wont in my old age, to ask her permission whether it is okay to dedicate "her book – Nickel Cross" to our beloved grandchildren instead? She is the stronger willed between us two - - but she also broke down weeping and said with tears in her eyes "Ding-has, its Gods will – Thy Will be Done". Well that settled it [I must admit I don't think she called me Ding-has at that exact moment – which is her wont – but. . .]

To Courtney, Brendan, Matthew, Lucy, Mia and Jake Pey's, I trust you will cherish the memories that we were blessed with spending time together with one another.

Solomon - the wisest man that ever lived said:

There is a right time for everything;
A time to be born, a time to die;

A time for war; A time for peace (and everything in between).
(Ecclesiastes 3:1-8.)

I say: "I wish that my Dad was alive – to tell me his stories".

ROLL OF HONOUR

The Roll of Honour (as per my Operations book, and purposefully not repeated here) testifies to the immortal words of my late father, SAAF Pilot, and I quote:

**"There are Old Pilots, and
There are Bold Pilots
BUT
There are very <u>few</u> Old Bold Pilots."**

AT THE GOING DOWN OF THE SUN, AND IN THE MORNING, WE WILL REMEMBER THEM

Rhodesians owe a debt to these (especially those killed in action), for they paid the supreme sacrifice for the survival of the country and the Rhodesian nation.

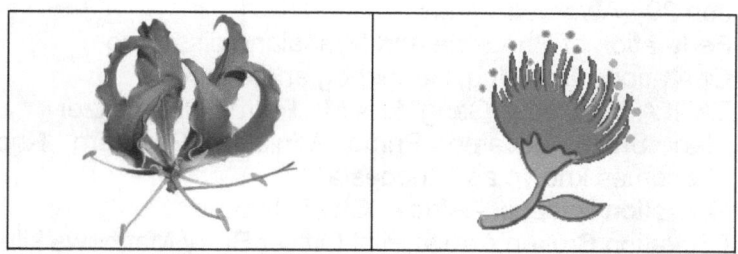

CHRONOLOGY OF EVENTS

1661 Barend Gildenhuisz made a Vryburger of the Cape Colony on 23rd September 1661
1870 Grandmother Lizzie Geldenhuys (nee Preller) born
1890 Pioneer column hoist Union Jack in Salisbury
1895 Mashonaland and Matabeleland renamed Rhodesia
1899- Anglo-Boer War. Lizzie Geldenhuys writes her "Oorlogsherinneringe"
1914-18 First World War. 25% of the total European (and 64% of available manpower) population of Rhodesia served in WW I
1916 A.C.F.Preller Geldenhuys born. Rustpan, Bothaville.
1922 Rhodesian referendum rejects Union with S.A.
1923 Southern Rhodesia granted self-government status
1939-45 World War II. No's 44,237 and 266 (Rhodesian) Squadrons excel.
ACFP Geldenhuys joins SAAF. First solo.
1943 Preller M. Geldenhuys born, Rustpan, Bothaville.
1946 Geldenhuys household emigrate to Copper Belt, Northern Rhodesia
1948 Pey (Preller) Geldenhuys first air experience, Piper Cub VP-RBG
1953 Referendum approves Federation of Rhodesia and Nyasaland
1959 African National Congress rioting and intimidation, Cranwell boys hostel guards Halton girls hostel, Thornhill High School
1960 Joshua Nkomo's Zapu formed
1961 Prop Preller Geldenhuys attests into Royal Rhodesian Air Force, 15 March
Aug 13 First Solo, Provost TMk I No 301
Zapu banned; first armed terrorist infiltration
1963 Feb 13 First Solo, Vampire T 11 jet
Zanu formed, Zanla (military wing) sends recruits to China for terrorist training

	Jun 29 - Awarded Wings
	Federation of Rhodesia and Nyasaland dissolved
1964	Operations Coondog, Hedgehog and Slipshod
	ZANLA "Crocodile Gang" kills Mr. Petrus Oberholtzer
	Ian Smith became Prime Minister, Southern Rhodesia becomes known as "Rhodesia"
	Operation Phoenix - African Chiefs Indaba
1965	Operation Broken Arrow; Pilot Officer Barry Matthews killed
	Appointed Pilot Attack Instructor. Won Commissioner's Trophy
	Ex. Panther, Longdrag, Operation Breampool & Ex Greentrees & Greenhills
	Operation Wizard - Rhodesia declares U.D.I. - 11 Nov 65
1966	UN sanctions imposed; Marriage to Rina Malan; Ex Armchair, VR - Preston, Cobra
	Appointed Instrument Rating Examiner
	Apr 28 Seven terrorists killed at Sinoia
	Jun 22 Operation Pagoda - Johannes & Barbara Viljoen murdered by terrorists
	Operation Armchair
1967	Ex Crocodile Fever, Fabric
	Aug 5-9 Kariba/Makuti ops - one terrorist killed and 13 captured
	Aug 12 Operation Nickel. ZIPRA and ANC (SA) terrorists mount the first major incursions into Rhodesia. Awarded Nickel Cross for first IS Pilot to log over 100 flying hours on specific operation
	South African Prime Minister John Vorster sends S.A. Police to Rhodesia
1968	HMS Fearless talks, in Gibraltar, fail
	Operation Cauldron
	Birth of Renene Delene, Gwelo, Rhodesia
1969	Frelimo agrees to Zanla transit through Tete, to infiltrate Rhodesia.
1970	Royal dropped from Rhodesian Air Force
	Sir Alec Douglas-Home and Ian Douglas Smith meet
	Pey Malan born, Gwelo
1971	Ian Smith accepts the Lord Home settlement proposals. Opposed by Bishop Muzorewa
	Dec – First two Zanla terrorists cross into Rhodesia from Tete
1972	Feb 13 – My father, Abram Carl Frederik Preller Geldenhuys, died in Pretoria.

Pearce Commission finds settlement proposals unacceptable to Rhodesian blacks.

Op Tempest – Armaments are carried through Tete to Rhodesia. 60 terrorists infiltrate

Dec 21 – Attack on Altena Farm in north-east Rhodesia – and the Bush War begins in earnest.

JOC Hurricane Operational Zone established, dealing with the north-eastern part of the country.

1973 Air Rhodesia acquires three sanction-busting Boeing 720 jets from an undisclosed source.

Terrorists abduct 295 African pupils and staff of St Albert's Mission.

1974 Caetano overthrown in Lisbon

Emperor Haile Selassie deposed from Ethiopia – Eritrea

Four South African policemen are gunned down in cold blood, within days of the ceasefire announcement.

1975 Mar – Herbert Chitepo assassinated in Lusaka. Josiah Tongogara imprisoned. Mugabe appointed leader of Zanu.

Aug – South African forces withdraw from Rhodesia.

1976 Feb – Operation Thrasher (Eastern Highlands) opens – to counter threat from Zanla Manica Zone

May – Operation Repulse (South-east Rhodesia) opens – for Zanla threat through Gaza province.

Aug – Operation Tangent opens – Botswana border, including Wankie and Victoria Falls areas.

Aug 9th – South Africa's Foreign Minister Dr Hilgard Muller, states that he supports majority rule in Rhodesia.

South Africa withdraws 26 of its 40 helicopters on loan to Rhodesia; 50 pilots and technicians also recalled.

Sep 24th – Kissinger and Vorster persuade Ian Smith to accept the principle of majority rule. There was to be no going back from this stance which marked the beginning of the end of white-ruled Rhodesia.

1977 Feb – seven white missionaries murdered at Musami by 12 terrorists. The British Government refuse Rhodesia's request to set up inquiry into the killings

Mar – Combined Operations (Comops) formed with Lt-General Peter Walls as commander, and Air Marshal Mick McLaren as Deputy Commander

Aug – Operation Grapple (Midlands) opens

Nov – Rhodesian Air Force, Special Air Service and Rhodesian Light Infantry mount a massive pre-emptive raid on Chimoio and Tembue terrorist bases in east and northern Mozambique, killing thousands. It is the biggest, most successful operation of the war.

1978 Ian Smith and the three internal black leaders sign the March 3 Agreement to form the Transitional Government.

Jun – Zanla murder nine British missionaries and four young children at Elim Mission, Vumba.

Operation Splinter (Lake Kariba) opens.

Sep – Nkomo's Zipra down Air Rhodesia Viscount; then slaughter 10 of the survivors. The other eight flee into the bush to survive.

Oct – Eleven sanctions busting Bell 205 helicopters, ideal for counter-insurgency work, with a far greater range capability and bigger load capacity than the Alouette IIIs arrive in Rhodesia. However, not all were used in the operational role. One was stripped down for spares and accidents claimed some. By the following June, only five were flying.

Dec – Fuel storage tanks severely damaged by fire after terror attack.

1979 Feb – Second Viscount shot down. All 59 people aboard killed and Nkomo claims responsibility.

Mar – Nkomo's Zipra shoot down two Zambian Air Force jets in Zambia.

The SAS begin training and operating with the Mozambique National Resistance (MNR)

Sep – Security Forces mount major offensive into Gaza Province of Mozambique.

Sep 10th – Lancaster House Conference starts in London

SAS destroy ten Zambian bridges in five days – to thwart Zipra invasion. Zambian President mobilises Zambia for full-scale war situation against Zimbabwe Rhodesia.

Dec 12th – British Governor, Lord Soames arrives in Salisbury. Legality is restored and sanctions removed. Agreement on new Constitution signed.

Dec 21st – A settlement is signed and a cease-fire takes effect.

1980 Mar – Robert Mugabe wins election

Apr – Black government in power.

SAS, RLI and Grey Scouts disbanded. Selous Scouts fade without formal disbanding.

1981	Dec – Preller Geldenhuys takes six months leave pending retirement.
1982	Jun 15th – Wing Commander Preller Geldenhuys retired from the Air Force of Zimbabwe.
	Jul – Hawker Hunter and BAC Hawk aircraft sabotaged at Thornhill Air Base. Air Vice-Marshal Hugh Slatter imprisoned
1986	Joaquim Chissano replaced Samora Machel, who was killed in a Russian aircraft crash.
1987	Ian Smith expelled from Parliament. White reserved seats abolished.
1989	Edgar Tekere expelled from Zanu (PF). Tekere forms Zimbabwe Unity Movement (ZUM)
1992	Grahame Jelley marries Renene Geldenhuys – Drakensberg, 6 June, a mere four days after Renene had been brutally assaulted, stabbed and hospitalised.
1993	Courtney Sacha Jelley born, 13 September.
1996	Brendan Vaughan Jelley born 15 November
1994	Pey marries Marion Muller.
1999	Jul - Joshua Nkomo died.
2000	USA trip. Masonite sends Prop Geldenhuys to the States for two weeks. Visits Disney World and Kennedy Space Centre.
	Zimbabwe so-called war veterans invade white farms.
	Grahame and Renene Jelley decide to immigrate to New Zealand.
	Pey and Marcelle tour Egypt and Israel
2001	First edition of Nickel Cross presented to Rina Geldenhuys. Decision taken to retire from Masonite (Africa).
2002	Retirement. First visit to New Zealand. Gentle Annie Reunion, and tour of North and South Island.
2003	Cape Trip
2006	Marcelle decides to leave Pey. Pey meets Eloise and Matthew Howard.
	Pey meets and gets engaged to Eloise Howard. New Zealand trip 2006.
2007	- Pey's marriage to Eloise Howard.
	- Renene, Courtney and Brendan's SA visit / Attend wedding.
	- Delene and Stu / Brinks visit to Africa.
	- Finding Oudad Jannie Geldenhuys's Anglo-Boer War diaries discovered at the Bloemfontein Vroue Monument Museum.
	- Courtney and Brendan performing at the Tauranga Arts Festival

- Rhodesian Air Force Operations with Air Strike Log book launched.
- Operation *Miracle* Hunter and Canberra remains found by Bob Manser
- Ian Douglas Smith dies in Cape Town on 20 November

2007 Jake Geldenhuys born, died 12 days later.

GLOSSARY

AFS = Advanced Flying School
AFZ = Air Force of Zimbabwe, formally Rhodaf and Royal Rhodesian Air Force - RRAF
AK = Kalishnikov or AK-47 rifle, used by most revolutionary units
Alpha bombs = One-kilogram bomb Rhodesian designed to bounce before exploding in the air
ANC = African National Congress
ANC = African National Council (Rhodesia)
ASF = Aircraft Servicing Flight
AWB = Afrikaners Without Brains, otherwise known as Afrikaner Weerstandsbeweging
BDF = Botswana Defence Force
BFS = Basic Flying School
Bluejob or Blues = Air Force personnel
BMATT = British Military Advisory and Training Team in Zimbabwe
BOSS = Bureau of State Security (SA)
Brownjob or Browns = Army personnel
BSAP = British South Africa Police
BSB = Burgelike Samewerking Bureau (refer also to Project Barnacle)
BT = Barbarian Terrorist
Bundu = Bush (see also Shateen/Kungen)
Can(s) = Canberra aircraft
Casevac = Casualty evacuation

Camo = Camouflage
CFI = Chief Flying Instructor
Charlie Tango = Phonetic CT
Chegutu = Hartley
Chibuli = Slang for beer
Chipinga = Chipinge
CIO = Central Intelligence Organisation
COINOPS = Counter Insurgency Operations
CO = Commanding Officer
Comops = Combined Operations
Contact = Contact with terrorists
Convex = Conversion exercise
CSI = Chief of Staff Intelligence (South African)
CT = Communist Terrorist
CV = Consolidated Village
Dak = Dakota DC 3 Aircraft
DDC = Directorate of Covert Collection
DH = direct hit
DME = Distance Measuring Equipment
DZ = dropping zone
EFTS = Elementary Flying Training School
Enkeldoorn = Chivu
ETA = Estimated time of arrival
FAC = Forward Air Control
FAF = Forward Air Field
FAPLA = Forças Armadas Popular para Libertacão de Angola (Popular Armed Liberation Forces of Angola)
FASOC = Forward Air Support Operations Centre

Fartsack = jargon for sleeping bag
Floppies = slang for terrorist (flopped, when shot)
FG = fixed gun
FFU = Field Force Unit
FN = Fabrique Nationale - semi-automatic and automatic NATO weapon
Fort Victoria = Masvingo
Frag = 20lb fragmentation bomb
Fran(s) = see frantan/napalm
Frantan = frangible tank, also called napalm bomb
Fred = Frigging ridiculous electronic device
Freds = Frelimo soldiers
Frelimo = Frente de Libertacão de Moçambique (Front for the Liberation of Mozambique)
FTS = Flying Training School
Fred/Freddie = Nickname for Frelimo
Fundi = Slang for expert
Funnies = Operations into Mozambique
Gatooma = Kadoma
Goffels = Coloureds (God's Own Forgotten)
Gomo = Mountain or hill
Gook = slang for terrorists
Goonie/Gooniebird = Dakota aircraft
G-Car = Alouette helicopter with twin ·303 Browning machine guns
GTS Ground Training School
GPS = Global Positioning System
Gwelo = Gweru
Hang-up = bomb or rocket which failed to fire or drop

Hartley = Chegutu
H-Hour = time attack due to start
Hot Extraction = ground troops uplifted from an emergency situation, using an 80 foot rope with a four-man crossbar slung beneath the helicopter
Hot-Pursuit = legal cross border pursuit of terrorists
IF = Instrument flying
IRE = Instrument rating examiner
ISOPS = Internal Security Operations
ITS = Initial Training School
JHC = Joint High Command (Zimbabwe)
JOC = Joint Operational Centre or Command
K-Car = Kill-car: Alouette with 20mm cannon, or 4 x ·303 machine guns, hydraulically operated
KIA = Killed in Action
Kopje = Small hill
Kraal = Rural village
Kungen = Bush
Lemon = Military operation that came to nothing
Lourenço Marques / L.M. = Maputo
Lynx = Twin-engine Cessna 337
LZ = Landing Zone
MAG = Medium automatic machinegun
Maningis/Mabuno = derogatory term for White (have many)

MK = Umkhonto we Sizwe (Spear of the Nation) the ANC/SACP's military wing
MNR = Mozambique National Resistance - see also Renamo.
MO = Medical Officer
Mujibas = kraal youths who acted as the eyes, ears and runners for terrorists
Muti = medicine
Nat JOC = National Joint Operational Command
Navex = Navigation exercise
NCO = non-commissioned officer
NDB = Non-Directional Beacon
Ndege = Aircraft
NF = night flying
NIS = National Intelligence Service (RSA)
NS/TF = National serviceman or territorial force member
NPA = Native Purchase Area
Nganga = witch doctor
OAU = Organisation for African Unity
OC = Officer Commanding
2i/c = Second in charge
OCC = Operations Co-ordinating Committee
OCU = Operational Conversion Unit
Op = Operation
OP = Observation Post
ORAFs = Old Rhodesian Air Force Sods
PAI = Pilot Attack Instructor
PATU = Police Anti-Terrorist Unit
Paras = Paratroopers
PF = Patriotic Front
PJI = Parachute Jumping Instructor
PV = Protected Village
Que Que = Kwekwe
R&R = Rest and Recuperation
RAF = Royal Air Force
RAMS = Radio Activated Marker Service
RAR = Rhodesian African Rifles
RATG = Rhodesian Air Training Group
Ratpacks = Ration packs
Recce = Reconnaissance
Renamo = Resistência Nacional Moçambicana (see MNR)
Rhodaf = Rhodesian Air Force
Rhodesia = Zimbabwe
RLI = Rhodesian Light Infantry
RPG-7 = Rocket launcher
RPD = Portable light machinegun
R and R = Rest and Recuperation
RR = Rhodesia Regiment
RR = Reconnaissance Regiment (SA)
RRAF = Royal Rhodesian Air Force
RV = Rendezvous
SAAF = South African Air Force
Salisbury = Harare
SACP = South African Communist Party
SADF = South African Defence Force
SAM = Surface to Air Missile
Sangoma = Witchdoctor (South African)
SAP = South African Police
SAS = Special Air Service

Selukwe = Shurugwi
SB = Special Branch
SF = Security Forces
SFTS = Service Flying Training School
Shabani = Zvishavane
Shamwari = Friend
Shateen/Bundu = The bush
Sinoia = Chinhoyi
Sitrep = Situation Report
Sleeping bag = lady of the night
Spoor = Tracks
Sqn = Squadron
SS = Selous Scouts
STD = Standard Letdown
Strela (or SAM-7) = Soviet manufactured heat-seeking missile
SWAPO = South West Africa People's Organisation
Terr = nickname for terrorist
TF/NS = Territorial force / National serviceman
TOT = time over target
Toyi-toyi = Political dance (SA)
Tsotsi = township thug, undesirable
TTL = Tribal trust land
TRC = Truth and Reconciliation Commission

UANC = United African National Council
UDI = Unilateral Declaration of Independence
UFO = Unidentified Flying Object
Umkhonto we Sizwe = Spear of the Nation, the ANC/SACP's military wing
Umtali = Mutare
UNITA = União Nacional para a Independência Total de Angola (National Union for the Total Independence of Angola
V.T.H. = Voortrekkerhoogte
Wankie = Hwange
WO = Warrant Officer
ZANLA = Zimbabwe African National Liberation Army
ZANU = Zimbabwe African National Union
ZANU P/F = Zimbabwe African National Union Patriotic Front
ZAPU = Zimbabwe African Peoples Union
ZIPRA = Zimbabwe Peoples Revolutionary Army
ZNA = Zimbabwe National Army
ZNDF = Zambia National Defence Force

CANBERRA AIR STRIKES

My own Air Strikes for 19th, 21st, 23rd February 1974, is well illustrated by this Sykes painting. Note – in this instance, the Canberras leading the Hunters! I remember it well.

Bill Sykes did not want to sell this particular painting to me because the colour scheme is not correct. Because the picture reflected the occasion where we took the lead at the "IP" (Initial Point – from which the bombing run is commenced), I persuaded him to part with it – more for accurately representing the air strike, rather than the painted colour scheme. When John McKenzie discovered I was using this painting, he quickly got his brother Ian to e-mail me a perfectly painted Hunter. However, this first edition of Nickel Cross will be published in black and white, so the colour is thus not crucial at this early stage.

A unique Bill Sykes painting

Geldenhuys Family – April 2007

Renene and Grahame Jelley – 6 June 1992

Gods' richest blessings to Oumie and Oudad - December 2000

Pey and Eloise – Wedding Waltz

A PROUD MOMENT FOR DAD – WHEN PEY GRADUATED WITH HIS DIPLOMA IN COMPUTER DATA PROCESSING

BIBLIOGRAPHY AND WAR STORIES

Geldenhuys, Abram Carl Frederik Preller, *Pilots Flying Logbook.*
Geldenhuys, Lizzie, *Oorlogsherinneringe van Lizzie Geldenhuys*
Geldenhuys, Preller, *Geldenhuys in Africa* (1999), *Pilots Flying Logbook* and *Rhodesian Air Force Operations with Air Strike Log* (Just Done 2007)
Andrew, Brother, *Battle for Africa*, (Revell, 1977)
Banana, Canaan, *Turmoil and Tenacity,* (College Press 1989)
Books of Africa, *Outpost, Stories of the Police of Rhodesia* (Gothic, Cape 1970)
Brent, Winston, *Rhodesian Air Force – The Sanction Busters* (Freeworld Publications 2001)
Brodie, Ian, *Warbirds over Wanaka,* (Reed, 2000)
Brown, James Ambrose, *A Gathering of Eagles* (Purnell, 1970)
Cocks, Chris, *Fireforce*, One Man's War in the Rhodesian Light Infantry (Galago, 1988)
Cocks, Chris, *Survival Course*, (Covos-Day Books, 1999)
Cole, Barbara, *The Elite,* (Three Knights, 1984)
Cole, Barbara, *The Elite – Pictorial*, Rhodesian Special Air Service (Three Knights, 1986)
Cole, Barbara, *Sabotage and Torture* (Three Knights, 1988)
Cowderoy, Dudley and Nesbit, *War in the Air. Rhodesian Air Force 1935–1980,* (Galago, 1987)
Flower, Ken, *Serving Secretly,* (Galago, 1987)
Gledhill, Dick, *One Commando*, (RLI Publishing, 1997)
Lovatt, John, *Contact,* (Galaxie Press, 1977)
Reid-Daly, Ron, *Selous Scouts, Top Secret War* by Peter Stiff, (Galago Press, 1982)
Reid-Daly, Ron, *Pamwe Chete*, the Legend of the Selous Scouts, (Covos-Day Books, 1999)
Salt, Beryl, et al *Encyclopaedia Rhodesia* (College Press 1973)
Salt, Beryl, *A Pride of Eagles,* (Covos, 2001)
Scannell, Ted, *Aviation in Central Africa,* (Horizon, 1960)
Smith, Ian Douglas, *The Great Betrayal,* (Blake, 1997)
Steele, Andrew and Ulli, Michael, *South African Portfolio* (Struik 1991)
Stiff, Peter, *The Silent War,* (Galago 1999)
Stiff, Peter, *Cry Zimbabwe,* (Galago 2000)
Thurman, Rob, *Half a Century in Uniform* (R.L. Courses 2000)

Venter, Al J., *The Zambezi Salient* (Howard Timmins, 1974)
Wood, Professor JRT, *The War Diaries of André Dennison* (Ashanti, 1989)
The *Gwelo Times* and the *Rhodesia Herald* newspapers

Plus inputs by the late Peter Cooke, Bill Sykes and Eddy Norris

SPECIAL ACKNOWLEDGEMENTS

A special word of thanks goes to Hugh Slatter, who kindly agreed to write the Foreword to my biography; to the late Peter, and Anne Cooke, for their valued corrections; to Bill Sykes for all the editing, correcting grammar and spelling errors and critical proof reading; to Maryna Swarts, editor/publisher of Covos Day Books for the use of the Operations Nickel and Cauldron maps; to Grahame Jelley who went over the original draft; to Professor Richard Wood for his airstrike log and valued input; to Winston Brent for use of his material; and of course my soul mate Rina, who not once raised a brow over the many hours spent on this project.

INDEX

A
Abbot, Lieut, 36
Abrahams, Dave, 135
Abrams, Chris, 310
Ackerman, Air Corporal B, 24, 25
Airey, Richard, 193, 199, 201, 202, 308, 309
Aitchison, Mark, 312
Aldrin, Edwin Buzz, 248
Amin, Idi, 143
Anderson, 46
Anderson, General Jock, 104
Anderson, Lieut, 38
Andrew, Brother, 326
Andrew, Lt GR, 39
Andrews, Lt Kenneth, 47
Anibal, Orlando, 295
Annan, Bob, 220
Annan, John, 228, 285, 310
Arbuthnot, Lt W, 40
Armand, SAC, 191
Armstrong, Ian, 310, 312
Armstrong, Neil, 169, 248
Arnott, Stella Nesta, 52
Ashford, Charles, 298
Atkinson, Geoff, 102, 133
Aust, Charlie, 223
Authers, Les, 262
Aveling, Commandant J, 204

B
Badenhorst, Major D, 204
Badenhorst, Pete, 99
Bak, Maria, 251
Baldwin, Baldy, 190, 283, 284, 285
Baldwin, Steve, 168, 189, 228, 308, 309, 311
Ballinger, Tony, 295
Banana, Canaan, 326
Banda, Hastings Kamuzu, 62
Bannerman, James "Tackie", 214, 290, 295, 299, 300
Barber, Jock, 88, 266
Bard, Lieut, 50
Barlow, Lt, 202
Barnard, Brigadier Bertie, 207
Barnby, M, 28
Barnes, John, 136, 148, 228, 289
Barrett, Garth, 231
Bass, Flg Off RW, 50
Bate, Paddy, 217, 290
Battle of Bangala, 207, 208, 279
Battle of Entumbane, 223
Battle of Inyantue, 139, 142, 201
Battle of Sinoia, 112
Battle of the Angwa River, 116
Bawden, Barry, 255
Baynham, Trevor, 167, 310
Bean, Rich, 99
Beaver, Caroline, 138
Beaver, Richard, 138, 139, 151, 154, 157, 159, 165, 167, 169, 170, 172, 193, 194, 199, 243, 307
Bedford, Colin, 159
Bekker, Major A, 204
Belstead, Beef, 310
Benecke, Cocky, 310
Bennett, Terry, 228, 271, 310, 311
Bennie, John, 119, 125, 127, 130, 135, 166, 167, 168, 199, 272
Bennie, the Cook, 266
Bentley, AVM, 9, 69, 88, 104, 144
Beretta, Joachim, 129
Bergman, Air Sgt, 39
Bernstein, Air Sgt, 38, 46
Bestbier, Andre, 231
Bester-Bond, Ian, 9, 70, 72, 76, 78, 80, 236
Bezuidenhout, Gerta, 116, 218, 259, 264, 266
Bezuidenhout, Hansie, 116, 134, 147, 210, 218, 264, 266
Bezuidenhout, Johan, 53, 211, 212, 217, 218
Binda, Alexandre, 208
Blackmore, Ron, 220
Blain, Ken, 228
Blocker, Lt, 202
Blowers, Roger, 295
Blythe-Wood, JR, 167, 311, 312
BMATT, 230, 319
Bogey, Mrs, 186
Bomford, Hugh, 273
Bopela, Thula, 142, 233, 256
Borlace, Michael, 311
Bos, Colonel W, 203, 204
Bosch, Lt Col, 48
Bosch, SL, 28
Boshoff, Willem, 55
Botes, JB, 28
Botha, Commandant P, 204
Botha, General Louis, 14
Botha, Helletta Lephina, 12
Botha, LC, 21
Botha, Mike, 295
Botha, Pik, 233
Bottomley, Arthur, 107
Bourhill, Dave, 295, 298, 311
Bouwer, Major J SAAF, 204
Bouwer, Rensha, 191
Boyd-Sutherland, 135
Brackely, Matthew, 291
Bradshaw, Dickie, 162, 163
Brand, Rich, 81, 150, 151, 158, 166, 167, 169, 172, 181, 191, 192, 193, 307, 312
Branfield, Gray, 232, 233, 234, 256
Breakwell, Bob, 171
Brent, Di, 262
Brent, Ted, 94, 97, 145, 170, 213, 312
Brent, Winston, 169, 172, 288, 326
Breytenbach, Jan, 240
Brink, Charlie and Chanli, 248, 259, 272
Brink, Commandant D, 204
Briscoe, Pete, 228, 254, 255, 272
Brislin, AC, 135
Britton, John, 311
Brockelhurst, Dave, 207
Brodie, Ian, 326
Brown, Alan, 219
Brown, James Ambrose, 23, 326
Brown, John "Wedge", 192, 199, 307, 308, 309
Brown, Sid, 163, 193
Bruce, Al, 70, 72, 78, 80, 175, 183, 184, 206, 236, 237, 309, 310, 311, 312
Bryson, Brick, 229, 298
Brytenbach, Jan, 238
Buckle, Bill, 117, 119, 125, 130, 133, 134, 135, 136, 151, 154, 157, 166, 167, 169
Burford, Peter, 112
Burger, S P, 125, 146
Burmeister, Ken, 159
Burniaux, FJ, 28
Bush, George, 255
Bushney, George, 310
Busoni, Colonel, 43

C
Callaway, Captain Mac, 238
Cameron, Joe, 264
Cappuccitti, Mike, 229
Carhart, John, 167
Carter, Gary, 217, 290
Chapman, Capt W, 39, 46
Chatburn, Mike, 243
Chegwyn, Lt RL, 52
Chichester, Wg Cdr 'Firpo', 49
Childs, Elaine, 262
Childs, John, 262
Chisnall, Tony, 220
Chissano, Joaquim, 318
Chitepo, Herbert, 317
Christie Road, 238, 250
Churchill, Winston, 13, 304
Claas, Coenelis, 13
Clarke, Nobby, 94, 99, 102, 266, 267
Clayden, Sir John, 7, 8, 9, 88, 89
Cloete, Dirk, 66, 67
Cloete, Jacob, 13
Clyde-Morley, Capt, 30, 34
Coaton, Major, 137
Cobbeldick, Lieut, 38
Cockcroft, Bud, 229
Cocks, Chris, 326

408

Coetzee, Gerry, 28
Coetzee, Jan, 240
Coetzee, Koetie, 61
Cohee, Angela, 295
Cole, Barbara, 326
Colleton, Colonel, 15
Collier, William, 55
Collins, Michael, 248
Collocott, Bruce, 9, 65, 70, 72, 80, 109, 159, 175, 236, 308, 312
Comops, 212, 222, 230, 317, 319
Conjwayo, Philip, 255
Conlin, Archie, 75, 76
Conn, Major, 116, 117
Cook, Vic, 151, 154, 157, 160, 161, 166, 167, 169, 312
Cooke, Anne, 261, 262, 271, 272, 326
Cooke, Peter, 139, 144, 165, 168, 169, 179, 186, 193, 219, 225, 228, 252, 261, 263, 272, 307, 326
Corbishley, Peter, 219, 220
Corrans, Keith, 84, 144, 154, 158
Coull, Lt Col, 28
Cowderoy, Dudley, 187, 326
Cox, John, 254, 255, 256
Cramp, John, 220
Crawford, Tom, 116
Craxford, Gerry, 93
Cronje, General, 14
Cronshaw, Graham, 9, 71, 72, 78, 80, 82, 108, 116, 131, 148, 166, 167, 170, 237, 275, 307, 310, 312,
Cruzamento, 287, 288, 289, 290, 292, 294
Culpan, Rick, 166, 168, 170, 309
Culpan, Vic, 167, 168, 190
Cunningham, Fynn, 310
Cunnison, Dad, 86
Currie, Dave "Spaz", 99, 105, 111
Curtain, Mike, 231
D
Dabengwa, Dumiso, 229
Dad. See Geldenhuys, ACF Preller
Dalgleish, Lt Cmdr J, 51
Dams, Chris, 145, 169, 274
Daniel, Brigadier H, 27
Daudpota, 255
Davidson, 2nd Lt, 48
Dayton, Rob, 159, 167, 174, 175
de Haas, Louis, 61
de Jager, Capt LJ, 52
de Kock, Harwood, 71, 72, 76, 78, 237
de la Rey, General, 14
De Simone, General, 34
de Waal, JHH, 19
de Wet, Commandant General CP, 14
Dean, Lt Cmdr FJ, 51
Delport, Mick, 168, 199, 307, 308, 309
Dennison, André, 205, 326
Deysel, Dux, 111
d'Hotman, Bob, 228

Dick, Lieut DB, 51
Dickie Fritz Shellhole, 208, 292
Dickinson, Chris, 228, 309
Diedricks, André, 232
Diggaden, Adrian, 267
Disney World, 241, 243, 246, 247, 318
Dixon, Chris, 9, 71, 72, 78, 80, 82, 88, 167, 189, 237, 264, 307, 308, 309, 310, 311, 312
Dixon, Guy, 214, 283, 295, 296
Doble, Lieut IJ, 52
Dominee Jackson, 127
Donaldson, Ian, 168, 199, 292, 308, 309, 311
Douglas-Home, Sir Alec, 107, 316
du Preez, Major J, 204
du Rand, Randy, 81, 94, 111, 131, 132, 148, 168, 193, 200, 265, 308, 309, 310, 311
du Toit, Andre, 71, 72, 76, 80, 237
du Toit, Capt, 39
du Toit, Mara, 295
Dumbutshena, Judge Enoch, 255
Duncan, McKenzie, 265
Dunn, Jerry, 53, 272
Durrett, Pat, 167
E
Eadie, John, 219, 220
Edden, Mike, 295
Edmond, John, 158
Edward, Bruce, 271
Edward, Erica, 271
Edwards, Ken, 107, 108, 109, 113, 114, 119, 125, 126, 127, 130, 133, 134, 136, 167
Elliot, Henry, 94, 101, 107, 108, 175
Ellis, Capt, 100
Ellis, Lt WE, 51
Engela, Capt, 133
Erasmus, Flt Lt, 108
Erasmus, Rfn, 208
Ernst, TJM, 229
Eva, Ken, 264, 266
Exercise "Askoek, 152
Exercise Armchair, 130, 135
Exercise Aurora, 131
Exercise Cobra, 135
Exercise Irish Stew, 175
Exercise Longdrag, 116
Exercise Panther, 115
F
Fawcett, Nick, 201, 202
Feinberg, L, 24
Feltcott, Captain, 245
Fenn, Geoff, 220
Fenton-Wells, Steve, 220
Ferreira, Louis and Anna, 146, 193
Few, Blake, 119, 166
Field, Winston, 99
Finnegan, Capt, 48
Flaxman, Ron, 161
Flemming, Flamo, 171, 310
Fletcher, Bob, 310
Flower, Ken, 99, 255, 326

Flygore, Veldcornet, 14
Fordyce, Bruce, 250
Fotheringham, Nigel, 136
Fourie, Fritzie, 147
Fowkes, Maj General, 41, 45, 47
Frans Josef glacier, 248
Frost, Capt, 28, 30
Fulton, Mick, 106, 108
Fylde, 231
G
Galbraith, George, 276
Galbraith, Lynn, 278
Galbriath, George, 278
Galbriath, Lynn, 2
Galloway, Wally, 83, 105, 145, 151
Garlake, Col S, 68
Garnett, Lieut, 99
Gassner, Tony, 96
Gaunt, Rob, 307, 308, 309, 310
Gazzera, Gen. Pietro, 31, 35
Geldenhuys, "Prop" Preller, 5, 9, 19, 29, 50, 55, 61, 64, 65, 71, 72, 78, 80, 82, 88, 89, 114, 125, 129, 132, 139, 154, 169, 172, 181, 189, 192, 194, 195, 198, 202, 228, 235, 264, 307, 308, 309, 310, 311, 316, 318
Geldenhuys, Abie, 251
Geldenhuys, ACF Preller, 19, 20, 21, 22, 23, 29, 31, 32, 33, 35, 36, 38, 39, 40, 41, 42, 46, 47, 48, 49, 50, 51, 55, 56, 57, 66, 67, 81, 191, 263, 316, 317, 326
Geldenhuys, Aircraftsman, 126
Geldenhuys, Anna Elizabeth "Lizzie", 12, 13, 16, 18, 316, 326
Geldenhuys, Capt M, 51, 152
Geldenhuys, Corporal, 48
Geldenhuys, Dawnie, 55, 56, 259
Geldenhuys, Delene, 15, 55, 56, 57, 58, 153, 172
Geldenhuys, Eloise, 322, 324
Geldenhuys, GJ, 51, 52
Geldenhuys, Henry, 19, 20
Geldenhuys, Jake, 3, 5, 13, 305, 318, 325
Geldenhuys, Jake, 304
Geldenhuys, Jan, 37, 39, 55, 56, 57, 248, 259, 260
Geldenhuys, Johannes Norval, 52
Geldenhuys, Joy, 266
Geldenhuys, Julia, 260
Geldenhuys, Karen, 260
Geldenhuys, Matthew, 305, 325
Geldenhuys, Oudad Jannie, 13, 14, 15, 16, 20, 29, 202, 272, 318
Geldenhuys, Oupa, 14, 15
Geldenhuys, Paul, 260
Geldenhuys, Petty Officer JCM, 51
Geldenhuys, Pey, 166, 170, 180, 186, 190, 193, 194, 211, 239, 240, 246, 248, 260, 262, 263, 264, 266, 270, 272, 278, 282, 305, 316, 318, 324, 325
Geldenhuys, Renene, 103, 151, 152, 153, 165, 166, 170, 179, 190, 193,

409

200, 211, 234, 239, 240, 248, 259, 260, 262, 263, 264, 266, 270, 278, 305, 316, 318, 322
Geldenhuys, Rina, 6, 7, 13, 50, 53, 58, 59, 64, 91, 105, 108, 109, 116, 125, 126, 127, 129, 134, 135, 136, 138, 139, 146, 147, 152, 153, 162, 165, 166, 171, 172, 173, 186, 190, 193, 195, 200, 205, 209, 211, 217, 238, 243, 247, 248, 250, 257, 258, 259, 260, 261, 263, 264, 265, 266, 270, 271, 305, 316, 318, 326
Geldenhuys, Ronald Olwen, 212
Geldenhuys, Stuart, 266
Geldenhuys, Tony, 204
Geldenhuys,"Prop" Preller, 237, 269
Genari, Pete, 220
Geraty, Spook, 167, 190
Gibb, Squadron Leader, 22, 48
Gibbs, Sir Humphrey, 89, 99, 221
Gibson, Blair, 296
Gibson, Snr Tech, 115, 130, 134
Gildenhuisz, Albert Barends, 13
Giles, Capt GA, 30, 34
Giles,Capt GA, 33
Gilson, Marcelle, 248, 318
Gledhill, Dick, 326
Goddard, Keith, 296
Gonella, Colonel, 41, 42
Goniwe, Jacques, 142
Gordon, Brian, 213, 217, 281, 284, 285, 286, 287, 289, 290, 291, 292, 296, 299, 306
Gordon, Elliot, 298
Gouws, Capt, 39
Graham, Pat, 310
Graves, Ian, 296
Graves, Robert, 294
Graydon, Butch, 109, 307
Green, Johnny, 262, 271, 276
Green, Noelene, 262, 263, 271
Grier, Mick, 228
Griffiths, Harold, 116, 125, 127, 130, 166, 167, 228
Griffiths, Rob, 228
Guiness, Air Lt, 210
Guy, Richard, 239
H
Haigh, Phil, 281
Hamence, Mick, 288
Hammond, Sgt, 50
Hammond, Terry, 141
Hani, Chris, 142, 233
Harding, 239
Harrison, Bruce, 280, 290
Hart, Winston, 232
Harvey, Ian, 93, 100, 224, 228, 310
Hawkes, David, 292, 311
Hawkins, Harold, 104, 115
Hayden-Thomas, Peter, 32, 34, 38, 40
Haywood, Wally, 251
Heane, Pete, 198
Heard, Barry, 167, 168, 175, 189
Hedebe, Zapu, 148, 149
Hepenstall, Dave, 274

Hertzog, General, 14
Hickman, John, 255
Hickman, Richard, 255
Hill, Mike, 93, 96, 97, 107, 133, 175, 179
Hill, Pat, 207, 279
Hitler, Adolf, 22, 29, 51, 67
Hlekani, Gandhi, 142
Hobbs, Eddie, 106
Hoefnagels, Margaretha, 13
Hofmeyr, FA, 28
Hofmeyr, Murray, 193, 307
Holmes, Charles, 296
Home, Sir Alec Douglas, 221
Honan, Corporal, 50
Hope, Paddy, 21, 22, 36, 42, 43, 44, 48
Hopkins, Roy, 71, 72, 76, 78, 80, 237
Hosking, Peter, 102, 133, 208
Houston, Mo, 159
Hove, Byron, 124
Howard, Eloise, 15, 272, 318
Howard, Matthew, 3, 318
Howe, Don, 220
Howman, Jack, 99
Hubble, Jack, 239
Hulley, Roy, 159, 167, 168, 174, 175
Hume, Dave, 99
Huson, Mike, 214, 287, 296, 312
Hutchinson, 2nd Lt B, 24
Hutchinson, Pilot Off, 25
I
Illsley, Sqn Leader, 46
Inyantue, Battle of, 142
Irvine, Captain, 208
J
Jacklin, Ted, 199
Jackman, ET, 229
Jackson, Guy, 131, 148, 167
James, Colyn, 228
Janeke, Tol, 81, 166, 168, 169, 172, 189, 191, 192, 198, 199, 209, 268, 275, 311
Janson, Ron, 159, 296
Jeffries, David, 278
Jeffries, Wally, 278
Jelley, Bill, 53, 81, 103, 116, 125, 130, 131, 134, 136, 138, 139, 144, 145, 146, 148, 150, 151, 152, 153, 154, 157, 161, 165, 166, 167, 168, 169, 193, 201, 263, 264, 278, 307
Jelley, Brendan, 3, 13, 52, 103, 165, 202, 218, 248, 257, 263, 264, 272, 305, 318, 324
Jelley, Brian, 218, 219
Jelley, Courtney, 3, 52, 202, 218, 248, 257, 263, 264, 272, 305, 318, 324
Jelley, Grahame, 81, 152, 193, 248, 260, 263, 264, 276, 318, 323, 326
Jelley, Keith, 260
Jelley, Leonard William, 218
Jelley, Margaret, 259, 264
Jelley, Renene, 272, 276, 318, 323
Jenkins, Jenkie, 311, 312
Jenkinson, Lt, 201

Joachim, Pilot, 129
Johnson, Aircraftman, 105
Johnson, Major, 100
Johnson, Rln, 208
Johnson, Robert, 296
Johnson, Sgt, 190
Johnson, WO, 157, 160
Jones, Dag, 132, 181, 228, 255, 307, 308
Jones, Terry, 135, 136, 166, 167
Jordaan, Steyn, 55
Joss, Mick, 135
Joubert, Willy, 290
Jovner, Capt A, 204
K
Kasrils, Ronnie, 92
Kaunda, Kenneth, 62, 210
KD. See Major Brian / Gray Branfield
Keeton, Sgt, 45
Keightley, Bert, 311, 312
Kemsley, Keith, 136, 166, 168
Ken Pierson, 142
Kennedy, President John F, 93, 248
Kerr, Major Jock, 204
Kesby, Steve, 130, 145, 151, 180, 181, 228, 269
Killey, George, 296
Kissinger, Henry, 317
Kitchener, Lord, 14
Kitson, John, 228
Knight, Mark, 311
Korb, Aubrey, 141
Kotov, Vladimore, 251
Kotze, FL, 28
Kriel, Capt, 48
Kruger, President Paul, 14
Krummeck, Maj, 48
L
Lamb, Nigel, 202
Lancaster House, 5, 218, 222, 230, 318
Lanham, Morgan, 268, 269
Laurel, 241, 243, 245, 246
Law, Ken, 134, 135, 166, 167, 310
Le Roux, Johannes, 112
Leaver, Terry, 275
Ledderboer, Basil, 74
Leitch, Gordon, 220
Lewis-Walker, Nigel, 255
Liebenberg, Kat, 233, 234
Liebenberg, Plt Off, 132
Light, Jim, 146
Litson, Mike, 168, 228
Littlewood, Clive, 220
Livingstone, David, 289
Lloyd, Barry, 255
Lockhart, Pat, 271
Logan, Colonel, 14
Loots, Fritz, 232, 233, 234, 240, 256
Louw, Sergeant, 46
Lovatt, John, 66, 326
Lovering, Dr Tim, 274, 338
Lucas, Capt / Major GW, 35, 36, 42, 47, 48
Ludgator, John, 229

Lunt, Ted, 150, 151, 154, 157, 167, 272
Luthuli, Daluxolo, 142, 256
Lynch, Jerry, 312

M

Maasdorp, Norman, 228
Mace, SAC, 162
Machel, Samora, 318
MacIntyre, Dave, 197
Macmillan, Harold, 227
MacMillan, Sgt, 33
Madzimbamuto, David, 142
Maingue, 213, 217, 286, 290
Maitland, Simon, 296
Major Brian, 232, 233, 234, 256, See Gray Branfield
Malan, Adolf, 112
Malan, Francois Daniel, 59, 125, 192
Malan, Frans, 58, 105, 173, 195, 197, 207, 231
Malan, Frans and Lettie, 58
Malan, Hendrik, 58
Malan, Kleinding, 173, 207
Malan, Philip, 58, 104, 105, 200
Malan, Sailor, 112, 114
Malan, Susanna Catharina "Rina", 58
Malan, Tant Lettie, 192
Malloy, Paddy, 71, 78
Maltas, Molly, 220
Mandela, Nelson, 92
Mann, Ted, 296
Manser, Bob, 213, 214, 280, 282, 286, 287, 288, 289, 290, 292, 295, 296, 299, 303, 304, 318
Mapai, 236, 240, 285, 286, 312
Marais, Major JC, 204
Marais, Major JL, 204
Marcussen, Fynn, 271
Mare, Neville, 271
Maree, Lieut, 47
Marshall, Lieut, 30
Martin, HJ, 28
Mashumba, Lt, 258
Masimbe, Dr Ben, 234
Masimini, James, 142
Masodja, 208
Mason, William H, 238
Masonite, 169, 236, 237, 238, 239, 240, 241, 244, 246, 250, 252, 258, 259, 260, 270, 318
Masuku, Lookout, 229, 230
Matthews, Barry, 105, 106, 109, 110, 175, 316
Maughan, Monty, 122, 124, 148
Maunder, Pete, 278
Maxwell, Flt Lt, 67
Mazaris, Jnr Tech, 99
Mc Roberts, Trevor, 237
McCabe, Pete, 310
McClurg, Peter, 135, 265
McColl, Delene, 50, 56, 173, 191, 248, 251, 258, 259, 260, 270, 316, 318
McColl, Stu, 15, 248, 259, 272
McConnell, Capt, 122

McCulloch, Sgt, 160
McGregor, Rob, 147, 156, 157, 181
McIntyre, CJ, 171
McKenzie, Ian, 187, 321
McKenzie, John "Kutanga Mac", 94, 99, 109, 111, 118, 135, 264, 265, 269, 270, 280, 290, 292, 321
McKenzie, June, 109, 264, 265
McKerron, Bruce, 95, 96, 101, 175
McLaren, Air Marshal Mick, 85, 86, 126, 130, 134, 136, 137, 138, 139, 198, 199, 230, 317
McLean, IF, 9
McLean, Mark, 119, 125, 127, 130, 148, 166, 167, 307
McMillan, Harold, 62, 64
McNeill, Rodney, 60, 61
McRoberts, Trevor, 9, 71, 72, 76, 78
Meddows-Taylor, Pat, 9, 81, 98, 116, 125, 134, 138, 166, 167
Meikle, Barry, 214, 287, 288, 290, 292, 293, 294, 295, 299, 303
Meikle, Brian, 145, 292
Meikle, Nick, 210, 228, 311, 312
Melville, SA, 24
Merber, Tony, 312
Meredith, Charles, 67
Meyer, Lt, 112
Middelton, Alistair, 229
Mienie, Jan, 312
Mitchell, Lieut, 40
Mninzi, Freddy, 142
Modise, Joe, 92
Moffat, Mary, 289
Mogentale, Tino, 296
Monte Cassino, 213, 217, 285, 286, 290
Moorcraft, Paul L, 66
Morgan, Paddy, 159, 162, 163, 192, 195, 199, 202, 225, 228, 309, 310, 312
Morris, Capt, 115
Morris, Roy, 86, 87, 161, 177, 180, 181, 186, 187
Moss, Basil, 121, 272
Mostert, Col MCP, 39, 41, 44
Mothusi, George, 142
Moyo, Cpl, 222
Moyo, Jonathan, 142
Mugabe, Robert, 143, 210, 222, 223, 229, 230, 256, 258, 260, 272, 304, 317, 318
Muller, Hilgard, 317
Muller, Marion, 318
Mulligan, Mike, 145, 167, 172
Murdoch, Brian, 166, 167, 175, 309
Murray, Steve, 168, 189
Mussell, John, 97, 100, 107
Mussolini, 22, 29
Mutch, Sandy, 99, 106, 107, 108
Muzenda, Simon, 229
Muzorewa, Bishop Abel, 210, 222, 255
Myburg, Ian, 268, 269
Mzondeni, Templeton, 142

N

Nash, JJ, 28
Nasi, General Guglielmo, 35, 36, 40, 45, 47
Nel, GJ Tpr, 281
Nel, Major D, 204
Nelson, Kevin, 209
Nelson, Rob, 209
Nesbit, Roy, 187
Nettleton, Gordon, 133, 179
Nettleton, Sqn Ldr JD, 67
New Orleans, 243, 245, 246
New Sarum, 281
Newton, Percy, 220
Nhongo, Rex, 229, 230
Nicholls, Pete, 225, 228, 234, 252
Nicholson, Rose, 265
Niemand, Pat, 81, 170
Nightingale, Nobby, 107, 113, 116, 125, 127, 130, 133, 181, 262
Nijkela, Siviwe, 274
Nkala, Enos, 222
Nkomo, Joshua, 62, 64, 104, 208, 210, 211, 222, 316, 317, 318
Norris, Eddy, 188, 213, 214, 271, 272, 273, 289, 290, 292, 295
Norris, Trish, 292
Northcroft, Don, 131, 132, 148, 167, 308, 309, 310
Nuttal, Miss, 58, 261
Nyajena, 207, 208, 279
Nyandoro, Edmund, 134
Nyerere, Julius, 62, 258

O

O'Neill, Gert, 281
Oakley, Tony, 168, 189, 214, 228, 290, 312
Oberholtzer, Petrus, 316
Ogilvie, Don, 171
O'Grady, Sqn Ldr S, 50
Olivier, Major B, 204
O'Neill, Gert, 296
Operation Bene, 314
Operation Bluebell, 314
Operation Breampool, 121, 316
Operation Broken Arrow, 109, 110, 316
Operation Bumper, 314
Operation Cauldron, 116, 121, 147, 149, 152, 263, 316
Operation Chessman, 193
Operation Coondog, 99
Operation Cowboy, 314
Operation Dice, 217
Operation Dingo, 281, 282, 314
Operation Eland, 281, 314
Operation Grapple, 317
Operation Griffin, 150
Operation Hedgehog, 99, 100
Operation Hottentot, 158, 168, 169
Operation Hurricane, 194, 201, 202, 205
Operation Junction, 158
Operation Knuckle, 153, 154, 156
Operation Lobster, 314

411

Operation Longdrag, 117
Operation Mansion, 150
Operation Mardon, 206
Operation Mascot, 314
Operation Maybuye, 92
Operation Miracle, 213, 281, 282, 283, 284, 287, 303, 318
Operation Mute, 238
Operation Neutron, 281, 314
Operation Nickel, 92, 106, 121, 138, 139, 142, 143, 152, 193, 201, 210, 263, 316
Operation Noah, 124
Operation Pagoda, 133, 316
Operation Paladin, 314
Operation Paradise, 126
Operation Phoenix, 105, 106, 107, 271, 316
Operation Polar, 163
Operation Quartz, 229
Operation Ranger, 209
Operation Reptile, 121
Operation Repulse, 206, 207, 317
Operation Sable, 314
Operation Sausage Machine, 227, 230
Operation Seed, 231
Operation Shovel, 314
Operation Show Plane, 68
Operation Slipshod, 108
Operation Snoopy, 314
Operation Spider, 64
Operation Splinter, 317
Operation Stripper, 314
Operation Tangent, 209, 317
Operation Tempest, 194
Operation Terminate, 314
Operation Thrasher, 317
Operation Tombola, 53
Operation Winter, 231
Operation Wizard, 122, 124, 316
Orbell, M, 229
O'Reilly, Paddy, 188
Orlando, 243, 246, 247
Ormsby, Lt Col, 45, 46
Osborne, Dick, 236
Osborne, Geof, 228
Osler, Capt, 48
Oswald, Lee Harvey, 93
Owen, Wilfred, 294

P
Paintin, Ed, 151, 157, 167, 311
Pallin, Major B, 204
Palmer, Ken, 296
Palmer, Richard, 296
Parker, Major, 134
Parsons, Lieut, 29
Pasea, Doug, 162, 163, 192, 195, 199, 228, 270, 307, 308, 309, 310, 311, 312
Patterson, Graham, 290
Patton, Brian, 137
Paxton, Charlie, 85
Paxton, Dick, 166, 167, 168, 175, 190
Peak, Lieut, 48

Peake, Mike, 162
Pearce, Dumpy, 148
Peinke, Kevin, 213, 217, 281, 285, 287, 292, 294, 295, 296, 299, 306
Penton, June, 262
Penton, Ozzie, 76, 92, 93, 94, 95, 97, 98, 100, 108, 133, 144, 156, 219, 262
Penver, Lt AW, 45, 46
Perhat, Rory, 312
Perioli, Paul, 213
Perry, John, 61
Peters, Pinky, 64
Petter-Bowyer, Beryl, 262
Petter-Bowyer, Peter, 9, 81, 82, 83, 93, 94, 95, 96, 101, 102, 131, 170, 202, 206, 232, 262, 274, 290, 308, 309
Pettersen, Air Corporal E, 24, 26
Phillips, Buff, 145
Phillips, Inspector, 141
Phillips, Sgt AC, 52
Pierson, John, 141
Pierson, Ken, 140, 141
Piggot, Peter, 122
Pigou, Piers, 274
Pile, Phil, 99, 228, 254, 255, 265
Pincher, Chapman, 124
Pingo, Mike, 229
Pink, Len, 204, 205, 228, 254, 255
Pinner, John, 111
Pirigongo, Lt, 222
Platt, General Sir William, 41
Pompe, Rob, 297
Porter, Giles, 159, 167, 174, 175, 266
Postance, Polly, 122, 123, 124
Potterton, Ed, 151, 157, 165, 166, 167, 170, 180, 181, 190
Preller, Abraham Christoffel Naude, 12
Preller, Abram, 16
Preller, Bob, 19, 37
Preller, Carel Friedrick, 23
Preller, Charlie, 14, 16, 17, 18, 135, 147, 148, 319
Preller, Dr Gustav, 18, 19, 23
Preller, Lizzie, 316
Preller, Mauritz Herman Otto, 23
Preller, Ouma, 15
Preller, Oupa, 14, 15, 16
Preller, RH Bob, 23, 24, 25, 26, 27, 28, 31, 34, 37, 38, 39, 48
Preller, Robert - RH Bob's father, 23
Preston, Tom, 258
Pretorius, Ben, 267, 268
Pretorius, Glen, 312
Pringle, Sgt, 190
Project Barnacle, 232, 233, 234, 238, 319
Pullar, Ian, 115
Purnell, Derrick, 115, 116, 136

Q
Queen Elizabeth, 8, 88, 100, 115, 124, 232
Quinell, Richard, 287, 290
Quirk, Capt, 21

R
RAA, 274
Rainey, Derrick, 134, 136, 141, 166
Rann, Sgt, 46
Rautenbach, Colonel, 233
Rawlins, Pete, 310
Rees, Doug, 298
Reid-Daly, Ron, 326
Reynolds, Mike, 108, 109, 110
RFMP, 278, 279, 290, 295
Rich, Capt, 122
Richards, N, 125
Rider, Heather, 264
Ringrose, Major, 39
Ritsko, Joe, 243
Robbertse, Flg Offr J, 52
Robbertse, P, 24
Roberts, Barry, 126, 127, 143, 145, 307
Roberts, Lord, 13, 14
Robinson, Brian, 100, 148
Robinson, Marshal, 220
Robinson, Tommy, 219, 220
Rodgers, Mr, 153, 186
Rogers, John, 148
Rogers, LAC, 50
Ronne, Mike, 158, 160, 161, 162, 191, 192, 193, 195, 201, 202, 310, 311
Roodt, Major G, 204
Rossiter, Jeff, 298
Roughead, Alec, 93, 96, 101, 175
Roux, Major General H, 238
Rowe, Dave, 213, 312
Rowley, Hugh, 99
Royce, 2nd Lt, 47
Ruby, Jack, 93
Russell, Jim, 206, 228, 310, 311, 312
Russell, Mike, 338
Rustpan, 14, 50, 55, 316
Ryan, Terry, 175

S
Sachse, Bert, 133, 231
Salt, Beryl, 53, 208, 272, 290, 326
Santoro, General, 40
SAS, 4, 53, 54, 64, 100, 148, 206, 211, 212, 217, 218, 224, 227, 229, 231, 240, 269, 276, 278, 283, 284, 292, 308, 318, 320
Saunders, Colin, 220
Saunders, Mike, 311
Scales, Peter, 106, 271
Scannell, Ted, 326
Schekhoven, Herman Fer, 13
Schikkerling, Hendrik and Elizabeth, 13
Schoeman, Commandant W, 204
Schooling, Phil, 192
Scott, Alec, 271
Seegmuller, Ziggy, 214, 229, 284, 285, 291, 297
Selassie, Haile, 92, 317
Serfontein, Dot, 15
Sewell, P, 24
Seymour Hall, Glen, 297
Shaik, Shabir, 278

Sharp, Alfred, 142
Shaw, Beaver, 297, 311, 312
Shaw, Major General John, 134
Shields, Alan, 311
Shires, Alan, 220
Shirley, Dave, 229, 298
Shuttleworth, Lieut., 21, 44, 51
Sibanyoni, Delmas 'Nsimbi', 142
Simmonds, Pete, 168, 189
Simon, Bryan, 297
Sinclair, Dave, 220
Sinclair, Doug, 311
Sisulu, Walter, 92
Sithole, Ndabaningi, 210
Skeeles, Jerry, 229
Skinner, RT, 229
Slater, Mike, 241
Slatter, Hugh, 5, 9, 71, 72, 78, 88, 93, 99, 100, 105, 108, 109, 113, 116, 125, 126, 127, 134, 166, 167, 205, 228, 237, 254, 255, 265, 309, 318, 326
Slaughter, Sgt, 51
Slovo, Joe, 92
Smart, John, 105
Smart, Lt - Scottish Guards, 105
Smit, Shirley, 153, 262
Smit, Tony, 130, 153, 262
Smith, Bill, 158
Smith, Bruce, 93, 101, 104, 105, 110, 113, 151, 154, 166, 167, 169, 170, 172, 174, 175, 272
Smith, Graham, 220
Smith, Janet, 264, 304
Smith, Mike, 255
Smith, Nic, 140, 142
Smith, Nick, 140
Smith, Prime Minister Ian Douglas, 53, 63, 99, 107, 123, 124, 135, 205, 221, 223, 230, 262, 264, 304, 316, 317, 318, 326
Smithdorff, Mark, 84, 86, 125, 132
Smithdorff, Tinker, 105, 307
Smuts, Field Marshal Jannie, 14, 49
Snelgar, Bruce, 290
Soames, Lord, 222, 230, 231, 318
Sowrey, Air Cde, 41, 47
Spence, Dennis, 262
Spence, Keith, 213, 214, 310
Spiret, Conex, 130
Spoor, Ken, 133, 135, 137
Spoor, Major, 21, 133
Springer, Bill, 113
Squance, Daryl, 228
Squires, Hilary, 277, 278
Stagman, Jim, 167, 174, 309, 310
Stallard, Col, 33, 34
Stanton, Peter, 297
Stead, Steve, 108, 109, 171, 310
Steele, Andrew, 326
Steele, Sandy, 105
Stevens, Starry, 160, 175, 191, 192, 193, 199, 308, 309
Steyn, Douw, 233, 240
Steyn, Lieut, 30

Steyn, President, 14
Stiff, Peter, 238, 256, 326
Stokes, Capt, 122
Stone, Corporal, 50
Stone, Dave "Unc", 109
Stone, Joan, 270, 271
Stott, Jo, 239
Stracken, John, 71
Strever, Ted, 106, 219
Strickland, Brian, 86
Strnad - name changed to Stracken, 9, 71, 72, 78, 80, 87, 88, 237
Strnad, John, 237
Strydom, Danny, 112
Strydom, JJ, 213, 217, 281, 285, 287, 294, 296, 299
Sutcliffe, Colin, 147
Svoboda, Danny, 167, 168, 190
Swanepoel, Pedro, 287, 290
Swart, Boet, 232
Swart, Sgt, 22
Swarts, Maryna, 326
Sykes, Bill, 139, 151, 152, 154, 156, 157, 166, 167, 169, 170, 171, 174, 175, 184, 187, 228, 252, 262, 263, 272, 290, 321, 326
Sykes, Mary Ann, 156
Syslo, Joe, 273
T
Tamana, Bethuel, 142
Tambo, Oliver, 92
Tasker, Capt, 23
Tasker, Rob, 81, 84, 86, 113, 116, 125, 130, 136, 166, 167, 228
Tau, George, 142
Taylor, Denise, 273, 292
Taylor, Rex, 228
Taylor, Shumba, 292
Tekere, Edgar, 223, 318
Terrorist Camps Nyadzonia, 281
Theron, Capt, 28
Thomas, Tudor, 134, 135, 136, 166
Thomson, Bob, 312
Thomson, Lt, 50
Thorne, Dave, 107, 228
Thornhill High School, 57, 58, 59, 64, 69, 111, 220, 263, 316
Thorogood, Al, 214, 229, 253, 290, 297, 298
Thring, AL, 14
Thurman, Rob, 97, 144, 326
Tidy, Kevin, 289, 299
Timitiya, Warrant Officer KIA, 140, 141
Todd, Greg, 167, 168, 189, 310
Tongogara, Josiah, 222, 317
Towanda, 241, 242, 243, 245, 246
Trenoweth, Sandy, 110
Tubbs, Charlie, 135
Tungumirai, Josiah, 230, 255
Turner, Harry, 220
Tylden-Wright, Lt PM, 52
Tyson, Cliff, 173
U

Ugolini, Colonel, 45
Umkhonto we Sizwe, 142
Upton, Mike, 170
V
van Aard, Lettie, 243
van der Riet, Willie, 214, 283, 290, 302
van Dyk, 2nd Lt G, 45
van Dyk, Peter, 297
van Malsen, Rick, 214, 223, 225, 292, 302
van Niekerk, Commandant M, 203, 204
van Niekerk, Johann, 239
van Riebeeck, Jan, 13
van Ryneveld, Flt Lt JF, 66, 70
van Ryneveld, Sir Pierre, 36, 47
van Schalkwyk, Boet, 137
van Wezel, Lt, 50
van Zijl, John, 297
Varkevisser, Amy, 264
Varkevisser, Fred, 233, 234
Varkevisser, Varky, 81, 103, 108, 109, 111, 113, 114, 115, 118, 125, 127, 135, 136, 139, 159, 167, 169, 170, 189, 265, 269, 310
Vass, Ron, 135, 167
Vaughan, Bernie, 159, 199, 228, 309
Venter, Al J, 326
Venter, Lieut, 28, 30, 34
Venter, WAJ, 52
Venter, Zelda, 274
Venton, Tony, 250
Venutti, Mario, 311
Vernon, Mark, 228
Viljoen, Air Sgt, 45, 46
Viljoen, Johannes and Barbara, 133
Vorster, John, 316, 317
W
Wahl, Air Sgt, 39
Wainwright, Paul, 239
Walker, General Sir Walter, 66
Wallis, IMW, 229
Walls, General Peter, 54, 66, 223, 230, 277, 278, 317
Walsh, Norman, 228, 255, 295, 307
Ward, Clive, 228
Warren, Brian, 148
Warrington, Flg Offr R, 52
Watkins, Bruce, 235
Watt, Roger, 167
Wauchope, General Andy, 14
Webb, L, 228
Webber, Derek, 297
Wehburg, Gavin, 214, 301, 302
Weinmann, Chris, 116, 117, 118, 119, 121, 125, 131, 132, 134, 135, 136, 140, 167, 175, 200, 275, 308
Weir, Jim, 132
Weir, Neville, 254, 255
Welensky, Sir Roy, 96, 97, 289
Wellington, OF, 28
Welman, Commandant F, 204
Welsh, Ken, 80

413

Wentworth, Chris, 151, 154, 157, 159, 165, 166, 167, 307, 312
Westwood, Al, 219
Wetherall, Lt General, 41, 47
White, Babs, 262
White, Cyril, 166, 170, 171
White, Guy, 268
Whitehead, Chris, 297
Whiteley, Alan, 52
Whyte, Doug, 102, 105, 137, 154
Wightman, Shirley, 211, 264
Wightman, Vic, 264, 265, 269, 290
Wigmore, Angie, 297
Wild, Alf, 167, 228, 269, 310
Wildsmith, Lieut / Capt, 39, 48
Wilkie, Fred, 240
Wilkinson, Eddy, 76, 78, 81, 86, 88, 131, 132, 148, 265
Williams, Lt, 50
Williams-Wynn, Abbey, 220
Wilson, Alan, 99, 241
Wilson, Archie, 9
Wilson, Graham, 206, 207
Wilson, Harold, 107, 124, 221
Wilson, R, 201
Wilson, Stan, 220
Winston-Burnett, Robert, 297
Wolhuter, Henry, 195, 197
Wood, JRT Richard, 205, 326
Woods, Kevin, 255, 256
Woodward, Bob, 81, 83, 85
Woolcock, Ellie, 157, 262, 270
Woolcock, Pete, 136, 156, 167, 170, 262, 276, 278
Wrathall, John, 54
Wright, Gordon, 228, 262

Y

Yeats, Capt R, 51
Young, Kenneth, 221

Z

Zuma, Jacob, 278

DEDICATED TO

BABY JAKE GELDENHUYS

Born: 18-12-2007   Died: 30-12-2007

Who graced our lives for 12 memorable days

AMAZING GRACE	TO ALL
Amazing grace! How sweet the sound That saved a wretch like me. I once was lost but now I'm found, Was blind, but now I see. 'Twas grace that taught my heart to fear, And grace my fears relieved. How precious did that grace appear The hour I first believed.	Do not cry, I did not die My time just came to part. But I will always be close to your hearts I am resting in a peaceful place. If you could see me now, I wear a happy face. God gives me a lot of care and love I am in heaven above. So do not cry, because I didn't die. Keep me alive in your hearts, Because from there I'll never part.

Through many dangers, toils and snares I have already come. 'Tis grace hath brought me safe thus far, And grace will lead me home. The Lord has promised good to me; His word my hope secures. He will my shield and portion be As long as life endures.	When I died I kept on living, I'm your angel up in heaven. You'll always have my love To see you through.

RHODESIAN AIR FORCE OPERATIONS with AIR STRIKE LOG REVIEWS

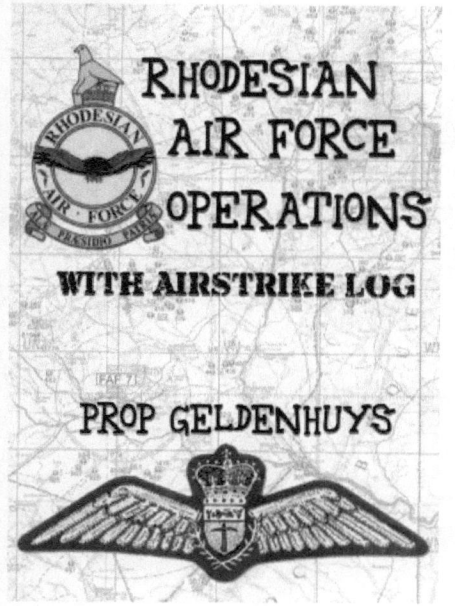

Dr Timothy Lovering - Research Fellow at the University of the West of England: Geldenhuys has produced a comprehensive account of the Rhodesian Air Force role in the war in Rhodesia. The work <u>includes one of the most detailed summaries of Rhodesian military operations to have been published</u>, and in this respect serves as an excellent work of reference. However, the book is much more than this, as the author's personal experience leaps from every page, producing a fascinating combination of memoir and historical account.

~~~OOO~~~

Peter Petter-Bowyer – author of *Winds of Destruction*: Considering <u>the political turmoil that brought about hurried separation and destruction of Air Force records in March 1980</u>, Prop's attempt to save whatever could be recovered for this work is highly commendable. Certainly there are errors and omissions that arise from late searches and faded memories. Nonetheless these records will prove most useful to historical researchers.

~~~OOO~~~

Mike Russell – Flame Lily Foundation - Review of "Props" War, for the Rhosarian publication

This book is a follow-up on Nickel Cross and is again a very personal account of the author's participation in the anti-terrorist war. A short introduction to the Rhodesian Air Force is followed by a detailed account of operations in which the author was involved, or of which he has received first hand accounts. The period covered is from the early start of counter-insurgency operations in 1964 up to the sabotage of aircraft at Thornhill in 1982 and the South African support to Renamo until 1983. The writer's feelings and reminiscences run through the narrative, making it exclusively "Prop's" war.

To order a copy, go to: http://www.peysoft.co.za/orderform.asp

Or to enquire, e-mail Prop Geldenhuys prop@peysoft.co.za

www.ingramcontent.com/pod-product-compliance
Lightning Source LLC
Chambersburg PA
CBHW020633230426
43665CB00008B/151